Student Mastery Guide to Accompany

Dunfee • Gibson • Blackburn • Whitman • McCarty • Brennan • Cohen:

MODERN

BUSINESS

LAW

The Regulatory Environment

Student Mastery Guide to Accompany

Dunfee • Gibson • Blackburn • Whitman • McCarty • Brennan • Cohen:

MODERN

BUSINESS

LAW

The Regulatory Environment

Third Edition

Nancy Kubasek
Bowling Green State University

McGraw-Hill, Inc.

New York   St. Louis   San Francisco   Auckland   Bogotá   Caracas
Lisbon   London   Madrid   Mexico City   Milan   Montreal   New Delhi
San Juan   Singapore   Sydney   Tokyo   Toronto

Student Mastery Guide to Accompany
Dunfee • Gibson • Blackburn • Whitman • McCarty • Brennan • Cohen:
Modern Business Law:
The Regulatory Environment

 This book is printed on recycled paper
containing 10% postconsumer waste.

1 2 3 4 5 6 7 8 9 0   SEM   SEM   9 0 9 8 7 6 5

ISBN 0-07-018217-5

The editors were Terri Varveris and Michelle E. Cox;
the production supervisor was Paula Keller.
Quebecor-Semline was printer and binder.

CONTENTS

INTRODUCTION

Complex as it is, the study of law can be made much easier for students by the application of a logical and systematic approach. The aim of the Student Mastery Guide is to provide you with an efficient and simple study technique for reaching an understanding of the legal concepts and principles developed in *Modern Business Law*, Second Edition. This guide has been designed to be a supplement to the text, not a substitute, and you will obtain the maximum benefit from it when you use it along with your text, as well as with your lectures and class discussions.

Following this introduction is a section entitled "Approaching Your Business Law Course." This section outlines:

- an effective, step-by-step study technique
- how to answer essay questions effectively
- the method of case presentation that you will encounter in *Modern Business Law*, Second Edition
- how to read, analyze, and brief a case

By means of an outline approach, the guide reinforces, highlights, and tests the key concepts and terminology presented in the text. Each chapter of the Student Mastery Guide includes six features to help you review and study the material:

1. a **Synopsis**, which gives an overview of the contents

2. **Chapter Objectives**, so that you are aware of the major learning goals

3. **Major Points to Remember**, a section that sets forth the important legal principles presented in the chapter and highlights again what the chapter is about

4. **Major Points of Cases**, a section that identifies the key principles of law illustrated by the cases

5. **Practical Considerations**, a section, in most chapters, that is designed to give you an insight into how the concepts covered in the chapter apply to real-life situations

6. **Self Test**, a section usually consisting of ten true-false questions, ten multiple-choice questions, and five completion questions that is designed to measure your mastery of the course material. Answers to the self-test questions are in the back of this Guide.

As you use this book, keep in mind that there is no substitute for a diligent, conscientious, analytical approach to the study of law. If you are to be successful in your quest for knowledge, you must work at it and be willing to expend the effort that will be required. Knowledge of the law once attained in this fashion will always be retained.

Finally, study the materials in the Student Mastery Guide so as to gain an understanding of the concepts. Avoid simply memorizing. An ability to recall the rules of law is not enough; you must be able to apply them to factual situations.

With the foregoing in mind, I wish you much success in your quest for knowledge.

Nancy Kubasek

APPROACHING YOUR BUSINESS LAW COURSE

Study Techniques

As you embark on your study of business law, you will encounter a detailed, and sometimes quite complex, body of rules. A conscientious approach to the materials is essential to reaching a full understanding of the various ramifications of the law.

It is important that you find a system of study with which you feel comfortable; however, it is suggested that the study technique described below be used for each chapter, since it represents a logical approach that will help you both to remember and to understand the material. Although the method of study described will require you to expend a considerable amount of time, its benefit to you as a student will amply justify its use.

Step 1.   Before you begin the text chapter, read the **Overview** and **Chapter Objectives** of the Student Mastery Guide for that chapter. The **Overview** will orient you to the contents of the chapter, and the **Chapter Objectives** will alert you to the learning goals that you should set for yourself.

Step 2.   Read the text chapter. In reading the textbook, you should make careful note of the manner in which the cases complement the text so as to clarify and illustrate the practical applications of the major concepts. You should read text and cases together in order to comprehend fully the legal ideas involved. As you read the chapter, take notes. These notes need not be elaborate but should highlight the critical concepts being discussed.

Step 3.   Attend the class presentation, recording class notes in a temporary notepad.

Step 4.   After class, transcribe the notes into a permanent notebook, comparing and integrating them with your own notes on the text. When you review all your notes in light of class discussion, the relevant concepts and terms should become much clearer and more understandable.

At this point you should read the remainder of the student guide chapter, except for the **Self Test** section. The guide provides you with a thorough review of the major concepts and legal principles that have been discussed in the text and cases, and thus provides another opportunity for you to examine them. It is hoped that the situation described in the **Practical Considerations** sections will bring to life for you the everyday and immediate relevance of the law.

Step 5.   Now take the **Self Test.** This will allow you to evaluate how much of the material you have actually understood and retained. To make the best use of these test questions, please refer first to the text for answers to those questions with which you had difficulty. Only after this should you check the answers that appear at the back of the guide.

Examinations

The most important factor in achieving success in examinations is preparation; reread the text and review your own notes and the Student Mastery Guide materials before taking examinations.

How to Answer Essay Questions Effectively

Essay questions generally allow for a wide range of possible solutions. In connection with questions involving the law, it is even possible that there is no specific correct answer to the hypothetical situation that is presented for resolution. Frequently, the examiner is seeking to determine:

1. whether the student is aware of the legal principles that affect the answer to the problem

2. how the student analyzed the critical facts involved, and

3. how the student develops a logical argument in applying the legal principles of the facts

As mentioned above, the correct answer is often only a collateral aspect of the problem-solving process. In view of this, an appropriate approach to answering an essay question is the following:

1. Read the entire problem from beginning to end in order to determine the nature of the situation presented.

2. Isolate the various legal issues that need to be considered (frequently there is more than one issue in each problem).

3. Make an outline (on scratch paper) of the specific rules that apply to the identified issues.

4. Isolate the facts of the cases as they relate to each of the identified issues.

5. Apply the rules of law to the facts in a well-reasoned, logical argument.

6. State your conclusions based on your application of the law to the facts.

A word of warning: Do not stray too far from the issues in stating your answer. A well-reasoned, logical argument does not have to be long to be effective. A short, informed answer is much better than a long uninformed, poorly reasoned answer that rambles aimlessly, and the latter is easily detected by your instructor.

Notes on Objective Questions

Objective examinations usually contain true-false and multiple-choice questions. Unlike essay questions, an objective question seeks a specific answer to a specific inquiry and generally involves only a single rule or principle. Use great caution in relying on the philosophy that you have a 50-50 chance of answering a true-false question correctly. When you apply the same theory to questions of this type, the odds of correctly guessing the answers are significantly reduced. Students usually have an advantage with multiple-choice questions in that the correct answer appears right on the examination paper. In answering these questions, always read all of the optional answers provided to you. Do not stop at the first answer that appears correct and presume that it is the only correct answer.

How to Read a Case

All of the cases in this textbook are decisions of appeals courts as opposed to trial court decisions. As these decisions are often quite long and involve several issues of law, the authors of the text have done several things to assist you, the student. They have edited the cases to eliminate portions of the opinions they feel are unnecessary. The cases, as edited, focus on the basic reasoning of the court in each case. Citations by the judges to cases, statutes, and other such matters have generally been removed - except where such a reference is essential to understanding the case. When cases discuss two or more issues of law, they usually have been edited so as to deal with only a single point of law.

Appeals courts typically have a number of judges - for example, the U.S. Supreme Court is composed of nine justices. In order to win a case, at least five of the nine must rule for the prevailing party. Although five or more justices may believe a given party to a suit should win, they may nonetheless disagree as to the reasons why. In such cases, the justices may write several opinions, each ruling for the same party, but for different reasons. In other cases, when justices may feel the majority has ruled for the wrong party, they may write a dissenting opinion. What counts, as far as the litigants are concerned, is the opinion of the majority. The majority's opinion also serves as a precedent for later cases dealing with the same issue. Generally, cases in this text have been taken from cases in which a majority of the justices all agree on the same result and reasoning. On occasion, very good dissenting opinions also appear.

A special effort has been made to simplify the major facts of each case. The first material that appears after the name of the case is the *authors'* - not the court's - summary of the major facts and the decisions of the lower courts, as well as the decision of the court whose opinion is reproduced following the summary of facts. The judge's name follows the summary, followed by an edited version of his or her opinion.

Your first task when reading a case is to determine the facts, that is, what happened between the parties that caused the case to be filed. Once you have determined what the basic *facts* in the case are, your next major consideration is to determine what the judge is being asked to decide. In other words, with what *issue* of the law is the case concerned? Sometimes the issue is clearly stated or identified in the case; at other times you must read the case more carefully. In trying to determine what the issue is, first look to see if the court (the judge) has identified it for you by using such language as "The court is asked to decide..." or "The issue in this case is..." If the court has not specifically identified the issue, try to determine what the plaintiff hopes to accomplish by instituting the lawsuit and why he or she wants to accomplish it. When you join the answers to those items together, the issue in the case should become clear.

After you determine what the facts and the issues are, the next item that should be considered is the *decision*, that is, for whom the judge has ruled. Determining this is quite easy because it is specified in the authors' summary of the facts just prior to the judge's opinion. The judge also states in the opinion for whom he or she has ruled.

The final element in reading a case is determining *why* the court ruled (or decided) for the plaintiff or the defendant, in other words, the *reasoning* or *rationale*. The decision of the appeals court comprises the bulk of the case. It explains how the court arrived at its decision and the principles of law upon which it relied. When reading the case, you should first try to extract the principles of law from the language used by the court. After doing this, then try to understand how the court used the rules of law in justifying its decision. It may be helpful to memorize the rules of law announced in the case for purposes of testing.

In order to develop a better understanding of the cases, you may wish to "brief" the case. Briefing the case means writing out and identifying the *facts, issue, decision,* and *reasoning* of the judge.

Let us consider an example taken from the case *Lucy* v. *Zehmer*, which appears in Chapter 10 dealing with offers. Try briefing the case, then compare your brief to the one that follows. The following brief is fairly short; you might wish to write more of the facts down when briefing a case. Compare this brief to the case.

FACTS: Zehmer and Lucy were farmers and had known one another for many years. While at a restaurant, and after drinking some liquor, Lucy inquired about the sale of Zehmer's farm. Zehmer doubted Lucy's ability to pay $50,000 for the farm, but he wrote on a piece of paper, "We do hereby agree to sell to W.O. Lucy the Ferguson Farm for $50,000 complete." Both Zehmer and his wife signed the paper. When Lucy attempted to enforce the contract for the sale of the farm, Zehmer refused to comply with the writing. He asserted that his offer had been a joke and, therefore, no contract ever came into existence. Lucy contended that he thought Zehmer intended to sell the farm, and as he had accepted Zehmer's offer to sell, a contract for the sale of the farm existed.

ISSUE: Did Zehmer's making an offer that Lucy accepted thus create a binding contract?

DECISION: Yes. The court ruled for the plaintiff, Lucy, that a valid offer had been made by Zehmer.

RATIONALE: The evidence showed that Lucy believed, and was justified in believing, that an offer had been made. To determine if an offer has been made, the courts look at the outward expression of a person as manifesting his or her intention rather than to the secret and unexpressed intention of the person. The law imputes to a person an intention corresponding to the reasonable meaning of his or her words or acts. If a person's words or acts, judged by a reasonable standard, manifest an intention to agree, what may be the real but unexpressed state of his or her mind is immaterial. If a reasonable person would have believed that Zehmer, by his conduct and words, had made an offer, then Zehmer may not escape from the contract by contending the offer had been made in jest.

Is your brief similar to this one? If so, you should have no problem spotting the issues and reasoning of the judges in the cases in the text. If not, you can develop this ability by trying to brief each case. Over time, spotting the issues and reasoning will become easier for you to do.

Each chapter of this Student Mastery Guide states the main point of each case in the text. Looking at this material in the guide also will be helpful to you in understanding a case.

The rule announced in each case may be used by your professor in class or on a test. You must understand the rule announced in each case and how to apply it. Very often, professors present students with similar facts to cases in the book and ask students how the case should be decided.

The best way to answer such a question is to state for whom a court should decide, then state the applicable rule of law, and then apply the rule to the facts of the case.

For example, suppose a test question reads as follows: Jack posted a notice on a bulletin board offering his Corvette for sale. Elmo asked Jack if he would take $18,000 for it. Jack said yes. They both signed a piece of paper that stated "I, Jack, agree to sell to Elmo, who agrees to buy, my Corvette for $18,000." The next day, when Elmo presented Jack with a check for $18,000, Jack refused to deliver the title to Elmo. Jack claimed he had been joking and no contract ever came into existence. Is Jack correct?

SAMPLE ANSWER: No. The court should rule that a contract was created when Elmo and Jack signed the paper. The applicable rule of law is that if a person's words or acts, judged by a reasonable standard, manifest an intention to agree, it is immaterial what may be the real but unexpressed state of his or her mind. This rule of law was announced in the case of *Lucy* v. *Zehmer* in the text. While Jack may have in fact been joking, this fact is irrelevant to the decision in this case. If a person in Elmo's position could reasonably have thought Jack was making an offer to sell the Corvette for $18,000, an offer has been made. As Elmo accepted the offer, a contract was formed. Thus, the court should rule for Elmo.

Read the cases slowly and carefully, with the precision that the law requires. A judge's decision is a well-reasoned piece of work that, when fully absorbed, can be very enlightening and informative. It must be analyzed and digested fully. When you do this, the case will open up a world of knowledge and the concepts of the law will take on additional meaning. You will also be well prepared for class and for any tests administered during the semester.

Chapter 1

THE FUNCTIONS AND SOURCES OF LAW

The terms "law" and "legal systems" escape precise definition; yet they are critical to the study of law. Chapter 1 examines the nature of legal systems and the law, some specific functions at which legal systems should be directed, and the sources and types of law that exist. Finally, this chapter discusses some alternative nonjudicial techniques for resolving disputes. In reading this chapter, you should try to acquire a feeling for what the law is and what it tries to accomplish, because only with such understanding can one fully appreciate the significance of the specific rules of law that will be presented in subsequent discussions.

CHAPTER OBJECTIVES

After reading Chapter 1 of the text and studying the related materials in this chapter of the Student Mastery Guide, you will understand:

1. The nature of legal systems
2. The specific functions and tasks of legal systems
3. The sources of law, including:
   a. constitutions
   b. judicial (common) law
   c. statutes
   d. administrative rules and orders
4. Alternative techniques for resolving disputes

MAJOR POINTS TO REMEMBER

Legal Systems

1. Legal systems establish rules (often called laws) that control human conduct in order to peacefully solve some of society's problems. Generally, legal systems also provide procedures for the formal and orderly enforcement of these rules.

2. Within our legal system there are numerous subdivisions, which include the courts, legislative bodies, law enforcement agencies, the practicing bar (lawyers), and administrative boards, commissions, and departments.

Secondary Sources of Law

3. Sources of law that are characterized as secondary, such as books and treatises, serve to describe and summarize the law and are valuable tools for legal research.

4. Restatements of the law are a particular type of secondary source that summarizes the common law in a particular field. Prepared by legal scholars, this type of source does not have the legal effect of statutes enacted by legislatures.

5. Although both may be applicable to a single event, civil law and criminal law are distinct in a number of ways. Civil law involves a violation of a given individual's rights, while criminal law pertains to infractions against society by the individual. Civil law focuses on compensating people whose rights have been violated, while criminal law concerns itself with punishing wrongdoers. Moreover, civil defendants are at worst found liable and are forced to pay damages, while criminal defendants found guilty can be sentenced to jail, forced to pay a fine, or even sentenced to death.

6. The common law system has judicial decisions as an important source of law, while civil law as it is known in continental Europe is more concerned with and reliant on statutory codes for its law.

7. Substantive law is what most of us think of as "law". This type of law delineates for us what we may and may not do as well as, sometimes, what we must do.

8. Procedural law are the steps that must be followed in holding anyone responsible for violations of substantive law.

9. Actions of law seek monetary damages, while an action in equity seeks an alternative form of relief, such as an injunction. Equitable relief entails no constitutional right to a trial by a jury, and it is generally granted only when monetary damages are not suitable.

Schools of Legal Thought

10. Natural law theorists believe a higher authority to be the source of all law, and that fundamental principles, applicable to all societies, can be derived from this authority by the use of reason.

11. Legal positivists hold that all law derives from the authority of whomever has the authority to enforce the law.

12. The historical school reveres long lasting legal principles that have lasted the evolution of the law over time, and it emphasizes the need not to change those principles abruptly.

13. Proponents of the sociological school assert that legal principles must evolve in a manner consistent with the achievement of economic and social justice.

Issues and Trends

14. Criticisms of the U.S. legal system include that there is too much law, too much litigation, and too many lawyers, as well as that the system is too slow and costly in resolving specific disputes. However, it must also be recognized that the population of the United States has grown dramatically in this century and that it has become an urban, heterogeneous, and industrialized nation that faces numerous and changing societal problems. Increasingly this

society has turned to the legal system as the forum for finding solutions to these problems, rather than relying on the family, church, or other local institutions.

15. Judicial interpretation of the U.S. Constitution has established the power of the federal courts to review the actions of the branches of the federal government and the states, when asked to do so through a lawsuit, to determine their compliance with the Constitution. This power of judicial review, however, remains a matter of considerable debate in this society between those who believe that courts should exercise restraint in interpreting the Constitution in order to limit judicial lawmaking and those who believe that the courts should be activists in interpreting the Constitution to protect individual freedoms and keep it relevant to the needs of modern society.

Law and Ethics

16. Law and ethics are not exactly the same conceptually or in practice. Ethics can require that a person voluntarily take actions beyond those mandated by law. Ethics deals with how one should act in regard to other persons and provides standards by which to evaluate human conduct in regard to whether it is right, just, and proper.

Sources of Law

17. Laws can be derived from many sources, including:
    a.   constitutions
    b.   judicial (common) law
    c.   statutes
    d.   administrative rules and orders

18. The authority of a constitution is absolute in regard to all the points that are contained in it.

19. Constitutions have three major functions:
    a.   to guarantee certain basic rights to individuals
    b.   to allocate power among the different branches of government (legislative, judicial, and executive)
    c.   to allocate power among political subdivisions

20. The U.S. Constitution grants certain powers to the three branches of the federal government. Actions by the federal government within these powers are supreme, or take precedence, over those of state or local governments. The federal government cannot take any action unless it is authorized by the Constitution, nor can the individual rights and liberties provided in it be violated.

21. State constitutions distribute powers to the branches of state government, provide for basic individual rights and liberties, and in some states delegate certain powers to local governments under "home rule" provisions.

22. The courts interpret and apply constitutional provisions. If the courts find that a government's action has violated a constitutional provision, the action in question is unenforceable.

23. The development of common law (judicial law) is based in part on the concept of *stare decisis*, which is a Latin phrase meaning "to abide by [or adhere to] decided cases." It holds that once a court has applied a principle of law to a certain factual situation, subsequent cases involving the same principle should follow the rule announced in an earlier case unless there is a compelling reason to do otherwise. The concept of stare decisis applies to factual situations that are governed by a constitutional provision, statute, or administrative rule as well as those to which only previous judicial decisions apply. Application of the stare decisis concept makes the law more predictable.

24. A court may refuse to follow a principle of law established by the doctrine of stare decisis where there:
    a. is a substantial distinction between the facts of the earlier case and the case under consideration, or
    b. has been a significant change in conditions

25. The federal courts and each state's courts are organized in a hierarchy in which a court is bound under stare decisis to follow the precedents of an appellate court that has authority over it. All courts must adhere to the precedents of the U.S. Supreme Court. In matters concerning state law, a state court must follow the precedents set by the highest court of that state, but not those of other states.

26. "Statutory law" refers to any rules or laws that are created by the action of a branch of government with lawmaking powers. Normally, statutes are general and prospective, whereas judicial decisions are specific and retrospective.

27. When the exact meaning of a statute is unclear, it is sometimes necessary for a court to interpret or construe the statute in question or determine its intended meaning. In reaching such an interpretation, the court will usually consider:
    a. the general purpose of the statute
    b. the plain meaning of the terms contained in the statute
    c. the manner in which specific provisions fit into the context of an entire legislative package
    d. the legislative history of the statute
    e. the interpretation given to the statute by administrative agencies that are responsible for enforcing it

28. Administrative agency rules and regulations are another increasingly important source of law today. These rules and regulations have the force and effect of law. Some administrative agencies also hear cases involving disputes arising under their rules and issue orders deciding them - a process called an *administrative adjudication*. Since administrative agencies implement statutes, they often must interpret statutes, and courts generally give great deference to such agency interpretations. (See Chapter 53.)

MAJOR POINTS OF CASES

Kelly v. Gwinnel (p.16)

As the note following this case indicates, the courts previously held that individuals, sober or drunk, were solely responsible for their actions. Subsequently, some states adopted "dram shop statutes" to make commercial entities liable to their customers and others for harm caused by a person to whom the business had served alcohol when that person was visibly intoxicated. This case, like those in some other states, addresses the questions of whether this liability should be extended to social hosts who serve alcohol to their guests.

The majority of the court held that social hosts have a duty of care to not serve alcohol to guests who are intoxicated and will be driving an automobile later. The majority concluded that the benefits to society of this rule, in the form of public driving safety and greater assurances of just compensation for victims of drunk drivers, exceeded the costs associated with placing restraints upon a common social activity. The dissenting opinion states that such a significant change in the law that would likely have a substantial impact on social hosts - a duty to determine intoxication and the risk of financial liability beyond that which they could buy liability insurance for protection - should be made in the legislature, not the courts, since it is the more appropriate forum for such issues.

Powell v. California (p.19)

In this case, the Court reversed an earlier decision of a lower court and allowed the relocation of the trial of four Los Angeles police officers accused of assaulting a civilian by force likely to produce great bodily injury. Such an allowance was made to ensure a fair trial for the accused.

In making its decision, the court opined that the videotape and subsequent media coverage of the alleged incident as well as the fact that the accused were police officers and racially distinct from the arrestee all made it impossible for the accused officers to get a fair trial. With Los Angeles County "saturated with knowledge of the incident", the court ruled that the totality of the circumstances indicated that the chances of the accused not receiving a fair trial because of a lack of requisite impartiality on the part of the jurors, more than surpassed the "reasonable likelihood" standard.

Edwardo v. Califano (p. 21)

Section 202(d) of the Social Security Act stipulates that any child of a person who dies a fully or currently insured individual is entitled to insurance benefits. Charlotte Diane Edwardo claimed that this section was applicable to her children, because their father John Richard Long was presumed to be dead after a seven year absence. At issue in this case was whether such a presumption of death was acceptable.

The court reversed the earlier decision and ordered that payments be made to the children. While acknowledging the existence of evidence indicating that Long was still alive, the court ordered the payments on the basis of Section 404.705(a) of the Social Security Act, which directed the secretary to presume dead any individual absent from his residence and unheard of for more than seven years. Thus, the court ignored the

Department of Health, Education, and Welfare's interpretation of the regulation because of its inconsistency with the controlling statute and shifted the burden onto to the secretary to show that the missing person is alive.

Equal Employment Opportunity Commission v. Trabucco (p.22)

In this case, the Equal Employment Opportunity Commission (EEOC) claimed that an earlier case that upheld the statutory mandatory retirement age of police officers at fifty should not be a binding precedent. At issue in this case was whether such a statute was a "bona fide occupational qualification" (BFOQ) or, alternatively, a violation of the Age Discrimination and Employment Act (ADEA).

The court upheld the decision of the lower court, indicating that the earlier case was a proper precedent because there had been no evidence presented that revealed a weak or ineffective presentation in the earlier case. Such a decision on the part of the court illustrates the meaning of stare decisis for legal proceedings.

SELF TEST

True-False Questions

_____ 1. All laws derive from the Constitution.

_____ 2. A court must always follow a principle of law that was established by the doctrine of stare decisis.

_____ 3. The authority of a constitution is absolute in regard to all the points that are contained in it.

_____ 4. When the exact meaning of a statute is unclear, a court can render an interpretation with respect to what the statute is intended to mean.

_____ 5. In the mediation technique for resolving legal disputes, the mediator renders a decision that the parties must obey.

Multiple-Choice Questions

_____ 6. Which of the following is a function of a constitution?
   a. to allocate power among political subdivisions
   b. to guarantee certain basic rights to individuals
   c. to allocate power among the different branches of government
   d. only a and b are correct
   e. a, b, and c are all correct

_____ 7. Which of the following is not a source from which laws can be derived?
   a.   statutes
   b.   constitutions
   c.   administrative rules
   d.   decisions of courts
   e.   all of the above are sources of law

_____ 8. The development of common law is based to some degree on:
   a.   statutes
   b.   treaties
   c.   administrative rules
   d.   constitutions
   e.   c and d are both correct

_____ 9. Statutory law refers to:
   a.   rules or laws created by judicial decisions
   b.   rules or laws created by the action of a branch of government with lawmaking powers
   c.   those rules or laws that entail harsh penalties for violation
   d.   all of the above
   e.   none of the above

_____ 10. The application of the concept of stare decisis makes law more:
   a.   understandable
   b.   equitable
   c.   predictable
   d.   effective
   e.   conservative

Completion Questions

11. _____ is any set of rules or regulations by which one's daily conduct is controlled or governed.

12. Pronouncements of legal concepts presented in a court's opinion that are not necessary to decide a case and that are not binding on other courts are referred to as

_____.

13. _____ is the process by which judge-made law is enacted into statute by legislative bodies.

14. The term that is used to refer to the practice of using court decisions as precedents in future legal actions that deal with similar factual situations and principles of law is

_____ _____.

15. _____ _____ is a substantial basis for the development of common law.

8

Chapter 2

LEGAL SYSTEMS

This chapter discusses the questions of how the law works and what mechanism is available to put the principles of law in motion. It discusses the interplay between the state and federal systems of law and the differences between them, and in doing so it considers such constitutional issues as the separation-of-powers doctrine, the Commerce clause, and the doctrine of full faith and credit. Also covered are the various elements that make up both the state and the federal court systems, jurisdictional issues related to each, and differences between the systems. Finally, the chapter examines the stages of the litigation process, including pretrial procedures, the trial itself, and the appellate stage of dispute resolution.

CHAPTER OBJECTIVES

After reading Chapter 2 of the text and studying the related materials in this chapter of the Student Mastery Guide, you will understand:

1. The nature of the federal and state legal systems
2. The nature and structure of the federal and state court systems, including:
   a. trial courts
   b. appellate courts
3. The concept of jurisdiction, including:
   a. federal court jurisdiction
   b. state court jurisdiction

MAJOR POINTS TO REMEMBER

Federalism

1. Under the federalism principle that is implicitly embodied in the U.S. Constitution, sovereign governmental powers are allocated between the state and federal governments. The Constitution delegates specific powers to the federal government, with all other powers being retained by the states. The federal government also has implied constitutional powers, which are those powers necessary and proper to carry out the delegated powers.

2. When the federal government acts pursuant to its constitutionally delegated or implied powers, these acts are supreme over state actions. Conversely, state actions pursuant to retained powers are supreme over federal actions. There are also concurrent powers that can be exercised by both the state and federal governments.

Regulation of Interstate Commerce

3. One of the federal government's important delegated powers is "to regulate commerce with foreign nations, and among the several states....." In response to changing needs in society,

the courts have interpreted this power first broadly and then more narrowly. However, since the Great Depression of the 1930s, this Commerce clause has been interpreted broadly to empower the federal government to regulate "interstate commerce," which includes not only commerce that flows across state boundaries but also wholly local intrastate commerce that could substantially affect interstate commerce.

4. Although the federal government's power to regulate interstate commerce is supreme, under their retained police powers the states can regulate interstate commerce if: (a) the state law serves a valid local purpose with only an incidental effect on interstate commerce; (b) the federal government has not expressly or impliedly preempted the states from regulating; and (c) the state law does not irreconcilably conflict with the federal regulations.

Separation of Powers

5. The concept of the "separation-of-powers" doctrine established by the U.S. Constitution provides that the government be divided into three branches, namely, legislative, judicial, and executive. It also provides that none of those branches shall exercise any of the powers belonging to the others. Most states follow this same doctrine.

6. Despite the separation-of-powers doctrine, each of the three branches of government does have some powers to act to check the other branches' exclusive exercise of powers in order to prevent abuses.

Court Structure

7. The court systems in the United States are divided into two types:
   a. the federal court system
   b. the state court system

8. The federal court system is made up of the:
   a. U.S. Supreme Court
   b. U.S. circuit courts of appeals
   c. U.S. district courts

   The U.S. district courts are the trial courts in the federal system. There are ninety-four districts in the federal system.
   The U.S. circuit courts of appeals are intermediate appellate courts. The United States is divided into twelve circuits.
   The court of last resort in the United States is the U.S. Supreme Court, the highest court in the nation.

9. The state court systems generally consist of:
   a. trial courts
   b. intermediate appellate courts
   c. appellate courts of final state review, often called supreme courts

Federal Court Jurisdiction

10. In order for a case to be tried in a federal court, the matter must involve a claim over which the federal courts have jurisdiction. Such matters include:
    a. the interpretation of the U.S. Constitution, a U.S. statute, or a treaty
    b. diversity of citizenship when the amount in controversy exceeds $50,000. Diversity of citizenship means that none of the defendants comes from the same state as any of the plaintiffs.

State Court Jurisdiction

11. Under the provisions of the full faith and credit clause of the U.S. Constitution, each state must acknowledge, recognize, and give full credit to the public acts, records, and judicial proceedings of every other state.

    Such recognition must be granted even though the second state does not have such a cause of action within its own jurisdiction, or feels that the judgement was the result of some legal error or contravenes its own public policy.

    A state is not required to recognize the judgment of a court in another state when it is determined that such court lacked jurisdiction over the subject matter or over the persons, or when the judgment was obtained without due process of law.

    The full faith and credit clause does not apply to criminal laws of the various states.

12. When a lawsuit in a state court has connections to more than one state, federal law does not apply to resolve it, and the laws of the connected states differ, the trial court must normally apply the substantive law of the state with the most substantial interest in the outcome under conflict of laws rules.

Pretrial Stage

13. In order for a court to have jurisdiction over a matter, it must normally have jurisdiction over the person of the defendant. Traditionally, such jurisdiction is established by locating the defendant within the state and serving him or her with certain documents.

    However, the various states today have enacted "long-arm" statutes that permit them to exercise jurisdiction over defendants in certain specified types of cases even though such defendants are outside the state. A typical long-arm statute is an act that permits a plaintiff to sue an out-of-state defendant who was involved in an automobile accident in the plaintiff's state. The long-arm statutes can also apply to certain business activities. However, constitutional due process of law requires that such statutes can apply only when a defendant has had such minimum contacts with a state to make it fair to require the defendant to be subject to that state court's jurisdiction.

Doe v. Sullivan (p.29)

The dispute in this case centered around Rule 23(d), which was issued by the FDA. Under this rule, the FDA could waive the consent requirement for certain unapproved drugs in combat-related situations. Not wanting to take unapproved drugs, a soldier challenged the rule but lost in a lower court. That court ruled that the courts do not have the power of judicial review over Rule 23(d) because the legislative and executive branches had authority over the actions of the military in times of war.

On appeal, the District Court reversed the decision of the lower court, ruling that the courts do have the power of judicial review concerning Rule 23(d). The reversal was not based on a revision of the legislative and executive branches' authority over the military. Instead, the court opined that the "military authority" exception was not applicable to this case. Upon review, the court upheld the validity of Rule 23(d).

Gafford v. General Electric (p.35)

The court's findings were favorable to the defendant of a gender discrimination suit on two separate grounds. First, the court upheld the District Court's decision to remove Gafford's claim from the Western District of Kentucky on the basis of diversity jurisdiction. The court rules that both requirements for such a decision had been met: the amount in controversy was over $50,000, and there was a diversity of citizenship. The latter requirement was determined by applying the total activity test.

Additionally, the court held that the plaintiff-appellant Gafford's claim to have been discriminated against for job promotions on the basis of gender was unfounded. The court stated that the suit rested "on a veritable plethora of multifarious grounds."

World-Wide Volkswagen Corp. v. Woodson (p. 38)

With its decision, the Supreme Court upheld the strict requirements previously established for personal jurisdiction. The plaintiff-appellant Woodson suffered an automobile accident in Oklahoma while driving an automobile both manufactured and sold in New York. Woodson brought suit in an Oklahoma court, but the court ruled that the incident did not meet the requirement of "minimum contacts" needed for a state to assert personal jurisdiction over a non-resident.

Moreover, the court dismissed the notion that "foreseeability" is a sufficient benchmark for personal jurisdiction. That is, just because the auto manufacturer could have foreseen the automobile's likely travel in another state, this alone does not justify the enactment of personal jurisdiction on the part of that state.

Allstate Insurance Company v. Hague (p. 41)

Despite the fact that the accident happened in Wisconsin, both parties involved were citizens of Wisconsin, and all three Allstate Insurance policies were delivered in Wisconsin, the court found that the accident victim's widow was justified in bringing suit in Minnesota, where life insurance benefits are greater.

This case is an illustration of when a state may assert personal jurisdiction over a non-resident. The court found three substantive contacts between the State of Minnesota and Allstate Insurance. Ralph Hague, the accident victim, commuted to and worked in Minnesota. His widow held current residence there. And, finally, Allstate's presence in Minnesota.

PRACTICAL CONSIDERATIONS

1. While under the full faith and credit clause of the U.S. Constitution each state must recognize the validity of a judgment entered by a court in another state, it is generally necessary to initiate additional legal proceedings in order to enforce that judgment in the second state. Consequently, the person who is entitled to the judgment must be prepared to expend additional money and time in an effort to enforce the judgment.

2. While the litigation process is intended to provide a speedy resolution of disputes, the legal requirements attendant on the preparation and prosecution of a lawsuit necessarily involve the expenditure of a great amount of time. Consequently, a person involved in a lawsuit should not expect it to be completed swiftly. It often takes several years before a dispute is finally resolved by trial; and that time may be further extended by the appellate process if one of the parties decides to appeal the decision or judgment rendered in the case.

SELF TEST

True-False Questions

_____ 1. The doctrine of separation-of-powers refers to the division of governmental authority among the legislative, judicial, and executive branches.

_____ 2. The powers that can be exercised by the office of the President of the United States are not affected by the doctrine of separation of powers as embodied in the Constitution of the United States.

_____ 3. An individual is subject only to laws of that state in which she/he is a resident.

_____ 4. In order for a case to be heard by the U.S. Supreme Court it is generally necessary first to obtain an order granting certiorari.

_____ 5. The police power that can be exercised by a state under the provisions of the U.S. Constitution will always prevail against ordinary businesspersons who argue that the Commerce clause requires a statute to be declared invalid.

6. A litigant who loses a cause of action (case) in the courts of one state is usually denied the opportunity to bring the same lawsuit in the courts of another state.

7. Under the terms of the full faith and credit clause of the U.S. Constitution each state must recognize any judgment rendered by a court of another state that had proper jurisdiction in the case.

8. In order for a state court to have jurisdiction in a particular case, the defendant must be physically present within the state at the time the action is commenced.

9. Federal courts have subject matter jurisdiction over cases involving citizens of different states.

10. In order to adjudicate a case a court must only have jurisdiction over the subject matter.

Multiple-Choice Questions

11. A case may be brought in either the federal or state court if:
   a. the plaintiff and defendant reside in differnt states and over $50,000 is at issue
   b. the case involves the interpretation of a federal statute or the United States Constitution
   c. a plaintiff is filing an action against multiple defendants
   d. a and b
   e. all of the above

12. Long-Arm Jurisdiction has:
   a. resulted from the expansion of business enterprises into national markets
   b. extended the jurisdiction of federal courts
   c. extended the jurisdiction of state courts
   d. b and c only
   e. a and c only

13. Functions of the full faith and credit clause include:
   a. requires the courts of the second state to recognize a judgment rendered by a court that does not have jurisdiction
   b. prevents states from refusing to recognize the judgments, public acts, and records of another state
   c. permits a litigant who wins a judgment in one state to take this judgment to the courts of another state
   d. all of the above
   e. b and c only

14. The amount in controversy required for diversity jurisdiction was increased for the purpose of:
   a. reducing the number of cases in all courts
   b. making people sue each other for greater amounts of money
   c. limiting the number of diversity cases that the federal courts have to decide
   d. all of the above
   e. none of the above

15. Federal courts have jurisdiction when the decision depends upon the interpretation of:
   a. the Constitution
   b. the federal statute
   c. a treaty
   d. all of the above
   e. none of the above

16. Powers of the state are referred to as:
   a. delegated powers
   b. implied powers
   c. retained powers
   d. concurrent powers
   e. none of the above

17. The provision of the U.S. Constitution that broadly empowers the federal government to regulate business activities is the:
   a. sovereignty clause
   b. privileges and immunities clause
   c. police power clause
   d. illegal search and seizure provision
   e. Commerce clause

18. What provision in the Constitution grants supremacy to federal law?
   a. Article I
   b. Article IV
   c. Article III, Section 2
   d. Article II
   e. none of the above

19. The separation-of-powers doctrine stipulates that:
   a. the authority of the government shall be divided among the judicial, legislative, and executive branches, and none of these branches shall exercise any of the powers belonging to the others
   b. the authority of the government shall be shared by the three branches, each helping the other with its functions

        c.   the legislature shall make the laws
        d.   a and c
        e.   none of the above

_____   20.   All of the following possess intermediate appellate courts:
        a.   federal system
        b.   state system
        c.   judicial system of heavily populated states
        d.   a and b
        e.   a and c

Completion Questions

21.   _____ _____ _____ improve the administration of
       justice by reducing the burden on the state's supreme court.

22.   A system that allocates the powers of sovereignty between the state and federal
       governments is known as _____.

23.   In World-Wide Volkswagen Corp. v. Woodson, Justice White ruled that _____
       was not a sufficient benchmark for personal jurisdiction under the Due Process Clause.

24.   Trial courts are known as courts of _____ _____.

25.   The authority of a court to hear a case and render a decision is referred to as its
       _____.

Chapter 3

CIVIL LITIGATION AND ALTERNATIVE DISPUTE RESOLUTION

This chapter examines the way in which U.S. court systems are intended to function. It begins by discussing the fundamental principle that characterizes litigation throughout the nation, the adversary principle. Then, the chapter notes the fact that most cases end in settlement and all of them involve issues of either fact or law. Next, the discussion moves to the judicial proceedings themselves, including pretrial procedures, the trial itself, and the appellate process. Finally, the chapter closes with a discussion of means other than the litigation process employed in the interest of dispute resolution.

CHAPTER OBJECTIVES

After reading the text presented in Chapter 3 as well as studying the related materials in this chapter of the Student Mastery Guide, you will understand:

1. Characterizations of the litigation process
   a. Adversary Principle
   b. Settlement
   c. Issues of Fact and of Law
2. Pretrial Procedures
   a. Pleadings
   b. Discovery
   c. Summary Judgments
   d. Pretrial Conference
3. The trial
   a. The jury system
   b. Burden of proof
   c. Trial stages
4. The Appellate Process
5. Alternative Dispute Resolution
   a. Arbitration
   b. Private Courts
   c. Mediation
   d. Minitrial
   e. Summary jury trial

MAJOR POINTS TO REMEMBER

Adversary Principle

1. Civil and criminal litigation places responsibility for the presentation of the evidence and legal arguments in cases on the disputing parties, since as adversaries with a personal stake in the outcome they have the incentive to do the best possible job. Attorneys often carry out these functions as representatives of the parties.

Settlement

2. The overwhelming majority of cases are settled. At some point in the litigation process, both parties agree on the terms under which a lawsuit will be terminated. Generally, the defendant agrees to pay some amount; however, both sides, because of the costs of the litigation process, usually save money by making this agreement.

Issues of Fact and Issues of Law

3. An issue of fact is one type of issue that may be presented in any litigation. When this issue is the one at hand, the two sides cannot agree on the facts of the case. Both cannot be right; thus, the judge or jury has the task of determining the real facts in order to resolve the dispute.

4. Another issue that may be presented in any litigation is one of law. This issue entails a disagreement about how the law applies to an agreed upon set of facts.

Issues and Trends: Too Many Lawsuits?

5. The overload of cases and the attendant delays in the litigation process have led many potential litigants to seek out alternative means of dispute resolution. Some court systems even require disputes to be sent to arbitration if the amount in controversy is less than a certain amount.

Issues in Ethics

6. The adversary principle can place attorneys in difficult situations, such as potential conflicts between the general duty to the courts to assist in obtaining justice and the duties to represent, within the law, the best interests of their clients. The Code of Ethics for lawyers does not allow a lawyer to knowingly make false statements in representing a client.

Pretrial Procedures

7. The initial stage of a civil lawsuit is normally referred to as the *pleadings* stage. The main pleadings include the complaint (or petition) and the answer. The purposes of the pleadings are to provide fair notice of each party's claims and define the differences between the parties on the facts and law.

8. Generally, a lawsuit is commenced by the service upon the defendant of a summons either with or without a complaint.
    After the defendant receives the complaint, he or she normally responds by serving upon the plaintiff an answer that typically contains:
    a. a denial of some or all of the allegations in the complaint
    b. affirmative defenses
    c. one or more counterclaims

9.   During the various stages of a lawsuit, the parties normally submit various *motions* to the court requesting that certain actions be taken or permitted.

10.   If the pleadings demonstrate that no issue of fact exists that needs to be resolved by the trier of facts, the court, upon motion, may grant an application for *summary judgment* in favor of either party. Before a court may grant such a motion, however, there must be no dispute as to any material facts. If there is a material dispute as to the facts, the case then proceeds to trial.

11.   The *discovery* stage of a lawsuit permits either party to obtain information regarding the case that will be presented by the other party.

12.   Most courts use pretrial conferences between a judge and the parties to expedite the litigation, reduce surprises occurring during the trial, and explore possible settlements.

The Trial

13.   Trials result when parties are unable to agree on the "facts" of the case, and they are used to process the information used to determine the facts.

14.   In civil litigation, the parties have a right to have a jury determine the facts, although this right may be waived.

15.   The plaintiff bears the "burden of proof" in civil litigation up until the point where his/her case crosses the threshold of establishing a prima facie case. At that point, the burden shifts to the defendant to rebut the plaintiff's claims. The "burden of proof" entails proving one's case by a preponderance of the evidence.

16.   The trial stage of a case is made up of several elements:
    a.   the selection of a jury
    b.   opening statements by the attorneys for the respective parties
    c.   the presentation of evidence
    d.   closing arguments in summation by the respective attorneys
    e.   the judge's instructions (charge) to the jury
    f.   deliberation and verdict by the jury
    g.   judgment for the successful party and execution

The Appellate Process

17.   The function of an appellate court is to review the legal rulings that one or both of the parties assert were incorrect. An appellate court does not normally review the facts.

18. The steps of an appeal are normally made up of:
    a. the submission of legal *briefs* prepared by the attorneys for the respective parties
    b. the presentation of *oral arguments* supporting the contentions of the respective parties
    c. the *decisions* of the court

Issues and Trends: Using the Judicial System to Intimidate the Public

19. In response to opposition from various groups, developers have employed what are called SLAPP suits: strategic lawsuit against public participation. The suit is based on defamation and while unlikely to succeed because of 1st Amendment rights to free speech, serves to drain the defendant financially with protracted litigation. Legislation has been introduced in some states to restrict SLAPP suits.

Alternative Dispute Resolution

20. This term describes any number of procedures designed to resolve disputes without litigation. These procedures have become popular due to the rising costs of litigation.

21. Examples of Alternative Dispute Resolution procedures include:
    a. Arbitration
    b. Private Courts
    c. Mediation
    d. Minitrial
    e. Summary Jury Trial

MAJOR POINTS OF CASES

Bioguardi v. *Duning* (p. 48)

This case demonstrates how liberal the court can be in terms of its requirements for what must be stated in the complaint. While the federal courts used to require a statement of "facts sufficient to constitute a cause of action," under the new rules of procedure, only "a short and plain statement of the claim showing the pleader is entitled to relief" is necessary.

Thus, the plaintiff's claim that the customs official made away with 2 cases of his tonic and sold the others in a manner incompatible with the public auction the official had announced was sufficient.

Ramseur v. *Beyer* (p. 52)

To establish an equal protection violation in the jury selection process, a defendant must demonstrate that there has been purposeful discrimination in the jury selection process. Three elements are required:
    1. The prospective juror allegedly discriminated against must be a member of a cognizable racial group.

2.   There must be a jury selection practice that permits discrimination by those so inclined.

3.   The defendant must show that the opportunity for discrimination was utilized.

In this case, where a judge intentionally tried to get a mixture of people of different races on the jury by not initially empaneling two black jurors was not discriminatory in light of the facts that there were already blacks initially selected for the jury, the judge was not trying to exclude all blacks, but rather was trying to get a mix that he thought roughly matched the racial demographics of the area, and the two jurors initially passed over because of their race were eventually empaneled.

In Re Japanese Electronic Products Antitrust Litigation (p. 53)

This case resolves a conflict between the seventh amendment's preservation of the right to a jury trial and the due process clause. The purpose of due process is to provide a set of procedures that will minimize the risk of erroneous decisions. When a case is so complex that a jury would not be able to understand the evidence and the law that applies, there is a danger that the jury's decision would be erratic and unpredictable, thereby undermining the ability of the parties to obtain a fair trial. In such a case, the plaintiff is not entitled to a jury trial.

Juries function to provide a check on judicial power. A jury unable to understand the rules and evidence cannot perform such a function.

J.C. Penny Insurance Co. v. *Varney* (p. 55)

This case makes the point that in a civil case, the preponderance of evidence standard applies, even when a factual matter being established is criminal in nature. In this case the insurance company had to prove by only a preponderance of evidence that arson caused the fire.

SELF TEST

True-False Questions

_____   1.   Everyone agrees that the adversary system is the best way to achieve justice because the parties will be motivated to bring out all the evidence and arguments that support their case.

_____   2.   Most cases that are filed are settled before trial.

_____   3.   Every year the number of state and federal lawsuits filed increases.

_____   4.   The initial stage of a civil lawsuit is generally referred to as the pleading stage.

21

_____ 5. If the pleadings in a case show that no issue of fact exists that needs to be resolved by the trier of facts, the judge can refuse.

_____ 6. A primary difference between depositions and interrogatories is that depositions are taken orally whereas interrogatories are answered in writing.

_____ 7. Only the defendant can made a motion for summary judgment.

_____ 8. A jury requires 12 persons.

_____ 9. Jury instructions are given to the jury by the judge prior to the opening statements so that the jurors will know what evidence to pay attention to during the trial.

_____ 10. Garnishment is the process by which a defendant's property is seized and sold to pay the judgment against him.

Multiple-Choice Questions

_____ 11. A function served by the pleadings in a lawsuit is:
a. to initiate or commence the lawsuit
b. to provide notice to the parties of the opposition's claims
c. to determine what differences exist between the parties
d. only a and c are correct
e. a, b and c are all correct

_____ 12. A person who does not want to file a lawsuit may use one of the following techniques:
a. arbitration
b. mediation
c. minitrial
d. summary jury trial
e. all of the above are correct

_____ 13. An attorney who excludes a prospective juror from serving on a jury and who gives no reason for such exclusion has exercised:
a. a peremptory challenge
b. a summary judgment
c. a garnishment
d. an allonge
e. only b and d are correct

14. Discovery procedures are used by attorneys to obtain:
    a. information about a prospective juror
    b. permission for an appeal of a verdict
    c. sworn statements from witnesses
    d. information on how to initiate certain legal proceedings
    e. all of the above are correct

15. Which of the following is *not* part of the appellate process?
    a. preparation and submission of briefs
    b. presentation of evidence
    c. presentation of oral arguments
    d. a decision issued by the court
    e. a, b, c, and d are all part of the appellate process

16. A defendant may include in his or her answer to the plaintiff's complaint:
    a. a preclusion order
    b. a garnishment
    c. a counterclaim
    d. a and c are both correct
    e. a, b, and c are all correct

17. Items discussed in the pretrial conference do not include:
    a. ways to narrow the legal issues
    b. ways to narrow the factual issues
    c. the number of witnesses to appear at the trial
    d. the date of the trial
    e. none of the above

18. An application made to a court for a special type of relief or order is:
    a. a motion
    b. a pretrial conference
    c. an appeal
    d. a subpoena duces tecum
    e. a trial de novo

19. Which of the following is a part of the trial stage of a case?
    a. opening statements
    b. jury selection
    c. closing statements
    d. presentation of evidence
    e. all of the above are correct

20. The authority of a court to hear any type of case presented to it and render a decision is referred to as:
    a. appellate jurisdiction
    b. original jurisdiction
    c. general jurisdiction
    d. limited jurisdiction
    e. exclusive jurisdiction

Completion Questions

21. A group of lay persons whose function is to decide issues of fact presented at a trial is known as a(n) _____ _____.

22. A motion to decide the case that is granted when no material issue of fact exists is a motion for _____ _____.

23. A document that directs a person to appear in court for the purpose of giving testimony as a witness is called a (n) _____.

24. The document that informs a defendant that he or she is being sued by someone else is the _____ _____.

25. A judgment that is contrary to the decision of the jury is called a _____.

Chapter 4

CONSTITUTIONAL LAW AND BUSINESS

Although Chapter 2 touched upon constitutional law's relationship to business with a discussion of the commerce clause, this chapter provides a broader treatment of this topic. An understanding of constitutional law is particularly important, because it is the source of all law in the United States. As a result, all behavior, including that of business, is subject to the rights provided by and the demands made by the Constitution. Businesses, like all legal actors, operate within the legal sphere of action created by the Constitution.

This chapter relates the ways in which legal rights, such as those to free speech and due process, affect the legal environment of business. Especially important to these legal rights effects has been their interpretation by the judicial system. In addition, the material presented will provide you with a better understanding of how federal power and business regulation are related.

CHAPTER OBJECTIVES

After reading Chapter 4 of the text and studying these related materials, you will understand:

1. Some major components of our federalist system under the Constitution, including federal supremacy, the preemption doctrine, the power of judicial review and state action.
2. The constitutional rights of businesses as legal entities, including those established by the First, Fifth, and Fourteenth Amendment.
3. Taxing and spending powers of the government.
4. The government's rights over international commerce.
5. The protection afforded free enterprise by the contract as well as the Privileges and Immunities Clauses of the Constitution.
6. Procedural and substantive due process.

MAJOR POINTS TO REMEMBER

Federalism

1. Federalism is a system of government in which power is shared by the federal, state, and local governments. In this system, the federal government possesses only limited enumerated powers, or those powers granted to it by the Constitution, while the rest of the powers are kept by the state and local governments. Through amendment and interpretation of the Constitution over time, the enumerated powers of the federal government have grown.

Federal Supremacy and the Preemption Doctrine

2. Under Article VI, Section 2 of the Constitution, federal law enjoys supreme status. Known as the supremacy clause, this article and section of the Constitution establishes the

preemption doctrine, which stipulates that all law must comply with federal law. In the event of a conflict between federal and either state or local law, the former prevails.

Judicial Review

3. Established by *Marbury* v. *Madison* (1803), the power of judicial review grants to the courts the authority to determine the constitutionality of governmental acts both legislative and executive in character.

The Evolution of the Constitution

4. Since its inception the Constitution has evolved through amendments as well as interpretation.

State Action

5. State actions are the public actions of governments and with the exception of slavery, the Constitution applies only to these. While legislation at all levels of government may apply constitutional principles to private action, state action is generally a prerequisite.

6. Private persons and organizations that function in ways traditionally exclusive to the state may have their actions treated as state actions.

Constitutional Rights

7. Provisions of the Constitution, both explicitly and implicitly, protect personal rights, thereby limiting government power. Although stated in absolute terms, these rights are seldom, if ever, absolute in practice. Personal rights and governmental powers often conflict, forcing the courts to use legal tests in creating a balance.

8. With few exceptions (e.g. the right to vote), constitutional rights refer to people or persons and not just citizens.

9. Since its inception, the Bill of Rights has applied to federal state action. Supreme Court interpretation of the 14th Amendment has extended this applicability to state state action as well.

First Amendment

10. Although the wording seems unambiguous in stating that no law shall limit an individual's rights to freedom of religion, speech, the press, and peaceable assembly, the First Amendment's protection is not absolute.

Freedom From and of Religion

11. The First Amendment's "Establishment Clause" protects individuals from being forced to adopt any religion. This clause stipulates that Congress is prohibited from making a law "respecting an establishment of religion."

12. The First Amendment's "Free Exercise Clause" prohibits Congress from making laws that prohibit the free exercise of religion.

Freedom of Speech

13. While spoken, written, or symbolic speech is protected by the First Amendment, to the extent that it is fraudulent, defamatory, obscene, or indecent and competes with other important interests, speech may be legally restricted.

14. Because its interest is balanced against that of the government in the regulation of commerce, commercial speech does not enjoy the same degree of protection that individual expression does.

15. Government can not only prohibit commercial speech if the prohibition is shown to serve substantial state interests, it can require speech as is the case with labelling.

16. An important distinction exists concerning offensive speech. Obscene language is not protected and may be banned, while indecent speech, offensive but not obscene by community standards, has limited protection.

17. Unlike constitutional freedoms concerning religion and speech, the press does not receive absolute protection in the Constitution.

Freedom of Peaceable Assembly

18. The right of the people to peaceably assemble is the final right protected under the First Amendment. When an assemblage is violent, however, it does not enjoy constitutional protection.

Equal Protection

19. Under the 5th and 14th Amendments combined, both natural and legal persons are afforded equal protection under federal as well as state and local law. However, laws contain many distinctions that are difference based, and the question is whether the differential treatment is permitted by the Constitution. There are different tests applied to a classification to determine its constitutionality, and the type of test applied is dependent upon the kind of classification that exists.

20. Suspect classes are those in which there is intentional governmental discrimination on the basis of race, religion, or state citizenship. Such classes receive the strict scrutiny test and

are unconstitutional unless the government can demonstrate its action is necessary to achieve a compelling state interest.

21. Quasi-suspect classes are those distinctions based on gender and illegitimacy, and they receive the intermediate scrutiny test. For the action to be constitutional, it must be shown to bear a substantial relationship to an important state interest.

22. In all cases excepting suspect and quasi-suspect classes, the government must only demonstrate that its action was reasonably related to a legitimate government interest without being arbitrary. In these cases, governmental regulation generally receives court deference.

Taxing and Spending Powers

23. The taxing power of the government, so long as it does not violate another part of the Constitution, is allowed under Article I, Section 8, Clause I, as well as the 16th Amendment (income) to achieve public policy objectives.

International Trade

24. Congress's international trade powers include the power to affect this type of trade unilaterally with tariffs and quotas as well as bilaterally and multilaterally with treaties and other agreements.

Contract Clause

25. This clause dictates that government can constitutionally modify contracts by law only to the extent that such modification is both reasonable and necessary to serve an important public purpose.

Privileges and Immunities Clause

26. Found in Article IV, Section 2 as well as the 14th Amendment, this clause protects the basic rights of citizens in states where they are not residents.

State Immunity

27. The Eleventh Amendment stipulates that states are immune from suits in federal court. Only if it consents, can the state be sued.

Due Process

28. The Due Process Clauses of the federal (Fifth Amendment) as well as the state and local governments (Fourteenth Amendment) requires deprivations of a person's life, liberty, and property to accompany a fair and reasonable procedure known as due process of law.

29. There are two components to the Due Process Clause, procedural and substantive. The right to procedural due process means that one is entitled to a fair procedure before s/he is deprived of life, liberty, and property. Generally, the more serious the deprivation of these rights, the more process that is due. Substantive due process provides that legislation and the legislative process cannot deprive anyone of due process.

MAJOR POINTS OF CASES

West v. *Atkins* (p. 67)

After receiving what he believed to be grossly inadequate treatment for a torn achilles tendon, a prison inmate, Quincy West, sued his state appointed physician, Samuel Atkins, for violating his Eighth Amendment right to freedom from cruel and unusual punishment. To support his claim, West was burdened with showing not only that there was such a violation, but also that Atkins acted "under the color of state law" in his treatment of West. The central issue in the case was whether a physician acting under contract with the state to provide medical services acts "under the color of state law" when treating an inmate.

The Court found in favor of the Plaintiff West, ruling that there was both a violation and that the violator, Atkins, acted "under the color of state law." Under the Eighth Amendment, the Court said, the state has a constitutional obligation to provide adequate medical care. Additionally, any public employee "acts under the color of state law" while performing in his/her official capacity and, thus, is subject to the same Eighth Amendment obligations. More importantly, neither the fact that the physician is a professional nor that he was contracted out releases him from this obligation, because medical treatment, the court said, is a state action.

Edenfield v. *Fane* (p. 70)

In this case, a CPA sued the Florida Board of Accountancy for its prohibition of uninvited, personal solicitation on the basis of its restriction of commercial speech. The Board justified its action by claiming that it was intended not only to protect consumers from fraud, but also that it was necessary to maintain the fact and appearance of CPA independence in auditing a business and attesting to its financial statements.

The court ruled in favor of the Plaintiff Fane, stipulating that personal solicitation is equivalent to commercial expression. Additionally, although laws restricting commercial speech need only to serve substantial state interest to be permissible, the court rules that this law did not serve such a function. The Court recognized that the Florida Board of Accountancy had substantial interests to serve, but it found that a blanket prohibition on solicitation did not serve them.

Turner Broadcasting System (TBS) v. *Federal Communications Commission (FCC)* (p. 73)

After losing in court concerning an FCC regulation requiring cable broadcasting companies to reserve channels for public broadcasting, Turner asked the Supreme Court to prevent enforcement of this regulation on First Amendment grounds until the Supreme

29

Court decided the case. Noting that an injunction is appropriate only if the legal rights at issue are "indisputably clear", the Court denied the injunction. Fundamental to its denial was the Court's undecided categorization of cable operators in First Amendment protection. Specifically, it had not decided whether cable operators' activities are more akin to newspapers (basically unrestricted) or radio (restricted). Thus, the legal rights were not "indisputably clear", and the injunction was denied.

Steffan v. *Aspin* (p. 76)

In this case, Joseph Steffan was dismissed from the Navy for admitting his homosexual orientation. The D.C. District Court upheld this dismissal, ruling that homosexuals did not deserve equal protection as a group because they are not a suspect class. Using a rational-review basis, the D.C. District Court found the Navy's action justified in that it served the legitimate goal of maintaining discipline, morale, et cetera.

Using a rational review basis itself, the Supreme Court overturned the District Court's decision. The Court found the argument that homosexuals had a "propensity" to break military law that prohibited homosexual activity to be illegitimate because it assumed a necessary linkage between thought and action. Additionally, the Court ruled that the Navy's concern about discipline, morale, et cetera was not sufficient to justify dismissing Steffan, because such dismissal cannot be legitimized on the basis of third part prejudices; in this case, those of the other midshipmen. The Court ordered Steffan's reinstatement.

United States v. *Good*

Good sued the United States for its seizure of his land on the basis of federal forfeiture law after his drug conviction. He claimed that this action violated his Fifth Amendment right to due process. Delivering the majority opinion, Justice Kennedy noted that such a property seizure is justified only if it fulfills a pressing need. Ruling that for the government there was neither a pressing need nor was there notice of an administrative burden - the Court found in favor of Good.

In dissent, Justice Rehnquist argued that the ex parte warrant requirement under the Fourth Amendment provides the justification necessary for the government's action; i.e. the government had the purpose of combatting illegal drugs. Also in dissent, Justice Thomas argued that Good had lost his property rights with the conviction, and the conviction itself served as proper notice for the seizure.

SELF TEST

True-False Questions

_____ 1. Under Federalism, any power not granted to the state and local governments goes to the federal governments.

_____ 2. The principle of federal supremacy stipulates that federal law prevails in a conflict with state and local laws.

30

3. Amendments to the Constitution have been the sole means for this document's changes over the years.

_____

4. Whether in practice or in theory, personal rights protected by the Constitution are absolute.

_____

5. The Free Exercise Clause of the First Amendment is a bulwark to freedom of speech.

_____

6. State action concerning commercial speech is subject to a lower level of scrutiny than in ordinary speech cases.

_____

7. Offensive speech is distinguished as either obscene or indecent.

_____

8. The Fifth Amendment guarantees persons equal protection in actions by all governments in the United States.

_____

9. Under the Privileges and Immunities Clause, state universities are now prohibited from charging non-residents extra fees for attending the university.

_____

10. The right to procedural due process is the guarantee to a fair procedure before the deprivation of one's life, liberty, and property.

Multiple Choice Questions

_____

11. The preemption doctrine stipulates that:
   a. the federal government has the right to seize control of the operations of any state or local government.
   b. state and local governing authority must be limited.
   c. the Supreme Court can decide the constitutionality of any piece of legislation.
   d. all law must comply with federal law.
   e. All of the above.

_____

12. Which of the following is/are true of judicial review?
   a. It has its origins in the 1803 decision *Marbury* v. *Madison*.
   b. It is a part of the system of checks and balances.
   c. It stipulates that the Court can determine the constitutionality of any challenged governmental acts.
   d. All of the above.
   e. a and c

13. Personal rights under the Constitution
    a. are implied
    b. are expressed
    c. limit government power
    d. All of the above
    e. None of the above

14. Which clause is the basis of the separation of church and state?
    a. Establishment Clause
    b. Free Exercise Clause
    c. Federal Supremacy Clause
    d. Church Freedom Clause
    e. None of the above

15. Advertising is an example of:
    a. commercial speech
    b. political speech
    c. non-political speech
    d. fraud
    e. a and c

16. Indecent speech is:
    a. speech that is offensive to any one person
    b. speech that is offensive to any reasonable person
    c. speech that is offensive by contemporary community standards but not obscene
    d. synonymous with obscene speech
    e. None of the above

17. A person's right to Due Process falls under what amendment?
    a. First
    b. Seventh
    c. Second
    d. Fourth
    e. Fifth

18. Intentional governmental discrimination is okay when:
    a. it is never okay
    b. it is on the basis of class
    c. it passes certain types of tests that are dependent on the type of discrimination
    d. a law is passed allowing for it
    e. None of the above

_____ 19. Rational basis review requires that discrimination be justified by:
a. the lowest standard test
b. the strict scrutiny test
c. the intermediate test
d. the rational person test
e. None of the above

_____ 20. Which of the following played an important role in the changes that have been made in Constitutional Law?
a. Amendments to the Constitution
b. court interpretation of the Constitution
c. the doctrine of stare decisis
d. All of the above
e. a and b

Completion Questions

21. _____ _____ is the public action of government.

22. Distinctions based on gender and illegitimacy are _____ classifications.

23. The _____ _____ stipulates that all law must comply with federal law.

24. _____ _____ is the type of speech that concerns business interests.

25. Persons are guaranteed equal protection in actions by state and local governments under the _____ _____ .

Chapter 5

INTRODUCTION TO CRIMINAL LAW

In contrast to Chapter 2, which dealt with civil litigation, this chapter presents an overview of the criminal justice legal system's procedures. It also briefly explains the mens rea, or criminal intent, element of many substantive crimes. From this foundation of criminal law the increasingly important areas of criminal liability of corporations, white collar crimes, and computer crimes are examined.

A fundamental understanding of criminal law is necessary for managers today. Businesses are not only victims of crime, but they can also be the criminals. As society comes to better comprehend the substantial costs it incurs from criminal activity related to business transactions, more resources are being devoted to the enforcement of existing criminal statutes, more business transactions and activities are being regulated by criminal statutes, and the punishments being imposed for convictions of these crimes are becoming more severe. Comprehension of this chapter will be important for the study of many of the subsequent chapters in this textbook.

CHAPTER OBJECTIVES

After reading Chapter 5 of the text and studying the related materials in this chapter of the Student Mastery Guide, you will understand:

1. The basis for criminal law and punishment
2. The basic procedures that apply to criminal cases, including those required by the Bill of Rights to the U.S. Constitution
3. The basis for corporate criminal liability
4. The nature and types of white collar crime
5. The evolving development of computer crimes

MAJOR POINTS TO REMEMBER

Basis of Criminal Law

1. Crimes are offenses against society that are established by local, state, or federal statutes and prosecuted by a public official on behalf of society. The victims of a crime generally must seek monetary compensation for their injuries through a civil lawsuit.

Punishment

2. Punishment for crimes can include a fine, imprisonment, or death, plus the loss of certain civil rights. One view of the purpose of punishment is that it acts as a deterrent to the commission of future crimes, while another is that it represents retribution by society against criminals.

Classification of Crimes

3. A felony is a crime punishable by death or imprisonment in a penitentiary, while misdemeanors are less serious crimes that are punishable by imprisonment other than in a penitentiary. Conviction of a felony also results in loss of certain civil rights. Felonies are often divided into categories or by degrees to reflect the varying seriousness of different criminal acts.

Criminal Act and Intent

4. Generally, for one to be convicted of a crime, she or he must commit a criminal act. This is known as the principle of actus reus. Additionally, she or he must be shown to have acted with criminal intent, a principle known by its Latin name of mens rea.

Regulatory Crimes

5. Sometimes a criminal statute imposes strict liability on those who commit the criminal act. Such statutes do not require proof of mens rea. Some of these statutes apply to businesses that are closely regulated by government. Strict liability crimes usually provide for less serious punishments than crimes requiring proof of mens rea.

Steps in the Criminal Justice Process

6. The steps in the criminal justice process normally are:
   a. A crime is reported to the police and they investigate to determine if there is probable cause to believe a specific person or persons committed it.
   b. If probable cause exists, an arrest can be made under an arrest warrant or a grand jury indictment upon which an arrest warrant has been issued. Warrantless arrests can be made based on probable cause, if, in the case of a felony, the suspect may not be easily located again and, for misdemeanors, when the crime is committed in the officer's presence.
   c. After the arrest, the defendant is taken to the police station for *booking* for the crime. For minor crimes *bail* for release from jail is now set. Defendants then have their *first appearance* before a court to be informed of the charges and their constitutional rights and to enter a plea. For felonies, the decision to release on bail can be made at this time, if a not-guilty plea was given. If the defendant pleaded guilty, then the court proceeds toward sentencing.
   d. If the arrest was not made based on a warrant issued from a grand jury indictment, a *preliminary hearing* would be held before a judge to determine if there is probable cause that the defendant should be bound over for, in some states, a grand jury hearing or, in other states, trial based on the judge's issuance of an *information* to formally charge the defendant. The defendant now enters a plea to the formal charges.
   e. After being formally charged and entering a plea, defendants in serious cases will decide whether to have a jury trial.

f. Plea bargaining between the prosecution and the defendant can occur at this time. If a plea bargain is reached to resolve the case without trial, it normally will be either an agreement for the defendant to plead guilty to a less serious crime than the one originally charged or one in which a guilty plea is given for a less severe sentence. Plea bargaining can be an ethical dilemma, especially when the defendant is suspected of murder, as was the case in the Ethics Box.

g. In criminal trials the government has the burden of proving that the defendant committed the crime charged by submitting evidence that establishes guilt beyond a reasonable doubt. Upon conviction the defendant is sentenced to a punishment ordered by the court as stated by the criminal statues.

Defenses

7. A criminal defendant may be exonerated from guilt for a crime even if she or he committed it if she or he has a valid defense. Valid defenses include:

a. Entrapment. This occurs when the accused is induced by a law enforcement officer or other government officials to commit a crime that he or she would not have committed otherwise. The idea for the crime does not originate with the accused.

b. A mistake of fact. This occurs, for example, when somebody inadvertently takes the wrong suitcase at a baggage claim. This is a sufficient defense, because the requirement of mens rea is not satisfied. Notably, a mistake of law is not a valid defense, for "ignorance of the law is no excuse."

c. Duress. This occurs when someone is coerced to commit a crime by the immediate threat of serious physical harm if she or he does otherwise.

d. Incapacity. This is a valid defense when the accused does not have the mental capacity to comprehend the moral consequences of his or her acts. Incapacity defenses include infancy, insanity, and intoxication.

e. Justifiable use of force. This defense is valid by virtue of the accused's attempt to protect his or her property by non-deadly force or his or her person with deadly force.

Criminal Procedure

8. A fundamental goal of criminal procedures is to avoid the conviction of an innocent person. Other goals include fairness, equality, and minimizing the burden of proof on the accused. Much of the Bill of Rights of the Constitution serves to accomplish these goals by protecting persons against actions of the federal, state, and local governments.

9. The Fourth Amendment to the U.S. Constitution protects persons against unreasonable searches and seizures, including arrests. Normally, a search or an arrest must be made pursuant to a warrant issued by a judge based on probable cause to believe that evidence will be found in a particular place, or that the person arrested committed a crime. There are situations, however, in which a warrant is not required to conduct a search or make an arrest, if probable cause exists and the facts also show that due to emergency circumstances a warrant could not be obtained first.

10. The individual liberties of the Fourth Amendment are protected by a judicially created remedy, known as the exclusionary rule. In general, the exclusionary rule requires that illegally obtained evidence cannot be used at trial to convict a criminal defendant whose rights were violated. There are, however, exceptions to this rule for circumstances in which the application of this rule would not serve to deter future violations of constitutional rights. As indicated by the "Issues and Trends" box, the Supreme Court has narrowed the application of the exclusionary rule. One recently established exception to the rule is the recognition of "good faith".

11. The Fifth Amendment to the U.S. Constitution provides through the due-process clause that civil and criminal procedures must be fundamentally fair. Under due process of law, persons must be given adequate notice prior to trial of the charges against them and a fair opportunity to defend themselves before an impartial court. The Fifth Amendment also protects persons from being tried criminally more than once by the same governmental entity for a single act. This amendment, however, does not bar the victim from bringing a civil lawsuit, or another governmental entity from filing a criminal action, for the same act.

12. Among other protections, the Sixth Amendment guarantees the right in criminal cases to be tried by an impartial jury and to be represented by an attorney. If a person cannot afford to hire an attorney in a criminal case, the court must, upon request by the defendant, appoint one to defend him or her.

13. Ethical questions arise when the accused allegedly has committed a crime that is horrific by popular standards and is still afforded a defense attorney. These questions attain even more depth when the accused's attorney even personally believes his or her client is guilty. Yet all accused criminals, guilty or not, have the right to counsel to insure the protection of their legal rights.

14. The Eighth Amendment prohibits excessive bail and excessive fines, as well as cruel and unusual punishment. Historically, this amendment has applied to criminal cases only. Recently, some people, especially businesses, have argued that it should also apply to punitive damages in civil cases, but the Supreme Court has not adopted this view.

Corporate Criminal Liability

15. Today, corporations can be convicted of strict liability crimes that do not require proof of mens rea, or a guilty mind. Corporations can also be convicted of crimes requiring proof of mens rea, since the mens rea of its agents or employees who committed the criminal acts on behalf of the corporation is attributed to the corporation. Under the majority rule, a corporation can be criminally punished when its agents and employees (except for lower-level employees in some states) commit crimes with the intent to benefit the corporation.

White Collar Crime

16. White collar crimes are those nonviolent crimes that are committed in a commercial context by managers or professionals either against their employers or for their employers against the public. Such crimes impose substantial harm and costs upon society.

17. Generally, bribery involves offering or giving or promising to give something of value to another with the intent to improperly influence decision making. Bribery statutes typically focus on bribery of public officials, but about one-half of the states also make commercial bribery illegal.

18. Larceny is often divided into grand larceny for property of substantial value and petit larceny for property of relatively minor value, with each having separate punishments. Related to larceny are the crimes of: (a) "robbery" in which the property is taken by violence or threats thereof; (b) "false pretenses" in which the property is taken with the owner's consent, but the consent was induced by intentional deceptions; and (c) computer fraud and fraudulent use of credit cards.

19. Embezzlement occurs when one who has been entrusted with the property of another acts to deprive the owner of that property or its value, regardless of whether he or she originally intended to take the property.

20. Forgery occurs when a person, with the intent to defraud, alters another's person's writing without authority or presents an unauthentic document as genuine.

21. Federal statutes make it illegal to use either the mail or wire in connection with any scheme to defraud.

22. Bankruptcy fraud occurs when either the debtor withholds assets or the creditor files a false claim.

23. When income is derived from illegal sources but made to appear legitimate, this act is known as money laundering and is illegal under the Money Laundering Control Act.

24. Conspiracy occurs when two or more people plan to commit a crime. Once a single person involved in a conspiracy acts covertly to further the criminal purpose, all conspirators are criminally liable.

25. Congress and the states have during this century enacted many other statutory crimes that apply to business. Some of these will be studied in later chapters.

Issues and Trends: Criminal and Civil RICO

26. The federal RICO statute was intended primarily to reduce organized crime's ability to use funds gained from racketeering (certain illegal) activities to acquire interests in legitimate businesses. There are both civil and criminal penalties for violating RICO. The courts have interpreted RICO broadly to achieve its purpose. Due to this broad interpretation, RICO has also become an important basis for civil lawsuits against legitimate businesses, since a business need not be convicted of any crime for it to apply. The civil penalties include the right to recover treble damages (three times the amount of the actual damages).

MAJOR POINTS OF CASES

State v. Wheat (p. 88)

This case illustrates that a crime can be committed even though the accused did not know the consequences of her acts of drinking and driving. The statutes in this case made it a crime to kill a human being by "criminal negligence," which is conduct grossly below the standard of care that a reasonably careful person would be expected to maintain under like circumstances. Even though the defendant had no specific or general criminal intent, the court held that the evidence was sufficient to prove she was driving drunk and that such conduct constituted criminal negligence under the statute.

In re Application of Dow Jones and Company (p. 96)

In this case, the Court ruled that, in the occasional conflict between First Amendment rights to free press and Sixth Amendment rights to a fair trial, the latter must have priority.

Applying its ruling to the case, the Court upheld the "gag order" imposed on the press immediately prior to the trial of prominent government officials. Such an order was justified, the court said, because there was a "reasonable likelihood" that pretrial publicity would prejudice a fair trial.

United States v. Coin (p. 100)

This case clearly establishes that repayment of embezzled funds is neither a defense to the crime, nor is it material to determining whether there was criminal intent when the restitution occurs after the crime has been committed. The crime was committed when the defendant expended tribal funds for personal uses, thereby depriving the tribe of deciding how to use those funds. Repayment after his indictment did not change the harm suffered by the tribe. Further, an intent to make restitution at the time the funds were embezzled could not be a defense to this crime.

Reves v. Ernst and Young (p. 104)

Interpreting the language of RICO's section 1962(c), the Court decided that outsiders are liable under its provisions only to the extent that they participate in the enterprise's operation or management. Applying this interpretation to the case, the Court ruled that Arthur Young's failure to tell the Co-Op board that the plant should have been given its fair market value did not constitute such participation. Thus, the Court upheld the lower court's ruling, which stipulated that Arthur Young is not liable under section 1962 (c) of RICO.

SELF TEST

True-False Questions

_____   1.   The primary purpose of criminal law is to remedy the harm done to victims by awarding them monetary compensation.

2.   Prosecutions of crimes are normally done by victims.

3.   Normally, a less severe punishment would be authorized for a misdemeanor than for a felony.

4.   All statutory crimes require proof of a specific mens rea.

5.   Criminal procedures are designed in part to minimize the risk of convicting innocent persons.

6.   State governments are bound to observe the individual liberties guaranteed by the Bill of Rights to the U.S. Constitution.

7.   If the police conduct a search and seizure pursuant to a warrant obtained in good faith, but which is invalid due to a lack of probable cause, the exclusionary rule requires that the evidence obtained be declared inadmissible in a criminal trial.

8.   A grand jury decides whether a defendant is guilty of the crime charged.

9.   The standard of proof is the same for civil and criminal trials.

10.   Companies that are victims of computer crime often do not report the crimes to the police.

Multiple-Choice Questions

11.   Punishment under the criminal law is believed to:
    a.   deter future crimes
    b.   constitute retribution by society against criminals
    c.   remedy the harm done to victims of crimes
    d.   both a and b are correct
    e.   a, b, and c are correct

12.   Generally, if the punishment for a crime can be death or imprisonment in a state or federal penitentiary, then the crime most likely is a:
    a.   felony
    b.   misdemeanor
    c.   petty offense
    d.   strict liability crime

13. The principle of actus reus holds that in order for a person to be convicted of a crime:
    a. there must be a preponderance of the evidence
    b. the accused must have had criminal intent
    c. the crime must have occurred no more than seven years before the formal charge
    d. the accused must have committed a criminal act
    e. None of the above

14. RICO's provisions:
    a. apply to criminal activity
    b. apply to civil activity
    c. include criminal sanctions
    d. were originally formed to deter organized crime from infiltrating legitimate businesses
    e. All of the above

15. A crime that requires no proof of mens rea is a _____ crime.
    a. specific intent
    b. general intent
    c. misdemeanor
    d. felony
    e. strict liability

16. Persons are protected from unreasonable search and seizures by the government under the _____ Amendment.
    a. Fourth
    b. Fifth
    c. Sixth
    d. Eighth

17. In general, due process of law requires:
    a. adequate prior notice of charges of wrongful conduct under the law
    b. a fair opportunity to defend before an impartial decision maker
    c. the same procedures for criminal cases as those for civil cases
    d. a and b are correct
    e. none of the above is correct

_____ 18. Under the Sixth Amendment to the U.S. Constitution, a criminal defendant is entitled to:
   a.   the assistance of legal counsel
   b.   a speedy and public trial
   c.   reasonable bail
   d.   a and b are correct
   e.   b and c are correct

_____ 19. An arrest of a person for allegedly committing a crime can be made pursuant to:
   a.   a warrant
   b.   nolo contendere
   c.   a plea bargain
   d.   probable cause in some situations
   f.   a and d are correct

_____ 20. The standard of proof in a criminal case is proof:
   a.   by a preponderance of the evidence
   b.   by clear and convincing evidence
   c.   beyond a reasonable doubt
   d.   beyond a shadow of a doubt

Completion Questions

21. Many criminal cases are resolved without trial through a _____
_____.

22. Nonviolent crimes committed in business settings by managers or professionals are _____ _____ crimes.

23. _____ is the crime of physically taking of another's property with the intent to deprive the owner of it or its value.

24. Evidence seized in violation of the Fourth Amendment is sometimes inadmissible in criminal trials under the _____ _____.

25. _____ _____ involves the obtaining of property from a person through misrepresentations of fact.

Chapter 6

INTENTIONAL TORTS

When a person breaches a duty owed to another party, he or she commits a tort. Torts can be either intentional or unintentional. This chapter examines the former type, specifically those torts against the person or against property interests.

There are a number of instances in which intentional torts are important to the field of business. Advertising can cross over into the region of falsehood, making a business liable under a defamation suit. Also, relatives of a worker killed on the job may sue the company for wrongful death. Private property rights are essential to businesses in the United States, and businesses are protected by torts against property rights. Whether intentional torts provide a threat or a protection for businesses, it is important that businesspersons understand both the basics and the nuances of intentional tort law.

CHAPTER OBJECTIVES

After reading chapter 6 and studying the related materials in the Student Mastery Guide, you will understand:

1. The different types of torts against the person.
2. The different types of torts against property rights.

MAJOR POINTS TO REMEMBER

Tort Categories

1. Intentional torts are one of three areas of tort law. Negligence and strict liability are the other types of torts. Intent to do a wrongful act is the cornerstone of intentional tort law. Negligence and strict liability are torts in which liability is assessed even when no wrongful intent is present.

Torts Against the Person

2. Torts against the person are those that are directed at an individual and include:
   a. battery
   b. assault
   c. false imprisonment
   d. defamation
   e. invasion of privacy
   f. intentional infliction of emotional distress
   g. wrongful death

3. An act that gives to a cause of action for battery can also, many times, violate the criminal law of a state or the federal government as well.

43

4. Words that are coupled with a threat to inflict immediate or imminent physical harm can constitute the tort of assault.

5. Under the common law, if a storekeeper detains a person against his or her will for suspicion of shoplifting, and it is later ascertained that the person did not steal anything, the storekeeper is deemed to have committed the tort of false imprisonment.

   Most states, however, have passed laws that permit storekeepers to detain suspected shoplifters for a reasonable period of time. These laws insulate the storekeeper from liability unless it can be shown that he or she acted either (a) without reasonable cause, or (b) in bad faith.

6. The tort of defamation of character is comprised of:
   a. libel-written defamation
   b. slander-oral or verbal defamation

7. A special type of defamation known as defamation per se exists when the statement that is published does any of the following:
   a. accuses the defamed person of committing a morally reprehensible crime
   b. claims that the defamed person has a loathsome communicable disease
   c. affects the defamed person's profession or business
   d. accuses a woman of unchastity
   If a matter is defamatory per se, the plaintiff need not establish anything other than the fact that the statement in question was made. Special damages need not be established.

8. If a statement claimed to be defamatory is actually true, no action for defamation exists. In other words, truth is an absolute defense against an action for defamation.

9. If the person making a defamatory statement has an absolute privilege, an action for defamation will not be successful. For example: the statement of a judge made while he or she is hearing a case in court.

10. There are four types of invasion of privacy:
    a. intrusion upon one's physical solitude;
    b. appropriation of one's name or likeness;
    c. misrepresentation of one in the public eye; and
    d. the public disclosure of private facts

11. With new technology that enables ever-increasing monitoring of individuals' behavior, the issue of right to privacy in the workplace has begun to pose even more ethical dilemmas.

12. Intentional infliction of emotional distress is now a separate tort, and it is actionable in cases where one person causes severe emotional suffering in another by means considered extremely outrageous by the average community member.

13. When a legal person by his or her willful or negligent behavior causes the death of another, he or she can be subject to a wrongful death action. Manufacturing firms are particularly susceptible to this type of suit.

Torts Against Property Rights

14. The tort of trespass consists of:
    a. trespass to land-intentionally entering upon another person's land and
    b. trespass to personal property-intentionally taking or damaging the personal property of another.

15. A tort that is similar to trespass to property is the tort of conversion. When conversion occurs, the measure of damages is the full value of the converted property. Conversion is the intentional exercise of control over personal property that so seriously interferes with another person's right of possession that the law requires the offending party to buy the property at full value.

16. A nuisance is an unlawful interference with real property (land). In order to be wrongful, the nuisance must be substantial and unreasonable and must outweigh any social usefulness derived from the activity.

17. The business tort of interference with contractual relations stipulates that one who intentionally and without justification causes a third person not to perform a contract with another is liable for the resulting damages.

MAJOR POINTS OF CASES

Katko v. *Briney* (p. 108)

The Briney case highlights and illustrates a particularly complex and sensitive issue. It holds that a person may use only such force as is reasonable under the circumstances to protect one's person or property. This principle applies even if the intruder intends to commit a theft or is a trespasser.

In this case, the court specifically ruled that Briney was unjustified in using a shotgun in an attempt to protect his property. It also held that a property owner was not justified in using deadly force, or force intended to seriously injure another, unless that person was in the process of committing a violent felony offense, an offense punishable by death, or an act that endangered human life. The case is somewhat unusual in that even though Katko entered the property with the intent to commit a theft, the court still ruled in his favor.

Goldfarb v. *Baker* (p. 111)

At issue in this case was whether a professor's reaction to being struck with a pie (he barred a student from the classroom and accused the student of blackmail) was so outrageous as to constitute the tort of intentional infliction of emotional distress. The court, while finding that the student had experienced some embarrassment, held that the suffering of the student was not severe enough to be actionable at law.

In affirming the earlier decision in favor of the plaintiff in this wrongful death suit, the court presented three principles. First, the court may not review the jury's resolution of conflicts concerning expert testimony that establishes causation. Secondly, for foreseeability to exist, all that is required is a risk of harm. If conduct is a substantial factor in the harm done, then a wrongful death suit is actionable. Third, the awarding of damages need not take only pecuniary losses into account. Damages arising from the loss of society, comfort, care, and protection afforded by the deceased are also legitimate factors in determining the appropriate compensation.

Edward Vartine Studios, Inc. **v.** *Fraternal Composite Service, Inc.* **(p. 114)**

In its decision, the court implicitly distinguishes between healthy competition and the tort of interference with contracts. Offering better prices, service, and/or quality signals only the existence of the former, and any responsibility for a breach of contract lies with the party terminating the contract. However, when a competitor offers another competitor's client an indemnity clause for breaking their contract, then that competitor is justifiably subject to a suit under the tort of interference with contracts.

PRACTICAL CONSIDERATIONS

When a burglar attempts to enter a person's home and the homeowner discovers the intruder, the homeowner's first reaction may be to become violent in an attempt to thwart the burglar's larcenous intentions. The standard that is applied is that the homeowner can use only as much force as is necessary to protect his or her property and safety and the safety of his or her family.

While the standard of conduct to be applied to the situation is easy to state, the actual application of the rule is difficult because it is hard to determine exactly how much force is necessary under the circumstances.

Example: Burt, age 28, who weighs 150 pounds, discovers that a burglar is in his home. The burglar is 6'5" tall and weights 260 pounds. Burt picks up a baseball bat with the intention of using it on the burglar.

The issue, of course, is whether Burt is justified in using the bat, and, if he is, where he can hit the burglar with it. Would Burt be justified in hitting the burglar on the head with the bat, in using it on the burglar's knees, or would he be justified in using it at all? The difficulty is that if the force used is not justified, the homeowner will be liable for the injuries inflicted on the burglar. To be justified in using force likely to cause death or serious bodily harm, one must be threatened by a person likely to cause death or serious bodily harm.

SELF TEST

True-False Questions

_____   1.   The three categories of intentional torts are negligence, strict liability, and trespass.

_____ 2. The difference between the torts of trespass to personal property and conversion is that conversion is a tort against real property.

_____ 3. Under certain circumstances, a single act may be deemed to be both a crime and a tort at the same time.

_____ 4. A storekeeper may detain a person suspected to be a shoplifter for any length of time, and will not be liable for false imprisonment even when the detained person proves that he or she did not steal anything.

_____ 5. In a lawsuit based on defamation per se, the plaintiff is required to establish and prove special damages.

_____ 6. A business commits a tort of interference with contractual relations when it advertises prices that undercut a competitor.

_____ 7. If a surgeon who has been authorized to remove a person's appendix only also removes the patient's gall bladder, which is seriously diseased, the surgeon has committed the tort of battery.

_____ 8. If Arnold throws a knife at George, who is aware that it is being thrown, and the knife misses George by one inch, George may sue Arnold for the tort of assault.

_____ 9. A person may commit the tort of trespass without personally entering onto another person's land.

_____ 10. A person who unreasonably interferes with another person's use of his or her land may be held liable for damages on the basis that his interference is a nuisance.

Multiple-Choice Questions

_____ 11. Liability for libel regarding a public figure will exist when:
    a. the statement in question is true, although the person who made it did not know the statement was true at the time
    b. the statement was made maliciously, that is, it was known to be false or made with reckless disregard as to its truth or falsity
    c. the defamatory statement was oral
    d. the statement was made in a daily newspaper
    e. b and c are correct

12. Which of the following is not an intentional tort?
    a.   battery
    b.   false imprisonment
    c.   negligence
    d.   conversion
    e.   all of the above are intentional torts

13. The intentional touching of another without justification and without consent is known as the tort of:
    a.   nuisance
    b.   assault
    c.   battery
    d.   b and c are both correct
    e.   none of the above is correct

14. A defense in an action based on defamation that will have the effect of preventing the plaintiff from recovering any money is:
    a.   lack of personal knowledge of the plaintiff
    b.   carelessness in making the statement
    c.   truth of the statement
    d.   carelessness in researching the facts
    e.   a and b are both correct

15. An example of a defense against the charge of defamation would be that:
    a.   the defamatory statement was not true
    b.   the defamatory statement was libelous
    c.   the defamatory statement was slanderous
    d.   no one other than the person defamed heard the statement
    e.   no crime was committed

16. Under the common law, a storekeeper who suspects that a customer is in the process of committing the act of shoplifting:
    a.   is prohibited from detaining the customer until police arrive
    b.   can detain the customer in the store for a reasonable time, but is liable for false imprisonment if the customer is able to show he or she was not stealing anything
    c.   can detain the customer for a reasonable time and is liable for false imprisonment only if he or she detains the customer after the police arrive
    d.   can detain the customer for any length of time without being liable for false imprisonment
    e.   cannot detain the person unless he or she actually saw an item of stolen property on the person of the customer

_____ 17. Which of the following is considered to be a tort against property interests?
    a.   trespass
    b.   nuisance
    c.   conversion
    d.   only a and c are correct
    e.   a, b, and c are all correct

_____ 18. If a person realizes that someone is breaking into his or her house without permission, the person who owns the house may:
    a.   use any amount of force to prevent the intruder from entering the house
    b.   use deadly force when the intruder is in the house under all circumstances
    c.   use only such force as is necessary to protect his or her property or personal safety
    d.   use force only after contacting the police and notifying them of the intruder's presence
    e.   not use force at all

_____ 19. The area of tort law that involves balancing the gravity and probability of harm resulting from the defendant's conduct against its social utility is:
    a.   nuisance
    b.   defamation
    c.   assault
    d.   conversion
    e.   none of the above is correct

_____ 20. Torts against a person include:
    a.   nuisance
    b.   defamation
    c.   prima facie tort
    d.   grand larceny
    e.   all of the above

Completion Questions

21. A civil wrong for which a court will provide a remedy is known and referred to as a(n)_____.

22. The intentional exercise of control over personal property that seriously interferes with another person's right of possession is called _____.

23. The intentional act of putting someone in immediate apprehension for his or her safety is the offense of _____.

24.   The intentional act of defamation by written word is known as _____.

25.   The intentional entering upon another's land or causing an object or third person to do so is the tort of _____ to land.

Chapter 7

NEGLIGENCE AND STRICT LIABILITY

Unintentional acts frequently cause injury to others. Occasionally a person who suffers such injury contributes to the unintended consequences by his or her own careless conduct.

This chapter discusses the concept of negligence and considers the various factors that render someone liable for damages as a result of his or her careless or reckless conduct. Before a person can be held accountable to another, that person must owe some obligation or duty of care to the injured person, and the injuries sustained must have resulted form the breach of that obligation. The chapter also considers two very important procedural considerations, as well as certain defenses that are available to a person who is sued for causing injury to another.

The chapter also discusses various legal concepts that impose liability for injuries sustained by another person even though the culpable party has acted responsibly and with a reasonable degree of care. This area of law, which includes "no-fault" liability as well as strict liability in tort, is a very perplexing one that requires a reorientation of philosophy, inasmuch as our society has generally considered that liability hinges on fault. When one considers the logic that has caused the development of the legal principles concerned with this area of law, however, the rules as issue appear to be rational and to have definite application to practical situations.

CHAPTER OBJECTIVES

After reading Chapter 7 of this text and studying the related materials in the Student Mastery Guide, you will understand:

1. The elements of negligence
2. The procedural doctrines that help a plaintiff establish negligence
3. The defenses to negligence
4. The elements of strict liability

MAJOR POINTS TO REMEMBER

Negligence

1. The tort of negligence does not depend on the unreasonableness of the tort-feasor's motive, but depends rather on the unreasonableness of his or her conduct. Liability is based on fault.

2. In order to establish negligence, the plaintiff must prove all of the following:
   a. the defendant owed a *duty of care* to the plaintiff
   b. the defendant *breached* the duty of care
   c. the plaintiff was *injured*
   d. a *causal relationship* exists between the defendant's conduct and the plaintiff's injuries
   e. the defendant's conduct was the *proximate cause* of the plaintiff's injuries.

3. In determining whether the defendant owned a legal duty of due care to the plaintiff, a court will balance such factors as risk, foreseeability, and probability of injury against the social utility of the defendant's conduct, the burden that would be created by a duty, and other consequences of imposing a duty.

4. In determining whether a person has breached a duty to use due care, the courts consider whether that person acted in the way that a "reasonable and prudent person" would have acted in the same or similar circumstances. If the defendant has not, the court will find that he or she breached the duty of care.

5. Under the trauma rule, it is required that a mental injury (mental distress) be manifested by a physical injury.

6. If a person's conduct was a "substantial factor" in causing injury to another, such person will not be excused from responsibility simply because other causes contributed to the injury that was sustained.

7. Under the doctrine of proximate cause, a defendant will be held responsible only for the natural, probable, or foreseeable consequences of his or her conduct.

Procedural Doctrines

8. While the plaintiff in a lawsuit has the burden of proving his or her case, in a negligence action two doctrines modify that burden:
   a. negligence per se
   b. res ipsa loquitur
   If a person violates a statute that is relevant to the case involved and the court determines that the statute was intended to apply as a standard of civil liability, a finding that such violative conduct is negligence per se (negligence as a matter of law) is justified. In order to make such a determination, the court must find both of the following:
   a. the statute was intended to apply to the case involved
   b. the injuries sustained by the plaintiff were of the type the statute was intended to prevent
   The doctrine of res ipsa loquitur applies when the only inference or conclusion that can be drawn is that the injuries that were sustained could have occurred only as a result of the negligence of another person. This doctrine can be invoked when the plaintiff can show both of the following:
   a. the injury sustained is of a type that does not ordinarily occur without the presence of negligence
   b. the defendant was in exclusive control of the instrumentality that caused the injury

52

Defenses

9. Two defenses with respect to an action based on negligence are:
   a. contributory negligence
   b. assumption of risk

10. The doctrine of contributory negligence acts as an absolute bar to the claims of the injured party in an action based on negligence. However, most states today follow the concept of comparative negligence instead. Under comparative negligence the relative fault of the parties is determined. If the plaintiff's negligence exceeds that of the defendant, then the plaintiff's claim is disallowed, similar to contributory negligence. However, if the plaintiff's negligence is less than the defendant's, then the plaintiff wins, but the amount of damages recovered reflects the percentage of fault assigned to the plaintiff's conduct.

11. Assumption of risk is a defense that applies when a plaintiff in a negligence case knew or should have known of a particular risk caused by the defendant's conduct and nonetheless voluntarily decided to encounter it.

Strict Liability

12. The doctrine of strict liability applies to situations in which a person's conduct creates an unusually great risk of harm even when reasonable care is exercised. In order for this doctrine to apply, however, the party who creates the risk must:
    a. be aware of the abnormally dangerous nature of the activity
    b. voluntarily engage in it

13. Liability under strict liability is limited to those consequences that can reasonably be expected as a result of the hazardous activities.

14. The doctrine known as *vicarious liability* (also referred to as *respondeat superior* or imputed negligence) holds that an employer is responsible for the negligent acts of his or her employee, provided that the negligent act was committed within the scope of the employee's employment.

    Although many rationales have been given (including legal history, evidentiary theory, enterprise theory, risk spreading, preventive management, social responsibility, and the deep-pocket principle), each recognizes that under respondeat superior the employer is held liable for the employees' torts because the employer can best bear the burden of paying for the harm done.

15. State-mandated insurance compensation systems have replaced the traditional tort litigation system in allocating losses in the areas of:
    a. worker's compensation
    b. no-fault automobile insurance

16. Common features of the workers' compensation statute of the various states are the following:
    a. employees are entitled to compensation for injuries regardless of fault (both their own or their employer's)
    b. compensation is received for job-related injuries (those incurred during the course of employment)
    c. employers are required either to contribute to a state-administered fund or to obtain private workers' compensation insurance
    d. claims for workers' compensation benefits are generally handled and administered by state agencies
    e. benefits are generally computed or determined according to an established schedule of compensation; the type of injury or disability determines the compensation to be received by the injured employee

17. Although no-fault automobile insurance varies from state to state, the basic idea is that persons who incur damages below a certain amount in automobile accidents are paid by their own insurance companies without having to prove negligence. Such statutes also benefit the states by removing automobile accident negligence cases from the courts for resolution.

Preventive Law

18. Manufacturers of products, particularly consumer products, have in recent decades been subjected to increasingly strict government safety regulations and greater risks of liability under negligence and strict liability law. To minimize the perceived need for more regulations and reduce the potential for tort liability, it has been suggested that manufacturers:
    a. create product safety committees
    b. utilize insurance safety audits
    c. keep informed of legal developments, consumer expectations, and technology changes
    d. develop plans to deal effectively with major product safety problems

Issues and Trends: Tort Reform

19. In recent years intense public debate has been waged regarding the tort law system. Some proposed reforms include:
    a. limit pain and suffering awards
    b. limit punitive damages
    c. the "English Rule" - losers required to pay winner's legal bills

MAJOR POINTS OF CASES

Doe v. *British Universities North America Club* (p. 120)

     The court held that there must be a legal duty on the part of the defendant for an actionable negligence claim to exist. A legal duty exists to the extent that the defendant could have foreseen the harmful implications of not exercising his/her duty. Foreseeability is tested by deciding whether an ordinary person in the defendant's position could have anticipated the general nature of the harm that was suffered.

Applying these principles to the facts of the case, the court found in favor of the defendant, BUNAC. The court ruled that, in the absence of any prior charges brought against him, no ordinary person could have foreseen the damaging conduct of the camp counselor recommended by BUNAC.

Westinghouse Electric Corp. v. *Nutt* (p. 121)

Plaintiff claimed that the defendant was negligent in designing the elevator in which his son was injured. This court held for the defendant stating that, although it had a duty to those expected to use its product to design a reasonably safe elevator, the plaintiff had failed to prove a breach of this duty. The required "reasonable care" depends on a balancing of the probability and severity of harm against the burden of avoiding the harm. A company's compliance with legal and industry safety design standards is evidence of reasonable care, but such compliance does not conclusively answer the question of whether a reasonable person would have taken additional precautions or included other safety features. However, proof of compliance with such standards causes the plaintiff to have to prove that the product was unreasonably dangerous for the lack of feasible safety features that a reasonable person would have incorporated. The plaintiff failed to prove this latter point.

Cimble v. *MacKintosh Hemphill Co.* (p. 124)

In this case the court held that an "act of God" is one that is not reasonably foreseeable. If an "act of God" occurs that could have caused the plaintiff's injury, regardless of any concurring negligence of the defendant, then the defendant cannot be held liable for negligence. However, whether an "act of God" caused the plaintiff's harm, rather than any negligence by the defendant, is a question of fact for the jury to decide. In this case the jury properly decided based on the evidence that the winds were a reasonably foreseeable event. Since they were foreseeable, the defendant breached its duty of due care by maintaining its roof in a defective condition. This breach, then, was the actual and proximate cause of the death of plaintiff's husband, even though the immediate cause was the wind.

Crenshaw v. *Hogan* (p. 127)

This case limits the scope of actionable contributory negligence claims. The plaintiff sued the defendant because she tripped and injured herself as a result of stumbling in a hole on the defendant's property. The court ruled that the plaintiff's suit was not actionable, because the hole was both open and obvious; thus, the burden or responsibility rests with the visitor, not the property owner. Only when a person is injured as a result of an obscured obstacle, hole, et cetera can he or she sue for damages under contributory negligence.

55

The court in this case overruled a past precedent that required in blasting cases that proof of negligence was required to recover damages unless the blasting caused an actual physical invasion of the plaintiff's property by the resulting debris. In so reversing past precedent, it established for New York the precedent that, given the inherently dangerous nature of blasting, regardless of the degree of care exercised, the party who voluntarily engages in blasting activities should be held absolutely liable for damages caused to others, even though no harm was intended and due care had been exercised.

PRACTICAL CONSIDERATIONS

1. When a lawsuit is based on the doctrine of respondeat superior, it is generally recommended that both the employer and the employee be made defendants in the action. This is so even when there is a strong likelihood that the employee has insufficient assets to pay any part of the judgement. One reason for this recommendation is that some states place restrictions on the ability to involve nonparty witnesses in formal pretrial discovery procedures. If the employee is made a party to the action, the effect of that restriction is eliminated. Another reason is the fact that though a party may have few assets at the beginning of a lawsuit, circumstances may change and that party's assets may become plentiful. A third reason lies in the fact that it may be easier to establish the plaintiff's claim against the employer by including the employee in the lawsuit. And fourth, the company may go bankrupt or reorganize - as in the case of the Manville Corporation - so that recovery from the corporation may be difficult or impossible.

2. A plaintiff in a negligence case often has difficulty deciding whether or not to bring a lawsuit. A plaintiff must weigh the likelihood of success in the action against the financial cost involved in preparing the case and presenting it for trial. In view of the fact that investigative reports are normally needed, pretrial procedures must be pursued, the testimony of expert witnesses must be presented at trial, the cost of a negligence lawsuit can be quite high. And these expenses must be paid whether or not the plaintiff is successful in his or her claim.

    It should be noted, however, that most attorneys will advance the necessary costs to the client. Furthermore, if suit is brought on a contingency basis, the plaintiff pays nothing for the attorney's services unless the attorney succeeds in obtaining a settlement or wins a verdict.

    Example: Abigail goes to a party with her friend, Andy. At the party Andy consumes several drinks containing alcohol and Abigail notices that he is a little unsteady as a result. Nevertheless, at the end of the evening Abigail gets back into Andy's car and proceeds homeward with him. Andy is able to drive the car straight and well until he feels the full effect of the alcohol; then, without warning, he passes out. The car strikes a tree, injuring both Andy and Abigail.

Abigail must now decide whether the risk involved in pursuing a negligence claim against Andy justifies the substantial expense that will be involved. In doing so, she must weigh the impact of her conduct with respect to the final outcome of her claim. Furthermore, she is unlikely to remain on the best of terms with Andy if she brings suit against him.

SELF TEST

True-False Questions

_____ 1. In order to succeed in a lawsuit based on negligence, it is always necessary for the plaintiff to establish that he or she was not guilty of contributory negligence.

_____ 2. A plaintiff who is able to show that the conduct of the defendant was negligent is usually entitled to receive punitive damages.

_____ 3. In order to establish a cause of action for negligence, it is necessary for the plaintiff to show that he or she suffered some injury as a result of the defendant's conduct.

_____ 4. The standard of behavior that has been adopted by the courts in determining whether a party has breached a duty to exercise care is the "reasonable and prudent person" standard.

_____ 5. A person who operates a motor vehicle at a speed of 70 miles per hour on a state highway and strikes a person who is running across the highway between oncoming cars will always be held liable for the injuries sustained by the person who ran across the road.

_____ 6. The terms "proximate cause" and "actual cause" mean the same thing.

_____ 7. Under the doctrine of respondeat superior, an employer's liability is based on the conduct of his or her employee.

_____ 8. Under workers' compensation statutes, an employee is entitled to receive compensation for injuries that he or she sustained even though the employee's negligence caused the injuries.

_____ 9. A defense that can be raised by a defendant in an action based on negligence is that of assumption of risk.

_____ 10. In order for the doctrine of res ipsa loquitur to apply, the plaintiff must show that the defendant was in exclusive control of the instrumentality that caused injury.

11. When a person violates a statute that was intended to apply as a standard of civil liability and another person sustains injuries of the type that the statute was designed to prevent, the wrongdoer will be considered negligent under the doctrine of:
    a. vicarious liability
    b. contributory negligence
    c. prima facie tort
    d. willful nuisance

12. Which of the following is an element that must be proved in order for a plaintiff to establish the existence of negligence?
    a. a duty of care owed to the plaintiff by the defendant
    b. a breach of the duty of care owed by the defendant
    c. proximate causation between the plaintiff's injuries and the defendant's conduct
    d. all of the above are correct
    e. only a and c must be proved

13. The doctrine that will act as a complete bar to a lawsuit based on negligence is:
    a. comparative negligence
    b. contributory negligence
    c. imputed negligence
    d. a and b are both correct
    e. a, b, and c are all correct

14. If a person was walking along a sidewalk and was injured by a safe that fell from a window on the tenth floor of the defendant's building, the plaintiff may establish that the defendant should be held responsible for the accident by asserting which of the following doctrines?
    a. res ipsa loquitur
    b. strict liability in tort
    c. assumption of risk
    d. b and c are both correct
    e. a, b, and c are all correct

_____15. The doctrine of strict liability in tort applies to injuries sustained as a result of:
a. a construction company's use of dynamite to excavate an area
b. a fall from a horse rented from a riding stable
c. being struck by an automobile that was traveling at 90 miles per hour
d. the crash of a commercial airliner
e. the sinking of a ship at sea by an enemy warship

_____16. In order for the doctrine of negligence per se to apply to a situation:
a. an inherently dangerous device must be involved
b. the defendant must have been engaged in an activity that is covered by strict liability
c. a plaintiff must show that the defendant's conduct violated a statute that was intended to apply as a standard of civil liability
d. all of the above are correct
e. only a and b are correct

_____17. If two or more defendants negligently caused a plaintiff's injuries, then in many states the plaintiff can recover the full amount of his or her damages from any one of the defendants, regardless of their respective degrees of fault, under the concept of:
a. strict liability
b. no-fault liability
c. absolute liability
d. joint and several liability

_____18. In workers' compensation cases, an injured employee may recover:
a. only if he or she was not at fault
b. regardless of fault
c. only if the company was at fault
d. only if another employee was at fault
e. a and d are both correct

_____19. A plaintiff who is guilty of contributory negligence in a state that has a comparative negligence rule may still recover damages when alleging negligence on the part of the defendant if:
a. the plaintiff's negligence is less than the defendant's
b. the defendant's negligence is less than the plaintiff's
c. the defendant was slightly negligent
d. the plaintiff may not recover under any circumstances

20. Which of the following is a common characteristic of workers' compensation statutes?
    a. they apply to job-related injuries
    b. benefits are determined by reference to an established schedule
    c. employers are required to contribute to a state fund or obtain special insurance
    d. all of the above are correct
    e. only b and c are correct

Completion Questions

21. A person who has committed a tort is referred to as a(n): _____.

22. Failure to exercise the care that a reasonable person would exercise in the same or similar circumstances is considered to be_____.

23. The doctrine that prevents a person from recovering damages from another person who was careless because the injured person was also careless is the doctrine of_____ _____.

24. An employer is liable for the torts committed by its employees within the scope of their employment under the concept of vicarious liability, also known as _____ _____.

25. Under the concept of _____ _____, tort liability is imposed on persons for voluntarily engaging in activities they should know are abnormally dangerous, even though they had no intent to cause others harm and they exercised due care.

Chapter 8

BUSINESS AND ETHICS

Media reporting of major incidents of illegal or unethical behavior by businesses has become common occurrence during the 1980s. As a consequence, the public and businesspeople have become increasingly concerned with business ethics. Businesspeople should understand not only what is required of them by law but also their ethical obligations. Law and ethics are not necessarily synonymous. In business seldom would it be ethical to not follow the law. However, merely following the law is not always sufficient to meet one's ethical obligations toward others. Ethics sometimes require a standard of conduct higher than that required by the law. The failure to meet ethical obligations can lead to negative reactions by society toward a business and may cause the legal restrictions imposed on businesses to be increased.

CHAPTER OBJECTIVES

After reading Chapter 8 of the text and studying the related materials in this chapter of the Student Mastery Guide, you will understand:

1. The arguments against business ethics
2. The theories of moral responsibility
3. The principles of business ethics
4. The use of business ethics in current problems

MAJOR POINTS TO REMEMBER

Ethics and Law

1. There are at least three widely used approaches to determining what is ethical: (1) consequential or utilitarian approaches; (2) deontological approaches; and (3) contractarian approaches.

Ethics in Business

2. *Ethics* involves formal consideration of the interests of others in deciding how to behave or act. Since all business actions impact outsiders directly or indirectly, ethical questions can and do frequently confront managers.

3. Some people argue that ethics are not absolute but instead are relative to the time and society in which an action is taken. Under relativism, ethics of business actions can be determined only according to the local rules or customs that exist at the time the action is taken. Some relativists argue that business itself has different ethical standards from those applied in other settings. Under this view, the companies of one nation when conducting transactions in other nations should follow the local customs.

61

The counter argument to relativism is universalism, which states that there are certain principles of ethics which transcend local custom. These universal ethics must be followed even if they conflict with local practices.

4. The psychological egoism concept states that humans can act only in their self-interest, and, thus, the interests of others are considered only as to how they affect the decision maker's self-interest. Ethical egoism, in contrast, states that everyone has the right to act in his or her self-interest. Under these views selfish behavior is restrained only by law.

   Adopting these approaches to ethics in business would increase substantially the costs of commercial transactions. These approaches also violate basic tenets of major religions. Although self-interest is part of standard business ethical analysis, the interests of others must also be considered.

Theories and Concepts of Moral Responsibility

5. Deontological theory, or duty-based ethics, requires adherence to the guiding principles to:
   a. act in a way that would be a good general rule for all individuals in society to obey, known as the *categorical imperative*;
   b. not treat people as means to an end;
   c. follow the Golden Rule of treating others as you would want to be treated.

   General duties can be derived from these principles. Specific duties for certain individuals in particular situations can supplement the general duties. However, problems can arise when two duties are in conflict in a specific case. Currently there exists no generally effective way of resolving all such conflicts.

   Codes of ethics do exist for some professions, but ultimately these codes should not be accepted without analyzing them under other general ethical theory.

6. Utilitarianism states that the ethical action is the one that provides the greatest net expected benefit to society as a whole.

   A significant problem, however, arises concerning how to determine society's best interests. The personal utility approach requires that in ethical analysis the guiding principle should be liberty of individuals to express their preferences in the marketplace and voting, since such actions will provide answers to what people believe are in the best interests of society. Actions that provide the greatest net expected good for society are deemed ethical. A disadvantage of this approach is that some individuals' personal preferences may be damaging to others in society.

   Another approach is to use the *pareto superiority* principle. Under this analysis a contemplated action would be ethical if it improved the condition of a person or group without harming anyone else. A disadvantage of this approach is that it accepts the status quo with all existing inequities. Contemplated actions, thus, are not evaluated in terms of whether they would improve current conditions.

   There are two forms of utilitarianism ethical analysis. In *act utilitarianism*, every action must be analyzed to determine the next expected impact on society. In *rule utilitarianism*, ethical analysis establishes general rules that should be followed, because it is assumed that following them will maximize the benefits to society. Situations covered by these rules are not specifically assessed.

Obviously, another major problem with utilitarian ethical analysis is how to measure costs and benefits that are intangible in nature. Finally, this approach can cause problems in recognizing and preserving rights to which a small minority of persons may be entitled.

7. The *social contract* approach to ethics focuses on how rights, benefits, and obligations among the members of a society are distributed. There is said to be a social contract among members of society establishing how people will behave toward one another. Theories of social contract often generate fundamental justice principles pertaining to the division of wealth, rights, and responsibilities in society.
   a. Several social contract theories are related to business ethics. One theorist worked out a theory of a global social contract for ethical behavior in international business transactions. He believes that people would want to establish a minimum floor of responsibility for global corporations. All corporations would respect a set of fundamental rights that would include:

   1. The right to freedom of physical movement.
   2. The right to ownership of property.
   3. The right to freedom from torture.
   4. The right to a fair trial.
   5. The right to nondiscriminatory treatment (based on race or sex).
   6. The right to physical security.
   7. The right to freedom of speech and association.
   8. The right to minimal education.
   9. The right to political participation.
   10. The right to subsistence.

Principles of Business Ethics

8. In making decisions with ethical dimensions, business managers may have formal industry, company, or professional society codes of ethics that can be helpful. The earlier discussion of various concepts of ethics can also be applied. The following are basic ethical guideposts for business decision making that can be justified under each of the major approaches toward ethics.
   a. *Honor confidentiality* of information provided by another.
   b. *Avoid even the appearance of a conflict of interest* with a duty owed by promise, contract, legal role toward another, personal or family relationships, or bylaws. Resolve potential conflict of interest by refraining from action or, when that is not practical, by making full disclosure to affected parties, having a neutral party certify the fairness of the transaction, and/or having an impartial person make the decision.
   c. *Willingly comply with the law*, because, although ethics can require a higher standard of behavior than the law, in virtually all business situations there is no ethical justification for not obeying the law.
   d. Businesspersons should *exercise due care* in the performance of their duties, or, in other words, act in a professionally competent manner, given their education, training, and experience.

e. Businesspersons should *act in good faith* - uphold promises, not make false representations, and meet other's reasonable expectations of them, among other things. Good faith means acting fairly by following just procedures and recognizing legitimate claims of others.

f. Businesspeople must also *observe fidelity to special responsibilities* imposed on them by acting in a trustworthy manner to satisfy fully the expectations of others.

g. Businesspeople must act with *respect for the liberty and rights of others*. People are the ends of business, not means to others ends. Limitations of employee liberties and freedoms must be clearly justified as business necessities.

Moral Development and Individual Ethics

9. Moral psychologist Laurence Kohlberg studied the reasoning patterns of boys and developed a theory that there are six stages of moral development an individual goes through. In the earliest stages the individual is selfish, the middle two stages focus on achieving peer or group approval, and the final stages are when one becomes a morally autonomous decision maker, acting in accordance with logical, consistent, universal moral principles.

10. Kohlberg's framework has been criticized because it was developed based on studies of only males and because it does not incorporate the relational and caring dimensions of ethics.

Specific Issues in Business Ethics

11. Business negotiations can often raise ethical issues, particularly in regard to deception versus honesty in disclosures. Some argue that deception is justified, because business is a game like poker or sports in which deception is important to success and also because everyone expects this type of behavior. However, even if some deception is tolerated, there must be some limits to protect those who reasonably expect honesty and to keep contracting costs lower than they would be if everyone was expected to act opportunistically. Further, under some circumstances the law imposes sanctions for this type of behavior.

12. False representations on resumes is a significant problem. With little chance of civil or criminal sanctions being imposed in most situations, this is primarily a matter of ethics. Such behavior breaches at least the duties of honesty and good faith.

13. Reported incidents of public and commercial bribery are common. The legal aspects of bribery were discussed in Chapter 3. Ethically, bribery in essence involves a conflict of interest and involves a duty owed to another. Moral culpability generally exists for both the payor and payee. Bribery may also involve theft and is unfair to the public or other businesses.

MAJOR POINTS OF CASES

Nix v. *Whiteside* (p. 141)

The legal issue presented to the Court was whether a criminal defendant had been denied the Sixth Amendment right to assistance of counsel and the due-process right to testify in his own behalf when his attorney told him that if he committed perjury, as the defendant had proposed, the attorney would withdraw as counsel and tell the judge about the perjury. Reversing the federal Court of Appeals, the Court held that the right to counsel is not denied if the response of the attorney is within the range of reasonable professional actions. The Court, then, held that under the professional code of ethics an attorney cannot as an advocate for a client knowingly use or allow perjured testimony or false evidence to be presented to a court, since it negatively impacts the truth-finding mission of the trial. The attorney here properly tried to dissuade his client from committing the crime of perjury. Since the defendant had no right to testify falsely, his attorney's actions had not denied him either the right to counsel or the right to testify truthfully. Finally, the Court held that the attorney had not threatened to breach his duty of confidentiality to the client, because this duty does not include keeping confidential a client's plan to commit future criminal acts.

National Society of Professional Engineers v. *United States* (p. 143)

The Court in this case faced a conflict between the engineers' code of ethics, which prohibited its members from competing based on the price of their services in order to insure greater public safety and minimize professional deception, and the policy of Congress, as stated in the Sherman Act, that restraints on competition are illegal. The Court affirmed the lower courts' rulings against the society, holding that the society cannot override through its code of ethics the national legal policies favoring competition expressed in the Sherman Act. The subjects of professional competence and honesty are certainly matters of legitimate concern for the society, but these concerns are not sufficiently connected to competition to justify a total ban on competitive bidding. The Sherman Act establishes that competition, as a general rule, is to be encouraged, not restrained, in the U.S. economy.

Soldano v. *O'Daniels* (p. 150)

This case presents the troublesome questions of under what circumstances the law should require a person to provide aid to another in an emergency. The Plaintiff here alleged that the refusal of defendant's employee to call the police or to allow a good Samaritan to use the telephone to call the police contributed to the wrongful death of his father. The traditional common-law tort rule was that, except when a special relationship existed to create a duty to come to the aid of another, a person has no such duty, even when the assistance can be provided with little or no cost, effort or danger. This court, however, held that the defendant's employee had a legal duty to call the police or permit the person requesting to use the telephone to call the police.

In so holding this court did not find that a person must always aid others in emergencies. Instead, it held that each case must be analyzed based on the following factors: (1) the foreseeability of harm; (2) the degree of certainty that injury will occur; (3) how closely the defendant's conduct is related to the person's injury; (4) the morality of the defendant's conduct; (5) the policy of preventing future harm; (6) the burden placed upon the defendant by requiring action; (7) the cost to society of requiring action to be taken with due care; and (8) whether insurance is commonly available for such risks.

Vokes v. *Arthur Murray, Inc.* (p. 155)

This case addresses the degree of deception tolerated by the law in contractual negotiations. In contracts the law traditionally has imposed few duties on persons to disclose facts within their knowledge. However, if they do choose to disclose facts, they are required to disclose the whole truth.

The plaintiff's complaint alleged that in convincing her to enter into numerous contracts for dance lessons costing over $31,000 the defendant had falsely represented the plaintiff's abilities. The defendant argued that its statements were mere "trade puffing" and were opinions, not facts. The court, however, held that falsely stating one's opinion is a representation of fact, particularly when there exists a special relationship between the parties or where one has superior knowledge, thus, the plaintiff should be allowed a trial to try to prove that the defendant had committed the torts of fraud or misrepresentation.

Umlas v. *Acey Oldsmobile*

The court in this case was presented with the problem of defining the parameters within which good faith is required in commercial transactions. The plaintiff's contract to purchase a new car established the trade-in value of the car he then owned at $650 but reserved the right to reappraise it at the time of delivery to account for the elapsed time that would occur. The plaintiff had a corresponding right to cancel his order for a new car if the reappraisal was unacceptable, which he exercised.

The court recognized the practical need for the reappraisal clause, but noted that it gave the seller substantial motivation to give too high an original appraisal for the purpose of securing an order and then to reappraise at too low a price when the buyer's new car is to be delivered. Under such circumstances the law implies an obligation that the reappraisal be done in good faith. This court then found that the defendant's reappraisal had not been done in good faith and that this constituted a breach of contract.

PRACTICAL CONSIDERATIONS

Personal ethics and the directions of a superior often conflict with each other. When they do, the employee of a corporation (or any other form of business enterprise) must decide whether to set aside his or her own professional business ethics and do as directed or refuse to follow the directive and risk the loss of his or her job. The employee must also consider the possibility of becoming involved in a lawsuit if the actions he or she is requested to perform may cause injury to third persons. The decision is a difficult one, and there are no simple solutions.

Example: While involved in the construction of a house that is to form one unit in a residential development expected to consist of 100 houses, Saunders is told by the vice-president of the company to use two-inch insulation in the walls instead of the four-inch insulation that the plans call for. He is also told to offer the building inspector a $100 gratuity in return for his "looking the other way" with respect to the insulation in the wall.

Saunders realizes that what he is being asked to do is improper. He also realizes that if he refuses to do as directed, his employer will blackball him and he will probably find it extremely difficult to obtain any further work in the construction industry. The decision regarding the most appropriate action to follow is a difficult one that must be considered most judiciously.

SELF TEST

True-False Questions

_____ 1. Under the concept of relativism an act could be ethical in one society but unethical in others.

_____ 2. Ethical obligations can always be satisfied by following the law.

_____ 3. Under the concept of universalism, some ethical obligations are deemed to be absolute and always should be followed.

_____ 4. According to the concept of ethical egoism, it is improper for people to consider their self-interest in determining a proper course of action.

_____ 5. Utilitarians are concerned that actions result in the greatest good for the greatest number.

_____ 6. Relativists believe that some business behaviors that would be unethical in the United States could be ethical in a foreign nation.

_____ 7. There are no circumstances in which it is ethical for an attorney to breach the confidentiality of client communications.

_____ 8. One problem with the deontological theory is that it does not assign relative weights to duties to enable people to decide which duty takes precedence over another when a conflict exists.

_____ 9. Historically, the common law of torts has not required people to come to the aid of other human beings who are in an emergency situation.

_____ 10. In business negotiations it is neither unethical nor illegal to intentionally misrepresent facts.

67

Multiple-Choice Questions

_____ 11. A decision by a U.S. company doing business in South Africa to obey and support that nation's apartheid laws would more likely be considered ethical under the concept of:
   a. universalism
   b. relativism
   c. equalitarianism
   d. the "veil of ignorance"

_____ 12. Which of the following is an ethical duty under the deontological theory of ethics?
   a. categorical imperative
   b. Golden Rule
   c. to not treat people as means
   d. a and b are correct
   e. a, b, and c are correct

_____ 13. Professional codes of ethics:
   a. are the final answer of what is ethical behavior for a professional
   b. take precedence over conflicting laws
   c. have been used to limit competition
   d. none of the above is correct

_____ 14. Which of the following is a basis for applying utilitarianism?
   a. personal utility
   b. pareto superiority
   c. personal conscience
   d. veil of ignorance
   e. a and b are correct

_____ 15. Allowing a free competitive marketplace to determine how the wealth of a society is distributed would be most acceptable under:
   a. act utilitarianism
   b. equalitarianism
   c. libertarianism
   d. altruism

_____ 16. Rights to procedural fairness, such as prior notice, a fair opportunity to be heard, and assistance of counsel, found in the U.S. Constitution, are most clearly illustrative of:
   a. social justice theories
   b. utilitarianism
   c. deontology
   d. relativism

17. Under business ethics when an actual conflict of interest arises, a manager:
   a. must refrain from acting
   b. should fully disclose the conflict
   c. should consider only his or her self-interest
   d. needs to refrain from acting only if it would be illegal

18. In contracts, the law today:
   a. allows persons to intentionally deceive others
   b. always requires full disclosure of all facts
   c. implies an obligation of good faith
   d. strictly follows the principle of caveat emptor

19. In regard to misrepresentations on resumes:
   a. the law is an effective deterrent
   b. it is ethically justified, since the practice is so prevalent
   c. an employer most likely could discharge an employee for falsely representing important facts
   d. none of the above is correct

20. In regard to bribery, which of the following is most correct?
   a. It is distinguishable from a gift by the requirement in bribery that the payee breach a duty to another.
   b. It is ethical in business situations in order to increase efficiency.
   c. The principle of relativism supports the approach of the Foreign Corrupt Practices Act.
   d. This is a legal and ethical problem only when public officials are involved.

Completion Questions

21. If an action improves the life of a person or persons without harming anyone else, then this action can be said to be _____ _____.

22. The approach to ethics that requires each act to be analyzed for its expected outcome is known as_____ _____.

23. The ethical obligation of businesspeople is to perform their duties with professional competence or, in other words, to exercise _____ _____.

24. The _____ _____ is a duty requiring people to act in ways that should be the general rule for all society.

25. _____ _____ is the belief that all persons have the ethical right to act in their own self-interest.

Chapter 9

SOCIAL RESPONSIBILITY OF BUSINESS

Public disclosures of major incidents of alleged illegal and unethical behavior by corporations in recent years have caused the debate regarding corporate social responsibility to be waged with new vigor. This chapter examines and evaluates the two basic competing concepts of corporate social responsibility. One position is that the singular purpose of a corporation is to maximize its shareholders' wealth while obeying the law. The other is that corporations have plural social responsibilities to a variety of stakeholders.

This chapter next examines the processes and strategies used by corporations to implement social responsiveness. It also explains some of the market and legal incentives for corporations to be socially responsible. Finally, it discusses some issues related to a corporation's obligations to its employees.

This chapter is important to understanding the complexity of a manager's task. Many different groups may bring pressure to bear on a corporation to achieve their objectives. These objectives may conflict with those of the corporation and even with one another. Further, the stakeholders' underlying concepts of ethics and social responsibility can be conflicting. If a corporation does not identify and respond successfully to stakeholders' claims, it can expect them to utilize economic, political, and legal power to the company's ultimate detriment.

CHAPTER OBJECTIVES

After reading Chapter 9 of the text and studying the related materials in this chapter of the Student Mastery Guide, you will understand:

1. The singular and plural purpose theories of corporate social responsibility
2. The methods and strategies for implementing corporate social responsibility
3. The consequences of failing to be socially responsible
4. The external incentives provided by the markets and law to act in a socially responsible manner
5. The nature of corporate obligations to employees

MAJOR POINTS TO REMEMBER

The Modern Debate Concerning Corporate Social Responsibility

1. The debate over corporate social responsibility is actually long-standing. At its essence this debate is about how far the management of a publicly held corporation should go in sacrificing the interests, primary financial, of the shareholders in favor of the interests of stakeholders, those outside the firm who are directly affected by its actions.

The Limited View: Profit Making as Social Responsibility

2. The arguments against corporate social responsibility include:
   a. Only people can have social responsibilities, not corporations, which are artificial entities.

b. Corporate executives are hired to make as much money as possible by the owners within the boundaries of law and ethics.

c. It is not within the authority or competence of corporate managers to make social decisions, since these are governmental functions.

d. Corporate social responsibility begins replacing the competitive market with political mechanisms for allocating scarce resources.

e. Shareholders invest for the purpose of receiving a financial return and should decide for themselves which, if any, social programs they wish to support.

3. Corporate social responsibility can involve acts to avoid or lessen harm to others or acts designed to provide other social benefits. The legitimacy of the latter actions are the most questionable under the above-described singular purpose theory of corporate social responsibility.

The Broader View: Corporations Have Plural Responsibilities

4. Although profit making is the primary goal of business, others argue that corporations have a long-term interest in maintaining a society conducive for their operations and, thus, must help to meet unmet social needs. This is the pluralism concept of corporate social responsibility.

5. In support of pluralism, it is also argued that managers are professionals, similar to doctors and lawyers, who have certain public service obligations.

6. In contrast to the singular purpose theory, some have concluded that a corporation, as a collective of humans which can have a culture that is not attributable to specific individuals, is morally accountable for its actions. Consequently, it can be viewed as a moral agent with duties to stakeholders. Hence, under this view a corporation can be held legally responsible, both civilly and criminally, for wrongful actions, as can its individual employees who actually commit the acts. Under limited circumstances this responsibility has been extended even to a corporation that purchases the assets of a corporation which had committed a wrongful act, although this is not the general rule.

7. Society has shown that it expects more from corporations than the singular purpose theory advocates. President Reagan's administration urged corporations to increase charitable giving and other social aid, called "voluntarism." The law supports such activities when at least a general, indirect benefit to the corporation can be reasonably expected. Thus, shareholders do not have a legal right to require managers to limit corporate activities to just those that maximize short-run profits.

8. Other arguments for the pluralism theory are that it is good business in the long run and that it reduces the need for government regulation, which often is expensive and inefficient.

Evaluation of the Debate

9. The singular purpose and pluralism theories are not universally advocated exclusively by conservatives and liberals, respectively. In practice, few publicly held corporations or their managers follow the singular purpose theory but instead engage to some degree in socially responsive actions.

Implementing Social Responsibility

10. There is no one standard managerial approach to making corporations ethical and socially responsible. Typical methods are codes of ethics, employee training, social auditing and reporting, changes in corporate structure, and ethics committees.

11. Most major corporations have and enforce codes of ethics. Many are beginning to provide training. In recent years the defense industry has had many problems with unethical conduct which is particularly troublesome due to the industry's importance to the security of the United States. In response, many defense contractors have publicly committed to programs to establish and implement codes of ethics that provide training to employees, are enforced, and create a culture in which violations are reported.

12. Firms are also increasingly emphasizing the concept of "stakeholder" management. This can be defined as identifying and responding to the legitimate interests of those individuals and organizations that have a real economic interest in corporate decisions but are not directly under the authority of corporate management. Engaging in these processes allows a corporation to develop more successful strategies to respond to forecasted future threats or opportunities to its operations.
    The typical types of stakeholder management are:

    a. identifying stakeholders
    b. identifying stakeholder interests
    c. prioritizing the interests identified by their immediacy and likely significance
    d. responding to important interests throughout the firm's strategic planning, ongoing business decisions, and public-affairs strategy.
    The failure to successfully engage in stakeholder management has led to stakeholder actions against corporations. These actions have included the use of economic, political, and legal powers.

13. In public-affairs management (PAM), a corporation can employ many strategies. These strategies must observe the legal rights of others. To counter corporate power, government regulations have sometimes been enacted to restrict corporations from utilizing certain strategies.
    However, corporations are "persons" under the law with many, but not all, of the same constitutional rights as natural persons. As examples, corporations are entitled to due process and equal protection of the law, but not the right of privacy or the privilege against self-incrimination. Further, corporations do have rights to free speech and free access to government, particularly in regard to public issues, but these rights are subject to limited government regulation to protect other important societal interests.

72

External Incentives for Social Responsibility

14. When the public becomes aware of perceived unethical or irresponsible actions by a company, it has sometimes reacted by not buying the company's products. In addition, a company may further suffer substantial reductions in the price of its stock. These results have often occurred in cases of defective consumer products.

15. It has also been argued that by law the internal structure and processes of corporations should be more closely regulated, in part to make directors and officers more directly and personally accountable to society. However, critics of these proposals argue that such government regulation would discourage people from taking such positions, reduce efficiency, and increase costs.

16. Other proposals for corporate structural change focus on "shareholder democracy" reforms that would increase the power of shareholders over directors and officers. Again, the critics of these proposals argue that they would increase costs while providing only marginal expected benefits.

17. Tort law, by imposing financial responsibility on corporations for harm caused to humans, can make firms more socially responsible in order to avoid large judgements. Naturally, some people argue that tort law should impose even greater responsibility on business, while others argue that the law has now gone so far as to become counterproductive. A side effect of our legal system, which allows each state substantial power to enact its own laws, is that corporations and plaintiffs are faced with widely divergent laws in different states on important issues, such as when punitive damages can be awarded in tort cases. Some states allow punitive damages only when the wrongful act was expressly authorized by the corporation, while others impose it for malicious or reckless action taken within the scope of an employee's job, and some when the act is committed by a person at the general management level.

18. The criminal law also provides incentives to act in a socially responsible manner by imposing substantial fines and even prison sentences for managers upon conviction of a crime. (See chapter 3).

Corporate Obligations to Employees

19. The employer-employee relationship is a fruitful one for legal and ethical questions. Beyond the law, ethics would recognize duties of the employer to not knowingly allow preventable harm to occur to employees in the workplace and to respect employees as persons. (See chapter 4). The latter obligation would significantly restrict an employer's right to interfere with activites unrelated to work.

20. More difficult questions arise when employers want to restrict a job-related activity that employees consider an important personal right. The law deals with some of these types of issues. For example, under the Civil Rights Act of 1964, which makes unlawful

employment practices that discriminate on the basis of race, color, religion, sex, or national origin, it has been held that employers must reasonably accommodate the religious needs of employees. This legal balancing of both the employer's and employee's legitimate needs is common to these problems.

MAJOR POINTS OF CASES

Charter Township of Ypsilanti, County of Washtenaw and State of Michigan v. General Motors Corporation (p. 169)

In this case the court had to determine the obligations that arise when a firm is given a tax break by a municipality. The court found that a tax abatement does not give rise to any legally binding promise to keep the firm open for any period of time.

First National Bank of Boston v. Bellotti (p. 173)

The Court was faced in this case with the legal issue of whether a state statute that did not allow corporations to spend money to influence votes on state proposals regarding a personal income tax or other matters not materially affecting the corporation violated the First Amendment freedom-of-speech provisions. The Court held that it did, stating that this statute restricted speech on public issues, which is the type of speech protected by the Constitution for the purpose of providing members of society the information necessary to make important decisions. The fact that corporations are the source of information does not remove it from the protection of the First Amendment. Finally, the Court found that the state had demonstrated no compelling state interest in protecting the integrity of the democratic process or shareholders that would justify this bridgement of freedom of speech.

SELF TEST

True-False Questions

_____ 1. Shareholders of a corporation legally own specific corporate assets.

_____ 2. Shareholders of a corporation have no legal right to control the directors and officers.

_____ 3. Economist Milton Friedman is an advocate of the view that corporations should be responsible only for maximizing profits while obeying the law and the basic ethical standards of society.

_____ 4. Corporations are for many purposes deemed to be persons under the law with many rights and obligations that are similar to those of natural persons.

_____ 5. A corporation that acquires another corporation cannot ever be held legally liable for the wrongful acts of the acquired corporation.

74

_____ 6. Under the law corporations can in certain circumstances be held responsible for wrongful acts committed by their agents and employees on their behalf.

_____ 7. In the United States today the law requires corporate directors and officers to act only to maximize profits.

_____ 8. Most publicly held corporations in the United States have implemented a formal code of ethics.

_____ 9. Stakeholders can exercise economic, political, or legal power to cause corporations to change their conduct.

_____ 10. Corporations are not legally entitled to freedom of speech rights under the First Amendment to the U.S. Constitution.

Multiple-Choice Questions

_____ 11. Which of the following can be an external incentive for corporations to act in a socially responsible manner?
   a. Unethical conduct can cause the demand for products or services to decrease and stock prices to fall.
   b. The civil law can be modified to require higher standards of corporate conduct and increase the severity of sanctions.
   c. Corporations and their managers can be punished criminally.
   d. b and c are both correct
   e. a, b, and c are all correct

_____ 12. Critics of the structure of corporations in the United States today have proposed, among other things, that:
   a. all or a majority of a corporation's directors should not be officers or employees of the corporation
   b. the law precisely defines the functions of directors and officers
   c. directors be subjected to unindemnifiable personal liability to breaching a legal duty
   d. b and c are both correct
   e. a, b, and c are all correct

_____ 13. Under tort law punitive damages are imposed on corporations:
   a. under standards that differ among the states
   b. under a single standard followed by all the states
   c. for negligence in all states
   d. none of the above are correct

14. In regard to the religious needs of employees, an employer under the Civil Rights Act of 1964:
    a. need do nothing
    b. must allow employees to meet their religious needs regardless of their impact on the employer
    c. is required to reasonably accommodate those needs
    d. cannot allow for differences in religions within their business policies

15. The view that corporate social responsibility is limited to profit making is supported by the argument that:
    a. only individuals can have social responsibilities
    b. social investments are really tax decisions that government should make
    c. social responsibility accepts the socialist view that resources should be allocated by political, rather than market, mechanisms
    d. a, b, and c are all correct

16. The broad view that corporations have plural responsibilities is supported by the argument that:
    a. corporate managers are similar to professionals, such as doctors and lawyers, who owe obligations to the public
    b. individuals, but not corporations, have social responsibilities
    c. acting ethically is good business
    d. a and c are both correct
    e. b and c are correct

17. In regard to meeting social responsibilities, the most common action by corporations today is to:
    a. change corporate structure
    b. implement a formal code of ethics
    c. have an ethics committee
    d. perform social audits

18. The process of stakeholder management involves:
    a. identifying stakeholders
    b. identifying stakeholder interests
    c. prioritizing stakeholder interests
    d. responding to important stakeholder interests
    e. all of the above are correct

19. As a public-affairs management strategy, a corporation's use of persuasive communications:
    a. with customers can be prohibited by law
    b. in the form of advertising can be prohibited by law, if the advertising attempts to influence voting in elections
    c. is protected by the First Amendment, although government can in limited circumstances regulate such communications
    d. none of the above is correct

20. Corporate managers today:
    a. most often follow the plural social responsibility approach
    b. strictly follow the singular purpose theory of profit making
    c. are clearly unethical
    d. clearly believe in socialism

Completion Questions

21. Employers generally are prohibited from discriminating in employment decisions against persons based on their race, color, sex, religion, or national origin under the _____ _____ _____ _____ _____.

22. The owners of a corporation are the _____.

23. Other than shareholders, _____ have real economic interests that are impacted by a corporation's actions.

24. Under the concept of _____ _____ _____, corporations are responsible for the consequences of actions taken by their agents and employees on their behalf.

25. The Reagan administration urged corporations to increase charitable giving and other social activities under a strategy called _____.

Chapter 10

INTRODUCTION TO THE LAW OF CONTRACTS

Probably no other area of law affects the activities of more persons than that of contractual relations. The law of contracts deals with the most basic relationships involving fundamental needs as well as the most complex business transactions involving the largest corporations. Yet the concept of the nature of a contract is quite simple. In its most fundamental form, as discussed in the main text, a contract is nothing more than an agreement between two or more persons that is enforceable in a court of law.

This chapter provides an overview of the nature and concept of a contract. It discusses some very basic but very important concepts that are essential to an understanding of contract law. It is, in other words, the prelude to the specific rules and principles that comprise the very structure of the law of contracts.

CHAPTER OBJECTIVES

After reading Chapter 10 of the text and studying the related materials in this chapter of the Student Mastery Guide, you will understand:

1. The nature and sources of contract law
2. The elements required for a valid contract
3. The different classifications of contracts, including:
   a. express and implied contracts
   b. quasi contracts
   c. valid, void, and voidable contracts
   d. bilateral and unilateral contracts

MAJOR POINTS TO REMEMBER

The Utility of Contracts

1. Contract law has several functions. First, contract law facilities exchanges between buyers and sellers in the U.S. free-enterprise system by protecting each of them from bad-faith conduct of the other. Second, contracts allow people to establish a private set of rules to govern their relationships by making known behavior that is expected. Finally, because contracts can be enforced through civil lawsuits, parties to a contract have an incentive to fulfill their obligations, and this, in turn, enhances the certainty of planning in transactions.

Elements of a Valid Contract

2. In order for a contract to be valid and legally enforceable, all of the following elements must be present:
   a. a valid offer
   b. a valid acceptance (i.e., mutual agreement)
   c. consideration

d.   absence of fraud, force, or legally significant mistake
e.   legal capacity of the parties
f.   consistency with general public policy
g.   proper legal form
h.   compliance with special rules governing the agreement

Sources of Contract Law

3.   Contract law is derived from:
   a.   the common law (precedents established by judicial decisions resolving contractual disputes)
   b.   statutes (including the Uniform Commercial Code, which deals with all aspects of sales transactions)

4.   For sales transactions the UCC rules control over any conflicting common-law rule, but if there is no applicable UCC rule the common law will still apply to sales transactions.

5.   In regard to contracts, it must be remembered that:
   a.   almost all contracts are fully performed both to avoid legal sanctions and to meet the good-faith ethical duty
   b.   there are numerous reasons why breaches of contract are often resolved without lawsuits
   c.   for many types of contracts there are special rules beyond the basic rules discussed in the textbook

Classification of Contracts

6.   Contracts can be described as being:
   a.   express or implied
   b.   unilateral or bilateral
   c.   executed or executory
   d.   valid, void, or voidable

7.   A *quasi contract* is not really a contract, in that the parties have not reached a mutual agreement. In order to prevent the unjust enrichment of one of the parties, however, the courts will create an agreement where none existed, even though the parties did not manifest an intent to contract. This is why a quasi contract is also sometimes referred to as an implied-in-law contract.

8.   In order for a court to recognize the existence of a quasi contract, both of the following elements must be present:
   a.   the benefited party received a benefit or unjust enrichment
   b.   no other legal recourse is available to the party who provided the benefit

9.   A *voidable contract* is one that can be set aside by one or sometimes either of the parties to it. The voidable contract is valid and enforceable until the party who has grounds to set it aside does so.

10. A bilateral contract is an exchange of a promise for a promise. A unilateral contract is a promise in exchange for an act.

Ethics Box: Ethics, Morality, and the Law

11. As indicated in the Marvin and McCall cases, contracts cannot violate "public policy," which includes community morals. Community morals are not synonymous with ethics. Since judges determine what public policy is, there is danger that their decisions will be influenced by their cultural biases and be unfair to certain groups. However, the flexibility of the common law often will allow unfairly biased precedents to be eventually modified or reversed.

Issues and Trends: An International Comparison of Contracting

12. Under U.S. law contracting is a rather formal process with the parties often entering into long contracts to cover foreseeable contingencies. In contracts, Japan uses a relational approach to contracts in which the parties agree to work out problems as they arise. The latter approach initially is less time-consuming and expensive. Contractual disputes between parties from different nations can involve very difficult legal questions. Consequently, such disputes are often resolved in a system of international arbitration, rather than the courts of the involved nations.

MAJOR POINTS OF CASES

Marvin v. *Marvin* (p. 184)

The court in this particular case held that if two persons voluntarily agree to reside with each other and they thereafter separate, an agreement previously made to share assets in a particular way upon such separation will be enforceable. The agreement must be more than a mere contract for the sale of sexual favors.

The court also stated that while agreeing to sell sexual favors is against public policy, it is not against public policy for two persons who reside together to agree voluntarily to provide for their financial security.

As the case note indicates, after trial an appellate court held in effect that plaintiff had not proven the contract alleged and was not entitled to any money to "rehabilitate" herself.

In the Matter of Baby M (p. 186)

The court in this case held that surrogacy contracts are unlawful. This particular state court judge found that an agreement to give up one's child violates public policy, and agreements in violation of public policy are null and void.

U.S. v. *Summit General Contracting Corp.* (p. 191)

This case demonstrates how the theory of quasi-contract will be used to prevent one party from being unjustly enriched by another.

In this case, there was clearly no agreement between the parties for the extra work performed on July 13, 1989. However, it was also clear that Falco performed the extra work only at Summit's request and that Summit would be unjustly enriched if they were to receive the benefit of Falco's work at no cost.

PRACTICAL CONSIDERATIONS

A contract, whether it be oral or written, is only as good as the person who stands behind it. In other words, the fact that a person has entered into a legally recognized contract does not necessarily mean that such person will perform his or her obligations.

Proof of a contractual relationship, however, provides an injured party with an opportunity to recover damages.

Example: S. Karp agrees to sell his house to N. Angel. Karp sells the same house to another party without notifying Angel or otherwise terminating the contract with him.

Under the circumstances, Angel would be able to sue Karp for the losses he suffered as a result of Karp's failure to perform the contract. Angel's ability to prove the existence of the contractual relationship would be critical. Angel must also determine whether the losses sustained would justify the commencement of a lawsuit.

SELF TEST

True-False Questions

_____ 1. All express contracts are required to be in writing in order to be valid.

_____ 2. In a unilateral contract the performance of the act requested constitutes an acceptance of the offer.

_____ 3. In order for a contract to be valid it must be supported by consideration.

_____ 4. An implied-in-fact contract is also known and referred to as a quasi contract.

_____ 5. A bilateral contract is created when A offers to pay $1,000 to B to paint A's house and B accepts by painting the house.

_____ 6. In order to be valid a contract must not violate the law.

_____ 7. A voidable contract is one that cannot be performed by the parties.

_____ 8. All legal principles that affect or govern the law of contracts can be found in statutory law.

_____ 9. An implied contract is formed by a verbal agreement of the parties that sets forth their respective undertakings.

_____ 10. Every agreement between two parties will be considered to be a contract.

Multiple-Choice Questions

_____ 11. Which of the following is an element that is required in order to have a valid contract?
   a. consideration
   b. mutual agreement
   c. competent parties
   d. a written document
   e. only a, b, and c are correct

_____ 12. In order for a party to prove the existence of a quasi contract, it is necessary to prove that:
   a. there was an implied agreement between the parties
   b. the party who received a benefit was unjustly enriched
   c. no other legal recourse was available to the party who provided the benefit
   d. b and c are correct
   e. a, b, and c are all correct

_____ 13. A contract in which some or all of the required performances remain to be done is referred to as a(n):
   a. express contract
   b. executory contract
   c. executed contract
   d. idiomatic contract
   e. quasi contract

_____ 14. A contract that can be set aside by one or sometimes either of the parties is referred to as a(n):
   a. executory contract
   b. executed contract
   c. voidable contract
   d. void contract
   e. valid contract

_____ 15. Which of the following statements is correct in regard to a contract?
   a. it is an agreement between two or more persons that will be enforced by a court
   b. it must always be in writing in order to be valid
   c. some verbal agreement must always be expressed
   d. every agreement between two people is a contract
   e. a and c are both correct

Completion Questions

16. A contract in which the obligations of the respective parties have been fully and completely performed is a(n) _____ contract.

17. Contract law originates from _____ and _____.

18. An implied-in-law contract is also known and referred to as a(n)_____ _____.

19. A contract that is formed by the words of the parties is called a(n)_____ contract.

20. When an agreement is determined to be invalid and unenforceable by the courts, it is considered to be_____.

Chapter 11

THE OFFER

The origin of every agreement is in the nature of an offer, which basically is a proposition to do something. An offer can consist of a simple gesture or an elaborate, coherent scheme.

This chapter discusses the nature of an offer and examines the various requirements that must be satisfied in order to establish its validity, including contractual intent, definiteness, and communication of the offer to the offeree. It also considers the various ways in which an offer can be terminated once it has been made.

In examining the materials contained in this chapter, the student should keep in mind that the offer is only the first step in the creation of a contractual relationship. It should also be kept in mind, however, that if the offer is not valid, the stages that follow in the contractual drama may be insignificant and meaningless.

CHAPTER OBJECTIVES

After reading Chapter 10 of the text and studying the related materials in this chapter of the Student Mastery Guide, you will understand:

1. The nature of an offer
2. The elements of a valid offer, including:
    a. intent to contract
    b. communication of the offer
    c. definite and certain terms
3. The different ways in which an offer can be terminated, including:
    a. lapse of time
    b. revocation of the offer
    c. rejection of the offer
    d. death
    e. illegality
    f. destruction of the subject matter

MAJOR POINTS TO REMEMBER

Requirements of an Offer

1. To be valid, an offer must be:
    a. based on an intent to enter into a binding contract
    b. definite and certain
    c. communicated to the offeree

Intent of the Parties

2.   A person's contractual intent may be described as actual or as manifest.

        A person has an intent to contract if he or she truly intends to enter into a contractual relationship with another person.

        A person will also be regarded as having an intent to contract if his or her actions or conduct, when viewed by a reasonable person, indicates that a contract is intended. Such intent may be found even when a person does not actually intend to enter into a binding contract.

3.   An offer for an agreement involving a purely social invitation does not give rise to a binding contract.

4.   An offer made in obvious jest or when the offeror is obviously excited will not give rise to a contract. If, however, it is not clear that the offeror is only joking, a contract could be created as a result. The intent to contract is determined by whether a reasonable person would think that an offer had been made by the offeror.

5.   Generally, an advertisement (sometimes referred to as an invitation to negotiate) does not give rise to a contractual obligation. If the advertisement is certain and definite as to all material terms, however, it could constitute an offer. No contract is created merely by an offer.

Definite and Certain Terms

6.   In order for an offer to be definite, it must:
    a.   identify the subject matter of the offer
    b.   define the essential terms of performance
    c.   set forth a quantity
    d.   identify the parties
    e.   specify the price (but see UCC Section 2-305 on sale of goods)

7.   Under Sections 2-204(3) and 2-305 of the Uniform Commercial Code, it is possible, in certain circumstances, to have a valid offer with respect to a contract for the sale of goods even though no price is set forth or agreed upon.

Communication of the Offer

8.   In order for an offer to be valid, it generally must be communicated by the offeror (or someone authorized by the offeror) to the offeree. In the case of reward offers, however, many states provide that a contract is formed when a person performs the act requested in the offer, even though they did not previously know of the offer. In contrast, some courts have refused to enforce fine-print provisions in consumer contracts under the theory that they were never communicated by the seller to the consumer.

Termination of the Offer

9. An offer may be terminated by:
    a. the lapse of time
    b. revocation of the offer by the offeror
    c. rejection of the offer by the offeree
    d. the death of either the offeror or the offeree
    e. subsequent illegality
    f. destruction of the subject matter of the offer
    g. a counteroffer

10. An offer that expressly states when it expires terminates after that day and time. Time limits on offers should be very specific to avoid ambiguities. If no time limit is expressly stated for an offer, it will terminate after a reasonable time for acceptance. A "reasonable time" will depend on the specific circumstances in which the offer was made.

11. Generally, in order for the revocation of an offer to be effective:
    a. the offer must be revoked before its acceptance by the offeree
    b. the notice of revocation must be communicated to the offeree

12. If an offeror has given an offeree an *option* with respect to an offer, the offer cannot be revoked until the option has expired.
    A *firm offer* is an offer for the sale of goods made by a merchant in which the offeror agrees to hold its offer open for a certain period of time. This offer may not be withdrawn within the period stated, or if no time is stated, for a reasonable period of time not to exceed three months.

13. In order for an *option* to be valid, it must be supported by consideration, but it does not always need to be in writing.
    In order for a *firm offer* to be valid, it must be evidenced by a writing, but no consideration is required.

14. When a court invokes the doctrine of promissory estoppel, the offeror is prohibited from revoking his or her offer or promise for a reasonable period of time.
    In order for the doctrine of promissory estoppel to apply, it usually must be shown that:
    a. the offeror's statement was one that the offeror expected the offeree to rely on
    b. the offeree did in fact justifiably rely on the statement
    c. the offeree suffered some loss or harm as a result of his or her reliance and actions

15. Once an offer has been rejected, the offeree cannot thereafter accept it. A rejection occurs when the offeree indicates that the offer will not be accepted, or the offeree makes a counteroffer that modifies the terms of the original offer.

16. Although the death of either party generally terminates an offer, death does not necessarily terminate contracts, including option contracts. (See Chapter 18).

17. If the law changes to make an offer illegal, it is terminated.

18. When an offer provides that the subject matter of the offer is to be provided generally, rather than come from a specific place or source, then the destruction of the subject matter will terminate the offer.

Preventive Law: Ambiguities in Negotiations

19. Ambiguous language is an inherent problem in negotiations and interpretations of contracts. The language used should be selected carefully to communicate one's intended meaning. For important contracts, the assistance of an attorney from the beginning of negotiations is important to minimize the risk of costly mistakes.

MAJOR POINTS OF CASES

Lefkowitz **v.** *Great Minneapolis Surplus Store* **(p. 197)**

This case illustrates the rule of law which provides that while generally an advertisement addressed to the public is nothing more than an invitation to make an offer, in certain cases an advertisement can constitute an offer that can be accepted by a member of the public. If the offer is sufficiently definite to qualify as a valid offer, it will be enforced by the courts. Whether the advertisement is sufficient to constitute an offer, however, must be determined on a case-by-case basis.

In this case, the court found that the advertisement relative to the sale of the lapin fur was sufficiently definite, and as a result ruled that the plaintiff's acceptance of the offer created an enforceable contract.

Simmons **v.** *All American Life Insurance* **(p. 199)**

The court in this case determined what constituted an offer in legally binding contracts. In order for there to be an offer, the court ruled that a subsequent unqualified acceptance must create "a meeting of the minds" concerning the contract's obligations for each party.

Applying this ruling, the court held that the life insurance policy between All American Life Insurance and the plaintiff's son was not a binding contract because the plaintiff's son died before the insurance premium was agreed upon. Without agreeing upon an insurance premium, there could not be a "meeting of the minds" in the offer and acceptance of the contract; thus, the contract was not valid. With this finding, the court ruled that the insurance company did not have to pay the $25,000 life insurance benefits.

Drouin **v.** *Fleetwood Enterprises* **(p. 202)**

In this case, the court ruled that the acceptance of a settlement offer within thirty days is not a sufficient condition to prevent litigation. Instead, the defendant must not only accept the offer within thirty days, he or she must also notify the plaintiff of acceptance within that same time period.

Applying this judgement to the case, the court affirmed the decision made in favor of the plaintiff who received more compensation from litigation than if the settlement offer had taken precedence. While the defendant did accept the June 14 settlement offer within thirty days, it failed to notify the plaintiff of this acceptance until August 6.

Werner v. *Norwest Bank South Dakota* (p. 205)

This case deals with the extent to which justifiable reliance as well as promissory estoppel are applicable to oral contracts. The court ruled that in order for justifiable reliance to be a legitimate claim concerning an alleged breach of an oral contract, the plaintiff must demonstrate that the oral agreement was certain enough for him or her to reasonably rely on it. The court also ruled that in order for promissory estoppel arguments to hold, the plaintiff must show that she or he altered his or her position detrimentally in the reasonable belief that a promise would be performed.

Applying these rulings to the facts of the case, the court held that Werner's claim to a breach of contract was not valid. The court found that Norwest Bank's response to Werner's oral request for a $70,000 - $80,000 loan did not constitute a promise on which Werner could reasonably rely. The bank had answered Werner's request by saying, "No problem."

PRACTICAL CONSIDERATIONS

While an advertisement is normally a mere invitation to negotiate and does not constitute an offer, advertisers frequently honor the terms of their advertisements even though they are aware that they are not bound to do so. The reason for doing so is that such action promotes goodwill between a company and its customers and consequently may represent good business judgment. Furthermore, failure to abide by the terms of an advertisement may cause a company to run afoul of state consumer protection laws.

Example: A company advertises a camera in a local newspaper. The newspaper misstates the price for the camera as $109 instead of the correct amount, $159. Although the company would not necessarily be required to sell the camera for $109, it may decide to sell it for that price anyway. Part of the reason for such a decision would be the fact that if the advertiser sells the camera at that price, the customer may return in the future for additional items. If the company does not sell the camera at that price, there is a good chance that the customer will be lost forever, along with the profits from his or her business.

SELF TEST

True-False Questions

_____   1.   In order for an offer to be valid, it must always be communicated to the offeror or by the offeror's authorized agent.

_____   2.   Death of the offeror will terminate all unaccepted offers.

3. In order for a firm offer made by a merchant to be valid, it must be supported by consideration.

4. An offer made in a fit of anger or disgust will not normally give rise to a contractual obligation.

5. An advertisement in a newspaper that gives specific information with regard to a product and states "First come, first served" may be considered to be a valid offer.

6. In order for an offer to be valid, the date on which the offer is made must be stated in the terms of the offer.

7. Under the Uniform Commercial Code, an offer for the sale of goods is always invalid unless a specific price for the goods is provided in the terms of the offer.

8. An offeror may sometimes be held responsible for and be bound by his or her offer even though he or she did not actually intend to enter into a contract.

9. Once an offer has been rejected, the offeree may still accept it later in certain circumstances.

10. An option must be in writing in all cases in order to be valid and enforceable.

Multiple-Choice Questions

11. In order for the revocation of an offer to be valid and effective, it must be:
    a. made in writing
    b. made before the offer is accepted by the offeree
    c. communicated to the offeree in the same way that the offer was communicated
    d. supported by consideration
    e. all of the above are correct

12. An element that is required in order for the doctrine of promissory estoppel to apply is that:
    a. the offeree must rely on a promise that was made
    b. the offeree must suffer some loss or harm
    c. a promise must be made to the offeree by the offeror
    d. all of the above are correct
    e. only b and c are correct

13. In order to be valid, a firm offer for the sale of goods:
    a. must be made between merchants
    b. must be made in writing
    c. does not need to be supported by consideration
    d. all of the above are correct
    e. only a and c are correct

14. Which of the following will terminate an offer for the sale of an automobile?
    a. the insolvency of the seller
    b. a manufacturer's recall of the automobile for repairs
    c. a counteroffer by the offeree
    d. all of the above are correct
    e. only a and c are correct

15. In order for an offer to be definite, it must set forth:
    a. the date on which it will expire
    b. the date on which the offer was made
    c. the identity of the parties to the offer
    d. all of the above are correct
    e. only a and b must be set forth

16. A person who makes a counteroffer becomes in effect an:
    a. offeror
    b. offeree
    c. obligor
    d. acceptor
    e. obligee

17. An agreement, supported by consideration, to keep an offer for the sale of a boat open for a specified period of time is:
    a. an accord
    b. an option
    c. a firm offer
    d. an illusory offer
    e. a confirmatory offer

18. In order for an offer to be valid, it must:
    a. be definite and certain
    b. be made in writing
    c. be for a tangible commodity
    d. a and b are both correct
    e. a, b, and c are all correct

_____ 19. An advertisement in a newspaper is generally considered to be:
   a. an offer
   b. an option
   c. an invitation to negotiate
   d. a surety agreement
   e. a firm offer

_____ 20. An offer for an agreement involving a purely social invitation:
   a. gives rise to a voidable contract
   b. does not give rise to a binding contract
   c. is unenforceable
   d. is illegal
   e. b and c are both correct

Completion Questions

21. The doctrine that prevents a person from withdrawing his or her offer or denying its validity is referred to as _____ _____.

22. The person to whom an offer is made is known as the _____.

23. When an offeree rejects an offer and thereafter responds by making an offer of his or her own, the offeree has made a(n) _____.

24. A(n) _____ is an agreement to keep an offer open for a certain period of time.

25. A(n) _____ is a proposition or suggestion that a contract be entered into.

Chapter 12

THE ACCEPTANCE

In order for a contract to be created, an offer must be made and accepted.

This chapter discusses the various considerations that are involved in the acceptance of an offer. It identifies the parties to a mutual agreement and considers the interrelationship between them. It also examines the various requirements that must be satisfied if an acceptance is to be valid and discusses special rules that apply to the law of sales under the Uniform Commercial Code. The chapter also discusses various problems that pose particular difficulties in regard to the acceptance of an offer.

Inasmuch as no contract can be created unless a valid acceptance is made, the student of law should acquire a thorough understanding of the rules that apply to this particular concept. While at times the rules may seem confusing, if they are approached in a logical manner their intended meaning becomes clear and the law of contracts is seen to be coherent.

CHAPTER OBJECTIVES

After reading Chapter 11 of the text and studying the related materials in this chapter of the Student Mastery Guide, you will understand:

1. The nature and effect of the acceptance of an offer
2. The elements of an effective acceptance, including:
   a. the intent to accept
   b. communication of the acceptance
   c. the variation of the terms of the offer by means of the acceptance
3. The ways in which an acceptance can be made
4. The cancellation of an acceptance

MAJOR POINTS TO REMEMBER

Requirements for Valid Acceptance

1. In order for an acceptance to be effective, it must:
   a. be made with an intention to enter into a contract
   b. be communicated to the offeror
   c. satisfy all conditions and terms established by the offer

Intent to Accept

2. The intent of an offeree to accept an offer is determined by an objective evaluation of his or her manifested conduct. In other words, the offeree's actions and conduct are relevant in determining whether an acceptance was made.

Communication of Acceptance

3. When an offer is made in connection with a unilateral contract, the offeree will accept the offer by rendering the performance that was requested.

   When an offer is made in connection with a bilateral contract, the offeree will accept the offer by giving a promise in return for the promise of the offeror.

4. Generally, an offeree may communicate acceptance of an offer to the offeror by any means and through any medium of communication that is reasonable in the circumstances.

   If, however, the offer specifies that it must be accepted in a particular way, then the offeree must accept the offer in the specified manner.

5. If the manner or means used by the offeree in accepting an offer is authorized by the offeror, then the acceptance is deemed to have been communicated to the offeror when the acceptance is delivered to the control of the communicating agency, even if the acceptance does not actually reach the offeror. An acceptance made by mail, for example, is effective as soon as it is deposited with the postal service.

   If the acceptance of the offeree is sent or made by any means not authorized by the offeror, the acceptance is effective only when it is received by the offeror.

Satisfying Terms of the Offer

6. Under the common law, any acceptance that changes the terms of the offer constitutes a counteroffer, and the offer is terminated as a result.

7. a. Under Section 2-207 of the Uniform Commercial Code, a clear and unequivocal acceptance of an offer *can* give rise to a contract even though the acceptance states terms that are additional to or different from those contained in the offer.
   b. If, however, the acceptance states or provides that it is expressly conditional on the offeror's agreement to the terms as they have been changed by the offeree, and the offeror does not agree to the changes, then no acceptance has been made and no contract exists.
   c. Between nonmerchants (i.e., either one or both of the parties is not a merchant) the terms added by means of the acceptance are treated as proposals for addition to the contract. In other words, the acceptance will be deemed made as to the original terms of the offer; and the additional terms will be part of the contract if they are accepted by the offeror.
   d. Between merchants, the additional terms automatically become a part of the contract unless:
      i. the offer expressly limits acceptance to the terms of the offer, or
      ii. the additional terms materially alter the offer, or
      iii. the offeror notifies the offeree of his or her objection to the additional terms within a reasonable time
   e. If it is clear from the conduct of the parties that they intend to be bound by a contractual relationship and the parties fail to enter into a formalized contract but perform anyway, and if the writings between them contain provisions that are in

93

conflict with each other, then the contract will consist of those provisions on which both writings are in agreement.

Acceptance Problems

8. Generally, silence in response to an offer does not constitute an acceptance of the offer. Silence may, however, be regarded as an acceptance when:
    a. the parties have had prior dealings with each other, and in the past silence was considered as an acceptance, or
    b. the initial agreement between the parties establishes that silence will be treated as an acceptance, or
    c. the offeree accepts the goods and uses them as if they were his or her own

9. Under the Postal Reorganization Act, a person who receives goods in the mail that he or she did not order or in some way request may keep those goods and is under no obligation to pay for them.

10. Under the terms of an auction sale, if the auction is being conducted "with reserve," the auctioneer may withdraw the item from bidding if the highest bid does not meet the predetermined minimum selling price.
    If an auction is being conducted "without reserve," the auctioneer must sell the item to the highest bidder, whatever it may be.
    Under Section 2-328 of the Uniform Commercial Code, an auction is deemed to be conducted with reserve unless an express statement to the contrary is made.

Cancellation of Acceptance

11. Generally, once an offer is accepted the offeree cannot thereafter reject the offer by canceling the acceptance. However, statutes in some states allow cancellation of an acceptance in certain circumstances. For example, in home solicitation sales made at the residence of the buyer, the buyer can revoke the offer or cancel an acceptance to buy consumer goods of more than $25, if it is done within a three-day "cooling-off period."

Preventive Law: Use of Forms

12. The common use of standard contract forms in business transactions is cost effective only when the forms are used for the type of transaction for which they were drafted. The use of standard forms for major transactions should be done with caution, since the importance of the deal indicates that it is not a common one. Obviously, all forms that are used should be read carefully by the parties to avoid later confusion and legal costs.

MAJOR POINTS OF CASES

Crouch v. *Marrs* (p. 211)

This case illustrates the fact that an offer may be accepted by means of the offeree's conduct as well as by an affirmative answer. The offeree's conduct may consist of performing an act or of refraining from an act. The case further shows that the exercise of control over the subject matter of an offer can also constitute an acceptance.

In evaluating the facts, the court found that when Purex Corporation endorsed and deposited the check it had received from Crouch, such conduct acted as an acceptance of Crouch's offer. Consequently, a contract for the sale of the property in question was formed and Purex breached the contract when it failed to complete the sale. The judgment of the lower court was therefore reversed.

Pribil v. *Ruther* (p. 214)

The court in this case stated that an express contract is created when a definite offer is unconditionally accepted by the offeree. If the offer requires a promise to be given by the offeree, it is essential that the acceptance be communicated to the offeror. If the acceptance is authorized to be made by mail, it becomes effective and a contract is formed as soon as it is placed in the mail with a proper address and proper postage.

The court stated that the act of the defendant's signing the purchase agreement did not in itself create a contract. It also stated that the act of giving the signed agreement to the real-estate agent was not a communication of the acceptance to Mr. Ruther because the acceptance was still within the control of the defendant. The evidence further tended to show that the letter containing the acceptance was mailed after Pribil had changed her mind and revoked her acceptance. Consequently, the court held that the acceptance had not been effectively communicated to the offeror and no contract was formed.

Newman v. *Schiff* (p. 216)

This case concerned an offer for a reward. The defendant made the offer on a nighttime news show. The plaintiff argued that his response upon seeing the offer on the morning news constituted acceptance. The court ruled in favor of the defendant on the basis of their finding that timely acceptance of the offer could only occur during the nighttime show. The court found that the morning news' rebroadcast of the offer was just that: a rebroadcast, not a renewal of extension of the offer. Therefore, no legal contract could be enacted on the basis of the plaintiff's response to that rebroadcast.

Air Products & Chem., Inc. v. *Fairbanks Morse, Inc.* (p. 220)

This case shows that under the provisions of Section 2-207 of the Uniform Commercial Code, a contract will not be formed if it is reasonable for the offeror to consider the response of the offeree as not constituting an acceptance or if the acceptance of the offeree is made expressly conditional on the offeror's agreement to terms that have been varied by the offeree. The case also shows that the statute in question is in derogation of the common law and provides that a contract can be formed even though the terms of the offer differ from those of the acceptance. Once it is determined that a contract has been formed, however, it must also be determined what the terms of the contract are. When such a determination is made, the statute should be interpreted so as to provide that different terms should be treated in the same way as additional terms for purposes of determining what terms are to be included in the contract.

When the court considered the facts of the case, it found that a contract had been formed between the parties. It also found that the provision of Fairbanks' "acknowledgment of order" form, which disclaimed warranty liability and liability for consequential damages, constituted a material alteration of the terms of the offer, and that under Section 2-207 (2)(b) of the UCC such provision does not automatically become a part of the contract. Further, the court held that inasmuch as Air Products did not agree to the provision, it did not become a part of the contract at all.

PRACTICAL CONSIDERATIONS

1. While the Postal Reorganization Act provides that a person is not obligated to pay for goods received in the mail under certain circumstances and conditions, a person who does receive goods under the applicable conditions should generally take some affirmative action to notify the seller that he or she did not order the goods, does not want them, and has no obligation to pay for them. Such notification should be made in writing, if possible, with a copy of the writing being retained by the party who refuses to make payment. The importance of the writing is self-evident, for when a collection agency starts to communicate with the person (as it often does), that person will have a written document to support his or her position. Such writing may also help to preserve the integrity of the person's credit rating.

2. When you attend an auction sale, be careful not to make any gesture that the auctioneer might interpret as a bid. If your gesture is so interpreted by the auctioneer, you may have difficulty convincing him or her that you don't want the item and that you didn't bid on it.

    Example: Jimmy, sitting next to his grandmother at an auction, notices that a bumblebee has entered the room through an open window and is heading for him and his grandmother. In an attempt to dissuade the bee from bothering them, Jimmy takes the card inscribed with both numbers that was given to them when they arrived at the auction and starts waving it at the bee. A moment later, to Jimmy's bewilderment, he learns that he has purchased a quartz desk set for $750. If the auctioneer is not an understanding and compassionate person, Jimmy may be hard pressed to succeed in his argument that he didn't bid on the item.

SELF TEST

True-False Questions

_____   1. An offeree may always accept an offer in any way he or she wishes, as long as the means selected is reasonable in the circumstances.

_____ 2. If an acceptance is mailed to the offeror by the offeree and mailing is an authorized means of acceptance, a contract is formed at the time of mailing even though the letter of acceptance never reaches the offeror.

_____ 3. An offeree may, in certain circumstances, be deemed to have accepted an offer even though he or she had no intention of accepting it.

_____ 4. In a transaction involving an offer for the sale of goods, a contract may be formed even though the offeree changes the terms of the offer in accepting it.

_____ 5. When an auction sale is being conducted with reserve, the auctioneer must sell an item for the highest bid made even though that price is less than the value the auctioneer had previously determined was required for sale of the item.

_____ 6. Silence on the part of the offeree may never constitute an acceptance of the offer being made.

_____ 7. Generally, an offeree may not revoke his or her acceptance of an offer once it has been communicated to the offeror.

_____ 8. An acceptance of an offer that was made by mail is invalid if the acceptance is made by means of a telephone conversation between the offeree and the offeror.

_____ 9. When an offer specifies that it must be accepted by performance of a particular act, the offeree can accept the offer by making a promise to perform the act at some time in the future.

_____ 10. Under the common law, in order for an acceptance to be valid and effective, it must be absolute and unconditional.

Multiple-Choice Questions

_____ 11. An element that is required in order for an acceptance to be valid is:
  a. a written expression of acceptance
  b. contractual intent
  c. a future commitment
  d. all of the above are correct
  e. only a and b are correct

12. An offer made in connection with a bilateral contract may be accepted by:
   a. a counteroffer
   b. anyone with knowledge of the offer
   c. a promise to perform
   d. an acceptance that is conditional on the occurrence of an event
   e. a and c are both correct

13. An offer made to Calvin Orbicks may be accepted by:
   a. Calvin Orbicks only
   b. Calvin Orbicks' mother
   c. any close personal friend of Calvin Orbicks
   d. a and c are both correct
   e. a, b, and c are all correct

14. An offer made by telephone to purchase a quantity of ripened bananas that are sitting in the sunlight on a railroad platform in Florida on August 10 may be accepted by:
   a. a letter indicating an acceptance that is sent by regular mail from California within 24 hours of the offer
   b. a telephone call
   c. any means the offeree chooses to use
   d. a letter to a messenger service in Florida for delivery to the offeree
   e. b and c are both correct

15. An acceptance that is made by mail becomes effective:
   a. when it is received by the offeror
   b. when it is received by the postal service in the offeror's town
   c. as soon as it is placed in a mailbox by the offeree
   d. all of the above are correct
   e. only a and b are correct

16. When a person remains silent in response to an offer:
   a. the silence will generally be treated as an acceptance
   b. the silence will be treated as an acceptance if silence has been treated as acceptance in prior dealings between the parties
   c. the silence will not be treated as an acceptance under any circumstances
   d. the silence will be treated as an acceptance if the offeree told a friend that he or she intended to accept the offer
   e. all of the above are correct

_____   17. A person who receives goods in the mail that he or she did not order:
    a.   may keep the goods without paying for them
    b.   must either return the goods or pay for them
    c.   may keep the goods but must contact the seller to negotiate a sales price
    d.   must keep the goods once the seller has sent a bill for them
    e.   c and d are both correct

_____   18. If a merchant accepts the offer of another merchant for the sale of goods but adds some terms to the offer by means of the acceptance, the additional terms:
    a.   always render the acceptance invalid
    b.   are always ignored
    c.   may automatically become part of the contract except in certain circumstances
    d.   are always treated as a counteroffer
    e.   must always be treated as binding upon the offeror

_____   19. When an offer for the sale of goods is made by one nonmerchant to another and the offeree unconditionally accepts the offer but adds some terms to it:
    a.   a contract is formed in which the terms of the agreement are those contained in the original offer unless the offeror agrees to the additional terms
    b.   no contract is formed
    c.   a contract is formed in which the terms of the agreement are those that are set forth by the offeree regardless of the offeror's objection to the additional terms
    d.   the additional terms automatically become part of the contract
    e.   c and d are both correct

_____   20. If an offeree accepts an offer on condition that the offeror agrees to changes or additions that the offeree has made to the offer:
    a.   no contract is created
    b.   a contract is formed only with respect to the original terms of the offer
    c.   a contract is created only if the offeror agrees to the changes or additions made by the offeree
    d.   the additional terms will become a part of the contract if the offeror does not respond to the offeree
    e.   all of the above are correct

Completion Questions

21. A person who deals in goods of the kind that he or she is selling is commonly referred to as a(n) _____.

22. The person to whom an offer is made is the _____.

23. Under the common law, an acceptance of an offer that changes the terms of the offer is considered to be a(n) _____.

24. A(n) _____ is a sales device in which the general public gathers at a central location for the purpose of making bids on items presented for sale.

25. Assent to an offer made by the offeror in connection with a contract is referred to as a(n) _____.

Chapter 13

CONSIDERATION

Though every contract is an agreement, not every agreement is a contract. In order for a contractual relationship to exist, the agreement must possess some adhesive quality that binds it and holds it together. That quality or element is *consideration*.

This chapter examines the nature of consideration and discusses the various forms it may take. The materials show that historically, consideration requires that one party must incur a legal detriment in exchange for that which is the subject of the bargain. The chapter also discusses specific rules that apply to particular situations such as illusory promises, output and requirements contracts, compromises of debts, and promissory estoppel.

When you examine the concepts contained in this chapter, you should try to acquire a comprehensive understanding of the nature of consideration rather than an isolated knowledge of the individual rules. Numerous rules apply to consideration, and there are exceptions to all of them. A general understanding of the concept will make the nature of consideration more meaningful and the exceptions less confusing.

CHAPTER OBJECTIVES

After reading Chapter 13 of the text and studying the related materials in this chapter of the Student Mastery Guide, you will understand:

1. The nature of consideration
2. The elements of consideration, including:
   a. legal detriment
   b. bargained for exchange
3. The different types of consideration, including:
   a. promise
   b. an act
   c. forbearance
4. Promissory estoppel

MAJOR POINTS TO REMEMBER

Nature of Consideration

1. Consideration is anything that is given in exchange for something else. It has also been described as a legal detriment that is incurred by a promisee as the bargained exchange for a promise.

2. Consideration consists of:
   a. a legal detriment
   b. a bargained exchange

Legal Detriment

3. A legal detriment is incurred where a person does something or promises to do something that he or she was not previously obligated to do, or refrains or promises to refrain from doing something that he or she had a legal right to do.

4. Consideration is legally *sufficient* if the promisee incurs a legal detriment in exchange for the promise given.

5. The *adequacy* of the consideration is immaterial when a court is considering the issue of consideration in connection with a claim, unless it is alleged that the contract involved was not entered into voluntarily. A person may, for example, exchange a pencil for an automobile. Courts generally do not examine the adequacy of the items exchanged.

6. An illusory promise is not sufficient consideration and is therefore unenforceable. An agreement with a clause allowing a party to terminate it at will is illusory and unenforceable, except in those states which hold that, if the parties clearly intended a contract, then notice of termination is implied, thereby making the promise not illusory and enforceable.

7. Today, under Section 2-306 of the UCC, output and requirement contracts include an obligation by the party who determines the quantity to act in good faith, which is sufficient to take these contracts out of the illusory category. Thus, they can be valid and enforceable, assuming that actual promises to buy or sell have been made.

8. Agreement to do something that a person is already under an obligation to perform does not constitute consideration under the preexisting duty rule. This rule does not apply, however, if the parties rescind the original contract and enter into a new contract. Further, if a contract is modified by agreement without new consideration but due to unforeseen difficulties in performance, then the modification is enforceable.

9. An agreement that modifies a contract that is under the purview of Article 2 of the Uniform Commercial Code does not need consideration in order to be binding (UCC Section 2-209). The code does, however, require consideration in order to create a contract.

10. Generally, partial payment on an undisputed debt that already exists will not discharge that debt unless there is an agreement to do so that is supported by consideration.

    If, however, there is a good-faith dispute over the amount of money that is actually owed, an agreement by the parties that the creditor will accept partial payment in full satisfaction of the debt will be enforceable.

11. If a bankrupt debtor whose obligations have been legally discharged desires to nonetheless pay part of it, then a creditor who agrees to accept only partial payment is bound to that promise, the consideration being the debtor's promise not to assert the bankruptcy defense.

Similarly, a debtor who cannot pay his or her debts in full, but does not want to file for bankruptcy, may enter into a composition agreement with creditors by which they all mutually agree to accept partial payment from the debtor in full satisfaction of the debts owed.

12. It is clear that a promise to refrain from asserting a legal right, or the act of doing so, is consideration sufficient to support a contract, provided that the legal claim is asserted in good faith. The out-of-court settlement of lawsuits is often accomplished by one party agreeing to give up the right to a trial in exchange for receiving consideration from the other party, normally the payment of money.

Bargained Exchange

13. Consideration must be bargained for - that is, something that the promisor requested in return for being bound by the promise - and exchanged by the parties.

14. If a promisor requests a specific form of consideration, the consideration provided by a promisee must be that which was requested.

15. Past consideration, under law, is no consideration, and therefore is insufficient to support a new contract. Further, no bargained-for consideration is normally present in gift situations or where promises are made based on a moral duty.

Promissory Estoppel

16. Promissory estoppel is a substitute for consideration.

17. In order for the doctrine of promissory estoppel to be invoked, the promisee must show that:
    a. the promisor made a promise that the promisor should reasonably expect the promisee will rely on
    b. the promisee justifiably relied on the promise
    c. the promisee incurred substantial economic detriment
    d. injustice can be avoided only by enforcement of the promise

18. Under the doctrine of promissory estoppel, a promisor will be prevented or prohibited (i.e. estopped) from denying the validity or existence of a promise that was made.

Preventive Law: Accord and Satisfaction

19. When a good-faith dispute arises between a debtor and creditor regarding the amount of money owed, the debt is unliquidated and the preexisting duty rule does not apply. Consequently, the debtor can offer an accord by sending the creditor a check marked "Paid in Full" with a note explaining the amount disputed. Upon receipt the creditor can:

 a. unconditionally accept the accord by cashing the check, and when it is paid, the remainder of the debt is discharged

 b. reject the offered accord by returning the check and attempt to collect the full amount claimed

 c. in some states and in cases governed by the UCC, notify the debtor that it accepts the check under protest, cash it, and proceed to try to collect the balance.

Ethics Box: Policy and Ethical Considerations in Enforcing Promises

20. Although the concept of consideration can seem abstract, it is critical to answering the legal and ethical question of when a person's promise should be enforceable as a contract. The consideration element of contracts limits enforceable promises to those that are given in a bargain-for and exchange relationship. The reasons for this limitation is that the courts should enforce only socially significant promises and those for which there was a reasonable expectation of performance.

     Critics of the consideration requirement argue that promises based on moral obligations and those that cause detrimental reliance should also be enforced. In response, the courts have sometimes invoked the promissory estoppel doctrine, and in the cases of firm offers and contract modifications the UCC has dispensed with the need for consideration. The question of what promises should be legally binding remains subject to debate.

MAJOR POINTS OF CASES

Hamer v. Sidway (p. 228)

     The court in this case indicated that forbearance is a sufficient consideration in exchange for a promise even if such forbearance has the effect of providing a benefit to the promisee or a third person. The forbearance, however, must involve the abandonment of some legal right that one party possesses at the present time or must limit his or her freedom of action at some time in the future.

     After examining the facts, the court found that the nephew, William E. Story, 2d, had refrained from doing something that he had had a legal right to do, and even though he may have realized some economic benefit as a result, his conduct constituted valid consideration for the promise made by his uncle. As a result, a valid contract existed between Story and his uncle, which could be enforced by Hamer, who was a successor in interest to the contractual rights of Story.

Ahern v. *Knecht* (p. 230)

This case demonstrates the exception to the general rule that the courts will not inquire into the adequacy of consideration. In cases where consideration is grossly inadequate and other factors such as gross inequality in bargaining power exist, the courts may deem the contract unconscionable and rescind or cancel the contract.

In this case, the court found the circumstances sufficient to set aside the contract as unconscionable. The defendant performed some services that had just been performed a few weeks earlier. The additional services he allegedly performed were in fact not substantially performed, and he exacerbated the problem he was supposed to remedy. There was also a gross disparity in bargaining power. The plaintiff was totally ignorant about air conditioners and was relying completely on the defendants expertise.

Levine v. *Blumenthal* (p. 233)

It is well established in law, according to the court, that a promise to do that which one is already legally bound to do does not constitute consideration. The court also stated that a partial payment made in connection with a debt does not discharge the entire debt unless the creditor agrees to accept the payment in full satisfaction of the indebtedness and the agreement is supported by consideration. The adequacy of such consideration is not significant. Likewise, according to the court, "the actual performance of that which one is legally bound to do" does not constitute consideration.

In applying the law to the facts of the case, the court held that the oral modification of the lease was not supported by consideration because Blumenthal was already required to pay $200 a month and nothing else was exchanged to support the reduced rental. Consequently, the court agreed that Blumenthal should be required to pay the unpaid balance of $25 a month and the full rent for the final month of the lease.

Allen M. Campbell Co. v. *Virginia Metal Industries, Inc.* (p. 238)

This case involves a lawsuit by a general contractor against a subcontractor for failing to perform as promised in its bid that was submitted to and used by the general contractor in winning a construction job. In order to fulfill its construction contract, the general contractor then had to obtain the products from another subcontractor at a higher price. In response to the lawsuit to recover the difference between the price paid and the defendant's bid, the defendant subcontractor asserted that no contract existed for a lack of consideration, since the general contractor had never communicated a promise of acceptance in exchange for the bid.

The court held for the plaintiff general contractor, however, despite the lack of consideration, by invoking the doctrine of promissory estoppel. The plaintiff's case, thus, could be that: (1) the defendant submitted its bid knowing that the plaintiff would rely on it in calculating the bid for the construction contract; (2) the plaintiff in fact did justifiably rely on the defendant's bid to its substantial economic detriment; and (3) there is no other way to avoid injustice other than to deny the defendant the right to revoke its bid, thereby making the plaintiff's ultimate acceptance valid. By application of the promissory estoppel doctrine, then, there could be a valid contract, which the defendant breached. Because the case had been dismissed before trial, the court remanded this case back to the trial court for trial at which the plaintiff would have the opportunity to prove its case.

PRACTICAL CONSIDERATIONS

1. Even though a promise to perform or discharge a preexisting obligation does not constitute consideration, the promisee may on occasion have no alternative but to agree to pay the other party the additional money that is demanded or requested, and thereafter look to the courts to recover the unjustified payment.

    Example: A agrees to build a house for B for $60,000. After the basement has been constructed, the house fully framed, and the roof completed, and B has notified his current landlord to terminate his lease, A informs B that as a result of increased costs, he cannot complete the house unless B agrees to pay an additional $5,000. Inasmuch as B will shortly have no place to live and also inasmuch as B cannot move into the house until he receives a deed and keys to the house from A, B may have no alternative but to pay the additional $5,000 and then, after he has moved into the house, sue A to recover the extra money.

2. When a person agrees to accept from a debtor less than the amount that he or she claims is due, the creditor should be certain to make an appropriate notation on the check received in payment of the debt so that he or she may take action to collect the balance due.

    Likewise, the debtor in the above situation, in order to protect his or her own interests, should indicate on the back of the check that the amount is being given as "payment in full." It should be noted that the law on this point does vary somewhat from state to state.

SELF TEST

True-False Questions

_____ 1. Promissory estoppel is a form of consideration.

_____ 2. In order for consideration to be present, the promisee must incur some legal detriment.

_____ 3. Past consideration is sufficient to support a contract involving the sale of precious jewelry.

_____ 4. If a court determines that the consideration provided in respect to a contract was inadequate, the court will usually permit the contract to be rescinded.

_____ 5. Rufer agrees to build a house for Kurt for $80,000. Thereafter, Rufer tells Kurt that he must pay an additional $10,000 because of increased building costs. If Kurt agrees in writing to pay the additional money, he will be required to pay the additional $10,000.

106

_____ 6. An illusory promise is unenforceable because it is not supported by consideration.

_____ 7. A promise by Arnold to pay his nephew William $5,000 if he doesn't smoke a single cigarette for the next two years is enforceable.

_____ 8. Two parties are involved in a dispute over how much money is actually owed by the debtor. The creditor accepts a lesser amount than he claims the debtor owes. The creditor may not thereafter sue the debtor for the balance allegedly owed.

_____ 9. A simple promise is sufficient consideration to support a contract.

_____ 10. A promise by an employer to provide an employee with an "all-expenses-paid" vacation to Hawaii for his or her past work would be supported by consideration.

Multiple-Choice Questions

_____ 11. Which of the following is a valid form of consideration?
    a. forbearance
    b. an agreement not to do something that one is legally bound to do
    c. an illusory promise
    d. a promise
    e. a and d are both correct

_____ 12. In order to establish the applicability of the promissory estoppel doctrine, a person must show that:
    a. a promise was made that the promisor should have known would be acted on by the promisee
    b. the promisee performed some act in reliance on a promise
    c. the promisee suffered a detriment
    d. all of the above are correct
    e. only a and c are correct

_____ 13. An element of consideration is:
    a. adequate value
    b. bargained exchange
    c. affirmative conduct
    d. all of the above are correct
    e. only a and b are correct

14. An agreement that modifies an existing agreement for the sale of goods:
    a. is invalid
    b. must be supported by consideration
    c. does not need consideration in order to be effective
    d. a and b are both correct
    e. a and c are both correct

15. Mrs. Hunt agrees to accept a lesser amount of money than she claims is due in connection with a debt owed to her. In order to protect against Mrs. Hunt later attempting to collect the balance, the debtor should mark the check:
    a. received without prejudice
    b. received with prejudice
    c. received without recourse
    d. all of the above are correct
    e. paid in full

16. A contract under which a party agrees to sell all of the product that he or she produces or manufactures is referred to as a(n):
    a. specialty contract
    b. requirements contract
    c. output contract
    d. productive commodity contract
    e. quasi contract

17. A promise made for inadequate consideration generally is:
    a. illegal
    b. enforceable
    c. required to be in writing
    d. void
    e. unenforceable

18. A payment that is made for the purpose of completing an accord is known as a(n):
    a. allonge
    b. codicil
    c. garnishment
    d. satisfaction
    e. partition

_____ 19. Which of the following is a correct statement with respect to consideration?
   a.   an illusory promise may sometimes constitute consideration
   b.   promissory estoppel is a form of consideration
   c.   a court will generally not consider the adequacy of the consideration provided for in a contract
   d.   past consideration is not valid consideration
   e.   c and d are both correct

_____ 20. If a local business offers to pay a reward to anyone who provides information leading to the arrest and conviction of the person who recently burglarized its store, which of the following persons would not be able to collect the reward?
   a.   the policeman who found the thief and arrested him
   b.   an employee of a business that competes with the company offering the reward
   c.   a resident of another state who was visiting a relative and witnessed the theft
   d.   a person who had previously been arrested on a theft charge
   e.   the persons identified in both c and d would be unable to collect the reward

Completion Questions

21.   Giving up or refraining from doing that which a person has a legal right to do is referred to as _____.

22.   An agreement under which a person agrees to buy from a particular seller all of a particular product that he or she needs is known as a(n) _____.

23.   Consideration consists of a _____ _____ _____ and a _____.

24.   An agreement that gives the promisor the option to perform a contract if he or she wishes or to cancel it if he or she so chooses is known as a(n) _____ _____.

25.   An agreement that is reached by means of negotiation and compromise is a(n) _____ _____ _____.

Chapter 14

GENUINE ASSENT

It has often been said that things are seldom what they seem. This statement is as true of the law of contracts as it is of anything else. Sometimes it may seem by all objective criteria that an agreement has been made and a contract exists. After an examination of the facts and circumstances surrounding the contract, however, it may be discovered that improper methods were used to bring about the agreement.

This chapter is concerned with factors that affect a party's ability to enter into a binding contractual relationship. It discusses the effect that another party's wrongful or coercive conduct may have upon an agreement that otherwise appears to be firmly intact. In particular, it discusses the nature and effect on a contract of fraud, duress, undue influence, and various types of mistakes.

CHAPTER OBJECTIVES

After reading Chapter 13 of the text and studying the related materials in this chapter of the Student Mastery Guide, you will understand:

1. The requirements for a genuine consensual agreement
2. The nature and effect of a misrepresentation of fact, including:
   a. fraud
   b. misrepresentation
3. The nature and effect of duress and undue influence
4. The types of mistakes and their effects on a contract

MAJOR POINTS TO REMEMBER

Nature of Fraud

1. In order to establish the existence of fraud, it is necessary to show all of the following:
   a. a misrepresentation of a fact
   b. the misstated fact is material
   c. knowledge of falsity with an intention to deceive
   d. reasonable reliance on the statement by the person claiming fraud
   e. damages

2. Generally, fraud is an intentional tort. As a result, punitive damages will be allowed upon a showing that the fraud was maliciously committed.

3. Fraud renders a contract voidable. It also subjects the wrongdoer to the possibility of responsibility for monetary damages caused by the fraud.

4. An unintentional misrepresentation renders a contract voidable but does not subject the person who made the statement to liability for money damages.

Elements of Fraud

Misrepresentation of Fact

5. A misrepresentation is an active concealment of a material fact or partial disclosure represented as full disclosure.

6. A misrepresentation can be express or implied.

7. Generally, failure to disclose information that another party would like to know does not constitute fraud, since there is usually no obligation to make such disclosure. However, some statutes impose a duty to disclose, such as the Truth in Lending Act's required financial disclosures in consumer credit situations.

8. Generally, fraud cannot exist in connection with the expression of an opinion, since an opinion is not a fact. An exception to this rule exists, however, when the opinion is rendered by an expert in connection with his or her field of expertise.

Ethics Box: Creative Resume Writing

9. Creative resume writing may sometimes go too far and become unethical behavior.

Materiality

10. The misstated fact must be one that is material to the contract. In other words, the misrepresented fact must be one that, had the truth been told, the contract in question would not likely have been agreed to by the party claiming fraud.

Knowledge of Falsity and Intent to Deceive

11. "Scienter" is also a required element of fraud. It means to knowingly misrepresent a fact for the purpose of deceiving another. In regard to this intent, one is presumed to intend the natural and probable consequences of voluntary acts. Further, this element is satisfied if one makes a statement of fact in reckless disregard of its truth or falsity.

Reliance

12. The person claiming fraud must have justifiably relied on the misrepresentation of fact. A person cannot claim reasonable reliance on the statement of another person if the person to whom the statement was made conducted his or her own investigation, or could have readily determined the truth of the representation.

Injury or Damage

13. The final element of fraud is that the party relying on the misrepresentation suffered harm as a consequence. The measure of the harm normally is the difference between the value of what was promised and relied on and that which was actually received.

Duress

14. The use of duress to induce a person to enter into a contractual relationship will render the contract thus formed voidable (but not void).

15. In order for a contract to be voidable on the grounds of duress, it is necessary to show that the acts or threats:
    a. were wrongful
    b. induced the contractual consent of the party so affected

16. Although economic duress or coercion can make a contract voidable, public policy reasons would seem to favor limiting it to cases involving individuals or weak companies that were induced to enter into involuntary agreements.

Undue Influence

17. The use of undue influence by a party to a contract will permit the person who was influenced to escape from the contract (it renders the contract voidable). In cases where a relationship between the contracting parties involves a high degree of trust by one in the other, then a contract that benefits the dominant party is presumed voidable unless the dominant party can prove that no undue influence occurred.

Mistakes

18. When a mutual mistake (bilateral mistake) has been made in regard to a material fact, the contract involved can be rescinded.

19. Generally, a unilateral mistake of fact has no effect on a contract, and the contract will be enforced as it exists. If, however, rescission of the contract would impose only a slight burden on the party not mistaken, while enforcement would be an undue hardship on the mistaken party, then the courts may grant rescission of the contract. Further, if a unilateral mistake is made that the other party knew or should have known was occurring, then the contract can be rescinded.

MAJOR POINTS OF CASES

Koral Industries v. Security - Connecticut Life Insurance Co. (p. 245)

The court in this case stated the proposition that failure to use due diligence to suspect or discover someone's fraud will not bar the use of the defense of fraud. Only actual knowledge of the falsity of the statement will act as a bar.

112

In this case, Koral actively misrepresented the medical condition of his employee by failing to disclose his history of hospitalizations and his recent treatment for alcohol abuse and depression. The misrepresentations were made to induce the insurer to enter into the contract. The insurer reasonably relied on the application.

Totem Marine T. & B. v. *Alyseka Pipeline, Etc.* (p. 247)

The principle illustrated by this case is that economic duress will render a contract voidable. The court indicated that in order to establish and substantiate an allegation of economic duress, there must be proof that the duress resulted from some wrongdoing on the part of the defendant and also that the coerced party had no other alternative, under the existing circumstances, but to agree with the terms and conditions suggested by the wrongdoer.

In this case, the appellate court did not rule that economic duress did in fact exist. It stated that such duress might have existed and returned the case to the trial court for a determination of that issue.

Odorizzi v. *Bloomfield School District* (p. 249)

This case illustrates the principle of law that provides that a contract can be set aside because of the exertion of undue influence on one of the parties to the contract. The court stated that undue influence "involves the use of excessive pressure" so that the will of the person exerting such pressure prevails over the will of the person being influenced in such a way as to prevent that person from being able to exercise independent judgement. In order for undue influence to exist, according to the court, the influenced party must be susceptible to influence and the pressure exerted by the influencing party must be excessive.

In this case, the court did not make a determination that undue influence had actually been exerted but did rule that, in the circumstances described, it was possible that undue influence was used. As a result, the matter was returned to the trial court so that a determination could be made on the basis of the evidentiary facts to be presented.

The court also discussed the nature of duress, fraud, and mistake in its opinion.

Frigaliment Importing Co., Ltd. v. *B.N.S.* (p. 252)

The plaintiff in this case sued for breach of warranty in a contract in which it was to buy "chickens" from the defendant. The plaintiff asserted that it intended to buy chickens suitable for broiling or frying, but the defendant instead delivered stewing chickens. The court examined the definition of "chicken" in the dictionary, as used in the poultry industry, as defined in government regulations, and in the marketplace. It found that this term encompasses the type of chickens delivered by the defendant. Since it was the plaintiff's burden to prove that its narrower definition of "chickens" was actually meant by the contract and it failed in carrying that burden, this was a case of unilateral mistake and its complaint must be dismissed.

M.J. McGough Company v. *Jane Lamb Memorial Hospital* (p. 254)

The holding in this case recognizes the general principle that a unilateral mistake of fact does not generally justify rescission of a contract. The court recognized that there are exceptions to this general rule and that in the case of the construction industry, if it can be shown that (a) there was a mistake that was so serious that enforcement of the contract would be unconscionable, (b) the mistake related to the substance of the consideration, (c) it occurred even though ordinary care was used, and (d) the other party suffered no real loss, then rescission of the contract would be allowed.

In this case, the court found that the contractor had established proof of the requisite elements and permitted rescission of the contract.

PRACTICAL CONSIDERATIONS

While it is easy to state the elements that make up the tort of fraud, the existence of those elements is often difficult to prove because the fraudulent party can frequently claim that there has been a misunderstanding, or that the claimant is simply wrong. Even the presence of witnesses at the time the fraud was committed will not always be sufficient to establish the existence of the fraud.

In view of the difficulty of establishing fraud, specific details of an agreement that are particularly important should be reduced to a writing whenever possible and stated in clear and precise language. That is not to say that all the terms of an agreement should always be in writing, but important terms and provisions that might otherwise be subject to different interpretations later should be clearly stated. So should any provisions that seem too good to be true.

Example: A offers to sell B an automobile that is generally sold for $75,000 and agrees to accept $20,000 for the car. When B inquires about the type of engine and its condition, A states that the car has its original engine and that it is in perfect condition. When B asks why the selling price is so low, A replies that he needs money quickly. In fact, the engine was taken from a car worth $5,000 and is not functioning properly. One week after the sale, B returns to A and demands his money back.

B may have difficulty proving fraud. A may now state that B was aware that the engine was not in good condition because A told B as much at the time of the sale. A may also contend that the price would have been much higher if the engine had been in proper condition and the correct type for the car.

Had the critical facts been put in writing at the time of the transaction, B would have a better opportunity to establish his claim.

114

SELF TEST

True-False Questions

_____ 1. All misrepresentation of fact will constitute the tort of fraud.

_____ 2. A unilateral mistake as to a matter of law will render a contract voidable.

_____ 3. The use of duress to induce a person to enter into a contractual relationship will render the contract void.

_____ 4. The failure of a person to speak will in certain circumstances constitute fraud.

_____ 5. A statement of opinion can never be the basis for an action based on fraud.

_____ 6. A bilateral mistake regarding a material fact will cause the contract that was formed in connection with the fact to be considered voidable.

_____ 7. When a person indicates that he will burn down another person's place of business unless that person signs the contract they are discussing, the contract thus created will be deemed voidable on the grounds of duress.

_____ 8. Undue influence will render a contract void.

_____ 9. In order to establish the existence of fraud, it is necessary to prove the presence of scienter.

_____ 10. The unintentional misrepresentation of a fact to another person will subject the person making the statement to liability for money damages.

Multiple-Choice Questions

_____ 11. Which of the following will render a contract void?
  a. duress
  b. bilateral mistake of fact
  c. fraud
  d. all of the above are correct
  e. only b and c are correct

115

12. Which of the following is an element of fraud?
   a. a material fact
   b. an intentional misstatement of fact
   c. reliance on a statement by the person to whom it was made
   d. all of the above are correct
   e. only b and c are correct

13. Ordinary persuasion and argument in connection with a contract of the sale of an item:
   a. are permissible and do not adversely affect a contract
   b. render a contract voidable
   c. constitute undue influence
   d. b and c are both correct
   e. a and c are both correct

14. Which of the following must be proved in order to establish the existence of duress?
   a. the person who exerted duress must be prone to violence
   b. the acts or threats that were used induced the consent of a party
   c. the person who allegedly exerted duress must have been in possession of a dangerous weapon
   d. the person who allegedly used duress was stronger than the other person
   e. b and d are both correct

15. Which of the following will render a contract voidable?
   a. undue influence
   b. fraud
   c. duress
   d. all of the above are correct
   e. only a and b will render the contract voidable

16. When both parties to an agreement have made an error in what they perceive the facts of the situation to be, their error is described as:
   a. a unilateral mistake of fact
   b. a bilateral mistake of law
   c. a bilateral mistake of fact
   d. a unilateral mistake of law
   e. a and d are both correct

_____ 17. Which of the following persons could commit fraud with respect to a statement of opinion?
     a. a jeweler in selling a diamond
     b. an airline pilot in selling his car
     c. a teacher in selling a boat
     d. a plumber in selling a television set
     e. all of the above are correct

_____ 18. A unilateral mistake of fact generally will:
     a. render a contract voidable
     b. render a contract void
     c. render a contract unenforceable
     d. have no effect on a contract
     e. b and c are both correct

_____ 19. If A and B are discussing the terms of a contract and A is aware of a fact that B does not yet know because he did not conduct an inquiry that would have readily disclosed the fact:
     a. A must inform B of the fact anyway
     b. A is under no obligation to disclose the fact
     c. B will be able to void the contract because of A's failure to disclose the fact
     d. the contract will be void
     e. a and c are both correct

_____ 20. A mutual mistake with regard to a material fact will:
     a. render a contract void
     b. render a contract voidable
     c. render a contract voidable only if there is a writing to support the fact of the mistake
     d. have no effect on a contract
     e. render a contract ex post facto

Completion Questions

21. A statement that constitutes the expression of a person's belief is referred to as _____.

22. _____ is the knowledge of the falsehood of a fact that was represented to be true.

23. The use of psychological coercion to induce another person to do something is known as _____ _____.

24. The use of force or a wrongful act or threat that overcomes the free will of another person is referred to as_____.

25. _____ refers to the unintentional misstatement of a fact that the person to whom it was made relied on to his or her detriment.

Chapter 15

CAPACITY TO CONTRACT

In order to fly, one must possess the necessary means to become airborne. Similarly, in order to be able to commit oneself to a binding contract, one must have sufficient capacity to enter into such a significant relationship.

This chapter examines the various factors that affect a person's ability or capacity to enter into a valid, binding contract. Included among the considerations in this chapter are the nature of minority, intoxication, and insanity and their effect on a contract.

In reading this chapter, keep in mind that a person must understand the nature of the contractual relationship and also the consequences of entering into a contract. If the person does not have full cognizance and awareness of these factors, a substantial question may exist with respect to his or her ability to enter into a contract or to discharge the commitments it entails.

CHAPTER OBJECTIVES

After reading Chapter 15 of the text and studying the related materials in this chapter of the Student Mastery Guide, you will understand:

1. The nature of contractual capacity
2. The effect of a lack of capacity on a contract, including:
   a. void agreement
   b. voidable agreement
3. The nature and effect of being a minor on a contract
4. The effect of intoxication on contractual capacity

MAJOR POINTS TO REMEMBER

Capacity in General

1. Generally, a person who seeks to set aside a contract has the burden of establishing incompetency. The incompetency must have existed at the time the contract was entered into and must make the person incapable of understanding the nature and effect of the transaction. The presumption is that all people making contracts have capacity.

Mental Incompetency

2. Generally, the contract of a person who has been adjudicated (declared or legally determined by a court to be) insane is void.

3. If a person has not been adjudicated insane by a court but suffers from an impairing mental illness that impairs his ability to understand the nature and consequences of his contract, that persons' contract will usually be considered voidable.

119

Intoxication

4. Generally, the contract of a person whose thinking is so impaired by alcohol or drugs that the person does not know what he or she is doing is voidable. However, some states do not allow the contract to be voided unless it is proven that the person claiming an enforceable contract was responsible for the other party's intoxication or, knowing of the intoxication, took unfair advantage of the intoxicated person.

5. To avoid a contract due to intoxication, the consideration received must be returned unless the other party has acted fraudulently.

6. A person who contracts for necessaries while intoxicated must pay for their reasonable value.

Minors

7. Generally, the contract of a minor is voidable at the option of the minor. (See p. 263 of the text for exceptions to this rule.)

8. When a contract that an minor enters into involves necessary items (food, clothing, shelter, medicine, etc.) that contract will not be considered voidable, but rather will be treated as completely valid and enforceable. However, the minor will be required to pay only the reasonable value of that which is provided to him or her under the terms of a contract for necessaries.

Ethics Box: Fair Treatment of Minors (p. 266)

9. In the *Kiefer v. Howe Motors, Inc.*, case presented in this chapter, the minor was emancipated, misrepresented his age, and apparently took advantage of or abused the general rule protecting minors. This type of conduct could be considered unethical. However, the legal policy of providing needed protection for minors is enhanced from an efficiency standpoint by not overturning the general rule or making too many exceptions to deal with the few persons who will act unethically.

Disaffirmance

10. A minor can disaffirm a contract at any time before reaching majority (becoming an adult) or within a reasonable time thereafter.

11. No particular or special form is required in order for a minor to disaffirm a contract. In other words, any actions, conduct, or words that inform the other party to a contract that the minor is disaffirming the contract are sufficient.

12. In most jurisdictions, a minor will be permitted to rescind or disaffirm a contract and recover any consideration given, even though he or she no longer possesses the consideration received when the contract was formed. A minority of jurisdictions, however,

require the minor to return the consideration received, or its value, in order to be able to rescind.

13. In cases in which a minor induces an adult to enter into a contract through misrepresentation of his or her age, the courts are split regarding the right of the minor to disaffirm the contract.

Necessaries and Parent's Liability

14. The law implies in contracts by minors to purchase necessities of life which are not being furnished by their parents that the parents are liable to the seller for the reasonable value of those items or services purchased. As a practical matter, adults will seldom contract with a minor when the purchase price is significant without taking steps to insure that some adult will also be bound on the contract, such as requiring an adult to co-sign a contract evidencing a minor's debt.

Ratification

15. If a minor fails to timely and effectively disaffirm and set aside a contract that was entered into while he or she was a minor, that contract will be enforced when the minor reaches adulthood and he or she will be obligated to perform the terms of the contract.

16. A minor can ratify a contract only after reaching adulthood. Any purported ratification that is claimed to have occurred before the minor reached adulthood will be invalid.

17. Any actions, conduct, words, or even inaction on the part of an adult that indicate his or her willingness or agreement to be bound by the terms of a contract entered into as a minor will act as a ratification of the contract.

MAJOR POINTS OF CASES

McGovern v. *Commonwealth State Employees Retirement Board* (p. 260)

This case demonstrates how the court determines whether a person's contract can be avoided because of diminished mental capacity. There is a presumption of mental capacity. The burden of proof is on the party claiming a lack of capacity. The fact that a decision to enter a particular contract was unwise or selfish does not indicate lack of capacity. Lack of capacity exists only when it can be proven that the person, at the very time he executed the document, because of mental illness or defect, was unable to understand the nature and consequences of his action or is unable to act in a reasonable manner regarding the transaction and the other party has reason to know of his condition.

Scott Eden Management v. *Kavovit* (p. 265)

This case stands for the principle that while a minor can disaffirm a contract, the minor cannot be put into a superior position to that which he would have occupied had he never made the contract. In the case, while the minor could disaffirm his contract with his agent, the agent was still entitled to his percentage return on the performance he had negotiated for the minor.

North Carolina Baptist Hospitals, Inc. v. *Franklin* (p. 268)

In this case, the court examines when a minor will be held liable for necessaries. The court ruled that the minor may be held liable for only the reasonable value of the necessaries, and only if the minor received the necessaries on his own credit.

In this case the nine year old was not liable for services provided to her because they were provided at her parents, not her, request.

Bobby Floars Toyota Inc. v. *Smith* (p. 270)

This case examines the issue of what constitutes ratification of a contract that was entered into by a person who was a minor at the time of contracting, but who had attained majority at the time of the attempted disaffirmance. The court in this case ruled for the seller, because it concluded that waiting for ten months after reaching majority to decide to disaffirm was an unreasonable length of time, given the constantly depreciating value of automobiles. Further, the court held that, even if an unreasonable length of time had not passed, the defendant had ratified the contract by retaining possession of the car and making the installment payments for those ten months.

PRACTICAL CONSIDERATIONS

1. While a minor is permitted by law to enter into a contract on his or her own behalf, most business people are reluctant to agree to such a contract unless an adult is willing to be responsible for the minor's obligations under the contract. Even if the minor later disaffirms the contract, they still can look to the adult for full performance.

    Example: Seventeen-year-old Edgar goes to the Gilford Foreign Car auto dealership and selects a car that he wants to purchase. When the salesman ascertains that Edgar is only seventeen years old, he tells Edgar that he will sell him the car only if his mother or father co-signs the purchase agreement.

    Note also that many sellers will refuse to deal with a minor on a contractual basis at all. They will tell any minor that they will deal only with his or her parents.

2. As has been pointed out previously, in most states a minor can disaffirm a contract even though the minor no longer has the item that was purchased under the terms of the contract. Even though the minor can disaffirm the contract, however, it is quite likely that the adult will refuse to return the money or other consideration received from the minor when the contract was created, especially when the minor is not returning the goods. Consequently, it is quite likely that the minor who wants the consideration returned will have to commence a lawsuit to get it back.

    Inasmuch as a lawsuit can become quite expensive, the minor must consider the benefit to be derived from such action and compare it with the cost involved. After doing so, the minor will be able to determine whether his or her disaffirmance of the contract had any real or practical effect.

SELF TEST

True-False Questions

_____ 1. A presumption exists in the law that a person is sane and has the legal capacity to enter into a valid contractual relationship.

_____ 2. The contract of a person who has been adjudicated insane is voidable.

_____ 3. All contracts entered into by minors are deemed to be voidable.

_____ 4. A minor may disaffirm a contract on the grounds of minority at any time before attaining adulthood or within a reasonable time after reaching adulthood.

_____ 5. A minor who intentionally misrepresents his or her age when entering into a contract may not rescind the contract in any state.

_____ 6. If a person is intoxicated at the time he or she enters into a contract, that person may always disaffirm the contract later.

_____ 7. A minor who buys a car and then sells it two days after reaching adulthood has ratified the purchase contract.

_____ 8. If, the day before reaching adulthood, a minor states to the other party to a contract that he will continue to be bound by the contract after his birthday, he will still be able to disaffirm the contract on the next day.

_____ 9. A minor must ratify a contract for necessaries in order to be bound by its terms after he or she becomes an adult.

_____ 10. If a male minor buys a diamond ring for his girlfriend and it is thereafter stolen, he may disaffirm the purchase contract even though he cannot return the ring.

Multiple-Choice Questions

_____ 11. A minor who wishes to disaffirm a contract may do so:
- a. at any time
- b. only at some time before reaching adulthood
- c. at any time before reaching adulthood or within a reasonable time thereafter
- d. only at some time after reaching adulthood
- e. all of the above are correct

123

12. A minor who enters into a contract for items that are considered to be necessaries is required by law to pay:
    a. the price marked on the item
    b. the reasonable price for the item
    c. the price he or she agreed to pay
    d. nothing
    e. the price he or she agreed to pay less 10 percent

13. The contract of which of the following persons will be deemed void?
    a. a person adjudicated insane
    b. an emancipated minor
    c. a drunkard
    d. a and c are both correct
    e. a, b, and c are all correct

14. In connection with the contract of a minor, which of the following is considered to be a necessary?
    a. food
    b. sporting equipment
    c. medicine
    d. a and c are both correct
    e. a, b, and c are all correct

15. A minor who disaffirms a contract must:
    a. return the consideration received, if he or she still has it
    b. notify the other party to the contract, in writing, of his or her intention to disaffirm
    c. pay the reasonable value of the item involved in the contract, if it has been stolen
    d. wait until he or she has reached adulthood
    e. all of the above are correct

16. Which of the following acts will constitute a ratification of the contract of a minor once the infant has attained adulthood?
    a. keeping the object that is the subject of the contract and using it regularly
    b. selling the object that is the subject of the contract to another person
    c. verbally acknowledging an agreement to be bound by the contract
    d. only a and b are correct
    e. a, b, and c are all correct

_____ 17. If a person has been declared by a court to be incompetent because of habitual drunkenness, his or her subsequent contracts will be deemed to be:
a. void
b. voidable
c. valid
d. subject to judicial scrutiny
e. all of the above are correct

_____ 18. If a person who has not been declared by a court to be a habitual drunkard is drunk but understands that he or she is entering into a contract and is aware of the consequences of the act, the contract will be deemed to be:
a. void
b. voidable
c. valid
d. unconscionable
e. all of the above are correct

_____ 19. Mental illness or disease will render a contract void when:
a. it has existed for a long time
b. there has been an adjudication of insanity by a court
c. it partially impairs the ability of the person to understand the nature of his or her actions
d. it is well concealed from the other party to the contract
e. all of the above are correct

_____ 20. If a minor signs a contract, his or her parent:
a. must pay for the reasonable value of the contract entered into by the child
b. must pay the full value specified in the contract entered into by the child
c. has no liability at all
d. must pay the full value specified in the contract if the contract states that the parent will be liable for payment
e. will be liable for payment under the contract but only if the minor fails to pay first

Completion Questions

21. _____ is the conduct of an adult that indicates agreement to be bound by the terms of a contract entered into as a minor.

22. The person who is appointed by a court to oversee and care for the activities and needs of another person is referred to as a(n)_____ _____
_____ .

125

23. The point at which a minor no longer depends on his or her parents for support is referred to as_____.

24. A person who has not attained the legal age of adulthood is referred to as a(n)_____.

25. The contract of an intoxicated person will be considered void if a court has previously declared that person to be incompetent because of _____ _____.

Chapter 16

ILLEGALITY

It would be unreasonable for a legal system to enforce agreements which encourage unlawful behavior. Accordingly, a necessary element in the formation of a contract is that its purpose or object be lawful. Even if every other requirement for a valid contract has been met, the agreement is unenforceable if either its formation or performance violates a statute or common law.

This chapter focuses on typical statutory provisions and court decisions based on common law principles to determine which contractual agreements are enforceable, and examines the effect of a statute or court decision declaring a contract to be illegal.

In general illegal contracts are void; they can not be enforced by either party to the contract. However, some exceptions do exist because of special public policy concerns. Furthermore, in certain cases where only a portion of the contract is illegal and unenforcable the remainder of the contract can be enforced.

CHAPTER OBJECTIVES

After reading Chapter 15 of the text and studying the related materials in this chapter of the Student Mastery Guide, you will understand:

1. The nature of illegal contracts
2. The four types of contract regulation that are frequently the concern of state statutes;
    a. wagering
    b. usury
    c. Sunday laws (also called "blue laws") and
    d. licensing laws
3. The classes of contracts that were condemned by the courts at common law, including:
    a. contracts with exculpatory clauses
    b. those that restrain trade
    c. unconscionable contracts and
    d. contracts against public policy
4. The distinction between refusing to enforce an illegal agreement and determining that no agreement has been made.

MAJOR POINTS TO REMEMBER

1. A contract involving an illegal subject matter is generally void and therefore unenforceable. Illegality is determined by reference to statutes and the common law.

Wagering Agreements

2. State statutes on wagering vary considerably, from making it legal in a few to those that generally prohibit it but allow certain kinds of wagering, such as social games, lotteries, and wagers for small amounts. Insurance and commodities future contracts are not considered illegal wagering.

Usury Agreements

3. Charging more than the legally permissible rate of interest on a loan is illegal. The effect of such conduct, however, varies from state to state.

4. In addition to entailing the civil penalties associated with usury, such conduct usually violates the criminal law as well.

5. The primary purpose of usury laws is to protect persons from having to pay excessive interest rates. However, their effect can be to reduce the availability of loans for people who need them most.

Blue Laws

6. Blue laws or Sunday laws, are those that make it illegal for work and business, or certain types of these, to occur on Sunday. Courts usually, however, enforce contracts, or those parts of them, which are made or performed on a day other than Sunday.

Licensing Regulations

7. Generally, if a person is required to possess a license pursuant to a revenue statute, a contract entered into by a person who does not possess that license will still be enforceable. In contrast, a contract made in violation of a regulatory licensing statute normally is unenforceable.

The Common Law and Illegal Contracts

Agreements in Restraint of Trade

8. Agreements "not to compete" can be legal if they are incidental provisions of another contract (such as the sale of a business in which goodwill is an important asset and employer-employee contracts in which the employee has access to valuable information), and the terms of noncompetition are reasonable in regard to the time period to which it applies, the geographic area covered, the burden placed on the party promising not to compete, the importance of the interests being protected from competition, and the rights of the public. If such agreements are found to be illegal, this illegality does not usually make the entire contract unenforceable, but courts often will refuse to enforce the entire agreement not to compete rather than merely limiting it to reasonable terms.

Exculpatory Clauses

9. Generally, an exculpatory clause that attempts to relieve a person of liability for his or her own negligent acts will be considered to be unenforceable. However, such clauses can be enforceable in contracts negotiated by two businesses with equal bargaining power if the public is unlikely to be harmed.

10. Exculpatory clauses in bailment relationships are frequently enforceable, but there are exceptions.

Unconscionable Contracts

11. Courts have the inherent equitable power to refuse to enforce contracts that are oppressive or too one-sided. Most claims of unconscionability, however, arise under Section 2-302 of the Uniform Commercial Code. The courts determine whether a contract is unconscionable by examining factors at the time of its making, such as the relative bargaining power of the parties, whether the parties have options to the contract in question, and the reasonableness of the terms in the specific circumstances of the transaction in question. Courts have most often invoked this doctrine of unconscionability to protect consumers from oppression by businesses. It is not intended to disturb allocations of risk in a contract that were reasonable at the time of contracting but that later become disadvantageous to one party.

12. If all or most of the terms of a contract are determined to be unconscionable, the court may refuse to enforce the entire contract. If, however, only some of the provisions are determined to be unconscionable, and those terms can be severed from the other without destroying the nature of the contract, the court will sever those terms or limit their application and enforce the balance of the contract.

Ethics Box: Unconscionability (p. 286)

13. The test of unconscionability comes as close to applying a principle of ethics as any part of commercial law. Some argue that the doctrine is unnecessary because we have fraud, duress, and undue influence. Others say unconscionability is inconsistent with the concept of freedom to contract.

Contracts Against Public Policy

14. If a contract or any part of it is injurious to the public or tends to interfere with the public's general welfare, safety, health, and so on, then it will be deemed to be violative of the public policy and will not be enforceable.

Effects of Illegality

15. If a contract contains provisions that are determined to be illegal and those provisions can be severed from the others without destroying the essence of the contract, then the remaining provisions will be enforced. If, however, the illegal provisions cannot be severed from the contract, then the entire contract will be deemed unenforceable.

Ethics Box: Using Sunday Blue Laws as a Competitive Tool (p. 277)

15. Blue laws also exist in Europe and Australia. Although moral arguments are made in their favor, there can be commercial motivations also, including causing harm to competitors who do most of their business on weekends. It is unethical to argue for blue laws based on moral

grounds, if limiting competition is the real motivation. This does not constitute acting in good faith.

Ethics Box: Unconscionability (p. 286)

16. By incorporating a concept of fairness into contracts, the doctrine of unconscionability in effect imposes an ethical standard as law. Critics of this doctrine argue that its applicability is ill defined, it increases transaction costs, and it is unnecessary due to other more definitive contractual defenses that guard against coercion and unfairness. Critics also argue that it violates the basic freedom-of-contract principle. Countering arguments are that the courts have reserved this doctrine for only outrageous cases of overreaching. Further, as the court in the *Allan* case argued, freedom of enterprise has been restricted by the development of huge companies, and consequently freedom of contract must be adjusted to meet the economic realities of today.

MAJOR POINTS OF CASES

Poyer v. *Sears Roebuck Co., Inc.* (p. 275)

Two issues arose in this case. First, whether a statute requiring retailers and wholesalers to give employees a sabbath was unconstitutional. Second was the question of whether a plaintiff who quit because she would have to work either Saturday or Sunday was constructively discharged in violation of policy to give workers their sabbath day off.

The Court found that the law was not unconstitutional because the sabbath is not necessarily a religious concept. A state may establish a policy of providing a day of rest every week for workers. As to the second issue, the state's policy was not violated by Sears' requirement that four clerks (including the plaintiff) work Saturdays and Sundays or be reassigned to another job that would pay slightly less but would allow her to have weekends off. That requirement was not so outrageous as to constitute constructive discharge and emotional distress.

Silver v. *A.O.C. Corporation* (p. 279)

The court examined the provisions of a specific statute dealing with services performed by someone who must possess a specific license, in this case an electrical contractor.

It has been held that a person does not need to be licensed in order to perform *minor* work, defined as work valued at $50 or less. According to the facts, the plaintiff was an electrician who performed *major* electrical repairs without being in possession of an appropriate license. As a result of his failure to be properly licensed, the court held that the plaintiff was not entitled to bring an action to recover the value of his services.

Gomez v. *Zamora* (p. 282)

This case examines the enforceability of agreements of employees not to compete with their employer after their employment relationship terminates.

The court found the agreement overly broad and therefore unenforceable. To be enforceable, limitations need to be reasonable in terms of time, geographic area, and scope of activity to be restrained.

Morgan v. *South Southern Bell Telephone Company* (p. 285)

The court in this case set forth what it believed to be the best and simplest rule: exculpatory clauses that are not in the public's best interest are invalid. Six criteria that render an exculpatory invalid as contrary to public interest:
1) It concerns a business generally thought suitable for public regulation.
2) The party seeking exculpation is performing a service of great importance to the public.
3) The party holds himself out as being willing to provide the service for anyone who seeks it.
4) Because of the essential nature of the service, the party invoking exculpation has a decisive advantage of bargaining strength against any member of the public who seeks his services.
5) In exercising this bargaining power, he presents the public with an adhesion contract without allowing members of the public to bargain away the exculpatory clause.
6) As a result of the transaction, the member of the public or his property is under the control of the party seeking exculpation, subject to the risk of his carelessness.

Personal Finance Company v. *Meredith* (p. 287)

The main principle presented by this case is that an unconscionable contract or clause is invalid and unenforceable. As a result, a court should determine the actual agreement between the parties.

The court stated that a waiver-of-defense clause in a contract is not always unconscionable. In this case, the court held that inasmuch as the defendants had ample opportunity to read the contract and to indicate any objections they might have had, and inasmuch as they were not precluded from understanding their rights, the waiver-of-defense clauses were not unconscionable.

Woodson v. *Hopkins* (p. 291)

This case represents the general rule regarding the enforcement of contracts that are illegal because they violate public policy. This rule is that the courts leave the parties where it finds them, even though one has benefited from the performance of the other without in return providing the bargained-for-consideration. In this manner the courts do not use their authority to aid and encourage illegal contracts. This court also explained that public policy is determined from constitutions, laws, and judicial decisions.

PRACTICAL CONSIDERATIONS

While usury may cause a loan to be considered void and therefore not subject to enforcement by the courts, an individual who lends money to another person at an illegal rate of interest is generally not interested in seeking the court's assistance anyway. Such a person will frequently resort to other means that he considers equally effective to collect the money he claims to be due him. Consequently, one should avoid dealing with another person who offers to lend money at illegal rates even when it seems that such a loan is the only way available to resolve an urgent problem.

SELF TEST

True-False Questions

_____ 1. The effect of so-called blue laws is to prevent companies from conducting business on the Sabbath.

_____ 2. An "agreement not to compete" is an agreement that restrains trade.

_____ 3. Exculpatory clauses seeking to relieve someone's liability for negligence are usually enforceable.

_____ 4. A contract that is considered unconscionable and contrary to public policy will be enforced if both parties have agreed to its provisions.

_____ 5. When a person sells his or her pizza business to another and the contract provides that the seller may not engage in a similar business within a radius of 150 miles for a period of twenty-five years, the restrictive provision will not be enforceable.

_____ 6. If a contract contains some provisions that are in violation of the law, no part of that contract will ever be enforced by the courts.

_____ 7. Generally, both parties to a contract that is determined to be illegal are considered to be *in pari delicto*.

_____ 8. Any contract that requires a borrower to pay more than the legal rate of interest is illegal.

_____ 9. Joseph, an unlicensed surgeon, performs successful neurosurgery on Cathy. Cathy fully recovers from the operation. She will be required to pay Joseph the reasonable value of his services, rather than the agreed-upon fee, even though Joseph does not possess a license.

10. Medical doctors are licensed under regulatory statutes.

Multiple-Choice Questions

11. Illegality with respect to a contract may be ascertained by reference to:
    a. the common law only
    b. statutory law only
    c. the commodity market
    d. statutory law and common law
    e. all of the above are correct

12. Which of the following persons would be regulated by revenue statutes?
    a. an orthopedic surgeon
    b. a landscaper
    c. a lawyer
    d. a and c are correct
    e. a, b, and c are all correct

13. An agreement in restrain of trade is:
    a. usually valid
    b. always void
    c. sometimes valid
    d. always considered to be unconscionable
    e. all of the above are correct

14. If a court finds that part or all of a contract is unconscionable, the court may:
    a. refuse to enforce the entire contract
    b. delete the portion of the contract that is deemed to be unconscionable and enforce the rest of the contract
    c. limit the application of the provisions that it considers unconscionable
    d. only a and c are correct
    e. a, b, and c are all correct

15. Generally, an illegal contract is considered to be:
    a. void
    b. voidable
    c. valid
    d. enforceable
    e. all of the above are correct

16. Generally, an exculpatory clause in a contract that attempts to relieve a person from his or her own negligence is considered to be:
    a. valid and enforceable
    b. valid but unenforceable
    c. invalid and unenforceable
    d. invalid but enforceable
    e. all of the above are correct

17. A person who lends money to another at a rate that is deemed to be usurious has violated:
    a. the civil law only
    b. the criminal law only
    c. natural law
    d. both the criminal law and the civil law
    e. antitrust laws

18. An agreement not to compete that is included in the terms of a contract is:
    a. valid if its terms are reasonable
    b. an agreement in restraint of trade
    c. invalid and unenforceable in all cases
    d. both a and b are correct
    e. both b and c are correct

19. An agreement to lend someone money at a rate of interest that is considered to be usurious is:
    a. valid
    b. void
    c. voidable
    d. unenforceable
    e. b and d are both correct

20. A contract will be considered to be violative of the public policy if:
    a. it interferes with the general welfare of the public
    b. it involves the sale of a handgun, no matter who the buyer is
    c. it involves a citizen of a foreign country
    d. a and c are both correct
    e. a, b, and c are all correct

Completion Questions

21. A_____ _____is one that the parties agree to pay money or transfer property upon the happening of an uncertain event.

22. In an illegal contract, the parties are considered to be_____ _____ if they are found to be equally at fault for something.

23. A contract that is considered to be grossly unfair by normal standards and that is not enforced by a court of law is considered to be _____.

24. A(n) _____ clause is a clause in a contract that relieves or limits a person's liability for certain specified acts.

25. Statutes that are primarily concerned with the regulation of a certain industry so as to protect the public are known as_____ _____.

Chapter 17

LEGAL FORM

While a written contract setting forth the terms of an agreement between two or more persons is frequently recommended, a contract need not always be in writing to be enforceable. An oral agreement, though more difficult to prove, is often valid.

This chapter deals with three very important concepts that are critical to the application of the law: the Statute of Frauds, the parol evidence rule (an evidentiary rule), and the interpretation of a contract's provisions. While the Statute of Frauds is somewhat complicated, it becomes quite easy to comprehend and its application is clear if it is approached slowly, systematically, and with attention to details. The parol evidence rule is a rule of evidence that deals with the admissibility at trial of oral testimony related to a written document. The section on interpretation of contractual provisions discusses factors to be considered when the provisions of a contract are not clear.

CHAPTER OBJECTIVES

After reading Chapter 17 of the text and studying the related materials in this chapter of the Student Mastery Guide, you will understand:

1. The nature of the Statute of Frauds
2. The requirements of the Statute of Frauds, including:
    a. a writing
    b. a signature
3. The contracts to which the Statute of Frauds applies, including:
    a. an executor's promise to pay for the debt of the decedent
    b. a promise to pay for the debt of another
    c. a contract for the sale of an interest in land
    d. a contract that cannot be fully performed within one year
    e. a contract for the sale of goods for $500 or more
4. The nature of the parol evidence rule
5. The interpretation of contractual provisions

MAJOR POINTS TO REMEMBER

In General

1. Oral contracts may be valid and enforceable even though nothing is in writing to substantiate them.

Statute of Frauds

2. Certain types of contracts must be in writing in order to be *enforceable*. Included among such contracts are:
    a. promise by the executor of an estate to personally pay the debts of the decedent

    b.   promise to pay the debts of another person

    c.   contract for the sale of land or an interest in land

    d.   contract that by its terms cannot be fully performed within one year

    e.   contract for the sale of goods in the amount of $500 or more

    f.   contract in consideration of marriage

3.   If a contract is of a type that is required to be in writing and it is not in writing, it will be considered unenforceable. The contract is still valid, however, even though it may be deemed unenforceable. Thus, unless a person raises the Statute of Frauds defense, the person is bound by the contract.

4.   The writing required by the Statute of Frauds does not need to be a formal contract prepared by an attorney. It may be a simple statement containing the necessary terms, written on any surface. That statement is referred to as a *memorandum*.

5.   In order for a memorandum to be sufficient, it must generally contain the following terms:

    a.   the identify of the parties

    b.   the subject matter of the contract

    c.   the basic obligation of the parties

    d.   the signature of the party against whom enforcement of the contract is sought

    e.   a quantity

6.   If a person signs a writing that satisfies the Statute of Frauds, but the other party does not sign, then the contract can be enforceable against the signing party, but not the one who failed to sign.

Contracts Required to Be in Writing

7.   Prenuptial agreements that involve property settlements must be in writing.

8.   If a person promises to be secondarily liable for the debt of another, it must be in writing to be enforceable. Secondary liability exists only if the creditor tries to collect from the original debtor first before holding the promisor liable. However, under the main-purpose doctrine, if the promise of secondary liability is made mainly to benefit the person making the promise, then no writing is required.

9.   Besides the sale of real property, a writing is also required to transfer other interests in land, such as easements, options, security interests, and leases. However, no writing is required to sell real property if one party has made substantial part performance in reliance on an oral promise to sell.

10.   Contracts that by their terms cannot possibly be fully executed or performed within one year from their making must be in writing to be enforceable.

11.   Under the Uniform Commercial Code, a contract for the sale of goods must be in writing if the price of the goods is $500 or more. Several exceptions to that rule exist, however.

In the following situations a contract does not need to be in writing in order to be enforceable:

a. the goods have been specially made (manufactured) for the buyer and cannot be readily resold in the ordinary course of the seller's business

b. the person against whom a contract is sought to be enforced admits, after a lawsuit has been commenced, that a contract existed; however, the contract will be enforced only up to the quantity of goods that are admitted

c. the goods have been received and accepted by the buyer

d. the goods have been paid for and the payment has been accepted by the seller

Equitable Estoppel and Promissory Estoppel

12. Where the doctrine of either equitable estoppel or promissory estoppel may be effectively invoked, the provisions of the Statute of Frauds will be held to be inapplicable. When a contract is enforced based on promissory estoppel, the winning party recovers only that amount necessary to return him or her to the position held prior to the detrimental reliance, instead of compensatory damages.

Preventive Law: Complying with the Statute of Frauds

13. As a practical matter in contracts, one should whenever feasible have them put into a signed writing.

Ethics Box: Raising the Defense of the Statute of Frauds

14. In many cases in which the Statute of Frauds is raised as a defense, there is little doubt that a contract was actually made by the parties. Can it be ethical to assert this defense even though it is legal? U.S. attorneys can ethically do so under professional ethics unless there is knowledge of fraud or other misconduct.

15. Under the parol evidence rule, parol evidence is not admissible at trial if it tends to:
a. contradict the terms of a final written agreement, or
b. change, modify, or amend the terms of a final written agreement

The Parol Evidence Rule

16. Parol evidence will be admissible at trial if it is introduced to:
a. clarify the meaning of ambiguous terms
b. complete the blank terms of a contract that is incomplete on its face
c. show that the contract is actually not a valid contract
d. prove the existence of a *subsequent* modification to the contract

17. Under the terms of the Uniform Commercial Code (Section 2-202), a writing may be explained or supplemented by:
    a. a course of dealing or usage
    b. a course of performance
    c. evidence of consistent additional terms unless the court finds that the writing was intended as the complete agreement between the parties

18. Many states have consumer protection statutes that make it illegal for sellers to fail to integrate all earlier agreements, oral or otherwise, into the final written contract. Once such oral agreements are proven under these statutes, then they are also proven for purposes of contractual enforcement.

Interpretation of Contractual Provisions

19. Even when contracts are in writing, there are many cases in which the courts must interpret the contracts to determine the reasonable intentions of the contracting parties. In order to discern the parties' objective intentions, the courts have developed specific rules of interpretation to apply.

Preventive Law: Contract Law and the Written Word

20. The Statute of Frauds, parol evidence rule, and rules of contract interpretation are based on sound public policy. Their application indicates that an oral contract should be evidenced by a writing or, when the subject matter is important, should be reduced to a formal written contract to avoid the costs of future litigation. Putting everything in writing is prudent.

MAJOR POINTS OF CASES

Martin v. *Scholl* (p. 297)

In defining the substantial part performance doctrine, the majority of the court explained that the acts must point clearly and unequivocally to the existence of the oral agreement to take the agreement out of the Statute of Frauds. The dissenting opinion argued that this doctrine should be applied such that once the proof of an oral agreement is established by other evidence, then the acts of performance need only constitute clear and convincing proof of the oral agreement, rather than being exclusively referable to an oral agreement.

Shervin v. *Ault* (p. 299)

This case demonstrates the application of the requirement that there be a written agreement when a contract cannot be performed within one year. This agreement included a specific date for termination. Because that date was later than one year from the making of the agreement, the court held that by its terms, the agreement could not be performed until that date.

Southwest Engineering Company v. *Martin Tractor Company* (p. 301)

In this case the court stated that a written memorandum of agreement for the sale of goods that sets forth a quantity and is signed by the "party to be charged" is sufficient to satisfy the Statute of Frauds. The court also indicated that once an agreement has been reached, the fact that the terms of payment for the goods have been omitted from the writing does not invalidate the writing, and it will be presumed that payment will be made at the time the goods are delivered. Finally, the court also stated that under the Uniform Commercial Code, a signature includes "any symbol executed or adopted by a party with present intention to authenticate a writing."

In evaluating the facts, the court found that a contract existed and that Hurt had signed a writing that contained all the terms required in order to satisfy the Statute of Frauds. Consequently, the contract was found to be enforceable and the judgement of the trial court was affirmed.

Allen M. Campbell Co. v. *Virginia Metal Industries, Inc.* (p. 304)

In this case the court had to decide whether the UCC Statute of Frauds requires a contract that falls within it to be in writing when that contract is based on the promissory estoppel doctrine. The court held that the promissory estoppel doctrine is, in effect, another exception to the general rule of the UCC that contracts for the sale of goods for $500 or more be in writing. Consequently, the lower court's judgment on the pleadings for the defendant was in error.

Masterson v. *Sine* (p. 307)

In this case the court held that when a written contract indicates that the writing embodies the final and complete terms of the agreement between the parties, parol evidence cannot be used to add to or vary the terms of the writing. Parol evidence can be introduced, however, when a writing does not constitute the entire agreement, but the evidence can be offered only to prove those elements that were not included in the writing. Further, in California, whether a writing contains the entire agreement of the parties must be determined "solely from the face of the instrument." The court stated, however, that the rule must be "based on the credibility of the evidence" and that "evidence of oral collateral agreements should be excluded only when the fact finder is likely to be misled."

According to the court, the contract between the parties did not explicitly provide that it contained all the terms of the agreement. It also found that in this case a collateral agreement "might naturally be made as a separate agreement." Therefore, the court ruled that parol evidence related to the option clause was proper and should have been permitted at trial.

The dissenting judge in the case felt that the option clause was clear on its face and that parol evidence should not be allowed.

PRACTICAL CONSIDERATIONS

1. Under the provisions of the Statute of Frauds, a writing is required to be signed by only one of the parties in order for the contract to be enforceable. The writing will be enforceable, however, only against the party who signed it.

    At the time that a contract is signed, neither party expects the other to fail to perform the respective obligations of the agreement and neither party expects the agreement to be breached. As a result, it is impossible to know which of the parties will subsequently seek to enforce the contract against the other. Consequently, as a practical matter, both parties to an agreement will execute the contract, and the contract (if the Statute of Frauds is otherwise fully satisfied) will be enforceable against both parties.

    Further, if one of the parties insists on refusing to sign the written contract but also insists that he or she does intend to honor the contractual obligations, the other party should take care to determine all of the risks involved before signing the agreement without the signature of the other party. Keep in mind that the other party will probably not be bound by the terms of the written agreement if he or she subsequently refuses or fails to perform the contract.

2. While the doctrine of promissory estoppel can be used to waive the requirement of a signed written agreement under the Statute of Frauds, the doctrine is frequently difficult to apply because of the nature of the proof required. Many times a person will be less than totally honest when someone claims that he or she made a promise and thereafter failed to keep his or her word. At other times it may be difficult to show that the promisee was in fact relying on the promise when he or she acted in a certain way. Further, although plans may have been made and certain arrangements completed, it may be difficult to show that the promisee sustained any damages.

    As a result, it is suggested that nothing can truly substitute for written documentation of the nature, extent, and terms of a contractual agreement. Further, even though the Statute of Frauds may not apply to a particular contract, it is generally advisable to have the significant terms of a contract put in writing. Remember, while fate and chance may often result in a positive situation, preparation, foresight, and attention to details in a contractual setting are prime considerations and should be attended to with great care.

3. During negotiations of the terms of a contract to be put in writing at a later date, it may be useful to take notes. At the end of the negotiation session, discuss the points agreed upon and perhaps have the other party sign the notes.

SELF TEST

True-False Questions

_____   1.   In order for a writing to be sufficient under the provisions of the Statute of Frauds, both parties to the contract must sign it.

_____   2.   A contract under which one person agrees to grant another person an easement in return for the payment of $300 must be in writing.

3. An oral promise by which a person agrees to pay for the debt of another person is never enforceable.

4. If a contract that is required to be in writing has been partially performed to a substantial degree, the Statute of Frauds does not apply and the contract is enforceable.

5. If on August 10, 1988, A agrees to become the accountant for B and further agrees to start work on January 4, 1989, the contract is not required to be in writing if it is agreed that it will terminate on October 10, 1989.

6. If a contract contains terms that are typed and also contains handwritten terms that contradict the typed terms, the handwritten terms prevail over the typewritten terms.

7. The parol evidence rule does not permit oral testimony to be admitted at trial if that testimony tends to show that one of the parties used duress to obtain the consent of the other party.

8. Every contract for the sale of goods must be in writing if the purchase price is over $500.

9. If a contract can be interpreted in two ways, one of which would make the contract legal and the other of which would make it illegal, a court will generally accept the interpretation that will render the contract legal.

10. If a contract is required to be in writing and it is not, the contract will be considered to be invalid.

Multiple-Choice Questions

11. The Statute of Frauds was designed to:
    a. serve an evidentiary function
    b. obviate the need for the parol evidence rule
    c. act as a guide for the courts in interpreting contracts
    d. eliminate unnecessary paperwork
    e. all of the above are correct

12. In order for a memorandum to satisfy the Statute of Frauds, it must set forth:
    a. the subject matter of the contract
    b. the identity of the parties
    c. the basic obligations of the parties
    d. only a and c are correct
    e. a, b, and c are all correct

13. Which of the following contracts is required to be in writing?
    a. a contract to buy a car for $300
    b. a contract to employ a barber for ten months
    c. a contract to act as someone's personal chauffeur for as long as the chauffeur is physically capable of driving a car
    d. a promise to pay the debt of another person
    e. all of the above are correct

14. Under the Uniform Commercial Code, a contract for the sale of goods is not required to be in writing if:
    a. it is supported by a memorandum
    b. the goods have been received and accepted
    c. the price of goods is over $500
    d. it accompanies a contract for the sale of real property
    e. all of the above are correct

15. If a contract is required to be in writing and it is not, the contract will be considered to be:
    a. void
    b. invalid
    c. unenforceable
    d. invalid but enforceable
    e. all of the above are correct

16. When a lawsuit has been commenced and the Statute of Frauds is involved, the writing that is offered in testimony is not sufficient if it has not been signed by:
    a. the plaintiff
    b. the defendant
    c. both the plaintiff and the defendant
    d. either the plaintiff or the defendant
    e. any person with knowledge of the contract

_____ 17. Parol evidence is not admissible at trial if:
   a.   the oral testimony tends to clarify the meaning of ambiguous terms
   b.   the oral testimony tends to show that no contract actually existed
   c.   the oral testimony tends to alter the terms of a written contract
   d.   the parties disagree on the facts on which oral testimony will be offered
   e.   all of the above are correct

_____ 18. When a court needs to interpret the intent of particular language used in a written contract:
   a.   specific provisions prevail over general provisions
   b.   technical words and terms will usually be given technical meanings
   c.   legal interpretations will be preferred over illegal interpretations
   d.   only a and b are correct
   e.   a, b, and c are all correct

_____ 19. Parol evidence will be held to be admissible at trial if it:
   a.   tends to clarify the meaning of ambiguous terms contained in a written contract
   b.   tends to alter, modify, or amend the terms of a written contract
   c.   tends to contradict the terms of a written agreement
   d.   only b and c are correct
   e.   a, b, and c are all correct

_____ 20. The legal term that is used for the idea that a person should not be allowed to avoid the consequences of a promise he or she made is:
   a.   collateral estoppel
   b.   promissory estoppel
   c.   equitable estoppel
   d.   _res judicata_
   e.   _res ipsa loquitur_

Completion Questions

21. An informal writing that gives evidence of the existence of a contractual agreement between two parties is referred to as a(n)_____.

22. Under the doctrine of _____ _____, a party will be prevented from denying the validity of a promise that he or she made.

23. _____ _____ is the term used to refer to an intention of the parties that is not contained within the specific terms of the contract between them.

24. The right to cross upon another person's real property is known as a(n)_____.

25. _____ _____ _____ requires that certain types of contracts must be in writing in order to be enforceable.

Chapter 18

RIGHTS OF THIRD PARTIES

A party to a contract may transfer rights acquired by the contract to a person who is not a party to the original contract. Such a transfer of rights is referred to as an *assignment*. The law also permits the transfer of contractual duties called a *delegation* - to a third party.

The most common type of assignment is that of a right to receive money, although other rights may be assigned. A person who acquires rights by assignment of a contract is in no better position than the person from whom he or she acquired the rights. The Uniform Commercial Code has special rules dealing with certain assignments.

In general, duties may be delegated except when the performance by another person would vary materially from performance by the original obligor, or when the original party to the contract has a substantial interest in performance of the duty by the original obligor. A good example of a nondelegable duty is the obligation of an artist to paint a picture. The artist could not transfer his or her other obligation to paint the picture to another artist.

In some instances, a contract may benefit a person not a party to the original contract, and the third party may sue. When a contract exists primarily for the benefit of the third party, for example, the courts will permit such a suit. In other instances, although a third party would benefit from the performance of the contract, he or she may not bring a suit on the contract.

The major concepts discussed in this chapter are thus assignments of rights and duties and contracts for the benefit of someone not a party to the original contract.

CHAPTER OBJECTIVES

After reading Chapter 18 of the text and studying the related materials in this chapter of the Student Mastery Guide, you will understand:

1. The rights of third parties in connection with a contract.
2. The different ways in which a third party may become involved in another person's contract, including:
   a. assignments
   b. third-party beneficiary
3. The nature of an assignment
4. The rights of the parties involved in an assignment, including the rights of the:
   a. assignor
   b. assignee
   c. obligor
5. The procedural requirements for making an assignment, including:
   a. the form of the assignment
   b. notice of the assignment
   c. prohibition of assignments
6. The nature and types of third-party beneficiaries, including the:
   a. donee beneficiary
   b. creditor beneficiary
   c. incidental beneficiary
   d. intended beneficiary

MAJOR POINTS TO REMEMBER

Nature of an Assignment/Delegation

1. An assignment results when a party to a contract transfers all or some of his or her rights under a contract to another person who was not a party to the contract.

2. *Delegation* is the transfer of duties or obligations under a contract to another party.

3. Generally, any right under a contract may be assigned or transferred to another person. This is particularly true of the right to receive money. If the transfer materially changes the obligor's duty to render a performance, however, that right may not be assigned unless the obligor consents to the transfer.

4. Assignments to the right to receive money are most common and the legal basis for several financing techniques. When businesses sell on credit, they often either sell the credit contracts for cash or obtain a loan using their accounts receivable as security. When a firm sells its accounts receivable, this is known as *factoring*.

5. Because assignments of the right to receive money are so important, few limitations are placed on such assignments. The UCC even makes prohibitions against assigning such rights ineffective. However, an assignment of future wages by an employee is limited in many states.

6. If a person's obligation under a contract requires him or her to render personal services that are unique or call for special skills or talent, that contract may not be assigned without the consent of the person who is entitled to receive those services.

Prohibition of Assignments

7. A prohibition of assignment clause in a contract is generally enforceable. In most states, such a clause means that the entire contract must be performed by the original parties to it, and they themselves must receive what they are entitled to under the contract. In some states, however, the provision is interpreted to mean that the obligations under the contract may not be delegated, but the rights can be assigned.

Rights of Assignee

8. Any defense to a lawsuit, or other action that is good against the assignor is also good against the assignee. An assignee is said to legally "step into the shoes" of the assignor. However, if the assigned rights are not received due to the legal fault of the assignor, the assignee can recover for breach of warranty from the assignor. Further, if an assignment of rights to money is expressly made with recourse and is uncollectible, the assignee can also collect from the assignor.

Notice of Assignment

9. Generally, notice of an assignment may be given to the other party to the contract by either the assignor or the assignee.

10. If the right being assigned is the right to collect money, and the person who is required to pay is not notified of the assignment, that party may continue to pay the assignor (even after the assignment) until he or she is notified of the assignment. In such a case, the assignee will not be able to collect from the obligor the money that was paid to the assignor. The assignee may, however, be able to recover the money paid to the assignor.

11. If the obligor is notified of the assignment and nevertheless continues to pay the assignor, the assignee can collect the amount due from the obligor again, even though the obligor already paid that amount to the assignor. Then the obligor must attempt to recover from this assignor.

12. If the assignor is able to assign the same rights twice due to the failure to notify the obligor, then there is a split among the states; most say the first assignee in time takes the rights, while others hold that the first assignee to give notice to the obligor has the superior claim to the assigned rights.

Form of the Assignment

13. Generally, an assignment is not required to be in writing in order for it to be enforceable. If the Statute of Frauds applies to the assignment, however, then the assignment must be in writing. Other statutes may also require assignments to be in writing.

Delegation of Duties

14. Generally, duties under a contract may be delegated to a third party unless the performance requires unique talents or experience, or the obligee has a substantial interest in receiving the performance of the original party.

15. The delegation of duties does not relieve the assignor of the obligation to perform in the event that the assignee fails to perform the contractual commitments unless the obligee has released the assignor under a novation from the duty to perform.

Third-Party Beneficiary

16. A third-party beneficiary relationship exists when a person who is not a party to a contract receives a benefit from it. That person, however, does not become a party to the contract as a result of the benefit.

17. There are several types of third-party beneficiaries:
    a. creditor beneficiary
    b. donee beneficiary
    c. incidental beneficiary
    d. intended beneficiary
    Creditor beneficiaries, donee beneficiaries, and intended beneficiaries may bring lawsuits to enforce the contracts under which they receive benefits.

18. An incidental beneficiary cannot sue to enforce a contract under which he or she benefits.

Preventive Law: Assignment of Leases

19. Commercial and residential leases often either forbid assignments or subleases or require the lessor's consent. If the lessee breaches these clauses, the lease terminates, but the lessee remains liable for the rent until the lessor finds another tenant. Although some states forbid the lessor from unreasonably withholding consent to an assignment, the traditional rule is that the lessor can withhold consent without any explanation. Leases, thus, should be examined with care and be written to minimize the chance of misunderstanding and litigation.

MAJOR POINTS OF CASES

Hurst v. *West* (p. 316)

This case stands for the proposition that a party to a contract may not assign his or her obligations under the contract without the consent of the other party if those obligations call for the unique skill or talent of the assignor or if the contract expressly forbids assignments of nonmonetary rights. However, since neither of these conditions was involved in the contract in dispute, the assignment was valid.

Chimney Hill Owners Association v. *Antignani* (pp. 317)

This case illustrates the fact that a defense that is good against an assignor is also good against the assignee.

Concordia College v. *Salvation Army* (p. 323)

This case demonstrates that if one was intended to be a beneficiary of a contract, one can sue to enforce that contract. George and Phyllis contractually agreed not to change their wills in the event that either died first. This agreement was clearly made to benefit the beneficiaries under those wills. When George changed his will, breaching the contract, the beneficiaries under the original will could sue to retain the benefits they were guaranteed under the contract.

Bain v. *Gillispie* (p. 325)

This case involved a claim by the owners of a store which sold University of Iowa memorabilia that they were third-party beneficiaries to a contract between the Big 10 athletic conference and a basketball referee. The court ruled that they were only incidental beneficiaries at best, since the contract showed no intent to make a gift to them, and neither of the contracting parties owed them any legal obligations that would be satisfied by the contract. As incidental beneficiaries, they had no right to sue to enforce the contract's alleged obligation by the referee to perform his duties competently.

PRACTICAL CONSIDERATIONS

1. Contracts are assigned all the time. If, therefore, a person who enters into a contract wants to make sure that he or she will be dealing only with the other party to the contract, a prohibition-of-assignment clause should be included in the contract.

2. Even though most assignments are not required to be in writing, it is a good idea to have a written agreement when a contract (or part of one) is assigned. Such a writing will greatly help a party to prove the existence of the assignment and will frequently have a psychological effect on all the parties involved such as to permit them more easily to recognize the reality of the assignment.

3. If someone gives a person notice that a contract has been assigned to him, it is wise for the person so notified to contact the original party to the contract and confirm that the assignment was actually made. Failure to make such confirmation may result in an expenditure of money without any reduction of a legal obligation and may have many other unpleasant consequences.
    Example: A and B enter into a contract for the sale of a boat. A agrees to pay B $500 upon delivery of the boat and also agrees to pay the balance of the purchase price in twelve equal monthly installments of $200 each. After making three of the required payments, A is notified by C that the right to collect the monthly payments has been assigned to him by B and that all future payments should be sent to him at his home. In fact, no such assignment had been made. A does not contact B to confirm the assignment and instead makes his next four payments to C. When B contacts A with regard to his failure to make the payments on time, A will have to pay him the money even though he has already paid it to C.
    If A had contacted B when C notified him of the claimed assignment, he would have discovered that C's conduct was fraudulent. A simple phone call could have saved a great deal of legal difficulties and expense.

SELF TEST

True-False Questions

_____   1. An assignment creates a new contract between the parties and the old contract is terminated.

_____ 2. Every assignment must be supported by consideration in order for it to be valid.

_____ 3. Most courts will enforce a clause restricting the assignment of a personal service contract.

_____ 4. An incidental beneficiary may sue to enforce the contract from which he or she derives a benefit.

_____ 5. If a contract is breached and the breaching party could cite the Statute of Frauds as a defense against the assignor, that defense can be made against the assignee of the contract as well.

_____ 6. Notice of an assignment must be given to the other party to the contract under all circumstances in order for the assignment to be valid.

_____ 7. A third-party beneficiary is a party to the contract.

_____ 8. Under the terms and provisions of a completed novation, the original obligor is released from all obligations under the contract and has no further liability under it.

_____ 9. All assignments are required to be in writing to be enforceable.

_____ 10. A builder contracted to construct a standard rectangular swimming pool. The builder must obtain the consent of the person for whom the pool is being built before the obligor can assign that contract to another pool contractor.

Multiple-Choice Questions

_____ 11. Which of the following persons is not permitted to sue to enforce the contract from which he or she derives a benefit?
a. a donee beneficiary
b. an incidental beneficiary
c. a creditor beneficiary
d. no third-party beneficiary can sue to enforce the contract
e. a and b are both correct

_____ 12. In order for an assignment to be valid, it must always be:
a. agreed to by all the parties
b. supported by consideration
c. in writing
d. a transfer of a legal right
e. a and b are both correct

13. Notice of the assignment of a contract may be given by:
    a. the assignor only
    b. the assignee only
    c. either the assignor or the assignee
    d. the obligor
    e. the creditor beneficiary

14. In which of the following contracts can the obligation to perform the contract be assigned without the consent of the other party to the contract?
    a. a contract for Andrew Wyeth to paint a portrait in oils
    b. a contract to paint the outside walls of a house
    c. a contract for Frank Sinatra to give a live performance in Las Vegas
    d. only a and c are correct
    e. a, b, and c are all correct

15. If a contract to build a standard rectangular swimming pool is assigned and the assignee breaches the contract in some way, the person for whom the pool was built may sue:
    a. the assignee alone
    b. the assignor alone
    c. both the assignor and the assignee
    d. only the obligor
    e. a, b, and c are all correct

16. A person who is not a party to a contract but who receives a benefit from it because one of the parties owes him or her money is referred to as:
    a. a creditor beneficiary
    b. a donee beneficiary
    c. an incidental beneficiary
    d. an intended beneficiary
    e. b and d are both correct

17. When no consideration is given with an assignment, the assignment is treated as:
    a. invalid
    b. unenforceable
    c. enforceable only if it has been fully completed
    d. void
    e. a, b, and d are all correct

18. The person to whom the rights and/or obligations under a contract are transferred is referred to as the:
   a. assignor
   b. assignee
   c. obligor
   d. beneficiary
   e. novator

19. A person who is named as the beneficiary under the provisions of a life insurance policy is an example of:
   a. an incidental beneficiary
   b. a creditor beneficiary
   c. a donee beneficiary
   d. an assignee
   e. an assignor

20. The legal release of one party to a contract from all obligations under the contract and the substitution of another person who assumes those obligations is referred to as:
   a. a novation
   b. a substitution
   c. an assignment
   d. an accord and satisfaction
   e. a and d are both correct

Completion Questions

21. A person who is not a party to a contract but who receives a benefit from it because he or she is a creditor of one of the parties to it is known as a(n)_____.

22. A _____ is a legal release of one party to a contract from his or her obligations under it and the substitution of another party who assumes those obligations.

23. A(n) _____ is a transfer by a party to a contract of all or some of his or her rights under the contract to a person who was not a party to it.

24. The party who owes an obligation to another person is referred to as a(n)_____.

25. One who transfers his or her rights under a contract to another person who was not a party to the contract is known as a(n)_____.

153

Chapter 19

PERFORMANCE, DISCHARGE, AND REMEDIES

Chapter 19 assumes a valid contract exists and goes on to consider the circumstances of performance and nonperformance of contractual obligations. Generally people make a contract and carry it out. Sometimes, however, circumstances change and one of the parties to a valid contract finds performance no longer desirable. The parties' duties to perform under a contract are determined by several important issues.

The parties contracting may make performance dependent on an event or circumstances happening or not happening. If so, these conditions must be met before a contract is enforceable.

Under the newer concept of "substantial performance" a party who has rendered a less than full and perfect performance may nonetheless discharge his or her contractual duties if the departure is slight and unintentional. However, if the performance has not met the essential purpose of the contract it is considered a material breach, and the innocent party is discharged from their contractual duties and may sue and recover damages.

A contract is said to be discharged when the legal duty or one of the parties has been terminated. Chapter 19 reviews a variety of ways contractual duties may be discharged.

A breach of contract is any failure to perform the contract without legal excuse. Even when it is clear that one of the parties has materially breached the contract disputes may arise about the remedies to which the injured party is entitled.

CHAPTER OBJECTIVES

After reading Chapter 19 of the text and studying the related materials in this chapter of the Student Mastery Guide, you will understand:

1. A party's duty to perform may be qualified by the happening of some event or condition.
2. The standards of performance for evaluating whether contractual duties have been performed.
3. The nature of breach of contract.
4. The variety of ways contract duties may be discharged.

MAJOR POINTS TO REMEMBER

Performance Dependent Upon Condition

1. If a person's performance under a contract is conditional upon the occurrence of some event or condition precedent, and that specified event or condition does not occur, then the person's obligation to perform will be excused (i.e., he or she will not be required to perform).

2. If performance under a contract is subject to a condition subsequent and that condition occurs, then such performance will not thereafter be required.

3. Conditions precedent that require the approval of some third party, or the other contracting party, of the performance rendered are narrowly interpreted by the courts. If the performance can be measured against a commonly accepted objective standard, and it meets that standard, then the courts will find it to have been satisfactory. Unless the contract expressly requires subjective, personal satisfaction, the courts will use an objective standard of whether a reasonable person would have approved the performance rendered.

Substantial Performance

4. Under the doctrine of substantial performance, if one of the parties to a contract has substantially and honestly performed that which he or she was obligated to do, then the other party will be required to do that which he or she was contractually obligated to do.
    However, inasmuch as the first party did not fully perform the contract, the other party will be entitled to a set-off for that portion of the contract that was not performed.

5. When one party materially breaches a contract, the other party is no longer required to perform his or her obligations and, in addition, may hold the breaching party liable for damages.

6. In connection with a contract for the sale of goods, the "perfect tender" rule applies. Section 2-601 of the Uniform Commercial Code provides that if goods tendered for delivery are not exactly what the buyer ordered, the buyer can:
    a. reject all the goods
    b. accept all the goods
    c. accept some of the goods and reject the rest
    However, the effect of this rule is mitigated by the buyer's obligation to give notice to the seller of the nonconformity of the goods and the seller's right to "cure the nonconformity of the goods and the seller's right to "cure the defects" within a reasonable time.

7. If the time of performance in a contract is missed slightly, normally this is not a material breach. However, if the contract expressly states that "time is of the essence" in performance, then performance must be made on or before the stated date, and the failure to do so is a material breach.

Discharge of Contracts

8. A contract may be terminated or discharged in any of the following ways:
    a. by completed performance
    b. by the occurrence of a condition subsequent
    c. by mutual agreement rescinding the original contract, substituting a new contract, or causing a release by novation
    d. by impossibility of performance
    e. by breach

9. When a contract is to be discharged by mutual rescission, the intent of the parties is that they will be restored to the same condition that they were in before they entered into the contract.

10. If, after a contract is formed, it becomes totally impossible (from an objective standpoint) to perform its terms, the contract will be terminated and the respective obligations of the parties will be discharged.

   Temporary impossibility, however, will not terminate the contract, but will only suspend its performance until such time as the condition causing the temporary impossibility is removed.

11. Generally, frustration of purpose will not discharge a party from his or her contractual responsibilities. Such frustration will, however, excuse a persons' nonperformance when all of the following conditions apply:
   a. the purpose that is frustrated was the principal purpose of the party in making the contract
   b. the frustration is substantial
   c. the nonoccurrence of the frustrating event was a basic assumption on which the contract was made.

   The concept of commercial impracticability is similar to frustration of purpose, but it applies to discharge of an obligation to perform where an unexpected event has made it extremely difficult for one party to perform the contract.

Anticipatory Breach

12. When there has been a clear anticipatory breach by one of the parties to a contract, the nonbreaching party may:
   a. treat the entire contract as being breached and immediately sue for damages
   b. ignore the repudiation and wait until the performance is due before taking any action
   c. rescind the contract and sue to recover anything furnished under the contract
   d. immediately start a lawsuit for a specific performance of the contract

Remedies

13. A party to a contract who has suffered a loss as a result of a breach of that contract is under an obligation to mitigate (keep to a minimum) his or her damages by reasonable actions under the circumstances.

14. The general remedy available for a breach of contract is to award the victim monetary damages sufficient to place him or her in the position that would have resulted from full performance of the contract. However, the breaching party is generally liable only for damages that were reasonably foreseeable. Special or unforeseeable damages must have been made known to the defendant and at least impliedly agreed to before liability for them arises. Finally, the amount of damages suffered must be proven with reasonable certainty to be recoverable.

15. Liquidated damages, in order to be valid, must have some reasonable relation to the anticipated or actual harm caused by a breach.

16. An action for specific performance will be available to a plaintiff only when money damages are not adequate and only when the contract involves the sale of real property, some unique subject matter, or goods that are not readily available elsewhere in the marketplace.

17. An injunction will not be issued in a matter involving a contract if the damages sustained by the injured party can adequately be compensated by an award of money damages. When allowed, an injunction orders the defendant to stop doing, or not do, something.

18. Rescission of a contract is allowed under the common law of torts and contracts. Statutes also provide for this remedy in certain situations today. Since the contract is to be canceled, both parties, if possible, must generally return the consideration received from the other under the remedy or restitution.

Preventive Law: Dealing with the "Impossible" Situation

19. The concepts of commercial impracticability and frustration of purpose expand the common-law doctrine of impossibility. However, because these newer concepts are not precisely defined, it is much better for the parties to provide for as many risks as possible in their contract. This will decrease the chance of problems arising that require litigation.

Ethics Box: Ethical Issues in Discharge of Contracts

20. Disagreements can arise regarding the meaning of conditions expressed in a contract that will discharge obligations. Ethically only honest interpretations should be raised, but legally it is difficult to discern whether a party actually intended a meaning for a contract provision at the time of contracting or is just raising it in self-interest, despite a contrary original intent.

Preventative Law: Allocating Risk with Contracts

21. One function of contracts is to allow parties who will be involved in a transaction with one another to allocate the risks that are anticipated. This can be done through the uses of conditions, provisions on damages, and other terms. It can be very important to the parties to identify the events that might occur during performance of the contemplated contract and expressly decide how the associated risks will be allocated between them.

MAJOR POINTS OF CASES

Russell v. *Salve Regina College* (p. 332)

This case deals with the legitimate extensiveness of the doctrine of substantial performance in breach of contract suits. Case precedent indicated that this doctrine had been applied only to construction contracts. The court noted that this limited application was due more to the limited variety of cases before the court concerning the doctrine of substantial performance than to the fact that courts ruled that construction contracts are the only contracts to which this doctrine properly applies.

In its judgement for the case at hand, the court ruled that the trial court acted properly in applying the doctrine of suit against Salve Regina College. In so doing, the Court of Appeals affirmed the trial court's decision which stipulated that the College in expelling Ms. Russell had breached its contract.

Plante v. *Jacobs* (p. 334)

The court in this case stated that in order for a person to be able to enforce the terms of a contract, he or she must have substantially performed his or her contractual obligations. A person's performance will be substantial if it meets the essential purpose of the contract. Recovery of compensation, however, must be adjusted to reflect any diminution in value on the basis of the degree of nonperformance or the replacement or repair costs associated with the nonperformance.

On the basis of the facts of the case, the court ruled that the plaintiff had substantially performed his obligations under the contract. The court applied both the diminished-value rule and the cost-of-replacement (repair) rule in determining the applicable award of damages. In doing so, the court held that the lower court had not made any reversible errors, and consequently it affirmed the decision of the lower court.

Mishara Construction Co. v. *Transit Mixed Concrete Co.* (p. 339)

The basic principle of law on which the court relied in this case is found in Section 2-615 of the Uniform Commercial Code, which provides that before performance of a contract can be excused, the performance must have been impractical and the impracticability must have been caused by the occurrence of a contingency the non-occurrence of which was a basic assumption on which the contract was made.

On the basis of the facts of this case, the court held that inasmuch as the possibility of a labor strike was within the risks and contingencies assumed by the parties at the time the contract was made, a labor dispute did not constitute an excuse for non-performance.

Stifft's Jewelers v. *Oliver* (p. 343)

In this case the court held that the amount of monetary damages that can be recovered upon breach of a contract are those which can be established to have been incurred with reasonable certainty. Monetary damages include those general damages that should be reasonably foreseeable to the party who breached a contract. Special damages are recoverable, however, only when the breaching party knew that they would be incurred upon a breach and at least tacitly agreed to assume responsibility for them. In this case the plaintiff's claim for the sentimental value of the lost diamond rings was not legally recoverable, since they did not prove the defendant's knowledge of their sentimental value or that the defendant tacitly agreed to be liable for such value. Further, the measurement of sentimental value is highly speculative and should not be allowed.

Parker v. *Twentieth Century-Fox Film Corp.* (p. 345)

The court in this case stated the rule that the measure of damages for the wrongful discharge of an employee is the amount of the agreed-upon salary less the amount the employer proves that the employee earned or reasonably could have earned from other similar employment. The employer must show, however, that any other such employment was comparable to that of which the employee was deprived. In addition, the employer is precluded from showing that the employee refused to seek or accept different or inferior employment

In applying the applicable rule of law to the facts involved, the court held that inasmuch as the substitute employment that was offered was significantly different from the original employment, the plaintiff was justified in rejecting the offer. By doing so, according to the court, the plaintiff did not fail in her obligation to mitigate damages, and consequently she was entitled to the damages that were awarded her.

PRACTICAL CONSIDERATIONS

It is quite easy to state the alternatives available to a person in circumstances that establish an anticipatory breach of a contract. The proper alternative to use in a particular situation, however, is often difficult to determine. One should be absolutely certain that a contract has been breached in an anticipatory manner before considering the contract terminated; otherwise the party who claims the breach may be in breach of the contract. A person who prematurely enters into a similar contract with someone else may find that he or she has two contracts for the same thing.

Obviously, such problems are not easily resolved. Perhaps the safest way to protect one's interests in such circumstances is to obtain, if possible, a written statement in which the breaching party acknowledges his or her breach and authorizes the nonbreaching party to obtain the goods or services elsewhere. Such a statement, of course, will usually be difficult to obtain. Absent such a statement, one should exercise extreme care in determining the appropriate course of action. The specific facts of each situation determine the appropriate alternative to take.

SELF TEST

True-False Questions

_____ 1. A nonbreaching party has an obligation to mitigate the damages he or she sustains as a result of the other party's breach.

_____ 2. A duty of performance in connection with a contract may be made conditional upon the nonoccurrence of an event.

_____ 3. If one of the parties to a contract has substantially but not fully performed his or her obligations under the contract, that party will be entitled to require the other party to perform his or her obligations as well.

159

_____ 4. The death of one of the parties to a contract will always terminate the contract.

_____ 5. Under the Uniform Commercial Code, if a contract calls for the sale of blue goods and those that are delivered are perfect except for the fact that they are red, the buyer may send all the goods back to the seller.

_____ 6. The phrase "time is of the essence" in a contract means that one of the parties to the contract would like performance to be rendered by a specified date, but it is not essential that the performance be rendered by that date.

_____ 7. A contract that is executory on both sides may be terminated by a simple express agreement between the parties indicating that neither party shall be bound to the contract any longer.

_____ 8. In a novation, a completely new contract is substituted for another contract and the parties to it remain the same as the parties to the contract that was discharged.

_____ 9. The general objective of all types of damages awarded by a court is to punish the wrongdoer for his or her conduct.

_____ 10. A party to a contract who claims that there has been an anticipatory breach of the contract by the other party must be able to show that the claimed repudiation of the contract was clear and unequivocal.

Multiple-Choice Questions

_____ 11. The type of damages that are most commonly awarded in a breach-of-contract lawsuit when the plaintiff has actually sustained losses are:
a. punitive damages
b. compensatory damages
c. nominal damages
d. reprehensible damages
e. all of the above are correct

_____ 12. An action for specific performance of a contract may be properly commenced in connection with a contract for the sale of.
a. a 1985 Rolls-Royce
b. an ordinary plot of land in Pennsylvania
c. a one-of-a-kind flower vase
d. only b and c are correct
e. a, b, and c are all correct

13. A contract may be discharged and terminated as a result of:
    a. subsequent illegality related to the subject matter of the contract
    b. a novation
    c. impossibility of performance
    d. an anticipatory breach
    e. all of the above are correct

14. Under the Uniform Commercial Code, if goods delivered to a buyer are not exactly what he or she ordered or asked for, the buyer:
    a. must keep the goods at a reduced price
    b. must accept redelivered goods that are proper regardless of when the seller redelivers them
    c. may reject the entire delivery
    d. may keep the goods without paying for them
    e. all of the above are correct

15. Which of the following contracts will be considered discharged by impossibility of performance?
    a. a contract to sell bananas in which the price to the seller has increased by 50 percent since the time the contract was signed
    b. a contract to sell a car that was blown up by rioters after the contract was signed but before delivery to the buyer
    c. the contract of a professional soccer player who fractured his arm
    d. b and c are correct
    e. all of the above are correct

16. The remedy that would be available to the owner of a professional baseball team to prevent the team's star player from playing for another team after the player has unilaterally breached his contract is:
    a. compensatory damages
    b. an injunction
    c. punitive damages
    d. a and b are correct
    e. all of the above are correct

17. Under the concept of substantial performance, a party who has not rendered full performance will still be able to enforce the contract if he or she can establish that:
    a. there was an unintentional departure from the terms of the contract
    b. there was an honest effort to comply fully with the requirements of the contract
    c. there was a substantial performance of the contract
    d. only a and c are correct
    e. a, b, and c are all correct

18. If there has been an anticipatory breach of a contract, the nonbreaching party:
    a. may begin a lawsuit for damages immediately upon the occurrence of the anticipatory breach
    b. must wait until the time scheduled for performance before starting a lawsuit for damages
    c. must perform his or her obligations under the contract until the date scheduled for performance by the other party
    d. may immediately treat the contract as breached, but must wait until the date scheduled for performance by the other party before starting a lawsuit for damages
    e. all of the above are correct

19. In order for the concept of frustration of purpose to relieve a party to a contract from his or her obligation to perform:
    a. the frustration must be substantial
    b. the nonoccurrence of the frustrating event must have been a basic assumption on which the contract was made
    c. the frustrated purpose must have been a principal purpose of the party in making the contract
    d. only a and c are correct
    e. a, b, and c are all correct

20. When a party has been paid money by mistake, the remedy he will most likely seek is:
    a. restitution
    b. injunction
    c. liquidated damages
    d. none of the above

Completion Questions

21. Under sales law, the standard of substantial performance does not apply, and performance is judged by the _____ _____ rule.

22. A substitution of a new party for one of the original parties is a _____.

23. The doctrine that excuses performance when it is literally not possible for a party to perform his or her contractual obligations is the _____ _____ _____.

24. An _____ _____ occurs when a party repudiates a commitment to a contract before performance is due.

25. A party must engage in _____ _____ _____ to minimize the loss he or she incurs when a contract is breached.

Chapter 20

INTRODUCTION TO SALES CONTRACTS

The law of sales in some way affects the life of everyone who lives in a money economy, for people need goods in order to survive. This chapter discusses the nature and creation of sales contracts, the scope of the Uniform Commercial Code, risk of loss, and other concepts that serve as the basis of the law of sales.

As you examine this chapter, pay special attention to the excerpted provisions of the UCC. It is to this code that lawyers and judges turn for the rules of law that govern contracts for the sale of goods. When you review the materials, however, make no attempt to memorize the applicable sections of the code; there are simply too many of them. Try rather to acquire an accurate understanding of the concepts they embody. Such an understanding will result in more lasting and effective retention of the rules of law.

CHAPTER OBJECTIVES

After reading Chapter 20 of the text and studying the related materials in this chapter of the Student Mastery Guide, you will understand:

1. The general characteristics and scope of the UCC
2. Offer and acceptance in a contract for the sale of goods
3. The creation of a sales contract under Article 2 of the UCC
4. Risk of loss between the parties to a sales contract, when:
   a. specific terms are agreed upon
   b. no specific terms have been agreed upon
   c. there is a breach of the contract
5. The nature of bulk transfers

MAJOR POINTS TO REMEMBER

1. All contracts are governed by the requirement of good-faith performance, which means "honesty in fact in the conduct or transaction concerned."

2. Merchants often have different and higher standards applied to them under the UCC.
   A merchant is described under Section 2-104 of the UCC as any of the following:
   a. a person who deals in goods of the kind that he or she is selling
   b. a person who by his occupation holds himself out as having knowledge or skill peculiar to the goods or practices involved in the transaction
   c. someone who employs another person who by his occupation holds himself out as having knowledge or skill peculiar to the goods or practices involved in the transaction

Scope of the UCC

3. Article 2 of the UCC applies to goods - tangible and movable personal property - and future goods; as well as unborn animals, growing crops, and timber to be cut.

4. A contract for the sale of goods includes both a present sale of goods and a contract for the sale of goods at a future time.

5. "Future goods" are described as goods that either do not now exist or are not identified to a contract, or are both nonexisting and unidentified.

6. Article 2 of the UCC does apply to transactions involving both goods and services, if the contract is primarily for goods with the services being incidental.

7. Contracts not covered include contracts for sales of real property, personal property other than goods, or services.

Creation of Sales Contracts

8. Under the UCC, as long as it is determined that the parties intended to enter into a contract, the contract will not be set aside for indefiniteness because one or more of the terms have been left open (UCC Section 2-204[3]

9. A contract for the sale of goods is not necessarily indefinite if the price has not been agreed upon. In such a case, UCC Section 2-305 provides that the price will be the reasonable value of the goods at the time of delivery.

   However, if the parties state that no contract will be formed unless the price is agreed upon, and the price is not thereafter agreed upon, then no contract has been created.

10. If no time for delivery of the goods is set forth in a contract for sale, then the goods must be delivered within a reasonable time (UCC Section 2-309[1]).

11. Unless it is otherwise agreed upon, all goods called for in a contract of sale must be delivered at the same time, and payment for the goods is due upon tender of delivery (UCC Section 2-307).

12. If no location for the delivery of goods is provided or specified in a contract for sale, then the goods are to be delivered at the seller's place of business with respect to those goods, or at his or her residence if the seller has no such place of business.

   If at the time of making the contract the parties know that the goods are located somewhere else, then that other place or location will be the place for delivery (UCC Section 2-308).

13. A quantity term must be specified to create an enforceable contract.

14. The meaning of a written sale-of-goods contract is construed with the aid of any course dealing, usage of trade, and course of performance, but if this leads to an unreasonable construction, then the written terms control. Further, course of performance controls over course of dealing, which in turn controls usage of trade when conflicts between any of them exist.

15. When the parties do not agree expressly on all the terms (but they intended to be bound and there is a reasonably certain basis for giving an appropriate remedy), the court will fill it in by looking to (in order) course of performance, course of dealing, and usage of trade. If this fails, the court will look to the "gap-filling" provisions of Part 3 of Article 2.

16. The Statute of Frauds under the UCC requires contracts for the sales of goods for $500 or more to be in writing.
    a. Between merchants, however, an oral contract is enforceable if it is followed up by a written confirmation that is not rejected by the party receiving the confirmation within 10 days of its receipt.

Acceptance

17. Under the Uniform Commercial Code, unless an offeror unambiguously indicates that his or her offer must be accepted in a particular way, the offeree can accept the offer in any way he or she wants as long as it is reasonable under the circumstances.

18. A seller can accept an offer to buy goods either by making a prompt promise to ship the goods or by a prompt or current shipment of conforming or nonconforming goods (UCC Section 2-206[1][b]). However, delivery of nonconforming goods without notice that it is made as an accommodation will also constitute a breach of contract.

19. If acceptance by beginning performance is reasonable, it will be valid, but if the buyer is not notified of this within a reasonable time, then the buyer can treat the offer as lapsed.

20. In 1987, Article 2A of the UCC was finished. This article applies most of the rules of Article 2 to personal property leasing transactions. In article 2A, the term lessor is generally substituted for the term seller, and lessee replaces buyer.

Ethics Box: Good Faith in Commercial Transaction

21. Good-faith actions is a basic principle of business ethics. However, within the law "good faith" has not yet been applied in the same sense as is meant in ethics. In contrast, "bad faith" action has a more definite legal meaning and has been used to impose punitive damages.

Issues and Trends:
Terms in an Incomplete Contract Will Be Supplied

22. Under the common law an agreement could be unenforceable for the lack of definiteness of terms. This does not occur under Article 2 of the UCC when there is an intent to be bound and a reasonable basis to determine the appropriate remedy. In such cases, the UCC automatically inserts terms left open (except the quantity term) by the parties to complete the contract.

MAJOR POINTS OF CASES

Decatur Cooperative Association v. *Urban* (p. 356)

This case illustrates the fact that a farmer who qualified as a merchant will be subject to the provisions of UCC Section 2-201(2), and an oral contract that is followed by a written confirmation is enforceable against such a person.

Under the facts of this case, the court held that Urban was only a casual or inexperienced seller and was not to be held accountable to the standards of a merchant with respect to the sale. Therefore, a written confirmation sent by the seller was not sufficient to bind him to the agreement in the absence of a written contract.

Keller v. *A.O. Smith Harvestore Products, Inc.* (p. 358)

This case illustrates the point that the parole evidence rule does not preclude a buyer from bringing a negligent misrepresentation case.

In this case, even though the contract stated that the written agreement constituted the full agreement the buyers could still bring in evidence of video tapes and brochures containing false information about the subject matter of the contract. The information was brought in as evidence of a tort, not to contradict the agreement.

Lancaster Glass Corp. v. *Philips ECG, Inc.* (p. 360)

This case demonstrates the principle that repeated acceptances of shipments of goods with ample opportunity to reject such shipments constitutes an agreement that those goods conform to the contract. Subsequent shipments of goods meeting the same standards cannot be rejected by the buyer as nonconforming.

Thus, in this case, Phillips' acceptance of the first shipment of bulbs precluded it from objecting to later shipments of bulbs that conformed to the same dimensions.

Pollack v. *Nemet Motor, Inc.* (p. 363)

This case illustrates that a writing sufficient to satisfy the Statute of Frauds does not have to be a formal agreement. In this case, a check for a deposit sufficed because it included the notation that the agreement was on the back, and the terms of the agreement were typed there.

PRACTICAL CONSIDERATIONS

1. An examination of the provisions of the Uniform Commercial Code shows that it frequently states that its rules apply when the parties have not made appropriate arrangements under the terms of their contract. In actuality, the parties to a contract often specifically provide all the necessary terms, including but not limited to price, delivery terms, dates for performance, and quantity. In such cases the provisions of the contract determine the primary rights of the parties except when the contract fails to deal with a given issue, in which case the code is controlling.

2. Under contracts providing for FOB deliveries and similar terms, even though the seller is required to pay the freight charges, that expense is generally added to the price of the goods being sold. As a result, the buyer is actually paying the cost of the freight charges, not the seller. Frequently the purchaser is unaware of the fact that he or she is paying the freight charges.

    Example: A, a buyer in New York, contracts with B, a seller in Oklahoma, for the purchase of a quantity of wheat. The terms of the contract for sale include a provision for the goods to be delivered to the buyer FOB New York, with the understanding that the seller will pay the freight charges between Oklahoma and New York. While B will make the actual payment for the freight charges, the price he quotes to A for the wheat will include such costs. Thus the buyer, A, actually absorbs the freight charges. (This arrangement is sometimes referred to as a "cost pass-along.")

SELF TEST

True-False Questions

_____   1. Article 1 of the UCC applies generally to transactions.

_____   2. Under the UCC, a sale is defined as a transaction that involves the passing of title from the seller to the buyer for a price.

_____   3. Article 2 controls only those sales involving "goods".

_____   4. Under the UCC, standards for merchants and nonmerchants are the same.

_____   5. A contract for the sale of goods is indefinite if it fails to make the price for the goods payable in money.

_____   6. If no time for delivery of goods is specified in a contract, then the goods must be delivered within a reasonable time.

_____   7. Contracts fail if it is not stipulated within them that the price will be paid in money.

_____ 8. Quantity is the only term that must be stated in a sales contract.

_____ 9. Under no circumstances are oral contracts between merchants enforceable.

_____ 10. If the parties to a contract for sale fail to provide for a location for the delivery of goods, the purchaser's place of business will be the place of delivery.

Multiple-Choice Questions

_____ 11. In a present sale:
a. the making of a contract occurs before the completion of the sale
b. the making of a contract occurs at the same time as a sale
c. a deposit is made before the contract is formed
d. the sale occurs before the making of the contract
e. none of the above

_____ 12. Contracts that are not covered by Article 2 are those involving the sale of:
a. all real property
b. all personal property
c. services
d. all of the above
e. a and c only

_____ 13. Under the Uniform Commercial Code, goods include:
a. a house
b. the unborn offspring of an animal
c. an automobile
d. both b and c are correct
e. a, b, and c are all correct

_____ 14. Course of performance relates to conduct:
a. after the execution of an agreement
b. one month after the execution of an agreement
c. prior to the execution of an agreement
d. at the same time as the execution of an agreement
e. none of the above

169

15. A contract for the sale of goods must be evidenced by "some writing" in order to be enforceable if the sale is for:
   a. $1,000 or more
   b. $750 or more
   c. $500 or more
   d. $250 or more
   e. any amount

16. In the absence of an agreement to the contrary, identification of goods occurs:
   a. at the moment of delivery
   b. when the goods are marked in some way or set aside as the object of a particular transaction
   c. when the goods are accepted by the buyer
   d. b and c are both correct
   e. a, b, and c are correct

17. All of the following would qualify as a "good", except:
   a. a watch
   b. a mobile home
   c. an idea
   d. a boat
   e. an appliance

18. Which of the following is not a definition of a merchant under the UCC?
   a. a person who deals in goods of the kind in question
   b. one who by his or her occupation represents himself or herself as having a skill peculiar to the practices or goods involved in the transaction
   c. a person who employs someone who qualifies as a merchant to act on his or her behalf
   d. all of the above
   e. none of the above

19. A contract for the sale of goods includes:
   a. only a present sale of goods
   b. only a contract for the sale of existing goods
   c. both a present sale of goods and a contract for the sale of goods at a future time
   d. only a contract for the sale of identified goods
   e. none of the above is correct

_____ 20. Unless the parties to a contract for sale agree otherwise, payment for goods must be made:
- a. at the time the contract is created
- b. within a reasonable time after delivery of the goods
- c. at the time the goods are shipped
- d. when the goods are tendered for delivery
- e. when notice of a future delivery date is given to the buyer

Completion Questions

21. _____ _____ is defined as "honesty" in fact in the conduct or transaction concerned.

22. Article 2 controls only the sale of _____.

23. _____ term is the only one that must be stated absolutely in a contract for the sale of goods.

24. Course of _____ relates to conduct between the parties prior to the execution of an agreement.

25. A _____ _____ is a contract for sale in which the making of the contract and the completion of the sale occur at different times.

Chapter 21

SALES: TITLE, RISK OF LOSS, AND INSURABLE INTERESTS

Before the adoption of the UCC, the concepts of title, risk of loss, and insurable interest constituted a conglomerate. Risk of loss and insurable interest rested with the holder of the title. However, with the UCC's adoption also has come a separation of these terms. Such a separation to some extent has complicated the court's determination of which party possesses the risk of loss or an insurable interest in given products.

This chapter explicates the new relationship between title, risk of loss, and insurable interest, especially by providing a treatment of them as separate entities. Additionally, the material presented in this chapter discusses bulk transfers.

CHAPTER OBJECTIVES

After reading Chapter 21 of the text and studying the related material presented in this chapter of the Student Mastery Guide, you will understand:

1. The definitions of:
   a. title
   b. risk of loss
   c. insurable interest
2. The interrelationship between these terms
3. Bulk transfers

MAJOR POINTS TO REMEMBER

Title

1. The following rules apply to the transfer of title to goods from a seller to a buyer:
   a. Generally, the parties to a transaction can make any agreement they wish relative to the time and place for the transfer of title to existing goods.
   b. If no agreement or provision for the passing of title has been made between the parties, title will pass at the time and place of delivery of the goods. The following rules apply when the parties have made a provision for delivery of the goods:
      i. If the seller is to ship the goods to the buyer but no specific destination is set forth, title to the goods will pass to the buyer at the time and place of shipment.
      ii. When the seller has agreed to ship the goods to the buyer at a specified destination (i.e., a destination contract), title to the goods will pass to the buyer when the goods are tendered for delivery at the specified destination.
      iii. If the seller's obligation under a contract is to deliver a document of title rather than the goods themselves, title to the goods will pass to the buyer at the time and place of delivery of the documents to the buyer.

Transfer of Title to Third Persons

2.   A purchaser acquires from the seller any title that the seller possessed or had the authority to convey.

3.   A thief acquires no title to property he or she has stolen; therefore, a person who subsequently buys the stolen property from the thief also acquires no title to it.

4.   A purchaser will obtain voidable title to goods that are purchased when:
       a.   the transferor of the goods was deceived as to the purchaser's identity
       b.   the purchaser gives the seller a bad check that a bank subsequently refuses to honor
       c.   the transaction provides that title will pass to the buyer after the seller has been paid
       d.   criminal fraud is involved in the purchase of the goods

5.   A third party who acquires goods from a person with a voidable title can retain the goods as against the original owner, if the third party was a good-faith purchaser for value of the goods. The third party can then transfer good title to others.

6.   If an owner entrusts goods to a merchant who deals in such goods and the merchant resells the goods in the ordinary course of business to a buyer who purchases in good faith and without notice of the rights of a third party, then the buyer has a clear, good title to the goods.

Risk of Loss

7.   Under the terms of an *FOB shipping point* (origin) contract, which is presumed if the contract is silent or ambiguous on this point, the seller is under an obligation to pay the freight charges required to get the goods to the carrier. The risk of loss with respect to the goods will shift from the seller to the buyer only when the goods are delivered to the carrier.
       Under the terms of an *FOB destination* contract, the seller is under an obligation to pay the freight charges required to get the goods to the named destination. The risk of loss will shift to the buyer only when the goods are tendered to the buyer at the named destination (UCC Section 2-319).
       Under a *CIF* or *C & F* contract, the risk of loss will shift from the seller to the buyer when the goods have been delivered to the carrier.
       Under an *ex-ship* contract for sale, the risk of loss will shift from the seller to the buyer when the goods are properly unloaded from the ship at the named port.
       If a destination contract contains a "no arrival, no sale" term, the seller is not liable if the goods do not arrive through no fault of the seller.

8.   Generally, under the UCC, the parties may make their own agreement as to the time and place at which the risk of loss will shift from the seller to the buyer even though the agreed-upon time and place are in contravention of the terms of the statute. If the agreed-upon risk of loss provision does contravene the UCC, however, the provision must be made in good faith and must not be unconscionable.

173

9. When no provision is made with respect to the shifting of the risk of loss and there has been no breach of contract:
   a. risk of loss cannot shift to the buyer until the goods are identified to the contract
   b. if goods are shipped by carrier, risk of loss passes to the buyer when the goods are delivered to the carrier under a shipping point contract and when the goods are tendered to the buyer under a destination contract
   c. if the goods are in the possession of a bailee and are to be delivered without being moved, and if a negotiable document of title has been issued, risk of loss will pass to the buyer when the document of title is delivered to the buyer
   d. if the document of title is nonnegotiable, risk of loss will pass to the buyer when the bailee acknowledges the buyer's right to possession of the goods
   e. in all other cases, if the seller is a merchant, risk of loss will shift to the buyer when the buyer actually takes physical possession of the goods; if the seller is a nonmerchant, risk of loss will shift to the buyer when the goods are tendered for delivery

10. If goods that do not conform to the contract specifications are tendered for delivery and the buyer rejects them, risk of loss remains with the seller at all relevant times.

11. If the buyer accepts delivery of goods and thereafter properly revokes his or her acceptance, the risk of loss will be considered to have remained with the seller to the extent that the loss exceeds the buyer's insurance coverage.

12. If the buyer breaches the contract, risk of loss is on the buyer for a commercially reasonably time to the extent that the seller's insurance is insufficient to cover the loss.

13. In a sale-on-approval situation, risk of loss will pass to the buyer when he or she approves the sale and accepts the goods. In a sale or return transaction, the buyer returns the goods at the buyer's expense and risk.

Insurable Interest

14. Under the UCC (Section 2-501), a buyer acquires an insurable interest in existing goods when they are identified to the contract of sale.
    The buyer obtains an insurable interest in future goods when they are shipped, mailed, or otherwise designated by the seller as goods to which the contract applied.

15. The seller of goods possesses an insurable interest in those goods so long as he or she retains title to them or has a security interest in them.

Bulk Transfers (Article 6)

16. The bulk transfer provisions of the UCC are intended as a means of preventing a merchant from selling all of his or her inventory without satisfying the rightful claims of creditors. Unless creditors of the seller are notified of the bulk transfer at least ten days before the buyer takes possession of the goods, the transfer will be ineffective against them.

Preventative Law Box

17.   A person can avoid bearing the risk of loss by including a specific contractual provision dealing with the risk of loss or by purchasing insurance.

MAJOR POINTS OF THE CASES

Kahr v. *Markland* (p. 371)

The court ruled in this case that a delivery or voluntary transfer is a prerequisite for the occurrence of an entrustment. Applying this ruling to the case, the court found that Goodwill's reception of sterling silver from the plaintiff did not constitute an entrustment, because the plaintiff unknowingly gave the silver to Goodwill. As a consequence, Goodwill did not have legal title to the silver and, thus, no right to sell it. The court ordered that the silver be returned to the plaintiff.

Jason's Foods, Inc. v. *Peter Eckrich & Sons, Inc.* (P. 377)

The goods sold in this case were to be transferred from the plaintiff to the defendant without being moved, because they were being held in a warehouse where both had accounts. After the warehouse made the transfer in its records, but before the buyer received a copy of the transfer receipt, the goods were destroyed by fire. UCC 2-509(2) provides in such cases that the risk of loss shifts to the buyer upon acknowledgment by the bailee of the buyer's right to the goods. The issue is whether acknowledgment to the seller satisfied this provision. The court stated the general rule that the risk of loss is placed on the party in the best position to prevent it. However, neither party was in a better position here. It concluded that, since the acknowledgment had not been made to the buyer, the risk of loss was still with the seller, even though the title had already passed to the buyer.

Martin v. *Melland's Inc.* (P. 379)

The decision in this case illustrates the principle that under the Uniform Commercial Code, title and risk of loss are two separate concepts. Title is no longer relevant in determining whether a buyer or seller bears the risk of loss. When the seller of goods, in this case Martin, is a nonmerchant, risk of loss passes to the buyer when the goods are tendered for delivery.

The court found that Martin had not tendered the haymover for delivery. Therefore, risk of loss did not pass to Melland's Inc., but instead fell on Martin.

Prewitt v. *Numismatic Funding Corp.* (p. 381)

This case involved a "sale on approval" contract for rare coins that the buyer returned to the seller within the prescribed time by certified mail and with partial insurance coverage for their value. The returned coins were never delivered. The court rejected the seller's arguments that through course of dealing and course of performance the

175

parties had shifted the risk of loss to the buyer. Instead, it held that the general rule of the UCC, which states that in "sale on approval" transactions, the risk of loss remains with the seller until the buyer accepts the goods, applies to this case.

SELF TEST

True-False Questions

_____ 1. Title to goods cannot pass from a seller to a buyer before identification of the goods to a contract for sale.

_____ 2. If a contract calls for the seller to ship goods to the buyer but doesn't require the seller to deliver them at a particular destination, title to the goods will not pass to the buyer until a destination point is agreed upon.

_____ 3. A thief can never transfer title to the goods he or she has stolen.

_____ 4. Valid title to goods can never be transferred to a person by someone who is not the owner of those goods.

_____ 5. If a document of title is negotiable, it can be transferred from one party to another.

_____ 6. A general philosophy reflected by the UCC is that parties must be under strict regulation when determining the details of a contract.

_____ 7. Under an FOB destination contract, risk of loss will pass from the seller to the buyer when the goods are tendered to the buyer.

_____ 8. Under the terms of the Uniform Commercial Code, the parties to a contract can agree on the time and place for the passing of the risk of loss from the seller to the buyer.

_____ 9. When a purchaser gives a seller a bad check in payment for goods, the title obtained by the purchaser is voidable.

_____ 10. When a buyer rightfully revokes an acceptance, the risk of loss still shifts to that buyer.

176

_____ 11. If a buyer who has obtained voidable title to goods conveys those goods to a third person, the third person may retain the goods if:
   a. he or she is a good-faith purchaser for value
   b. the original buyer informed the third person of the voidable title
   c. the goods were a gift to the third person
   d. the original buyer promises the third person to clear up the title problem but does not do so
   e. all of the above are correct

_____ 12. Which of the following transactions will give rise to a voidable title?
   a. the transferor of the goods has been deceived about the purchaser's identity
   b. the transaction is one in which the title to the goods will not pass until the seller is paid for them
   c. the goods were obtained by means of criminal fraud
   d. a bad check has been given in payment for the goods and a bank has refused to honor it
   e. all of the above are correct

_____ 13. Which article of the UCC deals with "bulk sale risk"?
   a. Article 1
   b. Article 2
   c. Article 2A
   d. Article 5
   e. none of the above

_____ 14. Under the terms of an FOB origin (shipping point) contract, the seller must:
   a. make a proper transportation contract
   b. obtain and deliver to the buyer all appropriate documents
   c. put the goods in the possession of the carrier
   d. notify the buyer of the shipment of the goods
   e. all of the above are correct

_____ 15. Risk of loss in a CIF contract shifts to the buyer:
   a. when the seller delivers the goods to the carrier
   b. when the seller delivers the goods to the buyer
   c. when the goods arrive at the carrier's office in the buyer's city
   d. at the time of contracting
   e. b and d are both correct

16. By possessing a void title, a third party:
    a. can sue the party who sold him this title to certain goods
    b. must immediately return the goods to the original owner or face a civil suit
    c. must immediately return the goods to the original owner or face criminal charges
    d. must return the goods to the original owner only if that owner demands them back
    e. none of the above

17. Under which of the following transactions will the price required to be paid by the seller include the cost of the goods being purchased, the cost of freight charges, and the cost of insurance premiums to insure the goods?
    a. no arrival, no sale
    b. FOB destination
    c. CIF
    d. FAS
    e. sale on approval

18. If no agreement for the passing of title has been made between the parties to a contract and the contract requires the seller to deliver the goods to a particular destination (i.e., a destination contract), title will pass to the buyer:
    a. at the time and place of delivery of the goods
    b. when the goods are shipped
    c. at the time the contract was entered into
    d. when the buyer sends an acknowledgment of delivery
    e. both b and c are correct

19. In a sale or return transaction:
    a. the buyer must return the goods within a reasonable amount of time
    b. the buyer must pay the cost of returning the goods.
    c. the goods must be substantially in their original position
    d. all of the above
    e. none of the above

20. Goods are sometimes transferred by:
    a. documents of title
    b. a bill of lading
    c. voidable title
    d. all of the above
    e. a and c only

Completion Questions

21. A warehouse receipt is a _____ _____ _____.

22. If a document of title can be transferred from one party to another it is said to be _____.

23. _____ is any delivery and any acquiescence in retention of possession.

24. The term _____ stands for cost, insurance and freight.

25. Title may not pass prior to _____ of the goods.

Chapter 22

SALES: PERFORMANCE

Once a valid contract for the sale of goods has been formed, the next consideration with which the parties need to be concerned is their respective rights with respect to the performance of their contractual obligations.

This chapter deals with the performance aspects of the contract of sale. The chapter considers the delivery element of the contract with respect to the time, place, and manner of delivery as well as the question of when payment for the goods will be due. It examines the rules related to the acceptance of goods and the rights of the parties when nonconforming goods are tendered for delivery. It also discusses the rights of the parties when one of them doubts that the other will perform his or her obligations and shows what can be done in such circumstances.

This chapter contains significant rules, which are detailed and specific. In view of the importance of these rules and the fact that they are frequently applied to business situations, take special care to familiarize yourself with them. Knowledge of these rules will certainly prove useful.

CHAPTER OBJECTIVES

After reading Chapter 22 of the text and studying the related materials in this chapter of the Student Mastery Guide, you will understand:

1. The manner in which a sales contract is performed, including:
   a. delivery provisions
   b. payment provisions
2. Rights of the parties to a sales contract in connection with:
   a. acceptance of the goods
   b. rejection of the goods
   c. revocation of an acceptance of goods
   d installment contracts
3. Rights of the parties to a sales contract regarding:
   a. assurance of performance
   b. anticipatory repudiation
   c. impossibility of performance

MAJOR POINTS TO REMEMBER

Terms

1. a. Unless the contract of sale or the circumstances indicate otherwise, the seller is obligated to deliver all the goods called for by the contract at one time.
   b. The buyer is obligated to pay for the goods at the time and place he or she is to receive the goods unless the contract provides otherwise.
   c. If the goods are delivered in lots, however, the buyer must pay for the lot at the time of tender of delivery, provided the price for that particular lot can be determined (UCC Section 2-307).

2. a. Unless the parties make specific provisions for delivery, goods that are being sold are to be delivered to the buyer at the seller's place of business or, if the seller has no place of business, at the seller's residence (UCC Section 2-308).

    b. If at the time the parties enter into a contract for the sale of identified goods they both know that the goods are located at some other place, then that other place will be the place for delivery.

3. If no time for delivery has been set under the contract, delivery must be made within a reasonable time.

4. If the seller tenders delivery of nonconforming goods and the buyer rejects the tender, the seller has a right to cure the defect in the tender of delivery of the goods. The seller must make a new tender on or before the original time for performance set forth in the contract, or within a reasonable time. If the seller intends to cure the nonconforming delivery, he or she must give reasonable notice to the buyer of such intention (UCC Section 2-508[1]).

    If the seller sends a nonconforming tender that he or she reasonably believes will be acceptable to the buyer and the buyer rejects the goods, the seller, if insufficient time is available to deliver conforming goods before the time for performance lapses, has a reasonable time to substitute performance.

5. The buyer of goods has the right to inspect the goods being delivered (to determine that they are conforming) before he or she accepts the delivery. Such inspection may be made at any reasonable time and place, and in any manner that is reasonable.

    An exception to the rule exists with regard to COD deliveries and payments made against documents of title. In such cases, the buyer must pay for the goods before inspecting them. In such circumstances, however, the buyer still has the right to reject the goods if upon inspection they are discovered to be nonconforming.

6. Generally, if delivery of goods is to be made by means of the delivery of a document of title, payment will be due at the time and place of tender of delivery of the document of title. The buyer still retains the right to inspect the goods and, if they are nonconforming, to reject them.

Acceptance

7. Under Section 2-606 of the Uniform Commercial Code, a buyer accepts goods if, after he or she has had a reasonable opportunity to inspect them, the buyer:

    a. indicates that they are conforming or that he or she will keep them even though they are nonconforming

    b. fails to make an effective rejection

    c. performs any act that is inconsistent with the ownership rights of the seller

8. A buyer who has accepted delivery of goods may not thereafter reject them. Under certain conditions, however, the buyer may be able to revoke his or her acceptance of the goods.

Rejection

9. A buyer who intends to reject a nonconforming delivery of goods must do so within a reasonable time after the goods are tendered for delivery and must reasonably notify the seller of his or her intention to reject the goods. The code permits a buyer to reject goods if the tender of delivery fails in any respect to conform to the contract. As a practical matter, however, the buyer cannot reject the goods because of trivial defects.

10. The only obligation of a nonmerchant buyer who has rejected a delivery of goods is to hold the goods with reasonable care and for a reasonable period of time so as to allow the seller to take possession of them.

    If a merchant buyer has rejected a delivery of goods and the seller has no agent or place of business at the location where the rejection occurred, then the merchant must follow any reasonable instructions given by the seller regarding the goods.

    If the seller fails to give any instructions to the merchant buyer and the goods are perishable or likely to depreciate in value quickly, then the buyer must make reasonable efforts to resell the goods on behalf of the seller. In such case, the buyer is entitled to be reimbursed by the seller for any expenses incurred.

Revocation

11. The fact that a buyer has accepted a delivery of goods does not necessarily mean that they cannot be returned to the seller thereafter. Under UCC Section 2-608 a buyer can revoke his or her acceptance of the goods if:
    a. the buyer knew of a defect in the goods but accepted them because he or she reasonably thought that the defect would be cured by the seller and it was not
    b. the defect could not readily be discovered upon a reasonable inspection of the goods
    c. the seller represented to the buyer that there were no defects in the goods, and as a result the buyer did not discover the defect

12. The buyer who revokes his or her acceptance of the goods must do so:
    a. within a reasonable time after he or she discovered or should have discovered the grounds for revocation
    b. before any substantial change in the condition of the goods (other than those inherent in the goods) occurs

13. A revocation of an acceptance is not effective until notice of it is given to the seller.

14. Many states have enacted statutes to give purchasers of new automobiles rights to revoke acceptance beyond those in the UCC. These statutes have been called "lemon laws." Typically such laws require that:
    a. the consumer notify the seller of defects within the warranty period or one year after delivery, whichever is first
    b. the seller be given a reasonable number of attempts to cure the defects, meaning four or more repair attempts or keeping the car out of service for no more than a total of thirty days in attempting to fix it
    c. if the seller is unable to cure the defects in a reasonable number of attempts, the seller must provide a replacement vehicle or refund the purchase price

Installment Contracts

15. A buyer can reject a nonconforming installment under an installment delivery contract if the nonconformity substantially impairs the value of the installment and it cannot be cured.

16. A buyer can reject or cancel the entire contract because of a nonconforming installment or installments if that nonconformity substantially impairs the value of the entire contract and cannot be cured.

Assurance of Performance

17. Under UCC Section 2-609, a party to a contract who reasonably believes that the other party may not perform his or her obligations may:
    a. suspend his or her own performance under the contract
    b. require adequate assurance of performance
    c. treat the contract as though it were broken if the grounds for insecurity are not corrected within a reasonable time

Anticipatory Repudiation

18. If a party indicates that he or she will not perform contractual obligations at some date in the future, the aggrieved party may immediately bring a lawsuit for breach of contract or wait a commercially reasonable time for performance. If the latter option is chosen, the repudiating party can retract the repudiation unless the contract has been canceled or the aggrieved party has materially changed positions.

Impossibility

19. When identified goods have been totally destroyed through no fault of either party to a contract and before risk of loss passes to the buyer, UCC Section 2-613 permits the contract to be canceled.
    The code also permits the contract to be canceled if the purpose of the contract has been frustrated or becomes impracticable because of either the occurrence of an event the nonoccurrence of which was a basic assumption of the parties or good-faith compliance with a government regulation.

20.   If a seller can partially perform despite the impossibility of full performance, then the seller must allocate the goods among customers in a fair and reasonable manner. In such a case, however, the buyer has a reasonable time to accept the allocation or to terminate the contract.

Preventive Law: Inspect Goods at Once

21.   Upon delivery of goods one should always inspect them for conformity with the contract, since the failure to do so within a reasonable time after the goods become available to the buyer can constitute an acceptance.

Preventive Law: Rejecting Goods

22.   Once goods have been properly rejected, the seller should be given notice of the defects immediately. The goods should also be clearly marked as rejected and not for sale to insure that other employees will not sell them, since a sale can constitute acceptance of goods.

Ethics Box: Duty to Perform

23.   There are basically two opposing views of the ethics regarding performance of contractual obligations. One view is that, since the law generally allows a person to choose between performance and paying the damages for breaching a contract, a person ethically can breach a contract. The opposing view is that ethically one should perform promises except in rare special circumstances, regardless of what the law may allow.

MAJOR POINTS OF CASES

T. W. Oil, Inc. v. *Consolidated Edison Co.* (p. 386)

This case illustrates the UCC rule that after a buyer has rightfully rejected nonconforming goods and notified the seller of the defects, the seller under Section 2-508[2] is allowed to cure the defects, if (1) it reasonably believed the tender would be acceptable; (2) it reasonably notified the buyer of its intent to substitute a conforming tender; and (3) the substitute tender takes place within the time of delivery in the contract or a reasonable time. The court concluded based on the evidence that the seller had met all these requirements. The buyer, thus, was required to accept the substitute tender of conforming goods, and its failure to do so was a breach of contract entitling the seller to recover its damages.

J. L. Clark Manufacturing Co. v. *Gold Bond Pharmaceutical Corp.* (p.391)

In this case, the court noted that any act by a buyer that is inconsistent with his or her rejection of the product constitutes acceptance. The court ruled that (as a matter of law,) the continued use of a rejected product constitutes acceptance, thus invalidating any rejection claims. Such continued use does not constitute acceptance only to the extent that both it is necessary for the buying business's survival and the product being used is eventually returned.

Applying this ruling to the facts of the case, the court found that in light of Gold Bond's continued use of J. L. Clark Manufacturing's product, Gold Bond's revocation of acceptance was invalidated. The court held that use on the part of Gold Bond was inconsistent with J. L. Clark's ownership of the product.

Colonial Dodge, Inc. v. *Miller* (p. 395)

The question presented in this case was whether the failure of the seller to include a spare tire with a new automobile is adequate reason for the buyer to revoke his acceptance of the vehicle. The court stated that revocation of acceptance could be made if the nonconformity of the goods "substantially impairs its value" to the buyer. Thus, even though the defect may be minor in comparison to the value of the goods, if the defect substantially reduces the value of the goods to the buyer and the other requirements for revocation are met, then the buyer is allowed to revoke the acceptance. Here, the buyer's special circumstances made a spare tire important to the value of the automobile to him personally. His position was reasonable under the circumstances, and his revocation was deemed valid.

Schumaker v. *Ivers* (p. 397)

This case illustrates the interaction of two grounds on which a buyer may revoke his or her acceptance of goods. A buyer can revoke an acceptance if (a) the goods that were delivered were defective but the defect could not be readily discovered, or (b) the goods were accepted because the buyer believed that the seller would cure a defect and the seller failed to do so.

In this case, the buyer discovered the latent defect after the organ was delivered, and agreed to give the seller an opportunity to correct the condition. After a reasonable time had passed, the buyer revoked the acceptance of the goods. The court ruled that the revocation was proper.

PRACTICAL CONSIDERATIONS

When both parties to a contract know that the goods are somewhere other than the seller's place of business or home when the contract is made, that place is the place for delivery. Many sellers will tell the buyer (who thought that the goods were at the seller's location at the time) that he or she must go elsewhere to pick up the goods. When the buyer demands that the seller deliver the goods at the present location, the seller may simply refuse to do so, notwithstanding the provision of the UCC. While the knowledgeable buyer may be able to quote the terms of the UCC to the seller, the seller may be equally knowledgeable in the ways of regretfully refusing to accommodate the buyer's demand. In such a case, the buyer must determine whether to remain firm in the face of the seller's refusal to comply or to do the pragmatic thing and pick up the goods. Often the more appropriate course of action will be to pick up the goods.

Example: Harry goes to a furniture store and selects a grandfather clock that he wishes to buy. After all the papers have been prepared and Harry has paid for the clock, he asks the salesperson to direct him to the store's loading platform so that he may put his clock in his pickup truck. The salesperson tells him to get into his truck and drive two miles east, to the company's warehouse. Harry refuses, claiming that as he hadn't been told that the clock was at the warehouse, he doesn't have to go there to get it. He demands that the clock be brought to the store.

While Harry has the right to make this demand, the more appropriate action would probably be to go to the warehouse and get the clock. By insisting on his rights, he will expend a great deal of time and energy and will probably get very frustrated and angry in the process. It is also unlikely that he will be successful in having the clock brought to him.

If, however, the clock is 250 miles away in another warehouse, then Harry may very well be acting properly in insisting that the store bring the clock to him.

A major point to remember is that common sense should prevail in this type of situation.

SELF TEST

True-False Questions

_____   1. If the contract of sale does not indicate when the goods are to be delivered and the parties have made no other agreement with respect to delivery, the seller may deliver the goods whenever he or she wants.

_____   2. The buyer has a right to inspect goods before accepting them.

_____   3. Tender of payment for goods is sufficient if it is made in a manner consistent with the demands of the seller for payment in legal tender.

_____   4. A buyer who intends to reject a nonconforming delivery of goods must do so within a reasonable time after tender of delivery.

_____   5. A buyer is always required to pay for conforming goods at the time they are tendered for delivery.

_____   6. If a seller tenders delivery of nonconforming goods and the buyer notifies him or her that the delivery is being rejected, the seller will always have the right thereafter to tender delivery of conforming goods.

_____   7. A buyer who has accepted goods delivered to him or her may not thereafter reject them.

_____   8. If goods are to be delivered to a buyer by means of the delivery of a document of title, payment is due upon tender of delivery of the goods represented by the document of title.

186

_____ 9. A nonmerchant buyer who rejects a delivery of goods must immediately return the goods directly to the seller even though the seller has given no specific directions with respect to return of the goods.

_____ 10. The revocation of an acceptance is not effective until notice of the revocation and of the defect in the goods is given to the seller.

Multiple-Choice Questions

_____ 11. Where a contract for the sale of goods makes no provision of the place of delivery, then the goods will be delivered to the:
a. buyer's residence
b. seller's place of business
c. buyer's place of business
d. buyer's warehouse
e. seller's designated agent

_____ 12. Under which of the following types of transactions must the buyer pay for the goods before he or she has an opportunity to inspect them?
a. FOB
b. COD
c. CIF
d. sale on approval
e. all of the above are correct

_____ 13. A buyer will be considered to have accepted a delivery of goods if he or she:
a. uses them in a sale on approval transaction and then returns them to the seller at the end of the trial period
b. permits them to be unloaded from the seller's truck even though the seller will not permit the goods to be examined
c. sells the goods to someone else
d. fails to make an effective rejection of the goods in a reasonable amount of time
e. a, c and d are correct

_____ 14. A buyer who rejects nonconforming goods tendered for delivery:
a. must reject the entire delivery
b. must accept the delivery if he or she can use the goods even though they are nonconforming
c. may accept the entire delivery
d. may immediately cover even though the seller has indicated an intention to cure the nonconformity
e. none of the above is correct

15. If a buyer has rejected a delivery of nonconforming nonperishable goods and the seller has given the buyer no instructions on what to do with the goods within a reasonable time, the buyer may:
    a. store the goods
    b. destroy the goods
    c. give the goods to a third person as a gift
    d. keep the goods without any obligation to pay for them
    e. give the goods to a local governmental agency

16. A buyer will be able to revoke acceptance of goods if:
    a. the buyer accepted the goods because he or she reasonably believed that the seller would cure the defect in the goods and the seller did not do so
    b. the goods cost more than $1,000
    c. the buyer did not discover a hidden defect in the goods until after he or she had accepted them
    d. a and c are both correct
    e. a, b, and c are all correct

17. Acceptance may be revoked:
    a. within a reasonable time after the buyer discovers the grounds for revocation
    b. at any time after delivery of the goods
    c. only if the buyer has previously notified the seller of his or her intention to reject the goods
    d. only if the seller has notified the buyer that he or she will not cure the defect
    e. b and d are both correct

18. A buyer may reject a nonconforming installment delivery if:
    a. the previous installment was nonconforming
    b. the nonconformity is substantial even though it can be cured
    c. the nonconformity substantially impairs the value of the installment and cannot be cured
    d. the buyer has inspected the goods and failed to notice a defect that should have been obvious
    e. b and d are both correct

19. When identified goods have been totally destroyed through no fault of either party to the contract, the:
    a. contract will be considered void
    b. contract can be canceled as long as the risk of loss has not passed to the buyer
    c. seller must provide suitable replacement goods
    d. buyer must accept substitute goods provided they are of comparable value
    e. buyer will bear the risk of loss in all cases

_____ 20. Acceptance can occur by the buyer's:
  a. express statements
  b. inaction
  c. reselling the goods
  d. a and b are both correct
  e. all of the above are correct

Completion Questions

21. After a buyer's proper rejection of goods, the seller is often entitled to _____ the defective tender of delivery.

22. A(n) _____ _____ is any unit of goods that by commercial usage is a single whole for purposes of sale and that cannot be divided without substantially impairing its character or value.

23. The term _____ refers to some action to be taken within the time provided in a contract, or within a reasonable time if no time was specified.

24. _____ _____ are those goods that in every way meet the specifications set forth in the contract for sale.

25. A(n) _____ is acknowledgment by a buyer that he or she has received the goods and will keep them.

Chapter 23

SALES: REMEDIES

This chapter addresses the crucial issues of what remedies are available to buyers and sellers in sale-of-goods contracts under Article 2 of the Uniform Commercial Code. First, however, this chapter examines the statute of limitations for sale-of-goods contracts, which establishes the period of time within which a lawsuit must be filed to enforce rights. Next, the sellers' primary remedy of resale, together with other available remedies, is explained. The buyer's primary remedy is to enter into a cover contract for substitute goods. Buyers, though, have other remedies available for circumstances when a cover contract is inappropriate. Finally, it is noted that the parties can limit or alter the remedies provided by Article 2 of the UCC.

The coverage of this chapter is crucial to understanding sale-of-goods contracts. The ability to enforce sales contracts and obtain an appropriate remedy gives ultimate legal and practical significance to contracts. In studying the remedies available to buyers and sellers, it may be helpful in keeping them separate to think about which party breached the contract, where the goods are, and what is needed to place the nonbreaching party in the position that would have been attained had there been full performance.

CHAPTER OBJECTIVES

After reading Chapter 23 of the text and studying the related materials in this chapter of the Student Mastery Guide, you will understand:

1. The Statute of Limitations for sale-of-goods contracts under Article 2 of the UCC.
2. The remedies available to the seller for breach of a sale-of-goods contract, including:
   a. resell the goods and recover damages
   b. recover damages
   c. recover the purchase price
   d. withhold delivery
   e. stop delivery
   f. cancel the contract
3. The remedies available to the buyer for breach of a sale-of-goods contract, including:
   a. cover
   b. cancel the contract and recover damages
   c. recover damages
   d. specific performance or replevin
   e. resell the goods
4. The rights of the parties to limit or alter remedies provided by Article 2 of the UCC.

MAJOR POINTS TO REMEMBER

Statute of Limitations

1. If the parties have by agreement reduced the time period to not less than one year in which to file a lawsuit to enforce a contract for the sale of goods, this reduction is binding

on them. If there is no such agreement, a party has four years within which to bring suit to enforce a sale-of-goods contract.

2.   Generally, the four-year statute of limitations begins to run on the date of the breach of contract. However, the time period for a breach of warranty starts from the tender of delivery, unless the warranty expressly extends to future performance and discovery of defects must await future performance, in which case the period begins when the breach is or should have been discovered.

Seller's Remedies

3.   Upon breach of a sale-of-goods contract by a buyer, the seller has several remedies available from which to elect or combine in order to achieve the UCC's primary purpose of placing the nonbreaching party in the position that would have resulted had there been no breach of contract.

4.   Among the remedies available to the seller are:
    a.   resell the goods and recover damages
    b.   recover damages for nonacceptance
    c.   recover the price
    d.   withhold delivery of the goods
    e.   stop delivery of the goods held by a bailee
    f.   cancel the contract
    g.   with respect to unfinished goods, stop work on them and sell them for scrap value

5.   The primary seller remedy is to resell the goods in good faith and in a commercially reasonably manner and sue to recover any damages. The recoverable damages are the contract price minus the resale price, plus incidental damages, and minus expenses saved due to the buyer's breach.
        The resale may be by private or public sale, whichever is commercially reasonable. The seller need only give the buyer notice of intent to sell privately, but for a public sale the notice must state the time and place of a public sale unless the goods are perishable or likely to decline rapidly in value. Both the buyer and seller can bid at the public sale.

6.   When the seller does not resell the goods, the measure of the recoverable monetary damages is the market place at the time and place for tender minus the unpaid contract price, plus incidental damages and minus expenses saved due to the buyer's breach.

7.   If the above formula for damages is insufficient to place the seller in the position that would have been attained with full performance, the seller can recover the profits (including overhead) from the sale plus incidental damages. This measure would be appropriate in the case of a lost-volume seller.

8.   The seller can recover the price in the following circumstances:
    a.   resale is impracticable
    b.   the goods were lost or stolen within a commercially reasonable time after the risk of loss has passed to the buyer

191

9. The right to collect damages means little if the buyer is insolvent. In such cases the seller:
   a. can withhold delivery, if the seller is still in possession, unless the buyer pays in cash all that is owed to the seller
   b. has ten days to demand them back from a buyer who took them on credit while being insolvent, but the ten-day rule will not apply if the buyer had in writing misrepresented its solvency within three months.
   c. can stop delivery by a carrier or bailee to the buyer (but if the buyer is not insolvent, the seller can stop delivery only for full-carload shipments) until the buyer receives the goods, documents of title are negotiated to the buyer, or the buyer receives notice from the carrier or bailee that the goods are available for the buyer

Buyer's Remedies

10. If a seller breaches the contract of sale by failure to deliver or by repudiation, or if the buyer rightfully rejects the goods or revokes his or her acceptance of them, the buyer may:
    a. cancel the contract and recover the consideration given to the seller
    b. cover (UCC Section 2-712)
    c. recover damages (UCC Section 2-713)
    d. gain possession of goods identified to the contract (UCC Section 2-716)
    e. resell the goods in the buyer's possession

11. A primary remedy for a buyer is to cover by purchasing substitute goods. If the cover is done in good faith and without unreasonable delay, the measure of damages will be the cover price minus the contract price, plus incidental or consequential damages, and minus any expenses saved by the seller's breach.
    a. Included in incidental damages are "any commercially reasonable charges, expenses or commissions in connection with effecting cover."
    b. Consequential damages include those the seller had reason to know of at the time of contracting and that could not have been prevented. A party can by contract limit or exclude liability for consequential damages except those for injury to a person.

12. Damages can be established by cover. However, the buyer can also establish its damages without reference to cover prices. This measure is the market price at the time the buyer learned of the breach minus the contract price, plus any incidental and consequential damages, and minus expenses saved. Market price is the price in the place the buyer would have effected a cover.

13. When goods are accepted and it is too late to revoke, but they do not conform to the applicable warranty, the buyer can recover the difference between the actual value of the goods and the value they would have had if they were as warranted, plus incidental and consequential damages.

14.   Specific performance is allowed when goods are unique or in other proper circumstances, such as when cover is not possible.

15.   When goods have been identified to the contract and the buyer cannot reasonably cover, the buyer has a right to replevin for the goods themselves.

16.   When the buyer is in possession of the goods after a proper rejection or revocation, and it has paid at least part of the price or incurred expenses in regard to the goods, then it has a security interest in the goods and can sell them to recover its damages.

17.   Reasonable liquidated damage clauses in contracts governed by the UCC will be enforced by the courts.

Limitation or Alteration of Remedies

18.   The parties can by agreement limit or alter the remedies provided under Article 2 of the UCC. However, a court can refuse to enforce such an agreement if it finds the terms to be unconscionable or to deprive either party of the substantial value of the bargain.

Preventive Law: Cover

19.   For buyers who do not receive contracted goods, the right to cover is often essential to the short-run continuation of their business operations. If they have to pay a higher price than the contract price, then the difference can be recovered as damages.

Issues and Trends: Computer Law - Limitations of Remedies

20.   Many computer software programs are sold with limited warranties and clauses excluding consequential damages. Since losses from software failure can be very large, buyers of computer software should carefully check the terms of the purchase contract in regard to their rights in the event the software fails to perform properly.

MAJOR POINTS OF CASES

Madsen v. Murrey & Sons Company, Inc. (p. 407)

In this case, the court deals with the appropriate determination of damages in the event that there is a nonacceptance or repudiation in a contract between a buyer and a seller. The court held that the seller must attempt to mitigate its damages due to the nonacceptance in the appropriate market, assuming that such a market exists. The seller is then entitled to the contract price minus the value received in the market for damages. In the event that the seller does not go to a market for the nonaccepted good, the buyer is entitled to the market value of the product if he or she paid for its manufacture.

Applying these holdings to the case, the court affirmed the trial court's judgement in favor of the buyer but discounted his damages. The Supreme Court of Utah found that the trial court had taken into consideration only the guidelines pertaining to the buyer in awarding damages. By factoring in the seller's entitlements and subtracting them from the damages award, the Supreme Court reduced the buyer's pecuniary award from $21,250 to $8,750.

Bill's Coal Co., Inc. v. *Board of Public Utilities of Springfield* (p. 409)

Noting that the normal award for a breach of contract is determined by the difference between the market and the contract price of the contract, the court held that sellers are only entitled to lost profits damages if they are a lost volume seller, a condition which the seller has the burden of proving.

Reviewing the evidence presented in this case, the court found that Bill's Coal Co. could scarcely fulfill the contract in question, let alone contract with a third party as well. In light of this finding, the court ruled that Bill's Coal Co. was not a lost volume seller and, therefore, was entitled only to normal damages.

Allied Canners & Packers v. *Victor Packing Co. of California* (p. 413)

In this case the court limited the buyer's damages to its actual economic loss rather than the higher amount that would have resulted from the application of the market-price formula. This interpretation was arrived at because the buyer had not covered, the buyer was not going to be held liable for breach of contract with its customers, and the seller had not acted in bad faith. Under these circumstances the buyer is placed in the same position as if the seller had fully performed by awarding damages equal to its actual economic loss.

PRACTICAL CONSIDERATIONS

Whether one is the buyer or seller of goods when the other party breaches, a rather confusing array of remedies is available. To help sort them out for the purpose of determining the most appropriate remedy or combination of remedies, it can be helpful to ask these questions:

1. Where are the goods at the time of the breach?
2. What is needed to put you in the position that was reasonably expected to be attained if the other party performed fully?
3. What are the circumstances of the breaching party that may limit the effectiveness of a particular remedy?

Since there are uncertainties with the application of some remedies and the breaching party's circumstances can limit their practical effectiveness, the parties to a sale-of-goods contract should consider the impact of a breach at the time of contracting. One should remember that, as is generally true, the parties can by their agreement alter the provisions of Article 2 of the UCC. In regard to remedies, the parties should consider whether to reduce the statute of limitation, provide for liquidated damages, or exclude, limit, or alter the remedies available. Finally, the parties should explicitly state any special circumstances that will increase their damages in the event of a breach that the other party would not reasonably foresee in order to preserve the right to collect those damages.

SELF TEST

True-False Questions

_____ 1. The primary purpose of the remedies under Article 2 of the UCC is to punish the breaching party.

_____ 2. Under Article 2 of the UCC, the statute of limitations in all cases starts to run from the time that a breach of contract actually occurs.

_____ 3. The parties to a sale-of-goods contract can by agreement reduce the statute of limitations to a period of not less than one year.

_____ 4. Under Article 2 of the UCC a seller is not necessarily required to pick one remedy to the exclusion of all others.

_____ 5. If a seller elects to resell goods after a buyer's breach, the seller is not entitled to also recover its costs or damages from the buyer.

_____ 6. If a seller elects upon a buyer's breach to resell the goods, but waits a commercially unreasonable length of time to do so, then the resale price will have little relevance in establishing the seller's damages.

_____ 7. A seller is not ever entitled to recover its goods after they are in the possession of the buyer.

_____ 8. A buyer who upon a seller's breach enters into a cover contract for substitute goods has no other additional remedies against the seller.

_____ 9. Under proper circumstances a buyer can "cover" by manufacturing goods itself in substitution for those that the seller was supposed to have delivered.

_____ 10. Liquidated damages in a sale-of-goods contract are always enforceable.

Multiple-Choice Questions

_____ 11. When the buyer has breached the contract of sale, the seller will be justified in:
   a. canceling the contract
   b. withholding delivery of the goods
   c. reselling the goods and bringing suit to recover damages
   d. stopping delivery of the goods by a carrier
   e. all of the above are correct

_____   12. The parties to a sale-of-goods contract can by agreement limit or alter the remedies provided by Article 2 of the UCC, except:
    a. if such an agreement is unconscionable
    b. if to do so would deprive either party of a substantial value of the bargain
    c. exclusions of liability for personal injuries
    d. b and c are both correct
    e. all of the above are correct

_____   13. Replevin is a remedy that can be available to a buyer upon the seller's failure to deliver goods as promised when:
    a. the goods are identified to the contract
    b. a cover contract for substitute goods is not reasonably available
    c. liquidated damages are greater than the price of the goods
    d. only a and b are correct
    e. only b and c are correct

_____   14. The buyer has accepted goods and cannot now revoke. However, the goods turn out to be in breach of warranty. The buyer is entitled to damages measured by:
    a. the purchase price
    b. the difference between the value of the goods if they had been as promised and their actual value
    c. the difference between the market price and the contract price
    d. the difference between the contract price and the cover price
    e. either a or c is correct

_____   15. A breach of sale-of-goods contract has occurred. Normally, under Article 2 of the UCC the nonbreaching party must bring a lawsuit:
    a. within one year of the breach
    b. within two years of the breach
    c. within four years after the cause of action has occurred
    d. within thirty days after learning of the breach
    e. none of the above is correct

_____   16. The statute of limitations for a breach of a sale-of-goods contract under Article 2 of the UCC begins to run from the time that the breach should have been discovered, if the breach is one of a:
    a. prospective warranty
    b. normal warranty
    c. limited warranty
    d. full warranty
    e. repair warranty

_____ 17. If a seller chooses to resell goods in a timely and commercially reasonable manner, it can:
   a. do so by private sale
   b. do so by public sale
   c. also recover incidental damages
   d. use the resale price to measure its damages
   e. all of the above are correct

_____ 18. The seller should recover its profits, including overhead, plus incidental damages, if it can show that the resale of goods:
   a. cost it a sale that would have otherwise been made
   b. was commercially reasonable
   c. was timely
   d. was impossible or impractical
   e. was for less than the contract price

_____ 19. To recover goods in the possession of the buyer, the seller must show that:
   a. the buyer was insolvent when it took possession
   b. the seller demanded return within ten days of the buyer taking possession
   c. the buyer committed fraud
   d. all of the above are correct
   e. only a and b are correct

_____ 20. A buyer's right to recover damages:
   a. is always based on the market price
   b. is sometimes limited to its actual economic loss
   c. is limited to incidental damages when a cover contract has been made
   d. is only based on its proven consequential damages
   e. none of the above is correct

Completion Questions

21. The remedy of _____ will allow the buyer to purchase in good faith goods in substitution for those that a seller failed to deliver under their contract for sale.

22. Those damages that are collaterally incurred by a person in connection with a particular transaction are referred to as _____ damages.

23. _____ damages are those incurred in connection with effecting a proper rejection, revocation of acceptance, or cover contract.

24. A _____ warranty is one that explicitly extends to the future performance of goods.

25.   The remedy of _____ _____ requires the seller to fulfill its contractual obligations by delivering goods that conform to the contract.

Chapter 24

WARRANTIES

While the concept of "caveat emptor" still lives, Article 2 of the Uniform Commercial Code has imposed an obligation upon those persons who provide goods to the public to insure that the goods will function effectively and perform in the manner in which they were intended and do so in a safe way. Article 2, however, has also provided such sellers with the necessary mechanism by which they can limit or even exclude their responsibility for products that they are selling on the commercial market or elsewhere.

This chapter considers the rules that affect the representations (usually referred to as warranties) that a seller makes to a buyer when the buyer purchases a product. It considers the nature of a warranty, the various types of warranties that exist, who is covered by a warranty, the manner in which a seller can limit or insulate him or herself from liability with respect to the applicable warranties, and various other considerations.

In a society in which the buyer as well as the product being purchased is becoming more sophisticated, the materials discussed in this chapter are of extraordinary importance.

CHAPTER OBJECTIVES

After reading Chapter 24 of the text and studying the related materials in this chapter of the Student Mastery Guide, you will understand:

1. The nature and extent of warranty liability
2. The different types of warranties
   a. express warranties
   b. implied warranties
3. Exclusion or modification of warranties
4. The nature and extent of claims for personal injury based on warranty liability

MAJOR POINTS TO REMEMBER

Types of Warranties

1. Warranties in connection with the sale of goods under Article 2 of the Uniform Commercial Code can be categorized as an:
   a. express warranty
   b. implied warranty

2. The implied warranties provided for by the Uniform Commercial Code are:
   a. implied warranty of title (UCC Section 2-312)
   b. implied warranty of merchantability (UCC Section 2-314)
   c. implied warranty of fitness for a particular purpose (UCC Section 2-315)

Express Warranties

3.   An express warranty consists of any specific representations with regard to the goods being sold. Express warranties can be created by:

     a.   an affirmative expression or statement of fact that becomes a part of the basis of the bargain

     b.   a description of the goods that becomes a part of the basis of the bargain

     c.   a sample or model that is identified as the same type to be delivered under the sale and that becomes part of the basis of the bargain.

4.   "Puffing" does not create an express warranty.

Implied Warranty of Title

5.   Under the Uniform Commercial Code, when selling goods, the seller impliedly warrants and represents that he or she:

     a.   is the owner of the property and has the right to transfer it, and

     b.   is transferring the goods free of any liens or encumbrances of which the buyer is not aware when entering into the contract (UCC Section 2-312[1]).

     These representations do not apply, however, if the buyer has reason to know that the seller is not the owner of the property.

     Any interference with the purchaser's use of the product sold because of questions concerning the warranty of title breaches this warranty.

Implied Warranty of Merchantability

6.   The implied warranty of merchantability relates to the quality of the goods being sold and provides that the goods shall be merchantable. The main standard followed by the courts in determining whether the goods are merchantable is whether they are "fit for the ordinary purpose for which such goods are normally used."

7.   Relative to the question of food or drink, UCC Section 2-314[1] provides that the service "for value [emphasis added] of food or drink to be consumed either on the premises or elsewhere is a sale." This means that when a person goes to a restaurant and has a four-course meal served to him or her, there has been a sale of the food and a warranty given that the food is merchantable.

8.   Section 2-314[2] of the Uniform Commercial Code identifies some of the conditions under which goods will be considered to be merchantable.

9.   The implied warranty of merchantability will be implied in a sale only when the seller is a merchant with respect to the goods being sold. A nonmerchant does not impliedly warrant that the goods being sold are merchantable.

Implied Warranty of Fitness for a Particular Purpose

10. When goods are sold, the seller may impliedly warrant or represent that the goods are fit for the particular purpose for which they are intended. However, in order for the warranty to attach to a sale under UCC Section 2-315, it must be shown that:
    a. the seller had reason to know the particular purpose for which the goods are intended, and
    b. the seller had reason to know that the buyer was relying on his skill or judgment in selecting or furnishing suitable goods.

11. In order for the implied warranty of fitness for a particular purpose to be made, the seller does not need to be a merchant with respect to those goods. A nonmerchant seller can impliedly represent that the goods being sold are fit for the particular purpose for which they are intended.

Exclusion of Warranties

12. A seller may attempt to exclude all warranties that attach to a sale. However, in doing so the seller must follow the provisions of the Uniform Commercial Code.
    a. Express warranties - they are disclaimed by any language or conduct which clearly indicates to the buyer that the product is being sold without the warranty (UCC Section 2-316[1]).
       If there is a conflict between any express warranty given and any disclaimer, the disclaimer generally will not be enforced.
    b. Implied warranty of title - excluded or disclaimed by specific language or conduct which informs the buyer that the seller does not claim to be the owner of the property. Also, this warranty is excluded by circumstances which give the buyer reason to know that the seller is not the owner.
    c. Implied warranty of merchantability - in order to disclaim this warranty:
       i. the language used must specifically refer to the term "merchantability"
       ii. the disclaimer may be made verbally or in writing. If the warranty is disclaimed in writing, however, it must be done conspicuously (UCC Section 2-312[2]).
    d. Implied warranty of fitness for a particular purpose - to disclaim this warranty:
       i. no specific language needs to be used
       ii. the disclaimer must be made in writing and must be conspicuous (UCC Section 2-316[2]).
    e. All implied warranties can be excluded or disclaimed by using phrases such as "as is", "with all faults," or any other language that calls the buyer's attention to the fact that there are no implied warranties being made (UCC Section 2-316[3]).
    f. Implied warranties can also be excluded or modified by:
       i. examination or inspection of the goods
       ii. course of dealings
       iii. course of performance
       iv. usage of trade (UCC Section 2-316[3](b))

Federal Trade Commission Warranty Rules

13. Magnuson-Moss Warranty - Federal Trade Commission Act
    a. Purpose - to give consumers opportunity to get knowledge, before a purchase, of the nature of any applicable warranties, and also to provide effective enforcement of the warranties.
    b. Scope - the act applies to any consumer product containing a written warranty. The act covers service contracts and consumer products costing $15.00 or more.
    c. Enforcement - the act can be enforced by the Federal Trade Commission, the U.S. Attorney General, or by a private party.
    d. Extent of warranty - if a consumer product costs over $10.00 and the seller provides a written warranty, the product must be labeled either a full warranty or a limited warranty. If it is a limited warranty, the product must be conspicuously labeled to reflect this.
    e. Disclaimer - the act prohibits disclaimer or modification of implied warranties under certain conditions.

Warranties and Personal-Injury Claims

14. Persons are generally allowed to sue for personal injuries caused by goods that are defective in breach of the warranty covering the goods. Privity of contract (which means a direct contractual relationship) need not be established in many states today in order to recover damages for injuries caused by breach of warranty. Under UCC Section 2-318 the states were allowed to adopt one of three alternatives.
    a. Alternative A allows the buyer's family members, household members, or guests to sue for personal injuries caused by a breach of warranty, if it was reasonable to expect that they would use, consume, or be affected by the product.
    b. Alternative B is similar to Alternative A, except that any natural person who it was reasonable to expect to be affected by goods is protected by a warranty.
    c. Alternative C expands the warranty protection to all natural and artificial persons (i.e., corporations).

15. Most states now allow manufacturers and wholesalers to be sued directly for breach of warranty by persons not in privity of contract with them.

16. Under UCC Section 2-607[3], in order for a buyer to be allowed to sue for breach of warranty, he or she must have given notice of the breach within a reasonable time after the breach was discovered or should have been discovered to every party who is a defendant in the lawsuit.

Ethics Box: Disclaimers

17. Historically, express written warranties have presented legal and ethical problems relating to how they are disclosed. Although normally persons are deemed to have agreed to terms in a written contract that they have signed, courts recently have tended to refuse to enforce disclaimers of warranties that are buried in fine print and coupled with other

statements that seemingly give warranty protection, particularly when the terms are not negotiated and the party with superior bargaining power did not explain the meaning of such clauses. It violates professional business ethics to intentionally use misleading contractual provisions. In addition, it violates the ethical duty of good faith for a party with superior knowledge to not inform the other party in such cases.

Issues and Trends: Federal Trade Commission Used-Car Rule

18. Used-car dealers are now required by the FTC to place in the windows of used cars stickers stating any warranties given, or that the car is being sold "as is" with the buyer responsible for any necessary repairs. The sticker must urge buyers to get an independent vehicle inspection and to have any oral promises placed in writing.

MAJOR POINTS OF CASES

Whitmer v. Schneble v. *House of Hoyt, Inc.* (p. 423)

This case applies the general rule that sales "puffing" will not constitute an express warranty. Further, it indicates that an express warranty in a contract can negate a conflicting prior oral express warranty. This case also states that an implied warranty will not be inferred from an express warranty when the alleged implied warranty runs counter to common sense. Finally, the court held that for an express warranty to be a prospective one it must be explicitly stated.

The buyers' claim in this case that the seller warranted the Doberman Pinscher dog they purchased to be a "docile dobe" was dismissed. The court found this statement to be puffing, in conflict with the written express warranty, and not a promise that the dog would never bite.

Interco, Inc. v. *Randustrial Corp.* (p. 424)

The Interco case discusses the meaning of Section 2-313 of the Uniform Commercial Code. Any affirmative statement of fact regarding the nature, condition, or quality of the goods being sold constitutes an express warranty. The court also holds that an advertisement in a catalogue or brochure can constitute an express warranty, provided that such a statement was a part of the basis of the bargain.

The court found the statement "Sylox will absorb considerable flex" to be a statement of fact on which the buyer could rely. However, the court ruled for Randustrial because the issue of whether Sylox would absorb considerable flex was a jury question. Inasmuch as the jury, after trial, found for Randustrial, it apparently thought that Sylox would absorb considerable flex.

Gates v. *Abernathy* (p. 427)

This principal concept illustrated by this case is that where a buyer, in purchasing a product, relies on the expertise of the seller in selecting the proper goods, and where the seller has reason to know what the product will be used for, the seller impliedly warrants

203

and represents that the product is fit for the particular purpose for which it was intended. The court relied on Section 2-315 of the Uniform Commercial Code in reaching its decision that the seller had breached this warranty by selecting clothes that were to be the correct size for the buyer's wife, but which in fact did not fit her.

Tarulli v. Birds in Paradise (p. 432)

The decision in the Tarulli case shows that if a purchaser is given the opportunity to examine or inspect the goods being sold, or a model or sample of such goods, the buyer accepts those goods in the condition they are in at the time of delivery, subject to whatever condition the examination or inspection revealed or should have revealed, and also subject to any latent conditions that could not have been discovered upon an examination. If the purchaser refuses or fails to inspect the goods, he also takes them subject to whatever condition such inspection would have disclosed. In order for this rule to apply, however, the seller must make a demand upon the buyer to inspect the goods.

Ismael v. Goodman Toyota (p. 436)

This case deals with the scope and meaning of the Magnuson-Moss Warranty Act. To receive damages under this Act, the court held that the plaintiff must demonstrate that she or he was damaged by the defendant's non-compliance to the contract obligation. Furthermore, as a general rule, "as is" purchases exclude the implied warranty of merchantability and, thus, are not protected by the Act. However, service contracts made within 90 days prohibit suppliers from disclaiming their contract obligations.

Applying this holding to the facts of the case, the court reversed the trial court's judgement and found in favor of Ismael. The plaintiff's damages were obvious in light of the limited mobility of the car. Additionally, despite the fact that the plaintiff purchased the car in "as is" condition, the service contract between the two parties prohibited the defendant from disclaiming responsibility.

PRACTICAL CONSIDERATIONS

1. If a purchaser notices that the contract of sale with the dealership contains a clause disclaiming the liability of the dealership for a breach of warranty, the purchaser should discuss this with the dealer and try to eliminate it from the contract. The fact that such a clause is contained in a contract does not require that it remain there.

    Example: A buyer seeks to purchase a new car. When signing the purchase agreement with the auto dealership, the buyer notices a disclaimer provision attempting to disclaim the liability of the dealership for all warranties except those expressly made to the buyer. The buyer may ask the seller to strike the provision from the agreement before the buyer signs it. The extent of the seller's reluctance to do so and the strength of the buyer's desire to procure the car should then determine how strenuously the buyer should pursue his or her position.

2. If a buyer is discussing the purchase of an item and senses that there may be some question as to the validity of the rights of the present owner, the buyer should make a

complete investigation to make sure that the seller is, in fact, the owner of the property. If the buyer purchases the property with out such an investigation, the buyer may lose the property at a later date if the seller was not the owner of it.

Example: A agrees to sell B a one-year-old Cadillac for $1,500. The car is in perfect condition and has 6,000 original miles of use on it. B agrees to buy the car.

B should be aware that the price of the car is so low that it is possible that the car was stolen or that A was not in fact the owner even though he had the right to be using it. An investigation of the title to the car might have disclosed who the owner was and what liens, if any, existed on the car. What will actually be discovered depends on the state in which the transaction occurred.

3.   Many breach-of-warranty situations, although legitimate, do not result in lawsuits because the damages sustained do not justify the expenses involved with the litigation. Therefore, before a person who has been injured or who has sustained damages due to the breach of a warranty begins a lawsuit, that person should determine whether the results will justify the expenses that will necessarily be incurred.

Example: A buys a piece of meat at her butcher's store. After cooking the meat, she begins eating it and in so doing bites into a piece of metal. Luckily, the only injury sustained by A is the mental discomfort of knowing that she had bitten into the metal. No actual physical injuries are sustained.

While a breach of warranty has undoubtedly occurred, the resulting injuries may not be considered serious enough to justify the expenses of a lawsuit. A will have to weigh the various factors and make a decision whether or not to sue.

SELF TEST

True-False Questions

_____   1.   A statement indicating that "this is the best car that this dealership currently has on its lot" constitutes an express warranty.

_____   2.   A person selling a surfboard to another indicates that the seller owns the surfboard even though nothing has been said to the buyer about such a fact.

_____   3.   When an accountant sells his or her car to another person, it is impliedly warranted that the car is merchantable.

_____   4.   The display of a sample or model that is described as being the same type of goods that will be delivered to the purchaser gives rise to an express warranty with respect to those goods.

_____   5.   When an uncle, who is a jeweler, gives his niece a watch as a birthday gift, the uncle impliedly warrants that the watch is fit for the purpose for which it was intended.

_____ 6. In order for a person to succeed in an action based on breach of implied warranty, that person must show that he or she was a party to the contract of sale.

_____ 7. A seller may not disclaim his or her liability for breach of warranty with respect to an express warranty.

_____ 8. All implied warranties can be disclaimed by the use of the term "as is."

_____ 9. The Magnuson-Moss Warranty Act applies to the sale of any and all consumer products.

_____ 10. The Magnuson-Moss Warranty Act can be enforced by the Federal Trade Commission.

Multiple-Choice Questions

_____ 11. An express warranty can be created by:
a. the buyer
b. a description of the goods that becomes a part of the basis of the bargain
c. puffing
d. all of the above
e. only b and c are correct

_____ 12. When a seller conveys goods to another person, there is an implied warranty that:
a. there have been no prior owners of the goods
b. the seller is currently in possession of the goods
c. the seller is transferring the goods free of any liens of which the buyer is not aware at the time of the contracting
d. all of the above
e. only a and b are correct

_____ 13. In order for a person to establish that there was an implied warranty of fitness for a particular purpose when goods were conveyed to that person, he or she must show that:
a. there was a sale
b. the seller had reason to know that the buyer was relying on his or her skill to provide proper goods
c. the seller had reason to know the particular purpose for which the goods were intended
d. all of the above
e. only a and c are required to be shown

14. In order for a seller to disclaim his or her responsibility for the implied warranty of merchantability, the disclaimer:
    a. must be in writing
    b. must be made verbally
    c. must specifically refer to merchantability
    d. may consist of any language indicating a disclaimer of liability
    e. b and d are both correct

15. All implied warranties can be excluded in a sale by:
    a. course of performance
    b. course of dealings
    c. usage of trade
    d. a and b are both correct
    e. a, b, and c are all correct

16. Persons to whom the implied warranty of fitness for a particular purpose extends (assume that the state has adopted Alternative A of UCC Section 2-318) include:
    a. an aunt of the purchaser who lives alone in Italy
    b. the purchaser's daughter who resides in the same house
    c. the purchaser's wife who is divorced from him and is living separately
    d. all of the above
    e. only a and b are correct

17. The implied warranty of merchantability applies to:
    a. a meal that is served at a restaurant
    b. a merchant who gives his nephew a hammer as a gift for his eighteenth birthday
    c. sales made by nonmerchant sellers
    d. all sales of goods
    e. a and b are both correct

18. In order for a seller to disclaim liability for the implied warranty of fitness for a particular purpose:
    a. no specific language is required to be used
    b. the disclaimer must be made verbally
    c. the disclaimer must be contained in all written documents
    d. the disclaimer need not be conspicuous if it is in writing
    e. b and d are both correct

_____ 19. The Magnuson-Moss Warranty - Federal Trade Commission Act can be enforced by:
   a. the governor of the state in which the goods are sold
   b. the state prosecutor
   c. the attorney general of the United States
   d. the Federal Communications Commission
   e. c and d are both correct

_____ 20. Where a sale of a product contains several warranties in conflict with each other:
   a. a sample from an existing bulk displaces inconsistent general language of description
   b. exact specifications will displace an inconsistent sample or general language of description
   c. express warranties will displace implied warranties other than an implied warranty of fitness for a particular purpose
   d. all of the above
   e. only a and c are correct

Completion Questions

21. An expression of opinion or an ordinary sales talk given by a seller in order to make a product more attractive is referred to as _____.

22. A direct relationship between parties as a result of a contract is known as _____ _____ _____.

23. A warranty created by operation of law and not as a result of anything stated or written by the seller of goods is referred to as a(n) _____ _____.

24. An undertaking by a seller to guarantee a product against defects is called a(n) _____ _____.

25. The implied warranty under which a seller represents that the goods being sold are conveyed free of all liens or encumbrances of which the buyer is not aware at the time of contracting is the implied warranty of _____.

Chapter 25

PRODUCT LIABILITY

Product liability refers to the liability of manufacturers and other sellers for injury caused by defects in their products. In most instances, we as consumers expect the products we purchase to be safe for use. However, if the product is defective, and as a result of the defect the purchaser is injured, the injured party may be able to recover damages.

The legal theories encompassed by product liability have been explored in preceding chapters. Chapter 10 reviews negligence, strict liability, and misrepresentation in the context of product liability and presents various defenses.

Unless you are paying close attention to the differences between strict liability and negligence you may find the concepts confusing. Keep in mind that negligence evaluates the conduct of a manufacturer, retailer, or wholesaler, whereas strict liability focuses entirely on the condition of the product.

CHAPTER OBJECTIVES

After reading Chapter 25 of the text and studying the materials presented in this chapter of the Student Mastery Guide, you will understand:

1. Three legal theories encompassed by product liability:
   a. negligence
   b. strict liability
   c. misrepresentation
2. The various defenses to product liability and the legal theory to which each apply:
   a. contributory or comparative negligence
   b. assumption of risk
   c. obvious danger
   d. abnormal use
   e. product changed condition substantially after leaving seller's hands
   f. puffing
   g. no reliance

MAJOR POINTS TO REMEMBER

Negligence

1. In order to establish a primia facie case for negligence, the plaintiff must establish: (review of Chapter 7)
   a. the defendant owed a duty to the plaintiff
   b. the defendant breached that duty by failing to exercise that degree of care a prudent person would have exercised under the circumstances
   c. the defendant's breach of duty caused an *injury* to the plaintiff
   d. the defendant's breach of duty was the *proximate cause* of the plaintiff's injury

Negligence of Manufacturers

2.   A manufacturer can be held liable for injuries to the purchaser that result from the manufacturer's failure to exercise reasonable care in assembling the product.

3.   A manufacturer can be held liable for injuries caused by a product that is defective because of poor design. Reasonable care in the adoption of a safe design is required of the manufacturer.

4.   The manufacturer generally must exercise due care to make certain a product placed on the market is safe. This includes reasonable tests and inspections to discover present or latent defects in the product.

5.   Sometimes the manufacturer has a duty to warn the public of the potential danger of a product.
      a.   a manufacturer must not only warn people of dangers associated with the proper use of the product, but also must warn purchasers of the foreseeable dangers associated with the misuse of the product.
      b.   if the danger of the product is not likely to be discovered by persons using the product (the danger is latent) a duty to warn exists.
      c.   a warning must be clear and intelligible.

6.   A manufacturer generally must make reasonable tests and inspections to discover latent defects in parts supplied by other companies to protect itself from liability.

7.   As the retailer actually has very little control over the product's design or assembly the retailer is not usually considered negligent for injuries sustained in use of a defective product. (see, however, the discussion of strict liability)

8.   Normally a retailer does not need to inspect or test the item sold if he or she neither knows nor has reason to know the product is dangerous. However, if the retailer should have known that the product was dangerous and could have inspected or tested the item, he or she may be liable.

9.   If the retailer advertises, labels, or packages a product in such a fashion that it appears that the retailer is the manufacturer, the retailer will be held to the same standards as the manufacturer.

Defenses Available in Negligence Cases

10.   Contributory negligence is a defense that says a person who is injured by a defective product but (a) did not employ the standard of care that a reasonably prudent person would use to protect his or her own safety and (b) contributed to his or her own injuries cannot recover from the defendant.

11. Many states have replaced the doctrine of contributory negligence with that of comparative negligence. In comparative negligence doctrine the court or jury weighs the relative negligence of the parties and reduces the amount of recovery in proportion to the plaintiff's negligence.

12. Assumption of risk is a defense in which the defendant must prove the plaintiff acted voluntarily with full knowledge and appreciation of the risk involved.

13. Some courts have denied relief to the plaintiff because the danger presented to the plaintiff was obvious or the plaintiff made an abnormal use of the product.

Strict Liability

14. Even if the seller exercises reasonable care and has not been proved negligent he or she may be liable for injuries caused by defective products if the following conditions apply.
    a. The defendant is in the business of selling the product.
    b. The product was expected to and in fact reached the injured party without substantial change in the condition in which it was sold.
    c. The product was in a defective condition.
    d. This defective condition rendered the product unreasonably dangerous to the user or consumer of his or her property.
    e. There was a causal relationship between the defect and the damage done to the plaintiff.
    f. This resulted in physical harm to his or her person or property.

15. In Section 402A the word "seller" applies to those in the business of selling the product: the manufacturer, the retailer, and any intermediate wholesaler or distributor.

Defenses Available in Strict Liability Cases

16. Two defenses in a strict liability suit are:
    a. assumption of risk
    b. product changed condition substantially after leaving the seller's hands.

Innocent Misrepresentation

17. When a seller misrepresents its product, and a buyer relies upon the misrepresentation, the buyer who is injured by the product may have a cause of action. Note that the seller may be held liable under *Restatement of Torts, Second*, Section 402B even if the misrepresentation is not made fraudulently.

Defenses Available in Innocent Misrepresentation Cases

18. Section 402B states that the misrepresented fact on which the plaintiff relied in making his or her purchase must be a *material one*. A defendant may assert that the fact was not material but a mere opinion or general praise referred to as puffing.

211

19.   The buyer must prove that the misrepresentation was of a material fact and he or she justifiably relied on the misrepresentation when making their purchase. If the buyer was unaware of the misrepresentation, or indifferent to it, or if the statement did not influence his or her purchase or subsequent conduct, the buyer may not recover.

MAJOR POINTS OF CASES

Richmond, Fredericksburg and Potomac Railroad Co. v. *Carrier Corporation Industries, Inc.* (p. 443)

This case illustrates the breadth of the manufacturers' duty to warn. In this case, the court held that the duty to warn extends beyond a mere duty to warn of foreseeable dangers arising from use of the product. A manufacturer must warn of known dangers that could possibly arise from the release of hazardous substance in the storage or handling of a product. However, the manufacturer has no duty to warn of the possible release of hazardous substances as a result of the destruction of the product for recycling purposes because this destruction is an unforeseeable alteration of the product.

McElyea v. *Navistar International Transportation Corp.* (p. 446)

This case illustrates the interaction of two doctrines used in product liability cases: the crashworthiness doctrine and the doctrine of avoidable consequences. In a crashworthiness case, the plaintiff must prove (1) an alternative safer design practicable under the circumstances, (2) the resulting injuries if the safer design had been used, and (3) the extent of enhanced injuries attributable to the defective design.

The doctrine of avoidable consequences provides that a plaintiff cannot recover for damages he or she could have reasonably avoided.

In this case, the plaintiff's failure to wear a seatbelt resulted in the plaintiff's being ejected from the car and consequently being severely injured. Had the plaintiff been wearing the seatbelt, these injuries would not have occurred. Therefore, they were avoidable. As a matter of law, the doctrine of avoidable consequences precludes the plaintiff from recovery because regardless of the "crashworthiness" of the design, the plaintiff could have avoided the injury.

Beuhler v. *Whalen* (p. 448)

This case demonstrates the applicability of strict liability in an automobile accident case. It shows that foreseeable use may also include accidents, if the good in question may be reasonably foreseen to be involved in an accident. Because it is reasonably foreseeable that automobiles may be involved in accidents, the auto designer has a duty to design a vehicle that will not be unreasonably dangerous to the consumer in the event of a collision.

The alleged defective design in this case was a gas tank design that allowed a fire resulting from a collision to spread into the passenger compartment in less than one minute. Because an alternative design could have slowed the speed by which the fire would have spread to the passenger compartment, a jury could find that the defendants had failed to design their car so as to reasonably reduce the likelihood of injury to the consumer.

Konowal v. *Heinrich Baumgarden Co.* (p. 450)

In this case, the court examines the question of which parties in the chain of distribution can be held liable under a theory of strict product liability. The court held that the theory of strict liability is intended to apply to not only the manufacturer of the defective good, but to the retailer and distributor as well. Thus, in this case, the middleman distributor, who simply sold the goods to the retailer, was not entitled to a summary judgment precluding the imposition of liability on him.

Klages v. *General Ordinance Equipment* (p. 453)

This case illustrates the type of misrepresentation for which a manufacturer and retailer can be held liable. In this case, the product was specifically advertised as deterring violence and protecting the user from harm in a dangerous situation. The product's sole purpose was to protect the user. These claims were not mere puffing, but were material misrepresentations about the products' function, thereby constituting the basis for a product liability action.

SELF TEST

True-False Questions

_____ 1. In a product liability negligence case it is necessary for the plaintiff to establish that the product was purchased directly from the defendant.

_____ 2. If reasonable care is taken in assembling a product the manufacturer has no liability if the product leaves the manufacturers premise in an unsafe condition.

_____ 3. Generally the retailer must conduct reasonable inspections or tests to discover present or latent defects in a product before it is sold.

_____ 4. The negligence theory holds a manufacturer of a defective product liable if the injury should have been foreseen.

_____ 5. Contributory negligence is generally not available as a defense in a strict liability suit.

_____ 6. In strict liability a plaintiff can win at trial merely by establishing that there was a defect in the product, regardless of whether his or her injury was caused by the defect.

213

7. Both federal and state governments have supplemented common law product liability theories by regulating certain standards of conduct.

8. To determine what the term defect means some courts will examine consumer expectations and whether the injured party was surprised by the dangers associated with the product.

9. Product liability suits may be based on warranty law.

10. If a misrepresentation is not made fraudulently or negligently the seller is not liable under the *Restatement of Torts, Second*, Section 402B.

Multiple-Choice Questions

11. The term puffing refers to:
    a. a statement of opinion or loose general praise
    b. a defense used in an innocent misrepresentation case
    c. an assertion used by the plaintiff which allows him or her to automatically recover
    d. a and b only
    e. a and c only

12. Legal theory(ies) encompassed by product liability is (are):
    a. negligence
    b. strict liability
    c. misrepresentation
    d. warranty law
    e. all of the above

13. A manufacturer has a duty to warn the public of a potential danger of a product when:
    a. the product is dangerous for the use for which it is supplied
    b. the product users are unaware of latent dangers
    c. the product is in an obviously dangerous condition
    d. the manufacturer anticipates foreseeable misuse
    e. a, b, and d only

14. In a product liability suit assumption of risk refers to:
    a. a defense used only in negligence cases
    b. a company engaging in ultra hazardous activities
    c. abnormal use of a product
    d. a situation where a person voluntarily performs an activity with full awareness and understanding of the risk involved
    e. the relative negligence of the parties

214

15. In a strict liability case the plaintiff needs to prove:
    a. he or she was injured
    b. the product was defective
    c. the injury sustained was related to the defect
    d. all of the above
    e. a and b only

16. In order to avoid being held liable for negligence a retailer needs to inspect or test items sold.
    a. within 24 hours of their arrival at his/her place of business
    b. after the customer has made the purchase and the package is opened
    c. if the retailer has a history of mishandling items sold
    d. if the retailer knows or has reason to believe the product is dangerous
    e. a retailer never needs to test and inspect items sold

17. A manufacturer must exercise reasonable care in:
    a. assembling a product
    b. designing a product
    c. testing and inspecting a product
    d. a and b only
    e. all of the above

18. In the chain of distribution of a defective product the following party(ies) is (are) strictly liable for the injuries caused by the product.
    a. manufacturer
    b. distributor
    c. wholesaler

19. The defense of contributory negligence is:
    a. a complete bar to the plaintiff's recovery
    b. a way to disperse the negligence over the chain of distribution
    c. a doctrine that reduces the amount of recovery in proportion to the plaintiff's negligence
    d. a voluntary contribution made by the defendant to compensate the plaintiff for his/her injuries
    e. the assertion that two or more persons were responsible for the product's malfunctioning

_____ 20. If a retailer advertises, labels or packages under their own name products that are manufactured by someone else, the retailer:
   a. is not liable for negligence because the retailer has no control over the product's design or assembly
   b. can always escape product liability by marking the goods "made for"
   c. will be held to the same liability standards as manufacturers
   d. is liable for negligence in testing and inspection, but not negligent of assembly and design
   e. none of the above

Completion Questions

21. The causal relationship between a defect in a product and the injury sustained by use of the product is called the _____ _____ of the injury.

22. _____ _____ is the apportionment of liability between two parties that are both negligent.

23. _____ _____ is imposed by law even though the defendant has exercised due care and has not been proved negligent.

24. To recover on grounds of innocent misrepresentation the plaintiff must show one misrepresentation was a material fact and that he or she _____ _____ _____ the misrepresentation.

25. _____ _____ _____ is a defense used in both the product liability theories of negligence and strict liability.

Chapter 26

INTRODUCTION TO NEGOTIABLE INSTRUMENTS AND DOCUMENTS OF TITLE

While cash is always acceptable as a medium for the payment of debts, the reality of the economic environment in which we live is such that payment for debts is usually made in some other acceptable form.

This chapter introduces the law related to those instruments that are accepted in place of cash in commercial transactions. It examines the nature of promissory notes, drafts, and checks, and also discusses the concept of documents of title as they relate to commercial transactions. The text also considers the various situations in which negotiable instruments have been used and identifies various parties who are associated with their use.

CHAPTER OBJECTIVES

After reading Chapter 26 of the text and studying the related materials in this chapter of the Student Mastery Guide, you will understand:

1. The nature and different types of documents of title, including:
    a. warehouse receipts
    b. bills of lading

2. The nature and different types of commercial paper, including:
    a. promissory notes
    b. drafts
    c. checks
    d. certificates of deposit

3. The uses of commercial paper

MAJOR POINTS TO REMEMBER

Documents of Title

1. Documents of title include a warehouse receipt and a bill of lading.

2. No particular form is required in order for a warehouse receipt to be valid. It must, however, contain:
    a. information about the location of the warehouse
    b. the date of issue of the receipt
    c. the name of the person or entity to whom the goods are to be delivered
    d. the amount of the storage or handling charges
    e. a description of the goods
    f. a statement regarding any liens or security interest

3. A warehouseman is required to exercise reasonable care with respect to the goods he is storing.

4. A warehouseman may impose a lien on any goods stored with him and that are in his possession if the owner or person entitled to the goods fails or refuses to pay the appropriate charges.

5. A carrier who issues a bill of lading in connection with the transportation of goods is required to exercise reasonable care with respect to those goods.

6. *A bill of lading* is a document that serves both as a receipt for goods being shipped and as a contract setting forth the terms and conditions under which the goods are being shipped. It may be either negotiable or nonnegotiable.

   A *letter of credit* is an instrument that is issued by a bank requesting payment to bearer or guaranteeing payment of a financial obligation for goods sold on credit.

Negotiable Instruments

7. In contrast to the assignment of ordinary contracts, the transferor of negotiable commercial paper may, in certain circumstances, transfer a better interest in the instrument than he or she possessed. This is allowed in order to encourage the use and acceptability of negotiable instruments.

8. There are four basic types of negotiable instruments:
   a. promissory notes
   b. drafts
   c. checks
   d. certificates of deposit (CDs)

9. A check is a special type of draft that is drawn on a bank.

Parties

10. The accommodation party signs for the purpose of lending his or her credit to another party to the instrument. An accommodation party may sign an instrument as a maker, acceptor, drawer, or indorser. An accommodation party is liable on the instrument in the capacity he or she signed.

Uses of Negotiable Instruments

11. Commercial paper can be used:
    a. to borrow money
    b. as a substitute for money
    c. as a credit device
    d. to create some evidence of debt

12. In order to qualify as a holder in due course, the holder of an instrument must be:
    a. a proper holder who is
    b. in possession of a negotiable instrument that
    c. was properly negotiated to him or her.

Preventive Law: Documentary Credits

13. Buyers in international transactions can have a reluctance to pay without assurance of delivery of the goods, while sellers do not want to deliver the goods without assurance of payment. To facilitate such transactions, the buyer can obtain a documentary credit from its bank and the seller can obtain a bill of lading from its carrier. The seller's bank can then deliver the bill of lading to the buyer's bank and the buyer's bank transfers the money on the documentary credit to the seller's bank.

MAJOR POINTS OF CASES

Guarantor Partners v. *Huff* (p. 467)

The court in this case reversed the trial court's decision on the basis of the lower court's mistake on a matter of law. The Court of Appeals ruled that a separate continuing guaranty is not a negotiable instrument, contrary to the trial court's holding. The only circumstance in which suit can be brought against a separate continuing guaranty is one in which the guaranty is so firmly affixed to a negotiable instrument that it becomes part of that instrument itself.

Applying this ruling to the facts of the case, the Tennessee Court of Appeals found Huff's separate continuing guaranty to be neither a negotiable instrument nor firmly affixed to a negotiable instrument. As a result, the Court reversed the summary judgement formerly in favor of the plaintiff.

PRACTICAL CONSIDERATIONS

Owing to the widespread use of standardized, preprinted forms in connection with commercial paper, most instruments that are prepared are negotiable. Generally, all that is required is that a maker or drawer complete the instrument by inserting the name of the payee, the amount for which it is payable, the date, the amount of interest (if applicable), and the due date (if applicable), and then sign the instrument in the appropriate place. As long as the maker or drawer completes the instrument properly, it will generally be negotiable.

Example: If Mike wants to issue a check to pay for a television set he is buying, he will take out his checkbook and write the check by filling in the date, the name of the payee, and the amount of the check (usually in numerals and words), and then sign it in the appropriate place. Assuming that the printing company that prepared the printed checks did not make a mistake that affects the instrument, the check will probably be negotiable.

SELF TEST

True-False Questions

_____ 1. A warehouse receipt enables the person in possession of the document to pick up the goods from the warehouseman.

_____ 2. A warehouseman is required to exercise extraordinary care with respect to the goods stored with him in order to avoid liability for damage done to the goods while in his possession.

_____ 3. A bank's obligation to pay under a letter of credit is independent of its customer's obligations under the contract for sale.

_____ 4. The transferor of a negotiable instrument may sometimes transfer a better interest in the instrument than he or she possessed.

_____ 5. A check is a special type of promissory note.

_____ 6. Fungible goods are interchangeable goods of which any unit is treated as the equivalent of any other unit.

_____ 7. A bill of lading is not usually transferable to another party.

_____ 8. A negotiable instrument is an ordinary obligation to pay money.

_____ 9. A draft is a written request to pay money.

Multiple-Choice Questions

_____ 11. Negotiable instruments may be used:
    a.   as a credit device
    b.   to create evidence of a debt
    c.   to borrow money
    d.   only a and c are correct
    e.   a, b, and c are all correct

12. The <u>principle</u> difference between a negotiable instrument and an ordinary obligation to pay money is that:
    a. the negotiable instrument's payer may default on his or her obligation without being subject to an actionable suit.
    b. an ordinary obligation to pay carries with it more advantages.
    c. the negotiable instrument's payee can, in certain circumstances, transfer to a third party rights that are greater than the rights of the payee.
    d. default on an ordinary obligation to pay cannot be subject to a suit
    e. none of the above

13. A person who signs a promissory note in the lower right-hand corner of its face is presumed to be:
    a. the drawer
    b. the maker
    c. the payee
    d. the endorsee
    e. the endorser

14. When a drawee of an instrument signs his or her name across the face of the instrument, that signature is regarded as:
    a. an acceptance
    b. a waiver of liability
    c. guarantee of payment of the instrument
    d. an accommodation endorsement
    e. none of the above is correct

15. An instrument is payable at a definite time if it is payable:
    a. on demand
    b. within ten days after the next heavy snowfall
    c. within seven days after demand for payment is made
    d. at any time before the next winter season
    e. a and c are both correct

16. An instrument bearing which of the following phrases would be considered to be bearer paper?
    a. pay to the order of cash
    b. pay to the order of John Jones
    c. pay to the order of bearer
    d. pay to Mary Smith
    e. a and c are both correct

_____ 17. Any negotiable instrument that is due at some particular date in the future is referred to as:
   a. a demand instrument
   b. a time instrument
   c. an accommodation instrument
   d. a guaranteed instrument
   e. an accepted instrument

_____ 18. A draft that has no documents or instruments attached to it is called a:
   a. clean draft
   b. trade acceptance
   c. letter of credit
   d. documentary draft
   e. fungible draft

_____ 19. The document that serves both as a receipt of goods being shipped someplace and as a contract setting forth the terms and conditions under which the goods are being shipped is a:
   a. warehouse receipt
   b. consignment statement
   c. bill of lading
   d. letter of credit
   e. trade acceptance

_____ 20. An instrument that is made payable to the order of Simon Seize and Richard Roe must be endorsed, for purposes of negotiation, by:
   a. the drawer of the instrument
   b. both Simon Seize and Richard Roe
   c. either Simon Seize or Richard Roe but not both
   d. Richard Roe and a guarantor for Simon Seize
   e. a and b are both correct

Completion Questions

21. _____ is a term used to refer to the transfer of a negotiable instrument from one person to another.

22. An instrument that is payable whenever the holder presents it for payment is referred to as a(n)_____.

23. A _____ _____ is a check that is drawn by a bank upon itself.

24. The person who is in possession of bearer paper is referred to as the _____.

25. A _____ is a person who executes an instrument that directs another person to pay a sum of money to a third person.

Chapter 27

NEGOTIABLE INSTRUMENTS: NEGOTIABILITY

As has been discussed in earlier chapters, there exist both negotiable and non-negotiable instruments. Each type of instrument has different types of characteristics. The negotiable instrument, we learned in the previous chapter, is the instrument to which Article 3 of the UCC applies. Thus, it is important to understand what constitutes a negotiable instrument. Developing such an understanding is the primary focus of this chapter.

CHAPTER OBJECTIVES

After reading Chapter 27 of the text and studying the materials presented in this chapter of the Student Mastery Guide, you will understand:

1. The requirements of a negotiable instrument, including:
    a. signature
    b. unconditional promise or order
    c. payable in a fixed amount
    d. payable on demand at a certain time
    e. payable to order or to bearer
    f. exclusive undertaking to pay the money
    g. dated

2. Rules of Construction

MAJOR POINTS TO REMEMBER

Negotiable Instruments

1. In order for an instrument to be negotiable, it must:
    a. be in writing
    b. be signed by the maker or drawer
    c. contain an unconditional promise or order to pay that is related to a sum certain (a definite amount) of money
    d. contain no other promise or order
    e. be payable on demand or at a certain date or after a certain period of time
    f. be payable to order or bearer
    g. have a maker or drawer who agrees to any other undertaking or instruction in addition to the payment of money.

2. Negotiation requires that the:
    a. instrument be transferred
    b. transfer be to a proper holder
    c. instrument be properly endorsed if it is an order instrument

3. Delivery of an instrument may be actual or constructive.

4. In order for a person to be held liable on an instrument, his or her name must appear on it. A person is liable on an instrument in the capacity in which he or she signs.

5. Oral statements do not affect the negotiable character of an instrument.

6. When a person signs an instrument in a representative capacity, that person must make sure that the signature clearly indicates that the instrument is being signed on behalf of another person. A failure to do so clearly may result in personal liability being imposed on the party (i.e., the agent) who signs the instrument.
    Some common ways to indicate a representative signature are:
    Herman Nudnick as agent for William Principal
    Herman Nudnick on behalf of William Principal
    William Principal by Herman Nudnick as agent
    Z Corporation by John Roe, President

7. Notes and certificates of deposit must contain an unconditional promise to pay, while drafts and checks must include an unconditional order to pay. The requirement of an unconditional promise or order means that the negotiability of an instrument must be determined from the instrument itself without having to refer to any other document. A holder in due course is not affected legally by any limitations contained in another related document.

8. To be negotiable an instrument has to be payable in money and in an amount that can be determined solely from the face of the instrument itself.

9. Additional information given in an instrument generally impairs its negotiability. The exceptions are:
    a. a statement that collateral has been given to secure the obligation
    b. an authorization to confess judgement or dispose of the collateral
    c. a waiver of the benefit of any law intended for the advantage or protection of a person who owes a debt.

Date

10. The holder of an undated instrument is permitted to fill in the date of the instrument but must do so before he or she negotiates it (UCC Section 3-115).

Time

11.   An instrument is payable at a definite time if it is payable:
   a.   on or before a stated date or after a specific period of time
   b.   at a particular period of time after sight
   c.   at a definite time subject to acceleration
   d.   at a definite time subject to extension at the option of the holder
   e.   at a definite time subject to extension at the option of the maker or acceptor, or automatically upon or after a specified act or event

12.   An acceleration clause in an instrument does not destroy its negotiability.

13.   A negotiable instrument can also be payable on demand, which means payable at sight, on presentation, or if it contains no time for payment.

Order of Bearer

14.   To negotiate order paper, the holder must transfer the instrument and endorse it.

15.   Bearer paper can be negotiated to a third person by anyone who is in possession of it without an endorsement by the bearer.

Rules of Construction

16.   In the event that an instrument has contradictory terms:
   a.   typewritten terms prevail over printed terms
   b.   handwritten terms prevail over both typewritten and printed terms
   c.   words prevail over numbers

MAJOR POINTS OF CASES

Resolution Trust Corporation v. *1601 Partners, Ltd.* (p. 475)

   This case dealt with the requirements for a negotiable instrument. The court held that to the extent that a note does not contain an unconditional promise it is not a negotiable instrument. Furthermore, the court stated that a holder of a note that is not a negotiable instrument cannot qualify as a holder in due course of that note.
   Applying this holding, the court ruled in favor of the defendant. The court found the note in question not to be a negotiable instrument because it "explicitly purports to incorporate the terms of the Deed of Trust." Because the note was not a negotiable instrument, the plaintiffs were ruled not to be holders in due course, and the defendant was released from liability.

Mumma v. *Ranier National Bank* (p. 479)

The court ruled in this case that a slash (/) between two payees on a check can be properly interpreted as a disjunctive rather than a conjunctive. Thus, the check containing such a symbol requires the endorsement of only one payee.

Applying this ruling to the facts of the case, the court upheld the trial court's decision. The court stated that the plaintiff Mumma, by using the symbol "/" between JHL Associates, Inc. and Fidelity, allowed either of these parties to deposit the check. Thus, no matter how wrong JHL was in depositing the check in its account alone the case was not actionable against either JHL or Ranier National Bank.

Galatia Community State Bank v. *Kindy* (p. 481)

The court held in this case that a conflict on the check concerning its amount does in and of itself provide the payee with a defense against the check's claim. Instead, any conflict is presumed to be a mistake and thus should be ignored.

With this holding, the court entered judgement against Kindy. The conflict between his check imprinting machine's figure on the word line and the numbers in the numbers box were not found to be a sufficient defense against the cashing of the check. The court ordered that the $5,500 written by the imprinting machine be paid by Kindy. The court chose the imprinting machine figure, because imprinting machines are presumably used to hinder alteration.

PRACTICAL CONSIDERATIONS

Owing to the widespread use of standardized, preprinted forms in connection with commercial paper, most instruments that are prepared are negotiable. Generally, all that is required is that a maker or drawer complete the instrument by inserting the name of the payee.

SELF TEST

True-False Questions

_____ 1. In determining whether documents are negotiable, the courts look to the documents themselves.

_____ 2. If an instrument is missing one or more of the requirements of a negotiable instrument, the instrument cannot be transferred.

_____ 3. An instrument lacking in just one requirement of a negotiable instrument is still governed by the rules in Article 3 of the UCC.

_____ 4. That payment is limited to a particular source or fund does not in and of itself make a promise conditional.

_____ 5. An instrument cannot be made payable to more than one person.

226

_____ 6. In order for an instrument to be negotiable, it must, among other things, contain an unconditional promise to pay a definite amount of money.

_____ 7. It is absolutely necessary for an instrument to be signed personally by the drawer or maker in order for it to be negotiable.

_____ 8. Oral statements do not affect the negotiable character of an instrument.

_____ 9. If an instrument is undated, the holder of the instrument may complete it before transferring it to another party.

_____ 10. The failure to include in an instrument the place where it is drawn and payable will affect the negotiability of the instrument.

Multiple-Choice Questions

_____ 11. Which of the following is required in order for an instrument to be negotiable?
   a. the signature of the payee
   b. the signature of the endorsee
   c. an unconditional promise or order to pay a definite amount of money
   d. a due date for payment of the money
   e. a and c are both correct

_____ 12. Through which of the following may transfer be achieved?
   a. unconditional delivery
   b. physical delivery
   c. de facto delivery
   d. constructive delivery
   e. b and d are both correct

_____ 13. To be negotiable, all instruments must contain an unconditional promise, except:
   a. notes
   b. certificates
   c. checks
   d. IOU's
   e. none of the above

227

14. The negotiability of an instrument must be determinable by:
    a. a reasonable person
    b. an examination of the face of the instrument itself
    c. an examination of one other document at the very most
    d. a and b are both correct
    e. none of the above

15. The requirement of "fixed amount" refers to:
    a. interest
    b. principal
    c. accrued interest
    d. discount
    e. a and b are both correct

16. Under the Code, money can be authorized by:
    a. the U.S. government
    b. a foreign government
    c. an intergovernmental organization
    d. all of the above
    e. a and c, only

17. If a note is payable "to the order of Dan Cook", that note is payable to:
    a. Dan Cook only
    b. Dan Cook or whomever else that Dan Cook designates
    c. Dan Cook or any immediate family member
    d. anyone possessing Dan Cook's identification card
    e. none of the above are correct

18. If an instrument is bearer paper:
    a. it cannot be negotiated without the appropriate bearer
    b. it cannot be negotiated
    c. any person possessing it has the power to negotiate it
    d. any person possessing it is liable
    e. none of the above

19. Example(s) of information that may be given in an instrument without impairing its negotiability, include:
    a. an authorization to collect collateral
    b. the waiver of authorization to confess judgement
    c. a statement that collateral has been given to secure a waiver of the benefit
    d. all of the above
    e. none of the above

_____ 20. The bank may pay a check before the date on the check under which circumstances?
     a. all circumstances
     b. if the drawer does not notify the bank of the postdating
     c. if the drawer has sufficient funds to cover the check
     d. no circumstances
     e. none of the above are correct

Completion Questions

21. To be negotiable, an instrument must contain a(n) _____ promise.

22. A negotiable instrument must be payable in a(n) _____ amount of money.

23. "Order" and "bearer" are _____ _____ _____.

24. If an instrument has contradictory terms, _____ _____ prevail over both typewritten and printed terms.

25. In order for the holder of an instrument to be a holder in due course, that instrument must be _____.

Chapter 28

NEGOTIABLE INSTRUMENTS: TRANSFER, NEGOTIATION, AND HOLDER IN DUE COURSE

This chapter is concerned with three important concepts in regard to commercial paper: the transfer and negotiation of commercial paper, the various types of endorsements used in connection with negotiable instruments, and the status of holder instruments, for if such instruments cannot be easily and properly transferred from one person to another, the concept of negotiability is meaningless.

The concept of holder in due course reveals the complexity of this area of law as well as the importance of the need to provide full and effective protection to the rights of the respective parties. The materials show how difficulties can be avoided by both the holder of a negotiable instrument and the party who executed it. They also reveal the various devices that are available to the parties to enforce their rights. Special attention should be given to the detailed requirements of the rules involved.

CHAPTER OBJECTIVES

After reading Chapter 28 of the text and studying the related materials in this chapter of the Student Mastery Guide, you will understand:

1. The methods of transferring commercial paper
2. The different types of endorsements that may be used in connection with the negotiation of commercial paper, including:
    a. bank endorsements
    b. special endorsements
    c. qualified endorsements
    d. restrictive endorsements
3. The nature of a holder in due course
4. The requirements for qualification as a holder in due course, which include:
    a. taking an instrument for value
    b. good faith
    c. no notice of any defense or claim

MAJOR POINTS TO REMEMBER

Transfer and Negotiation

1. The issuance of an instrument is effected when it is delivered by a maker or drawer to a payee. The maker or drawer will not be liable for the instrument until it is issued.

2. Personal defenses usually arise out of the transaction in which the instrument was originally issued, and such defenses include break of contract and lack of consideration. These defenses may not be asserted against a holder in due course.

3. Delivery of an instrument may be effected by:
   a. physical delivery
   b. constructive delivery

4. If the maker or drawer of an instrument is in physical possession of it, there is a rebuttable presumption that no delivery of the instrument was intended.

   If someone other than the assignee of the instrument is in physical possession of it, there is a presumption that its delivery was intended.

5. If an instrument is nonnegotiable, the law of contracts as opposed to the law relating to negotiable instruments will apply to it. The assignee of the instrument will make it subject to any defenses or claims that could have been raised against the transferor or any prior party to the instrument.

6. *Order paper* is negotiated by endorsement and delivery. *Bearer paper* is negotiated by delivery alone.

Endorsements

7. Various types of endorsements can be used in connection with negotiable instruments, including:
   a. blank endorsement
   b. special endorsement
   c. qualified endorsement
   d. restrictive endorsement

8. A *blank endorsement* is created when the endorser signs his or her name on the back of the instrument. It specifies no particular conditions, nor does it specify any particular endorsee.
   Example: "[Signed] Bernard Blimp."

9. A blank endorsement changes an order instrument to bearer paper.

10. A *special endorsement* is one that sets forth the name of a specific endorsee.
    Example: "Pay to the order of Mary Jones, [signed] Herman Snee."
    This endorsement makes or keeps the instrument an order instrument.

11. A *qualified endorsement* is created by the words, "without recourse" or similar words in connection with the endorsement.

12. When an endorser uses a *qualified* endorsement, the secondary or conditional liability as an endorser is eliminated.
    Example: "Without recourse, [signed] Gilbert N. Sullivan."

13. A *restrictive endorsement* is one that puts certain limitations on the use of the instrument by the endorsee. It does not, however, prevent the further negotiation of the instrument.

14. There are several types of restrictive endorsements, including:
    a. conditional restrictive, which requires the endorsee and other transferees, except intermediary banks, to act consistently with the stated condition
    b. prohibit further transfer, which cannot, however, prevent further negotiation
    c. for deposit or collection, which limits who can be a holder and the purpose of transfers
    d. trust endorsement

15. A *trust endorsement* is a restrictive endorsement that states that it is for the benefit or use of the endorser or another person.

Holder in Due Course

16. In order for a holder of an instrument to become a holder in due course under Section 3-302 of the Uniform Commercial Code, he or she must take the instrument:
    a. for value
    b. in good faith
    c. without notice that the instrument is overdue or has been dishonored, or of any defense against or claim to it on the part of any person

    The holder must also show that:
    d. the instrument involved is a negotiable instrument
    e. he or she is a holder of the instrument

17. Under Section 3-303 of the UCC, a holder takes an instrument for value:
    a. when he or she gives a negotiable instrument for it, or
    b. when he or she makes an irrevocable commitment to a third person, or
    c. to the extent that the agreed consideration has been performed, or
    d. when he or she acquires a security interest in or a lien on the instrument otherwise than by legal process, or
    e. when he or she takes the instrument in payment of or as security for an antecedent debt

18. A person who takes a security interest in an instrument takes the instrument for value.

19. A holder gives value when she or he takes the instrument in payment of or as security for an antecedent claim, whether or not the claim is then due.

20. A holder who gives a negotiable instrument in exchange for a second negotiable instrument gives value for the second negotiable instrument.

21. An executory promise to give value does not constitute value for purposes of holder-in-due course status.

22. In order for a court to determine whether a person took an instrument in good faith, it must ascertain whether the person acted honestly. The "reasonable man" standard does not apply to this determination.

23. A person has notice of a claim or defense that could be raised against an instrument if the:
    a. instrument is incomplete
    b. instrument appears to be forged or altered or is so irregular as to call into question its validity, terms, or ownership
    c. instrument creates an ambiguity as to who is entitled to payment
    d. person has notice that the obligation of any party is voidable or that all parties have been discharged
    e. person takes a time instrument that is past due, or a demand instrument after demand has been made or more than a reasonable time after its issue
    f. person takes an instrument knowing or with reason to know it has been dishonored
    g. person takes an instrument knowing or with reason to know there is a claim to or defense against it

24. A *defense* to an instrument is some reason why payment that is claimed to be due should not be made.
    A *claim* to an instrument is an argument that is interposed by a person who feels he or she has a right to the instrument.

Shalter Provision

25. A holder through a holder in due course receives the same rights and is entitled to the same protection as a holder in due course.

Payee as a Holder in Due Course

26. Generally, a holder in due course takes the instrument free from any defenses of a party to the instrument with whom he or she has had no dealings.
    However, a holder in due course does take the instrument subject to the real defenses of the maker or drawer.

FTC Modification

27. As a result of a trade regulation rule adopted by the FTC in 1976, the holder of a consumer credit contract that was given in connection with a consumer credit installment sale which is covered by the Federal Trade Commission Act takes the instrument subject to all claims and defenses that the debtor could assert against the seller of the goods.
    This rules does not apply to credit card transactions. However, the federal Fair Credit Billing Act does provide protection to consumers who use a credit card for a purchase of greater than $50.00 from a seller within 100 miles of the consumer's home.

Ethics Box: Taking an Instrument from a Merchant

28.   To become a holder in due course of a negotiable instrument, a holder, among other elements, must take it without notice of defenses against or claims to it and in good faith. Notice is an objective standard imposed in regard to a particular instrument. Good faith is a subjective standard that requires honesty in fact in the relevant transaction. Thus, even if a note is taken from a person or company that is known to have in the past acted illegally in similar transactions, the transferee has acted in good faith and without such notice so long as there is no other reason to question the validity of the instrument in question. Ethically, however, the transferee, given the knowledge of the subject company's past business practices, is obligated to first investigate this company's present business practices.

Issues and Trends: Destruction of Holder-in-Due Course Doctrine.

29.   Besides the FTC rule, which has virtually eliminated the holder-in-due course doctrine in consumer credit contracts, some states have adopted the Uniform Consumer Credit Code which prohibits sellers from taking negotiable instruments, other than personal checks, in consumer-credit sales and leases. The FTC rule and the UCC together have virtually eliminated the application of the holder-in-due-course doctrine in consumer-credit transactions.   This doctrine remains applicable to negotiable instruments issued in commercial credit transactions.

MAJOR POINTS OF CASES

M.G. Sales, Inc. v. *Chemical Bank* (p. 487)

In this case, the court ruled that the Chemical Bank as a matter of law acted appropriately by charging the plaintiff's account for checks presented to the bank after the stop payment period had passed. The court also ruled that even if the bank did have a policy against prohibiting the cashing of doubly endorsed checks, which it did not have at the time, it would have been irrelevant to the decision because the UCC contained no such prohibition.

Kolmann v. *Sol, K. Graff & Sons* (p.489)

In reaching its decision in this case, the court relied on Section 3-204 of the UCC which provides, in part, that "any instrument specially endorsed becomes payable to the order of the special endorsee and may be further negotiated only by his endorsement." The course also indicated that under Section 3-201(1) of the UCC, "transfer of an instrument vests in the transferee such rights as the transferor has therein."

In applying the code provisions to the facts of the case, the court ruled that inasmuch as Kolmann had transferred each promissory note to his daughter by means of a special endorsement, only she was capable of negotiating it thereafter. When Kolmann later changed the endorsement by inserting his wife's name, he had no authority to do so because he no longer retained any interest in the promissory notes. As a result, the court held that Kolmann's endorsement to his wife was invalid and consequently she had no interest in the notes.

Schwegmann Bank & Trust Co. of Jefferson v. *Simmons* (49)

In this case, the defendant claimed that the plaintiff's knowledge of three facts provided them with notice of Simmon's three defenses to the note: failure of consideration, federal securities law violating, and fraud. The court ruled that these facts could not alert the plaintiff Schwegmann of any of these defenses. Moreover, the court held that the facts did not create a material fact issue as to whether Schwegmann acted in bad faith. As a consequence of its ruling, the court affirmed the decision for Schwegmann, ordering Simmons to repay the loan.

American Federal Bank, FSB v. *Parker* (p. 500)

The court reordered two related rulings in this case. First, where promissory notes are left blank and signed, responsibility for loss regarding the note is placed upon the party who signed the note and left it incomplete. Secondly, the court also ruled that banks receiving notes that are facially valid hold no responsibility to contact the involved.

Applying these rulings to the facts of the case, the court held that American Federal acted properly in executing the note that Parker had left blank and signed. The court stated that Parker bore the responsibility for the excessive amount of the note by virtue of the fact that he left it blank and signed. Furthermore, because the note was facially valid when it was presented to the bank by Kirkman, the bank bore no special responsibility regarding it.

Smith v. *Olympic Bank* (502)

The court in this case ruled that a bank bears responsibility for the amount in question when it has knowledge that the guardian of an account is breaching his or her judiciary duty. After Charles Alcombrack acting as guardian used his son's estate for personal use, the court held that the bank was liable for such misdirected use, because it was aware of the misuse. Thus, the court entered a judgement in favor of the new guardian, ordering the bank to repay him the amount squandered by the former guardian.

Tinker v. *De Maria Porsche Audi, Inc.* (p. 505)

The case involved the operation of the FTC trade rule that requires consumer-credit contracts to contain a conspicuous notice that any assignee of the contract is subject to all defenses that could be asserted against the seller. The court ruled that this notice allows the buyer to withhold the balance of the purchase price when the seller does not fulfill its obligations, and, if the consumer is sued, it gives the consumer a complete defense to payment. Since the buyer could prove fraud or misrepresentation by the seller, he could withhold payment to the assignee bank and had a complete defense to a suit to collect the balance owing. The effect of this rule is to shift the costs of seller misconduct away from the consumer and on to the creditors who in effect provide the financing for such transactions.

PRACTICAL CONSIDERATIONS

1. Even though the Uniform Commercial Code provides that bearer paper is negotiated by delivery alone, most banks and other informed persons will require it to be endorsed as well. Such endorsement is usually demanded because of the fact that in the event that the instrument is later dishonored, the transferee will sometimes be unable to hold the transferor liable on the instrument unless such person's signature appears on it. As a result, the transferee may have recourse only against the defaulting party, and if that person is insolvent, the transferee may be left with no remedy at all.

    Example: A delivers a check to B without endorsement, since the check was made payable to bearer. B accepts the check and gives A the money for which the check was made payable. Thereafter, B presents the check to D's bank, which dishonors it because there are insufficient funds in D's account. When B goes back to A to try to get her money back, she will find that A is under no obligation to honor B's demand because A is not an endorser of the check. If D is insolvent, B will find herself in possession of a worthless check and will be unable to do anything to secure payment until D becomes solvent again.

2. While most people use blank endorsements freely and without concern for the possible consequences, one should actually be very careful when endorsing an instrument in blank. A blank endorsement has the effect of making an instrument bearer paper, so that anyone who is in possession of it is entitled to payment. If an instrument that is endorsed in blank should be lost, the finder would probably encounter little difficulty in cashing or negotiating it. Consequently, it is generally advisable to use a special or restrictive endorsement when negotiating an instrument whenever possible.

    Example: James Stone receives a check from Laura Wilson in the amount of $100.00. Stone decides to deposit the check in his bank account, and in order to save time at the bank he decides to endorse the check before he leaves his house. He uses a blank endorsement. On the way to the bank, the check falls out of his pocket. Tom Roman finds the check on the ground about an hour later.

    Because the check was endorsed in blank, it is possible that Roman could cash the check and receive the funds for it. Stone will probably have a very difficult time getting Wilson to provide him with an additional $100.00. The more prudent thing for Stone to have done would have been to endorse the check "For deposit only, James Stone."

    The various types of endorsements have been created for use in the appropriate types of situations. It seems that the most judicious conduct is to use them properly in the appropriate circumstances.

SELF TEST

True-False Questions

_____   1. In determining whether a delivery of an instrument took place, a court will examine the intent of the parties.

_____ 2. Order paper is negotiated by delivery alone.

_____ 3. A blank endorsement has the effect of making an instrument bearer paper.

_____ 4. When a person negotiates an instrument by means of a qualified endorsement, that person will have no secondary liability as an endorser if the instrument is dishonored at a later time.

_____ 5. A restrictive endorsement prevents the further negotiation of an instrument.

_____ 6. If an instrument states on its face that payment is due on December 3, 1988, and it is transferred to a holder on December 5, 1988, that holder can qualify as a holder in due course of the instrument.

_____ 7. A holder in due course takes an instrument for value if he or she acquires a security interest in it.

_____ 8. It is possible for a person who does not qualify as a holder in due course to have the same rights as a holder in due course of an instrument.

_____ 9. If Susan receives a promissory note from one of her debtors and thereafter gives it to her son Carl as a birthday present, Carl can qualify as a holder in due course of the promissory note.

_____ 10. Intermediary banks are bound by conditional restrictive endorsements.

Multiple-Choice Questions

_____ 11. Transfer of an instrument may be effected by:
   a. physical delivery of the instrument
   b. a letter stating that the transferor will transfer the instrument
   c. constructive delivery of the instrument
   d. both a and c are correct
   e. a, b, and c are all correct

_____ 12. The endorsement "Without recourse" is referred to as:
   a. a restrictive endorsement
   b. a qualified endorsement
   c. a blank endorsement
   d. a special endorsement
   e. an unqualified endorsement

13. In order for a person to qualify as a holder in due course of an instrument, that person:
    a. must take the instrument for value
    b. must take the instrument in good faith
    c. must take the instrument without notice of any defense that could be raised against payment of it
    d. must be a holder of the instrument
    e. all of the above are requirements

14. A holder takes an instrument for value when such person:
    a. takes the instrument in payment of an antecedent debt
    b. makes a revocable commitment to a third person
    c. makes a promise to perform a specified act
    d. acquires a security interest in the instrument
    e. a and d are both correct

15. A holder through a holder in due course takes an instrument:
    a. subject to the limited defenses of the maker or drawer
    b. subject to the universal defenses of the maker or drawer
    c. free of any defenses that could be raised against payment
    d. subject only to the defense of prior payment
    e. a and b are both correct

16. A holder of an instrument has notice of a claim or defense that can be interposed against it if:
    a. the instrument appears to be forged
    b. the instrument is undated
    c. there is some ambiguity as to who is entitled to payment
    d. a and c are both correct
    e. a, b, and c are all correct

17. A bank to which an instrument is transferred in the course of collection is referred to as:
    a. an intermediary bank
    b. a depository bank
    c. a payor bank
    d. a drawee bank
    e. a secondary bank

18. A restrictive endorsement that states that it is for the benefit or use of the endorser is known as:
    a. a depository endorsement
    b. an allonge
    c. a trust endorsement
    d. a constructive endorsement
    e. a conditional restrictive endorsement

_____ 19. An endorsement on the back of an instrument that states "Pay to the order of Roger Dodger" is:
   a. a restrictive endorsement
   b. a qualified endorsement
   c. a blank endorsement
   d. an unqualified endorsement in blank

_____ 20. Order paper is negotiated by means of:
   a. endorsement and delivery of the instrument
   b. delivery of the instrument only
   c. an assignment of the contract rights to it
   d. endorsement of the instrument only
   e. a qualified endorsement and delivery only

Completion Questions

21. A _____ _____ is a bank at which an instrument is deposited.

22. The failure or refusal to pay or accept an instrument when it is due or presented is referred to as a(n) _____.

23. A(n) _____ is a piece of paper that is firmly attached to an instrument and on which endorsements are written.

24. An endorsement that specifically sets forth the name of the endorsee is a(n) _____ endorsement.

25. _____ is the term used to refer to the transfer of an instrument in such form that the transferee becomes a holder.

Chapter 29

NEGOTIABLE INSTRUMENTS: LIABILITY, DEFENSES, AND DISCHARGE

The previous chapters introduced you to the various types of commercial paper that are used today. This chapter examines in more depth the potential liability of those who use commercial paper in business and the defenses available against honoring such instruments.

CHAPTER OBJECTIVES

After reading Chapter 29 of the text and studying the materials presented in this chapter of the Student Mastery Guide, you will understand:

1. When a party may be liable on an instrument
2. The real defenses that a drawer or maker may raise against all holders, including:
   a. forgery
   b. material alteration
   c. fraud in the execution
   d. infancy
   e. duress
   f. illegality
   g. discharge in bankruptcy
3. The personal defenses that may be raised against all holders except holders in due course.

MAJOR POINTS TO REMEMBER

Liability

1. Liability on an instrument is conferred upon an individual upon either his or her signing of that instrument or an agent of the individual signing on his or her behalf. The signature need not be handwritten, but there must be an intention to authenticate the writing.

2. Any persons who sign another person's name to a promissory note without authorization may themselves be held liable.

3. In cases where the signature of more than one person is required to constitute the signature of an organization, the absence of even one requisite signature renders the organization's signature unauthorized, and the organization does not confer liability.

4. There are several instances where an unauthorized signature is effective:
   a. ratification
   b. the impostor rule
   c. fictitious payee rule
   d. double forgeries
   e. substantially similar signature

5. When an employee is entrusted with responsibility for an employer's checks, that employee's fraudulent indorsements are the responsibility of the employer, who alone bears the risk of loss.

6. The comparative fault provision may result in the shifting of loss to the party who receives an instrument if that party fails to exercise ordinary care and that failure substantially contributes to the loss.

Negligence

7. When the failure to exercise ordinary care contributes substantially to either the alteration of an instrument or the making of a forged signature, the person who failed to exercise ordinary care may not use alteration or the forged signature as a defense against a person who in good faith paid the instrument, took it for value or for collection. However, a comparative fault standard may be applied to cases such as these.

Types of Liability

8. The *maker* of a promissory note has primary liability for its payment in that he or she assumes an unconditional obligation based on the instrument's promise to pay.

9. The *drawee* on a draft has primary liability for payment of the instrument once he or she has indicated acceptance. Before accepting the instrument, the drawee has no liability on the draft.

10. The following parties have secondary liability for the payment of an instrument:
    a. an *indorser* of a negotiable instrument
    b. the *drawer* of a draft
    It is important to note that a dishonor of an instrument must occur before a party can be held responsible for the payment of an instrument on the basis of secondary liability.

Establishing Secondary Liability

11. In order for indorsers or drawers to be held liable or responsible for payment of an instrument, there must be:
    a. presentment
    b. a dishonor
    c. notice of dishonor
    In some situations, protest is also required.

Presentment

12. Under Section 3-501 of the UCC, presentment of a draft for acceptance is required where the:
    a. draft requires it
    b. draft is payable at some place other than the drawee's residence or place of business.
    c. time of payment depends on the date of acceptance

13. If an instrument is not properly presented for payment, all indorsers are discharged completely, and in some cases the drawer may be relieved of liability (see UCC Section 3-502[1][b]).

14. Presentment of an instrument may be made:
    a. by mail
    b. through a clearinghouse
    c. at a place of acceptance or payment specified in the instrument

Dishonor

15. Subject to any requirement for the giving of notice or protest, when an instrument is dishonored, the holder of it has an immediate right or recourse against the drawer and/or indorsers of the instrument. Upon presentation a party may take time to examine the instrument, but payment must be made by close of business on the day of presentment or otherwise dishonor occurs.

Notice of Dishonor

16. Upon dishonor the holder must give notice of dishonor by midnight of the third business day after dishonor to his or her immediate transferor and can also give notice to any other prior transferors. Prior holders must then give notice to holders prior to them by midnight of the third business day after notice of dishonor is received. Banks, however, must give the notice before midnight of the banking day following the one on which they received an item or notice of dishonor.

17. Notice of dishonor can be made in any reasonable manner, but must identify the instrument and the fact of dishonor.

Protest

18. When a draft that is drawn or payable outside of the United States is dishonored, protest must be made in order to provide acceptable evidence of the dishonor.

Extent of Secondary Liability

19. If the holder of a draft unreasonably delays in making a presentment of it for payment after it is due, and during that time the drawee becomes insolvent, the drawer's liability will be limited to the extent that the drawee's insolvency deprives the drawer of funds with which to pay the payee or holder.

20. If a holder fails to properly present and give notice of dishonor, affected indorsers are discharged immediately and completely.

Establishing Warranty Liability

21. Warranty liability is not contingent upon signing an instrument, nor is it contingent upon presentment, dishonor, and notice of dishonor.

22. Unqualified indorsers who transfer a negotiable instrument for consideration impliedly warrant to the indorsee and all subsequent holders that:
    a. he or she has good title to the instrument
    b. all signatures are genuine and authorized
    c. the instrument has not been materially altered
    d. no defense of any party is good against him or her
    e. he or she has no knowledge of any insolvency proceeding instituted with respect to the maker or acceptor of an unaccepted instrument

23. Qualified indorsers make the same five warranties, except that they warrant only that they have no knowledge of any defense of any party that is good against them.

24. A person who transfers a negotiable instrument without an indorsement makes the same warranties as a qualified indorser, except that those warranties run only to the immediate transferee.

Real Defenses

25. A holder in due course takes the instrument subject to the real defenses of the maker or drawer.

26. Real defenses include the following:
    a. forgery
    b. material alteration
    c. fraud in the execution
    d. infancy
    e. duress
    f. illegality
    g. discharge in bankruptcy

27. The holder in due course of an instrument that has been altered in a material way may enforce it, but generally only up to the amount for which it was originally made payable.

28. While fraud in the execution is a real defense, fraud in the inducement is only a personal defense that will not usually be successful against a holder in due course.

Personal Defenses

29. A holder of an instrument who does not qualify as a holder in due course takes the instrument subject to the real and personal defenses of the maker or drawer.

30. Personal defenses are those that are based on some legally acceptable reason for failure to perform a contract.

31. Personal defenses
    a. the absence of consideration to support the contract
    b. non-issuance
    c. fraud in the inducement
    d. incapacity
    e. duress and illegality
    f. claim in recoupment

MAJOR POINTS OF THE CASES

Knight Communications v. *Boatmen's National Bank* (p. 510)

In this case, the court ruled that where more than one signature is required for authorization the absence of any one of the authorized signatures renders the signatures unauthorized. The signature card agreement for Knight Communications stipulated that the corporate checking account required the signature of at least one of the Browns and one of the Knights. When Boatmen's Bank began honoring checks not containing a signature of the Browns, the Browns brought suit. Applying its ruling to the case, the court ruled in favor of the Browns.

Clients' Security Fund v. *Allstate Insurance Company* (p. 512)

This case deals with the extent to which the impostor rule applies as an exception to the general rule that a forged instrument is ineffective to pass title. The court ruled that the impostor rule applies only where a person (the forger) represents him or herself as another.

Applying this ruling to the facts of the case, the court held that Yucht could not be considered an impersonator. As an attorney, Yucht did not pretend to be his clients but instead he acted falsely as their agent. The court recognized this distinction in applying the impostor rule and affirmed the dismissal of First Fidelity's cross-claim against Allstate.

Kid Gloves v. First National Bank of Jefferson Parish (p. 515)

The court in this case considered who was the negligent and thus liable party in a forgery case. Sather charged that the checks cashed by Larry Andrews contained Sather's forged signature and therefore were not valid. The bank asserted that it was not negligent in cashing the checks, because it used reasonable commercial standards.

Reviewing the facts of the case, the court ruled in favor of the bank. The court stated that by giving Andrews open access to the company checkbook, Sather's actions constituted negligence; therefore, he was expected to bear the costs.

National Loan Investors, L. P. v. Martin (p. 520)

This case deals with the applicability of the fraud in factum defense. The court ruled that a maker who signed a blank note is not entitled to such a defense.

Applying this ruling to the facts of the case, the court reversed the trial court's ruling which voided William Martin's promissory notes. Martin signed blank notes and allowed bank officials to fill in the proper amount at a later date. Even though an unauthorized person filled in an incorrect amount, the court held that Martin surrendered a fraud in factum defense against the enforcement of these notes by signing them while they were blank.

Federal Deposit Insurance Corporation v. Culver (p. 522)

The court ruled in this case that a person is not excused from liability for a promissory note on which she or he put her or his signature simply because the note was presented to him or her in a deceptive manner. To the extent that any person can read and understand the English language she or he has a responsibility for knowing the contents of any document on which he or she places a signature.

Applying this ruling to the facts of the case, the court ruled that Culver was liable for a promissory note that he signed. Although the note was misrepresented to him, Culver could not be excused from liability because he possessed the faculties to fully understand the note before placing his name on it.

New Jersey Mortgage & Investment Corp. v. Berenyi (p. 524)

The decision in this case illustrates the rule that a holder in due course takes an instrument subject to the real (universal) defenses of the maker or drawer. It also stated, however, that if the defense that is raised is that of illegality, it will be considered a real defense only if the illegality makes void the payment required for the underlying transaction.

On the basis of the facts in the case, the court held that while the conduct of Kroyden violated the injunction issued against it, there was no statute in New Jersey that makes void a note obtained in violation of an injunction. Consequently, the defense of illegality was ruled to be a limited (personal) defense that was not effective against New Jersey Mortgage & Investment Corp., which was considered to be a holder in due course of the note.

SELF TEST

True-False Questions

_____ 1. The maker of a promissory note assumes an unconditional responsibility for payment of it when the instrument is negotiable.

_____ 2. Once the drawee of a check has indicated an acceptance of it, the drawee has primary liability for the payment of the instrument.

_____ 3. Until a drawee indicates an acceptance of the draft, such party has no liability for the draft.

_____ 4. An unqualified indorser has no liability on an instrument once it has been transferred to an indorsee.

_____ 5. The maker of a promissory note must be given notice of dishonor in order to be held liable for payment of it once there has been a dishonor.

_____ 6. Presentment for payment is a necessary step in establishing the liability of a secondary party when an instrument has been dishonored.

_____ 7. If a promissory note is due upon demand, in order to fix the liability of secondary parties, presentment for payment can be made at any time.

_____ 8. If a draft has been dishonored, protest will always be required in order to enable a secondarily liable party to be held responsible for the instrument.

_____ 9. A holder in due course takes an instrument subject to the real defenses of the maker or drawer.

_____ 10. A check that is signed by the drawer but not completed as to the payee or the amount may be enforced against the drawer by a holder in due course who has obtained the check from a thief after the thief has filled in the name of the payee or the amount.

_____ 11. If presentment of an instrument is due on a day that is not a full business day for either party, presentment is due:
- a.   within a reasonable time thereafter not in excess of ten days
- b.   on the next full business day
- c.   within three business days
- d.   on the day specified for presentment
- e.   on the day before the day specified for presentment

_____ 12. Which of the following is a real defense?
- a.   failure of consideration
- b.   fraud in the execution
- c.   forgery
- d.   breach of contract
- e.   b and c are both correct

_____ 13. A holder in due course who is in possession of an instrument that has been materially altered may:
- a.   enforce it in its altered form as long as he or she is unaware of the alteration
- b.   enforce it for the original amount for which it was made payable
- c.   hold the drawee, but not the drawer, fully responsible for the payment of the entire amount
- d.   not enforce the instrument at all
- e.   a and b are both correct

_____ 14. Presentment of a draft for acceptance is required:
- a.   in all cases
- b.   when the draft requires it
- c.   only when it has been dishonored
- d.   when the draft is payable at some place other than the drawee's residence or place of business
- e.   b and d are both correct

_____ 15. A personal defense can be successfully raised:
- a.   only against a holder in due course
- b.   only against the drawer
- c.   only against the payee of the instrument
- d.   only against an ordinary holder
- e.   against both an ordinary holder and a holder in due course

16. Which of the following is a personal defense?
    a. fraud in the inducement
    b. forgery
    c. material alteration
    d. a and b are both correct
    e. a, b, and c are all correct

17. In order for an indorser or drawer to be held responsible for payment on an instrument, there must be:
    a. notice of dishonor given to the party
    b. a dishonor
    c. presentment of the instrument
    d. only b and c are correct
    e. a, b, and c are all necessary

18. presentment of an instrument may be made:
    a. by mail
    b. only through a clearinghouse
    c. at any place that the holder decides on
    d. only at the drawee's place of business
    e. only at the drawer's residence

19. Which of the following circumstances constitutes a dishonor of an instrument?
    a. the maker of a promissory note refuses to pay it when it is presented by the holder on the due date
    b. the drawee of a draft refuses to pay it when it is presented by the holder on the due date
    c. the maker of a promissory note refuses to pay it when it is presented by the holder on the day before the due date
    d. only a and b are correct
    e. a, b, and c are all correct

20. The purpose of a certificate of protest is:
    a. to provide acceptable evidence of dishonor
    b. to make a demand for a new draft
    c. to make a demand for a promissory note
    d. to discharge a draft
    e. b and d are both correct

Completion Questions

21. Fraud in the execution is also referred to _____ _____
    _____ _____.

248

22.   _____ is an official certificate of dishonor given by a consular officer of the United States, a notary public, or other person authorized to certify a dishonor by the law of the place where the dishonor occurs.

23.   The procedure by which the holder of an instrument submits it to the drawee or maker for acceptance or payment is referred to as _____.

24.   A(n) _____ _____ is a draft that is drawn or payable outside the United States.

25.   The party who has the primary liability for the payment of a note is the _____.

Chapter 30

NEGOTIABLE INSTRUMENTS:
CHECKS

There are many factors that one should be aware of in order to protect one's rights when a check is either given or received in payment of a debt or for any other reason.

This chapter considers the nature of a check and the relationship between a depositor and his or her bank. It examines the rules affecting stop-payment orders, certification of checks, and payment of a check that contains the forged or unauthorized signature of the drawer or indorsers. It also considers the effect of an alteration of a check and the factors and rules involved when a person intentionally or unintentionally fails to complete a check fully.

The problems discussed in this chapter affect everyone. Consequently, a good knowledge of the various rules governing checks and electronic fund transfers can be very useful in avoiding some major difficulties.

CHAPTER OBJECTIVES

After reading Chapter 30 of the text and studying the related materials in this chapter of the Student Mastery Guide, you will understand:

1. The nature of a check and the relationship between the parties to it
2. The effect of the following upon a check:
    a. the death or incompetence of a customer
    b. stop payment of a check
    c. certification of a check
    d. unauthorized signatures on a check
    e. alteration and improperly completed checks
3. The nature and effect of electronic fund transfers

MAJOR POINTS TO REMEMBER

The Bank and Its Customers

1. Banks are broadly construed as being "a person engaged in the business of banking, including a savings bank, savings and loan association, credit union or trust company."

2. The relationship between banks and their customers is governed by Article 9.

3. The relationship between a bank and its customer is dependent upon the status of the customer. Generally, a customer is a depositor.

4. The authority of a bank to pay a check ceases when its depositor dies, but it may continue to pay checks presented for payment until it receives notice of the death.

The Uniform Commercial Code does permit a bank to pay on a check for up to ten days after receiving notice of a depositor's death. If, during that ten-day period, a person claiming an interest in the account directs the bank to stop payment on a check, however, the bank must honor the order.

5. The following are specialized types of checks:
   a. certified checks
   b. cashier's checks
   c. traveler's checks

6. A certified check is a check accepted by the bank on which it is drawn.

7. Typically, in the event that a person wishes to substitute the bank's credit for his or her own, he or she will purchase a cashier's check from the bank.

8. Traveler's checks are typically used because of the degree of safety that they provide their holder. Because they contain an authorized signature before they are even used, traveler's checks are protected from use by an unauthorized person.

9. Money orders come in the form of an ordinary check, a teller's check, or a postal money order.

10. A certified cashier's or teller's check, when taken as payment, discharges one's financial obligation.

11. A bank can never refuse to pay a check based on the remitter's defense. However, a bank can refuse payment based on its own defense as long as it has sufficient grounds for such a refusal.

12. In the event that a claimant's check is lost, stolen, or destroyed, she or he may submit a "declaration of loss" to the bank who then must reissue a check within the ninety day period following the original issuance date of the cashier's check. While the bank's liability is discharged upon reissuance, the claimant must pay a holder in due course, if the check is found by him or her.

13. The check collection process traditionally has justified a hold period on deposited checks. However, the Expedited Fund Availability Act places strict guidelines on the amount of time allowable for a hold period. Banks have responded to these stricter guidelines with electronic presentation of information, which hastens the check collection process.

14. Anyone who presents an instrument and obtains payment or acceptance of it is deemed to make certain presentment warranties to the payor or acceptor.

15. A depository bank need not put an indorsement on an instrument in order to be a holder of that instrument.

16. A check does not constitute an assignment of funds in the hands of the drawee.

17. The negotiability of an instrument is not affected by the fact that it is undated, antedated, or postdated (UCC Section 3-114[1]).

18. A bank owes an obligation to its depositor (the drawer) to pay a check that is properly presented to it as long as the account has sufficient funds. In the event that the bank wrongfully dishonors the check, it will be liable to its depositor for any damages proximately caused by such dishonor.

19. Under Section 4-404 of the UCC, a bank is under no obligation to honor a check that is presented for payment more than six months after the date that appears on its face. This type of check is referred to as a "stale" check.

     While the bank is not obligated to honor a stale check, it may do so if it acts in good faith.

Stop Payment

20. A stop-payment order may be made only by the drawer of the instrument and may be made orally or in writing.
     a. An *oral* stop-payment order is good for fourteen days but cannot be renewed.
     b. A *written* stop-payment order is good for six months and can be renewed for additional six-month periods.

21. While the drawer has the right to place a stop-payment order with his or her bank, such an order does not alter the drawer's relationship with the payee or holder, and the drawer may still be liable for the payment of the debt for which the instrument was given.

22. When a bank honors a check and pays it even though its customer has submitted a stop-payment order, the bank acquires the rights of its customer if it is forced to recredit the customer's account. Conversely, if a bank pays a holder in due course over its customer's stop-payment order, the bank acquires the rights of the holder in due course and can still collect from its customer, absent the existence of a real defense to the check.

23. Banks are given a right of subrogation in the event that they pay a check over a stop-payment order. Subrogation to the rights of another party constitutes being able to pursue or defend a claim to the same extent as the party to which the rights are subrogated. For banks, these parties include:
     a. the holder in due course
     b. the payer or other holder
     c. the drawer

24. A customer of a bank is obligated to examine the periodic statement prepared by the bank as well as all the paid items that accompany such statement in order to determine whether any forgeries or alterations have been made.

     If a forgery or alteration has been made on a check, the customer must notify the

252

bank promptly. Failure to give prompt notice will generally result in the customer's inability to raise the forgery or alteration as a defense to the bank's claim that it suffered a loss as a result of lack of proper notice (UCC Section 4-406). In addition, a customer who fails to notify the bank within fourteen days of unauthorized signatures or alterations suffers the losses from similar future acts by the same wrongdoers.

25. If a bank is required to restore to its customer's account funds that were paid improperly by reason of a forgery or alteration, the bank may proceed against the party who presented the check to the bank for payment.

Forged Signature of Drawer

26. When the signature of the drawer of a check is forged, subject to the provisions of Section 4-406 of the UCC, the drawer has no liability for the check even as against a holder in due course (UCC Section 3-401[1]).

27. When a person forges the signature of the drawer, that signature operates as the signature of the unauthorized signer in favor of any person who in good faith pays the instrument or takes it for value (UCC Section 3-404[1]). Consequently, if a bank pays a check over the forged signature of the drawer, it may proceed to recover the funds from the person who made the unauthorized signature (i.e., the forger).

28. If the bank pays a check with a forged drawer's signature in good faith and in observance of reasonable commercial standards, it can charge a drawer's account whose negligence substantially contributed to the forgery or material alteration.

Right of Bank to Charge Customer's Account

29. Under UCC Section 4-401(1), when a bank, in good faith, pays an instrument that was altered, it can charge its customer's account according to its original tenor.

30. If an incomplete instrument is improperly completed, the bank may enforce it according to its tenor as completed.

Payment on Forged Indorsement

31. It is improper for a bank to charge its customer's account for the payment of a check that contains a forged or unauthorized indorsement.

Full-Payment Checks

32. When a good-faith dispute exists regarding the amount of money owed by a debtor to a creditor, the debt is an unliquidated one that can be satisfied by a partial payment through an accord and satisfaction. In such instances the debtor may give the creditor a check marked "paid in full" for less than the full amount owed. If the creditor indorses such a check "under protest" and cashes it, the courts differ on the legal result. Some follow the

common-law rule that the "under protest" notation is of no effect and that an accord and satisfaction has occurred which discharge the balance of the debt. Others follow Section 1-207 of the UCC to hold that the creditor has by this notation reserved the right to sue to collect the balance owing.

Preventive Law: Full-Payment Checks

33. Because the laws of the states differ in their treatment of the cashing of a check marked "paid in full" by indorsing it "under protest," one should not cash such a check without knowing the law of the state in which the transaction occurs. If this is impractical and one wishes to preserve the right to collect the full amount believed to be due, then the check should be returned to the debtor.

MAJOR POINTS OF CASES

Specialty Flooring Co. v. *Palmetto Federal Savings Bank of South Carolina* (p. 532)

The court in this case made two rulings. First, a bank has a right to stop payment on its check so long as that check is written on another bank. Secondly, a party does not have a valid claim to a breach of contract when a bank stops payment on a check when that party knows that it has insufficient funds to cover the check issued in consideration of the bank check.

Applying this ruling to the facts of the case, the court held that Palmetto Federal Savings Bank had every right to stop payment on its check because it was drawn on Citibank. Further, the court held that the stop payment did not constitute a breach of contract, because Specialty Flooring knew that its funds were insufficient to cover the check.

Pulaski State Bank v. *Kalbe* (p. 537)

This case illustrates the rule of Article 4 of the UCC that a check which is otherwise proper, but creates an overdraft, can be honored by the drawee bank, and its payment is implicitly a loan to its drawer customer that must be repaid. Checks creating overdrafts need not be honored by the drawee, and it incurs no liability for dishonoring such checks. Thus, the decision to pay or dishonor is an option available to the drawee bank under the UCC. The option to pay is not terminated in these cases due to the amount of the overdraft created. However, as with all contracts, good-faith performance is required.

Under the facts of this case, the court held for the drawee bank. It found no evidence that it paid the check in bad faith, and, consequently, it had the right to collect the amount of the overdraft from its customer.

Rhode Island Hospital Trust National Bank v. *Zapata Corporation* (p. 541)

In this case, the court ruled that banks do not necessarily fail to exercise ordinary care simply because they do not examine every check to prevent forgeries. Instead, banks can be exempt from this charge by following a procedure both consistent with their prescribed procedure as well as generally acceptable in the banking industry.

Zapata Corporation suffered check forgeries at the hands of one of its employees and subsequently sued Rhode Island Trust. Applying the above ruling, the court found in favor of the bank. Not only was the bank's procedure in handling Zapata's checks consistent with its general practices, this procedure also was more stringent than that which can be found in the banking industry overall.

PRACTICAL CONSIDERATIONS

A stop-payment order is a very useful device, but it must be used properly in order to be effective.

An oral stop-payment order is most useful in emergency situations or when it is impossible to submit a written order promptly. It is effective, however, only for a short period of time, and it is possible that the check for which the order was issued will be paid anyway and the bank may not be responsible for the restoration of the funds that were paid. Consequently, it is generally recommended that an oral stop-payment order be followed by a written order as soon as possible.

Example: Alex is in need of cash and consequently has his wife give him a check made payable to cash so that he can ask someone to cash it for him. After he gets on the train, he reaches for the check and discovers that it is missing. As soon as he arrives at his destination, he telephones his wife and tells her to stop payment on the check. In view of the fact that the check is made payable to cash, Alex's wife would be well advised to call her bank immediately and orally order that payment be stopped on the check. Then, in order to provide better protection against the improper payment of the check, she should deliver or mail to the bank a letter containing a written stop-payment order as soon as she possibly can. Certainly she should do so within fourteen days, before the oral order expires.

SELF TEST

True-False Questions

_____ 1. A check is always payable on demand.

_____ 2. The relationship between a bank and its depositor is considered to be a debtor-creditor relationship.

_____ 3. The negotiability of an instrument is not affected by the fact that it is postdated.

_____ 4. An oral stop-payment order is effective for a period of thirty days.

_____ 5. When the drawer of a check places a stop-payment order with his or her bank, he or she remains liable to any holder of the instrument for payment under all circumstances.

_____ 6. If a bank is notified of the death of its depositor, it may still make payment on checks that are presented within ten days of the date of death.

_____ 7. The holder of a check may have it certified by the drawer's bank.

_____ 8. Under EFTA, a financial institution is liable for all damages proximately caused by its failure to credit a deposit of funds.

_____ 9. The issuance of a check is considered to be an assignment of the funds in the drawer's account.

_____ 10. A depositor of a bank has an obligation to notify the bank of any alterations made to a check and must do so within fourteen days of the date of the alteration.

Multiple-Choice Questions

_____ 11. A written stop-payment order is effective for a period of:
   a. three months
   b. four months
   c. five months
   d. six months

_____ 12. A customer may direct his or her bank to stop payment on a check provided the bank has not:
   a. paid the check in cash
   b. received the check
   c. accepted the check
   d. only a and c are correct
   e. a, b, and c are all correct

_____ 13. When a bank wrongfully dishonors a check, it will be liable for damages to:
   a. any holder of the instrument
   b. the drawee
   c. the drawer
   d. a and c are both correct
   e. a, b, and c are all correct

14. If a bank makes payment on a check that contains the forged signature of the drawer and it is required to restore the funds to the drawer's account, it may recover those funds from:
    a. the drawee
    b. the person who made the unauthorized signature
    c. a prior indorser
    d. anyone who knew of the forgery
    e. b and c are both correct

15. If a check is dated August 3, 1988, it will be considered stale on:
    a. December 3, 1988
    b. February 15, 1989
    c. November 3, 1988
    d. October 18, 1988
    e. November 18, 1988

16. The transferor of a negotiable instrument warrants that:
    a. he or she has no knowledge that the signature of the drawer is unauthorized
    b. the signature of the drawee is authorized
    c. he or she is a holder in due course of the instrument
    d. the instrument will be paid when it is presented for payment
    e. b and c are both correct

17. Which of the following actions materially alters an instrument?
    a. Changing the amount from $1 to $50
    b. inserting a missing date on a check
    c. correcting the spelling of the payee's name
    d. changing the check number on a check
    e. a and d are both correct

18. A bank may stop payment on a:
    a. cashier's check
    b. certified check
    c. teller's check
    d. none of the above
    e. all of the above

19. If a customer does not have enough money in her or his account when a properly payable check is presented for payment the payor bank can:
    a. honor the check and create an overdraft
    b. refuse to honor the check
    c. pay whatever funds are in the customer's account
    d. a and b only
    e. a and c only

257

_____ 20. The loss for a series of forged checks or alterations falls on:
- a. the bank, if notified of the forgery within 30 days of the time the customer received the first forged check
- b. the bank, which must have procedures for detecting forgeries
- c. the customer for any forged check written after 30 days of the receipt of the first forged check up until he or she notifies the bank
- d. a and c only
- e. none of the above

Completion Questions

21. A(n) _____ is a draft drawn on a bank and payable upon demand.

22. Banks have been subject to strict guidelines on the amount of time that they can put holds on most checks since the _____ _____ _____ Act of 1987.

23. When a bank pays a check over a stop-payment order, then to the extent necessary to prevent a loss by the bank, the bank is given a right of _____.

24. A(n) _____ check is dated with a date in the future.

25. A(n) _____ check has been outstanding for more than six months.

Chapter 31

ELECTRONIC FUND TRANSFERS

The way in which money is exchanged in our society has evolved over the course of time. Electronic fund transfers are the latest development, and the volume of funds transferred by this means currently exceeds that exchanged by checks or bank cards. The emergence of electronic fund transfers has resulted not only in a loss of jobs due to automated tellers but also in customers becoming accustomed to banking from home.

The materials presented in this chapter have two main topics within their purview. This chapter discusses not only the law relating to the various systems that are revolutionizing the ways in which consumers bank and make payments but also the regulation of electronic fund transfers.

The increasing importance of electronic fund transfers necessitates your mastery of this material in order to make you a more informed student as well as citizen.

CHAPTER OBJECTIVES

After reading Chapter 31 of the text and studying the related materials in this chapter of the Student Mastery Guide, you will understand:

1. The different types of electronic fund transfers.
2. The laws relating to electronic fund transfers.
3. The regulation of those electronic fund transfers used in large commercial transactions.

MAJOR POINTS TO REMEMBER

Electronic Fund Transfers

1. Several types of electronic fund transfers (EFT) are currently being used, including the following:
    a. point-of-sale terminals
    b. automated tellers and cash dispensers
    c. pay-by-phone systems
    d. preauthorized direct deposits and automatic payments

2. The Electronic Fund Transfer Act (EFTA) is primarily concerned with protecting certain rights of consumers with respect to electronic fund transfer systems.

3. EFTA requires that a financial institution:
    a. disclose the terms and conditions of the electronic fund transfer services to a customer at the time he or she contracts for them
    b. provide written documentation of a transfer each time a customer initiates one

c. with respect to certain preauthorized transfers, either provide notice to its customer when a payment is made as scheduled or negative notice when a payment is not made as scheduled

d. disclose, at the time the customer contracts for the service, the manner in which notice of preauthorized electronic transfers will be handled

4. In order for a customer to be held liable for an electronic fund transfer, it must be shown that:
    a. the transfer was the result of the use of an accepted means of access, and
    b. the customer had been provided with a means of identifying himself or herself to that means of access

5. Generally, the liability of a customer for the unauthorized electronic transfer of funds will not exceed the lesser of $50 or the amount obtained before the time the financial institution becomes aware that an unauthorized transfer has been or may be effected. The customer's liability, however, can be up to $500, if he or she fails to notify the bank within two days of the loss or theft.

    However, the customer is under an obligation to examine the periodic statements provided to him or her and to report any unauthorized transfers or account errors to the financial institution, usually within sixty days. Failure to so notify the bank makes the customer responsible for all unauthorized transfers that the bank can show were caused by this failure to notify.

6. A financial institution is not required to reimburse its customer for a loss if the loss was caused by the customer's failure to report the loss or theft of a card or other means of access within two business days after learning of the loss or theft.

7. Generally under EFTA, a financial institution is liable to a customer for all damages proximately caused by:
    a. its failure to make an electronic fund transfer in the correct amount or in a timely manner when properly instructed to do so by the customer, unless
        i.   the electronic terminal does not have sufficient cash to complete the transaction, or
        ii. the customer does not have sufficient funds in his or her account
    b. its failure to credit a deposit of funds
    c. its failure to stop payment of a preauthorized transfer from a customer's account

Commercial Electronic Fund Transfers

8. Electronic wire transfer systems meet businesses' increasing demand for "same-day funds". Wire transfer systems can finalize transfers within a day.

9. The New York Clearinghouse Interbalance Payments System, with the exception of Fed Wire, is the most notable wire transfer system. Known as CHIPS, this system consists of both "settling" and "participating" banks, the former of which are the primary players.

10. Formerly, regulations promulgated by the Board of Governors of the Federal Reserve guided Fed Wire operations, while CHIPS was governed by its own internal rules. However, because neither of these methods of regulation was a comprehensive framework, Article 4A of the Uniform Commercial Code (UCC) was created which is mutually exclusive with respect to the EFTA in regulating transfers.

11. The basic parties to an Article 4A transaction are the originator and the beneficiary, which are the payment maker and the payment receiver, respectively.

12. Generally, Article 4A applies to "fund transfers", which consist of one or more payment orders. A payment order is an instruction that meets certain conditions, including:
    a. the payment order must either state an amount to be paid that is either fixed or that can be determined by the receiving bank
    b. the instruction's condition of payment must be consistent with the time that the payment is to be made
    c. the receiving bank must be reimbursed.

13. While Article 4A does not require a receiving bank to accept a payment order, the bank may have a separate agreement in effect requiring the bank to do so.

14. The execution date of a payment order is the date on which the receiving bank may execute the payment order. The execution date may not precede the day on which the receiving bank receives the payment order.

15. The payment date is the day on which the beneficiary is properly payable by the beneficiary bank, and it can be no earlier than the day that the beneficiary's's bank receives its payment order.

16. Section 4A-305 addresses the rapidity of the funds transfer. Senders who stipulate that the most expeditious means possible must be employed in making the transfer have a right to have this stipulation honored, and this section imposes liability on receiving banks that cause a delay in a fund transfer.

17. The sender's obligation to pay the amount of the order arises from the receiving bank's acceptance of the payment order. If the beneficiary's bank does not ultimately accept the order, then each sender's obligation is excused and the senders are generally entitled to a refund with interest for any payments that had been made.

18. The receiving bank is obligated to follow the sender's instructions or to pass these instructions along to the intermediary bank unless the receiving bank has made a good faith determination that the funds transfer system designated by the sender would unduly delay the funds transfer's completion. In the absence of such a determination, the receiving bank is liable for the sender's expenses if it fails to either follow or pass along the sender's instructions.

19. Receiving banks that erroneously issue payment orders in an amount less than the sender's order can correct the mistake by issuing a new payment order. However, the new payment order must be issued by the execution date.

20. Receiving banks that execute a payment order by issuing its own payment order to the wrong beneficiary exonerate the sender and all previous senders from their obligation to pay for their orders.

21. Banks and their customers are encouraged to jointly add security procedures to their payment order in order to protect each payment order from fraudulent practices. Common security procedures include:
   a. codes
   b. passwords
   c. callback procedures

22. As long as the sender can demonstrate that it complied with the security procedure and the error would have been detected had the receiving bank done the same, the sender is not required to pay the excess amount in the event that it erroneously sends a payment order greater than the amount intended. However, the sender must notify the receiving bank of the error within 90 days after receiving the bank's notice or else it is liable for any resulting loss to the bank.

MAJOR POINTS OF THE CASES

Wachter v. *Denver National Bank* (p. 549)

This case deals with the applicability of the Electronic Funds Transfer Act and the proper meaning of an "electronic fund transfer" within this act. The court ruled that the mere use of an electronic device to process a transaction does not constitute an electronic funds transfer within the Act's meaning. Not only must an electronic device be used, the court stated, it must be used in place of face to face banking transactions. Furthermore, the electronic device must be used to debit or credit an account.

Applying this ruling to the facts of the case, the court found in favor of the defendant. Because the transaction between Wachter and the Denver National Bank was face to face and did not entail the debiting or crediting of an account, the court reasoned, it was removed from the scope of the Act's coverage, regardless of the fact that an electronic device was used. This ruling was sufficient for dismissing the plaintiff's claims, for they were based on the Act.

Feinman v. *Bank of Delaware* (p. 552)

In this case, the court ruled that the threat of a bank's client to overdraw an ATM is a security reason sufficient to justify the bank's implementation of changes in the terms of the client's account without prior notice to the client. The court added, however, that the bank is liable for its failure to execute an electronic fund transfer when it is instructed to do so by the consumer.

Applying this ruling to the facts of the case, the court found that the Bank of Delaware was justified in its restriction of the Feinman's access to ATM funds, because the Feinmans presented the security risk of overdrawing their fund. Furthermore, the court found the Bank to be liable for any loss incurred by the Feinmans between February 29 and March 2, because this time period represented the date on which the Feinmans requested renewed ATM access (February 29) as well as the date on which it was restored (March 2). However, the court held that there were no damages and, thus, the Bank had no financial obligations to the Feinmans.

Shawmut Worcester County Bank v. First American Bank & Trust (p. 560)

This case deals with erroneous transfers, and the court made two separate rulings. First, a bank that erroneously receives a payment and then credits the beneficiary's account is not obligated to reverse the transfer. Secondly, where security procedures of a receiving bank are adequate and adhered to, this bank has no liability for accepting erroneously made payments.

Applying this ruling to the case, the court held that the First American Bank & Trust as a receiving bank did not have to reverse the transfer erroneously made by Shawmut. Furthermore, the court held that First American possessed no liability for accepting these mistakenly transferred funds because it complied with reasonable security procedures in examining the transfer for errors.

SELF TEST

True-False Questions

_____ 1. An automated teller machine (ATM) is an example of an electronic funds transfer.

_____ 2. Point-of-Sale terminals allow businesses to transfer funds to individual accounts.

_____ 3. Under the EFTA, a consumer is any natural person.

_____ 4. The financial institution bears full liability for unauthorized transfers.

_____ 5. "Electronic wire transfer systems are important in meeting businesses' demand for "same-day funds."

_____ 6. "Participating banks" are the primary players in the CHIPS system.

_____ 7. Neither Fed Wire nor CHIPS transactions are covered by the EFTA.

8.   In regulating electronic fund transfers, Article 4A and EFTA contain sufficient overlaps and further revision is needed.

9.   Article 4A is limited to electronic transfers.

10.   Receiving banks bear the loss for erroneously issuing a payment order in an amount less than the sender's order.

Multiple-Choice Questions

11.   All of the following is true of the EFTA, except:
    a.   It became effective in 1978.
    b.   It is part of a larger piece of legislation known as the Financial Institutions Regulatory and Interest Rate Control Act.
    c.   Its primary objective is to protect certain consumer rights in dealing with electronic systems.
    d.   The consumer under this act is any natural person.
    e.   all of the above

12.   The EFTA stipulates that the terms and conditions of electronic fund transfers be disclosed:
    a.   before a customer contracts for such services
    b.   at the time a customer contracts for each service
    c.   within 10 days after a customer contracts for such services
    d.   within 72 hours after a customer contracts for such services
    e.   The EFTA contains no such stipulation.

13.   The financial institution's documentation of a customer's transfer must contain:
    a.   the date of the transfer
    b.   the type of transfer
    c.   the location or identification of the electronic terminal involved.
    d.   all of the above
    e.   none of the above

14.   In order for a preauthorized electronic fund transfer that debits a customer's account to be used:
    a.   the customer must agree in writing
    b.   the customer must furnish a copy of the authorization
    c.   the bank must receive permission from the Federal Reserve
    d.   all of the above
    e.   a and b, only

15. A customer may notify his or her financial institution of any errors in a financial statement within how many days after receiving the report?
   a. 30
   b. 60
   c. 90
   d. 120
   e. none of the above

16. After discovering the loss or theft of a card or other means of access to an electronic fund transfer, how much time does the customer have to notify the financial institution?
   a. 12 hours
   b. 36 hours
   c. 48 hours
   d. 10 days
   e. 5 business days

17. Which of the following exceptions excuse financial institutions from liability for failing to make an electronic funds transfer?
   a. the electronic terminal does not have sufficient cash to complete the transaction
   b. the customer has overdrawn his or her account more than three times in the past
   c. the customer does not have sufficient funds in his or her account
   d. a and b only
   e. a and c only

18. Article 4A is applicable to which type of transfers
   a. electronic transfers
   b. any transfers
   c. all transfers, except those made by mail
   d. mail transfers
   e. none of the above

19. The basic parties to an Article 4A transaction include:
   a. the participating banks
   b. the settling banks
   c. the beneficiary
   d. all of the above
   e. a and b only

_____ 20. The execution date of a payment order is:
     a. the date on which the sender notifies the receiving bank of its intention to pay
     b. the date on which the receiving bank will execute the payment order
     c. the date on which the receiving bank accepts the sender's payment
     d. dependent upon the amount of the payment order
     e. none of the above

Completion Questions

21. A(n) _____ bank is a receiving bank other than the originator's bank or the beneficiary's bank.

22. Article 4A encourages _____ _____ to ensure that each payment order is properly authorized and is not issued in error.

23. Section _____ of Article 4A deals with payment orders erroneously transmitted by a sender.

24. _____ is the largest wire transfer system.

25. _____ _____ are the primary players on the CHIPS system.

Chapter 32

SECURED TRANSACTIONS

A creditor normally expects to be paid for the indebtedness owed to him or her by a debtor; but an element of risk is always present when credit is extended to another person. As a result of such risk, and also because of the desirability of maintaining economic stability and continued use of credit in commercial transactions, the law has provided creditors with certain devices that are intended to reduce the risk factor.

This chapter considers the means by which creditors can increase their security with respect to credit they have extended to other persons in certain commercial transactions. It discusses the elements involved in establishing an enforceable security interest, the perfection of such interest, priority of claims when a person is indebted to more than one creditor at the same time, and the rights of the parties when an installment contract that is accompanied by a security interest has been assigned. Finally, the text discusses the rights and remedies available when there has been a default in payment.

As you examine the chapter, keep in mind that the rules that are presented apply to credit transactions in which personal property is involved. The rules affecting real property are considered in Chapter 40.

CHAPTER OBJECTIVES

After reading Chapter 32 of the text and studying the related materials in this chapter of the Student Mastery Guide, you will understand:

1. The nature of a secured transaction
2. Secured transactions under Article 9 of the Uniform Commercial Code
3. The requirements for establishing an enforceable security interest
   a. the security agreement
   b. attachment
4. The methods of perfecting a security interest
5. The priority scheme applied to security interests
6. The rights of parties upon default

MAJOR POINTS TO REMEMBER

Article 9

1. Article 9 of the Uniform Commercial Code provides comprehensive rules for administering the various types of financing arrangements in which personal property is used as security. It applies to personal property and fixtures.

2. Goods are classified as:
   a. consumer goods: those that are used or bought for use primarily for personal, family, or household purposes (UCC Section 9-109[1])

b. equipment: those goods used primarily in business other than inventory, farm products, or consumer goods (UCC Section 9-102[2])

c. inventory: goods held by someone for sale or lease or to be furnished under service contracts or if they are raw materials, work in process, or materials used or consumed in business (UCC Section 9-109[4])

d. farm products: crops, livestock, or supplies used or produced in farming operations, or products, crops, or livestock in their manufactured states and in possession of a debtor engaged in raising, fattening, grazing, or other farm operations.

Establishing an Enforceable Security Interest

3. A security interest in collateral attaches when the:
    a. parties agree that the secured party has a security interest (i.e., a security agreement exists)
    b. debtor receives value
    c. debtor has rights in the collateral

    The attachment of the security interest creates rights between the secured party and the debtor.

The Security Agreement

4. The security agreement creates or provides a security interest (UCC Section 9-105[1]).

5. Except for those situations in which the collateral is in the possession of the secured party, a security agreement must be in writing and must:
    a. contain a description or identification of the collateral
    b. give the names and addresses of the debtor and secured party
    c. be signed by the debtor

6. If a security agreement contains an "after-acquired property" clause, the secured party acquires a "continuing general lien" on property acquired by the debtor to replace the original inventory.

7. A security agreement may provide that future advances will be covered by the terms of the agreement. When a clause making future advances secured by the collateral is combined with an "after-acquired property" clause, a floating lien is created.

8. Even though under an agreement a purchaser acquires property to which the seller retains title, the purchaser has rights in those goods that are sufficient to support the security interest of a creditor. The debtor must also receive value for attachment to occur. Value includes any consideration sufficient to support a simple contract.

Perfection of a Security Interest

9. A security interest in goods may become a "perfected security interest" by:
    a. the filing of a financing statement in the appropriate public office, or
    b. the taking of possession of the collateral, or
    c. attachment of the security interest

10. A merchant who sells consumer goods (other than motor vehicles or fixtures) to a buyer on credit automatically obtains a perfected security interest when his or her interest in the collateral attaches. This interest is known as a *purchase-money security interest*.

11. A financing statement, when properly filed, serves notice to the public in general that the creditor has a secured interest in the collateral that is identified in the agreement.

12. A security interest may be perfected by filing either:
    a. a financing statement or
    b. the security agreement

13. If a secured party perfects his or her security interest by filing a financing statement any subsequent amendment of that statement must be done by a writing that is signed by both the debtor and the secured party.

14. The place of filing of the appropriate security document will be determined by the type of collateral involved.

15. When a financing statement (or security agreement) is filed, it is effective for a period of five years from the date of the filing. Thereafter, a continuation statement (which is required to be signed only by the secured party) must be filed in order for the security interest to remain perfected.

16. A security interest in accounts or general intangibles must be perfected by the filing of the appropriate document.

17. A security interest in money or negotiable instruments will be perfected only by taking possession of the collateral.

Priority

18. The following are rules regarding the priority of claims related to debts:
    a. The holder of a perfected security interest has priority over a nonperfected security interest.
    b. As between two secured parties who have unperfected security interests, the party whose security interests attached first will have priority.
    c. The holder of an unperfected security interest has priority over general creditors of the debtor who have established no lien on the collateral.

d.   A general creditor who obtains a judgment against the debtor and has the sheriff levy against the debtor's property will have priority over an unperfected security interest.

e.   If someone furnishes services or materials in the ordinary course of business and state law gives that person a lien on goods in his or her possession with respect to those services or materials, that lien will take priority over a perfected security interest. So, for example, a mechanic's lien will take priority over a perfected security interest.

Conflicting Security Interests

19.   Conflicting security interests are given preference according to priority in time of filing or perfection; that is, the first to file or perfect has priority over subsequent secured parties who thereafter file or perfect their respective security interests.

    The holder of a purchase-money security interest has priority over conflicting security interests in the same collateral if the purchase-money security interest is perfected within ten days of the time the debtor takes possession of the collateral.

20.   Under Section 9-312(3) of the UCC, a purchase-money security interest in inventory has priority over a previously perfected security interest if:

a.   the purchase-money security interest is perfected at the time the debtor receives possession of the inventory

b.   the purchase-money secured party gives notification in writing to the holder of the conflicting security interest, provided the holder had filed a financing statement covering the same types of inventory:

    i.   before the date of the filing made by the purchase-money secure party or

    ii.   before the beginning of the twenty-one-day period during which the purchase-money security interest is temporarily perfected without filing or possession.

c.   the holder of the conflicting interest receives notice within five years before that debtor receives possession of the inventory

d.   the notification states that the person giving notice has or expects to acquire a purchase-money security interest in inventory of the debtor, describing the inventory by item or type

21.   A security interest in chattel paper can be perfected either by filing or by taking possession of the chattel paper.

Protection of Buyers of Goods

22.   A buyer in the ordinary course of business takes goods free of a security interest created by his or her seller even if it is perfected and the buyer knows it (UCC Section 9-307[1]).

23.   If a security interest in goods is perfected and those goods thereafter become a component part of a product or mass and lose their identity as a result, the security interest continues in the product or mass of which the goods become a part.

24. A buyer who purchases consumer goods takes them free of any perfected purchase-money security interest created by his or her seller as long as the buyer purchases them without knowledge of the security interest before a financing statement is filed.

25. A security interest in fixtures is perfected by means of a "fixtures filing", which is a financing statement that is filed in the office where a mortgage on real property would be recorded and that covers the goods that are or are to become fixtures.

26. A buyer who does not qualify as a buyer in the ordinary course of business may under some circumstances purchase goods free of security interest even when these goods are subject to security interest. This is possible when the security interest secures future advances made after the secured party either becomes aware of the purchase, or after 45 days, whichever comes first.

ASSIGNMENT

27. Generally, the UCC does not permit the original purchaser under an installment contract for the sale of goods to restrict the assignment of the contract. A clause in the contract restricting assignment will not prevent it from being assigned.

28. Unless otherwise provided, when an installment contract and security interest are assigned, the rights of the assignee are subject to the terms of the contract between the account debtor and assignor and also to any defense or claim that arises from it.

29. A waiver-of-defense clause in a business transaction installment contract is permissible and effective as to an assignee of the contract provided the assignee takes the instrument for value, in good faith, and without notice of a claim or defense to it. Therefore, an account debtor will not be able to raise a defense against the assignee unless it is one that could be asserted against a holder in due course of a negotiable instrument.

Default

30. When a debtor defaults under a security agreement, the secured party may:
    a. reduce the claim to a judgment
    b. foreclose on the security interest
    c. enforce the security interest by any available judicial procedure
    d. take possession of the collateral (unless otherwise agreed)

31. After a debtor has defaulted, a secured party may sell, lease, or otherwise dispose of the property in order to satisfy the indebtedness. The disposition, depending on the circumstances, may be by public or private proceedings, but it must be commercially reasonable in all respects.

32. Even though a debtor has defaulted, either the debtor or any other secured party may redeem the collateral provided that the secured party has not disposed of it, entered into a contract to dispose of it, or completed the process for retaining it.

271

33. Purchasers of seized collateral generally take free of interests subordinate to that of the secured party.

34. When seized collateral is sold, the proceeds are distributed as follows:
   a. to pay for reasonable expenses of repossession and disposition
   b. to pay the unpaid debt and other lawful charges
   c. to pay written claims made by those holding subordinate secured parties
   d. any excess goes to the debtor

35. A secured party who does not comply with the UCC can be stopped from disposing of the collateral, held liable for losses caused by an improper disposition, prohibited from applying sale proceeds to the debt, or barred from collecting a deficiency judgment.

Preventive Law: Minimizing the Risk of Nonpayment by a Debtor

36. To increase the chance of being paid, the creditor should:
   a. have a sufficient written security agreement
   b. where appropriate, include after-acquired or future-advance clauses in the security agreement
   c. perfect the security interest and establish an early priority by filing or taking possession of the collateral

MAJOR POINTS OF CASES

Banque Worms v. *David Construction Co., Inc.* (p. 572)

The decision in this case involved a very strict interpretation of a statutory provision. The court ruled that the plaintiff's claim to a perfected security interest in the truck purchased by the defendant was not valid because Banque Worms filed a continuation statement two days prior to the beginning of the proper time period, thus invalidating this statement. The plaintiff's resulting unperfected security interest had rights subordinate to the status of the defendant, who was an unsecured purchaser as well as not a buyer in the ordinary course of business. Importantly, the court also ruled that the defendant would have had to have actual, not constructive, knowledge of the unperfected security interest for the plaintiff's claim to be valid.

In re Ivie & Associates, Inc. (p. 576)

In this case, the court ruled that IPI's security interest in two-thirds of the scrapers was not perfected, because they failed to perfect the security interest within fifteen days of Ivie's taking possession of the scrapers. As a result of the security interest not being perfected, the bank's prior security interest took priority over that of IPI.

Important to this decision was the court's interpretation of "possession" under O.C.G.A. language. Consistent with a precedent, the court held that because the lease agreement was dated back to the time of delivery, it was at that time that "possession" occurred.

Davis County Savings Bank v. *Production Credit Association* (p. 581)

The decision in this case revealed the extent to which claims to proceeds as a prior perfected security party are limited. When a party is a buyer, in the sense that the party "purchased" collateral under the language of the Iowa Code, that party is free of a bank's claimed interest if a future advance clause is not filed within 45 days of the purchase. Additionally, any successor to that party is free of interest as well.

Applying this ruling to the facts of the case, the court reversed the decision in favor of the PCA. Because the bank did not file the future advance clause within the 45 day time limit, Dan and Amber as well as their successor, PCA, are free of the claimed interest.

Capital Factors, Inc. v. *Caldor, Inc.* (p. 584)

In this memorandum decision, the court held that parties receiving goods from suppliers must remit their payment to any company that has taken a security interest in those suppliers, so long as the company has provided the parties with actual knowledge of the change.

Applying this ruling to the facts of the case, the court affirmed the ruling in favor of Capital Factors. Having taken a security interest in the supplier of Caldor, Inc., as well as having notified Caldor, Inc. of this fact, the court determined that Capital Factors was entitled to the payments from Caldor, Inc. directly.

Mbank El Paso, N.A. v. *Sanchez* (p. 585)

With its decision, the court held that a secured creditor does not escape the duty of peaceable repossession simply by delegating it to an independent contractor. While such a creditor may employ either judicial or nonjudicial means to attain a repossession, in the event that the latter is employed, the creditor still is burdened with the duty to public safety in the course of the repossession.

With this ruling applied to the case, the court found in favor of Sanchez, who was the victim of tortious acts during the repossession of her car. The repossessor was El Paso Recovery Service, an independent contractor, therefore, Mbank was liable.

PRACTICAL CONSIDERATIONS

While the Uniform Commercial Code makes extensive provisions with respect to priority of claims, it should be remembered that these provisions are relevant and important only when a person is indebted to more than one creditor at the same time, and even then only if the debtor is not meeting his or her financial obligations. As long as the debtor is paying his or her bills, and each creditor's indebtedness is being satisfied, the security interest that exists and the priorities that have been established with respect to them serve as a means of providing comfort, security, and protection to the creditors. They are similar to the parachute that a test pilot wears when testing the performance of a new plane: He doesn't expect to use it, but it's certainly nice to know that it's there. If the debtor should default on his or her debts, then the provisions of the code with respect to priorities become very important to the creditors involved, for they will determine which creditors will receive payment and which may be the unlucky ones to find themselves holding debts on which they cannot collect. It should also be remembered that as long as the debtor has assets that are sufficient to satisfy all of his or her debts, the priorities established by the UCC in effect create a waiting list and establish the order in which the debts will be paid. Creditors may thus have to get in line to be paid, but they are likely to be paid eventually.

SELF TEST

True-False Questions

_____ 1. A security agreement must always be in writing in order for it to be valid and enforceable.

_____ 2. If a security agreement contains an "after-acquired property" clause, the secured party acquires a continuing general lien on property acquired to replace the original inventory of the debtor.

_____ 3. A security interest can be perfected by the filing of either a financing statement or the security agreement of the parties.

_____ 4. A financing statement can be filed only after a security agreement has been made.

_____ 5. A security interest in accounts or general intangibles can be perfected only by the filing of a financing statement or security agreement.

_____ 6. A security interest cannot be perfected until a security interest attaches to the collateral.

_____ 7. A buyer in the ordinary course of business takes the goods being sold free of a security interest created by the seller even if such security interest is perfected.

_____ 8. A security agreement generally does not create a security interest.

_____ 9. A security interest in negotiable instruments can be perfected only by taking possession of the collateral.

_____ 10. An unperfected security interest will always be given priority over a general creditor whose claim has not been reduced to a judgment.

274

_____ 11. Goods can be classified in which of the following categories?
    a. inventory
    b. equipment
    c. chattel paper
    d. a and b are both correct
    e. a, b, and c are all correct

_____ 12. A security agreement that is required to be in writing must contain in its terms:
    a. the amount of the debt
    b. a description of the collateral
    c. the signature of the debtor
    d. b and c are both correct
    e. a, b, and c are all correct

_____ 13. Which of the following actions perfects a security interest in goods?
    a. taking possession of the collateral
    b. recording a description of the goods with a court
    c. executing a security agreement
    d. executing a financing statement
    e. a and d are both correct

_____ 14. A provision relating to which of the following is usually found in a security agreement?
    a. terms of repayment
    b. name of the debtor's employer
    c. acceleration of payment rights
    d. rights of the state attorney general
    e. a and c are both correct

_____ 15. A financing statement must be signed by:
    a. the creditor only
    b. the debtor only
    c. both the debtor and the creditor
    d. either the debtor or the creditor
    e. anyone with knowledge of the secured interest

_____ 16. A security interest may be perfected by the filing of:
    a. a negotiation statement
    b. the security agreement
    c. a financing statement
    d. b and c are both correct
    e. a, b, and c are all correct

_____ 17. A financing statement that has been filed is effective for:
a. two years
b. three years
c. five years
d. seven years
e. ten years

_____ 18. If a secured party perfects his or her security interest by filing and thereafter allows the filing to lapse, the:
a. security interest will lapse
b. security interest will become unperfected
c. creditor will lose his or her right to collect payment on the debt
d. time for payment of the debt will be automatically extended
e. lapse will have no effect on the perfection of the security interest

_____ 19. When a debtor defaults under a security agreement, the secured party may usually:
a. automatically enter a judgment against the creditor
b. foreclose against any property owned by the debtor
c. retake possession of the collateral
d. take possession of any property owned by the debtor
e. b and d are both correct

_____ 20. A debtor may redeem his or her collateral after a default:
a. at any time
b. only with the permission of the secured party
c. if the secured party has not disposed of it or contracted to dispose of it
d. if the secured party has not completed the process to retain the collateral
e. c and d are both correct

Completion Questions

21. An agreement that creates or provides a security interest is known as a(n) _____ _____.

22. A(n) _____ _____ is any lender, seller, or other person in whose favor there is a security interest.

23. A writing that evidences both a monetary obligation and a security interest in specific goods is referred to as _____ _____.

Statutory Liens

5.   There are three types of statutory liens:
     a.   Common law liens for service providers.
     b.   "Mechanic's Lien".
     c.   Those involving common carriers and warehouse operators.

6.   Improvements to real property without payment entitle the service provider to a security interest in the property. This is known as the "mechanic's lien."

7.   According to Article 7 of the Uniform Commercial Code (UCC), common carriers and warehouse operators can foreclose on the debtor's goods when they are unable to collect payment. Additionally, even after the goods are transferred to a third party, the common carriers and warehouse operators retain their security interest in the goods.

Tax Liens

8.   Upon making a tax assessment accompanied by a notice and demand for payment, the Internal Revenue Service (IRS) acquires an automatic lien against all the taxpayer's property, and the lien is valid for ten years.

9.   The IRS can seek a lien foreclosure to enforce its tax lien; however, it does not acquire secured creditor status unless the Service files a Notice of Federal Tax Lien.

Judicial Liens and Prejudgment Remedies

10.   A creditor may seek collection of the debt through the judicial process. Also, either before a formal lawsuit or pending the case's outcome, the creditor may seek prejudgment remedies. The best example of a prejudgment remedy is attachment, which allows the creditor to seize the debtor's property pending an outcome if that creditor procures a writ of attachment from the court.

11.   Replevin is another prejudgment remedy; however, it permits secured creditors to reach only the property that is security or collateral for the loan, while attachment can be used to seize any non-exempted property.

12.   As both a prejudgment and postjudgment remedy, garnishment enables the creditor to reach the debtor's cash assets. Under the Consumer Credit Protection Act a garnishment action is limited in that a debtor can retain either 75% of his or her weekly after tax, disposable income or the amount equal to thirty hours' paid work at the minimum wage level, whichever is greater.

13.   Receivership is both a prejudgment and postjudgment remedy used in exceptional cases. Such a remedy appoints a neutral third party to take control over the assets.

Judicial Liens and Postjudgment Liens

14. Because acquiring a judgement is far easier than actually collecting a debt, the creditor has available to him or her postjudgment remedies:

    a. Execution is a separate judicial process that allows the creditor to seize debtor's assets that are not exempted by state statutes. The debtor does have a brief period during which he or she can buy back his or her property by paying the owed amount. This is known as the right of redemption.

    b. In the event that a writ of execution does not satisfy the creditor's lien, a supplementary proceeding provides for an investigation of the debtor for any assets that may have escaped the execution process.

    c. Postjudgment garnishment stipulates that the debtor must turn his or her assets over for sale to satisfy the lien.

Debtor's Alternative Remedies

15. In a number of states, the debtor can assign property title to a trustee. Although the assigned property's value is usually less than the total debt outstanding, those creditors who accept the assignment receive an equal share of the proceeds upon the assets' sale. Creditors do have the option to reject this process.

16. Creditors who enter into a "composition of creditors' agreement" can expect to receive less than the full amount owed to them. Dissenting creditors are not bound by such an agreement.

17. With the creditor's consent, the debtor can seek a time extension for his or her debt repayment and is protected by an enforceable contract from collection actions for that period of time.

Suretyship

18. Creditors can seek extra protection in debt extensions by requiring that a third party accepts debt liability. This creditor-third party relationship can be constructed as either a surety or as a guaranty arrangement, both of which are governed by contract law.

19. A suretyship agreement requires the third party to pay the debtor's obligation on the due date regardless either of the requirements made of the debtor or the actions taken by the creditor up to that point. Suretyship differs from a guaranty agreement in that a guaranty agreement requires the third party to pay the debt only if the debtor defaults.

20. An indemnity agreement protects the debtor from the non-payment of the debt by the third-party.

Surety and Guarantor Rights

21. Both the surety and guarantor have rights to reimbursement, contribution, and subrogation.

Surety and Guarantor Defenses

22. By raising certain defenses, the surety or guarantor may be able to avoid paying the creditor. Generally, whichever defenses are available to the debtor are also available to the surety or guarantor.

Lender Liability

23. Counterclaims filed by debtors fall under an area of law known as "lender liability". While such claims range from common law fraud and negligence to environmental violations, the basis for most claims involves a charge that the lender put the debtor's business in financial jeopardy by either its actions or lack thereof.

Common Law Claims

24. A legal relationship often forms prior to a contractual agreement, holding the lender accountable for its commitment to a certain loan amount. If such an amount is not provided in the actual contract, the lender can be sued for a breach of contract.

25. Often times loan agreements may be negotiated without putting them into writing, and the Statute of Frauds may be applicable in the event that one party defaults. However, states sometimes require that loan amounts greater than an established amount must be in writing. Such a requirement can be detrimental to debtors who rely on verbal agreement to renew a contract.

26. Acceleration clauses allow the lender to demand full payment in certain circumstances such as the failure to make a principal and/or interest payment. Although the debtor can correct minor breaches, the lender does have the option of foreclosing on the property securing the loan if such corrections are not made.

27. Debtors can file suits claiming fraudulent behavior on the part of the lender during the negotiation process. However, because the burden of proof for fraud is so great, debtors will often include an allegiance of negligence in the complaint, which are based on a breach of the lender's duty of care owed to the debtor.

28. Other common law claims include:
    a. Economic Duress
    b. Control
    c. Good Faith

Statutory Claims

29.   Many statutory claims are based on a state's consumer protection act (CPA). Consumers can sue for victimization by unfair and deceptive trade practices.

30.   Lending institutions that foreclose on real property that is contaminated by toxic or chemical waste may be responsible for cleanup under the federal Comprehensive Environmental Response, Compensation, and Liability Act (CERCLA) of 1980. The Fleet Factors decision further expanded lending institutions' liability, making them responsible not only in cases where they have actual participation in hazardous waste decisions but also where they could have impacted a decision of this type.

Remedies

31.   Traditional contract and tort law remedies are the remedies most often used by debtors who initiate lender liability suits.

32.   The applicability of punitive damages is dependent upon the lender's level of tortious misconduct. Generally, the demonstration of fraud or other intentional misconduct is necessary for the allowance of punitive damages.

33.   Specific performance is not a typical remedy, due to the court's hesitancy to keep together two parties in a desiccated contractual relationship.

34.   Depending on the debtor's ability to establish a cause of action, she or he may have statutory remedies available. These statutes have great appeal, because they typically provide for recovery of treble damages.

Fraudulent Transfers

35.   To the extent that creditors can demonstrate that debtors transfer property to a third person in order to prevent seizure, creditors can win fraudulent conveyance lawsuits. Circumstantial evidence is acceptable in such suits.

36.   Creditors can rely on both the common law and statutory provisions to establish a fraudulent conveyance cause of action. The creditors' range of remedies include:
    a.   they can seek to have the transfer avoided and set aside
    b.   they can attempt to execute against the property in the hands of the transferee
    c.   they can file a motion for injunction

Bulk Transfers

37.   To prevent "bulk transfers" designed to avoid seizure of property, Article 6 of the UCC requires that a seller of a significant part of her or his inventory must notify the buyer of all creditors as well as inform all creditors of the intended bulk sale. Such a provision makes the buyer accountable.

38.   A 1988 report by the National Conference of Commissioners on Uniform State Laws (NCCUSL) and the American Law Institute (ALI) stated that bulk transfer regulation was unnecessary. This report offered a revised Article 6 which greatly weakened such regulation and encouraged states to adopt it.

Debtor Protection Statutes

39.   Additional protection to consumer debtors is provided by:
a.   The Equal Credit Opportunity Act
b.   The Truth in Lending Act
c.   The Fair Debt Collection Practices Act

Issues and Trends: Prejudgment Attachment

40.   To the extent that a state prejudgment attachment statute is filed without proper notice to the defendant as well as without a hearing prior to its filing, such a statute is unconstitutional on due process grounds unless the affiant can demonstrate exigent circumstances. This principle comes from the 1988 Supreme Court case, Connecticut v. Doehr.

Issues and Trends: How Bank Policies are Changing

41.   Because of the degree to which courts sympathize with plaintiff-debtors in cases concerning oral agreements between the debtor and lender regarding loan terms, lenders are now increasingly protecting themselves by including mandatory arbitration provisions in loan documents. Under these clauses, the debtor waives his or her right to a jury trial and in favor of arbitration for resolving loan agreement disputes.

MAJOR POINTS OF CASES

Alabama Farm Bureau Mutual Casualty Company v. *Lyle Service Ambulance Wrecker* (p. 593)

This decision determined the applicability of common law and statutory liens. The court ruled that neither of these liens are acquired by a party that merely tows and stores property, specifically a vehicle. Statutory liens apply only in the event that the party contributes to the "production, manufacture or repair" of a vehicle. Similarly, there is no common law lien unless the party claiming such a lien has imparted additional value to the vehicle. Applying this ruling to the facts of the case, the court reversed the earlier decision in favor of Lyle, who merely towed and stored the Farm Bureau vehicle.

McLaws v. *Kruger* (p. 597)

In this case, the court affirmed the trial court's decision, which determined the status of proceeds from the voluntary sale of homestead real property in relation to exemption from garnishment. The court ruled that Kruger's sale of his homestead changed the status of his property from real to personal. Because voluntary sales of homesteads do not fall under personal property exemptions, such an exemption is not appropriate. The court noted that it relied on the explicit language of the statute.

Layne v. *Gardner* (p. 603)

In its decision, the court held that no cosurety or coguarantor can enforce any right of contribution against any person liable to the debt unless full payment has been made. Applying this ruling to the case, the court found that Garner's suit against the Laynes was not justified. The debt had not been fully paid, protecting the Laynes from such a suit by virtue of the finding that they were a liable party.

United States v. *Maryland Bank and Trust Co.* (p. 607)

The court ruled that lending institutions that foreclose on land are equally responsible for the cleanup of hazardous wastes on that land under CERCLA as any other owner would be. Important to this decision was the court's finding that lending institutions are not covered under CERCLA's exemptions. The court stated that lending institutions do not hold ownership in land primarily to protect its secured interest. Applying this rule to the facts of the case, the court ordered Maryland Bank and Trust to repay the Environmental Protection Agency for its cleanup of the bank's land.

First National State Bank of New Jersey v. *Commonwealth Savings and Loan Association of Norristown* (p. 610)

In its decision, the court's reasoning rested on two principles. First, in the event that an investment venture is a financial failure, specific performance is perfectly appropriate. Secondly, the risk of a financial venture belongs on the holders of the permanent, not construction, lender, because it is this lender whose primary security rests on the capitalized value of the projects.

Applying these principles to the case's facts, the circuit court affirmed the district court's decision to grant First National's request for specific performance and order Commonwealth to close the permanent loan agreement. Mathema Developers' project was a financial failure, and it was Commonwealth as the permanent lender who had primary security on the venture.

SELF-TEST
True-False Questions

_____ 1. Interest rates and debt collection practices are no longer rigorously regulated by the government.

_____ 2. Real and personal property liens can be created only by consensual agreement of debtor and creditor.

_____ 3. The artisan's lien applies only as long as the service provider has possession of the personal property.

_____ 4. Allowing the creditor to seize the debtor's property pending the outcome of litigation, attachment is the most used prejudgement remedy.

_____ 5. The Due Process Clause affects state prejudgement attachment statutes.

_____ 6. Replevin is similar to attachment but gives the lender more power in that it allows him or her to seize any property owned by the debtor.

_____ 7. The assignment for the benefit of creditors allows the debtor to pay less than the full amount owed as complete satisfaction of debt with participating creditors.

_____ 8. Both surety and guaranty agreements are governed by contract law.

_____ 9. Upon paying the debtor's obligation, sureties and guarantors almost always have rights to reimbursement, contribution, and subrogation.

_____ 10. Subrogation permits the recovery of expenses incurred by surety or guarantor in performing agreement.

Multiple-Choice Questions

_____ 11. The area of law referred to as "lender liability":
    a.   is relatively new, arising in the last decade or so.
    b.   has been around for centuries.
    c.   is typified by debtors' counterclaims that contend that the lender acted or failed to act in a manner which put the debtor's business entity in jeopardy.
    d.   a and c
    e.   b and c

_____ 12. The debtor-lender relationship is established formally when:
    a.   each party agrees to equitable funding
    b.   a contractual agreement to lend money is reached
    c.   the contract negotiation process begins
    d.   the lender agrees to lend any amount of money
    e.   none of the above

_____ 13.   _____ loan agreements may be valid.
                       a.   oral
                       b.   written
                       c.   third-party
                       d.   mediated
                       e.   a and b only

_____ 14.   Acceleration clauses in promissory notes:
                       a.   permit the debtor to pay 90% of the debt if she or he pays
                             that percentage within 75 % of the loan period
                       b.   are meaningless under recently revised law
                       c.   permit the lender to demand full payment upon the
                             happening of a certain event
                       d.   allow third parties to pay some of what is owned by the
                             debtor in return for a quickly approved loan by the lender
                       e.   none of the above

_____ 15.   Consumer protection acts:
                       a.   exist in every state
                       b.   protect consumers from excessive taxation
                       c.   provide consumers with the right to sue in the event that
                             they are victimized by unfair and deceptive trade practices
                       d.   a and c
                       e.   none of the above

_____ 16.   The Fleet Factors decision:
                       a.   indirectly imposed on consumers' rights to protection
                       b.   expanded the potential liability of the lending institution
                             where it simply could have impacted on hazardous waste
                             decision
                       c.   was implicitly rejected by the EPA in the issuance of a rule
                             in 1992
                       d.   all of the above
                       e.   b and c only

_____ 17.   The types of statutory liens include:
                       a.   common law liens
                       b.   "mechanic's lien"
                       c.   the liens provided in Article 7 of the Uniform Commercial
                             Code
                       d.   all of the above
                       e.   a and b only

_____ 18. A UCC Article 7 Lien pertains to:
- a. services for labor and materials to repair personal property
- b. unpaid lodging charges
- c. services for labor and materials to repair real property
- d. both a and c
- e. none of the above

_____ 19. Garnishment is:
- a. a prejudgment remedy
- b. a postjudgment remedy
- c. permits the creditor to reach the debtor's cash assets
- d. all of the above
- e. b and c only

_____ 20. What distinguishes garnishment as a postjudgment remedy is that:
- a. the debtor is ordered to turn over the assets so that they can be sold to satisfy the judgement lien.
- b. it is used only in exceptional cases
- c. it is an injunction rather than a remedy
- d. it protects the debtor
- e. none of the above

Completion Questions

21. Under the postjudgment remedy of _____, the court orders a third party to take control of a debtor's assets.

22. A _____ represents a claim against the debtor's property that requires satisfaction before the property can be made available to other creditors.

23. Common law provides a(n) _____ _____ for a creditor who provides for labor and materials used to repair the debtor's personal property.

24. A tax lien is valid for a period of _____ years unless the IRS reduces its lien to judgement.

25. A prejudgment and postjudgment remedy used in exceptional cases is _____.

Chapter 34

BANKRUPTCY

This chapter is concerned with legal devices that have been developed to deal with the adverse conditions that result from economic failure or difficulties. It discusses the nature and content of the Bankruptcy Act, procedural aspects of the Act, and the factors that are considered in determining the extent of a debtor's estate and its distribution to the various creditors. The materials also discuss the discharge of debts, business reorganizations, Chapter 13 regular income plans, and Chapter 12 family farmer plans.

CHAPTER OBJECTIVES

After reading Chapter 34 of the text and studying the related materials in this chapter of the Student Mastery Guide, you will understand:

1. The nature and effect of bankruptcy
2. The types of bankruptcy proceedings, including:
    a. liquidation
    b. reorganization
    c. regular income method
    d. family farmer plans
3. The mechanics of a bankruptcy proceeding
4. The nature, extent, and distribution of a debtor's estate
5. The discharge of debts

MAJOR POINTS TO REMEMBER

Background of Today's Bankruptcy Law

1. Bankruptcy laws are regulated completely by the federal legal system.

2. The Bankruptcy Amendments and Federal Judgeship Act of 1984 created courts to deal with bankruptcy matters (called bankruptcy courts) under the control of federal district courts.
    Bankruptcy judges, who are appointed for terms of fourteen years, preside over these courts.

3. The 1984 Act also limited the right of a debtor to unilaterally reject a collective-bargaining agreement with a union when it has filed for business reorganization under Chapter 11 of the Bankruptcy Code.

4. The Bankruptcy Judges, United States Trustees, and Family Farmer Bankruptcy Act of 1986 created a temporary right for family farmers to file for reorganization under a new Chapter 12, which was added to the code.

5. In a bankruptcy proceeding, the estate of the debtor is administered by a trustee in bankruptcy.

6. Bankruptcy laws provide for various kinds of proceedings, which include:
   a. liquidation
   b. reorganization
   c. regular income plan
   d. family farmer reorganization plan

   In all of the above except liquidation the debtor is allowed to keep assets, pay the creditors in part under an approved plan, and have the rest discharged legally.

The Bankruptcy Proceeding

7. Liquidation (also known as straight bankruptcy) is of two types:
   a. voluntary: the debtor initiates the proceeding
   b. involuntary: a creditor or creditors of a party initiate the proceeding

8. The filing of a voluntary proceeding for liquidation automatically gives the bankruptcy court jurisdiction over the debtor and the debtor's property.
   When a debtor files a petition for bankruptcy, creditors are precluded from beginning new lawsuits or seeking enforcement of existing judgments against the debtor, except in certain matters such as criminal matters and collection of alimony or child support.

9. An involuntary proceeding for bankruptcy cannot be filed against any debtor who is:
   a. a farmer
   b. a nonprofit corporation

10. If a debtor has twelve or more creditors and a petition of involuntary bankruptcy is filed against the debtor, at least three of the creditors must join in the petition. If a debtor has fewer than twelve creditors, any one creditor may file an involuntary bankruptcy petition.
    Additionally, regardless of the number of creditors a debtor has, the total amount of his or her unsecured indebtedness must be $5,000 or more before a petition for involuntary bankruptcy can be filed.

11. If a debtor challenges the petition of a creditor for involuntary bankruptcy, the creditor must establish either:
    a. that the debtor has not been paying his or her debts as they become due, or
    b. that the debtor's property has been placed in receivership or assignment for the benefit of creditors.

    In the event that the creditor(s) cannot establish either of these conditions, the petition is dismissed.

12.   If a creditor has a claim that is secured by a security interest or other lien on specific property of the debtor, that creditor may use that property to satisfy the indebtedness owed to him or her.

The Debtor's Estate

13.   The debtor's estate includes all property owned by or on behalf of the debtor as of the date of the filing of the bankruptcy petition.

Property Added to the Estate

14.   Property acquired within 180 days after the date on which a petition for bankruptcy was filed will be included in the debtor's estate if it was acquired:
        a.   by inheritance
        b.   by a property settlement or divorce decree
        c.   as settlement of a life-insurance policy

15.   Some payments made to a creditor before the filing of a petition for bankruptcy may be considered preferential and therefore capable of being set aside by the trustee. The trustee may set aside a transfer or payment of funds if it was made:
        a.   by the debtor within ninety days before the filing of the petition, and
        b.   at a time when the debtor was insolvent, and
        c.   for a larger amount than the creditor would have received through bankruptcy

16.   As of the date of filing of the bankruptcy petition, the trustee in bankruptcy is deemed to be a lien creditor with respect to the debtor's property. Therefore, the trustee may add that property to the debtor's estate which is subject to a creditor's unperfected lien and that property which is subject to a lien that had not become effective as of the date of the filing of the petition.

17.   Any transfer made by or on behalf of the debtor *after* the date of the filing of a petition can be set aside (voided) by the trustee within two years after the transfer or before the bankruptcy is concluded, whichever occurs first.
        A fraudulent transfer made within one year before the filing of a petition may be voided by the trustee and the money restored to the debtor's estate.

Exemptions from the Estate

18.   The Bankruptcy Reform Act of 1978 permits debtors to exempt certain property from their estates for purposes of the bankruptcy proceeding. It also permits debtors to use the exemptions allowed under state law, and allows states to require debtors to use the state exemptions. The many items of exempt property can be kept by the debtor, and the debtor's debts are still discharged.

Distribution of Debtor's Estate

19.   After the trustee has liquidated the debtor's estate, claims are paid in the order of their priority. Each class of claims is paid in full before any payment is made for claims of a lesser priority.

20.   Claims are paid according to the following priority system:
   a.   costs and expenses involved in administering the bankruptcy proceeding
   b.   expenses incurred in the ordinary course of the debtor's business or financial affairs after the petition is filled out before the appointment of the trustee (this applies only in the case of an involuntary bankruptcy proceeding)
   c.   claims for wages, salaries, or commissions earned within ninety days before the filing of the petition or the termination of the debtor's business (up to $2,000 per individual)
   d.   claims for contributions to employee benefit plans relative to services rendered within 180 days before the filing of the petition or the termination of the debtor's business (limited to $2,000 per individual and can be combined with category c only to the extent that the total of both does not exceed $2,000)
   e.   claims for deposits made on consumer goods or services that were not received up to a maximum of $900
   f.   tax claims submitted by governmental agencies
   g.   claims of general creditors

21.   The excess amount of a claim that exceeds the allowance for a particular category becomes a general claim. For example, if an employee has a wage claim for $3,000 and $2,000 is entitled to a priority, the balance of $1,000 is a general claim.
       After all classes of priority claims have been paid, any remaining property is distributed on a pro rata basis to all unsecured creditors with general claims against the estate.

Discharge of Debts

22.   An individual petitioner can receive a discharge from debts that remain unpaid after his or her estate has been liquidated and creditors paid according to the priority schedule.

23.   A discharge of remaining debts will not be granted if:
   a.   a petition for bankruptcy for the debtor had been filed within six years before the current filing, or
   b.   the debtor, either within one year before the filing of the petition or at any time thereafter, intentionally concealed or transferred assets with the intent to hinder, delay, or defraud creditors, or
   c.   the debtor conceals, destroys, falsifies, or fails to keep records related to the debtor's financial condition or business transactions, or
   d.   the debtor fails adequately to explain the loss of assets, or
   e.   the debtor refuses to obey a lawful order of the bankruptcy court, or
   f.   the creditor makes any fraudulent statement or claim in connection with the bankruptcy case

24.	The following types of claims cannot be discharged by bankruptcy proceedings and the debtor will remain liable for them:
	a.	claims for back taxes accrued within three years before the bankruptcy
	b.	claims arising from the debtor's embezzlement, fraud, or larceny
	c.	claims based on the debtor's willful or malicious torts
	d.	claims for alimony or child support
	e.	unscheduled claims
	f.	certain fines and penalties payable to government units
	g.	educational loans that become due and payable less than five years before the filing of the petition

Business Reorganization

25.	A petition for reorganization may be filed by either the debtor or the creditors.

26.	Reorganization makes it possible for a company (including a railroad) that is experiencing financial difficulties to continue in operation while its financial resources and obligations are restructured.

	The court appoints a creditor's committee to examine the affairs of the business and decide whether the business should remain in operation.

27.	Under Chapter 11 reorganizations, either the debtor or any other interested party may file a plan for reorganization, but during the initial 120 days following the filing of a reorganization petition only the debtor may file such a plan. If the debtor files a plan within that time, he or she has an additional sixty days to have it approved by the creditors.

	If a satisfactory plan is not devised by the debtor within the permissible time period, a creditor or the trustee may thereafter submit a plan for approval.

28.	To be approved the reorganization plan must, among other matters:
	a.	specify the treatment of all classes of claims and treat all claims within a class the same unless a creditor agrees to a less favorable treatment
	b.	demonstrate that the plan's payment terms can be met
	c.	give to all claimants at least as much as they would receive in a Chapter 8 liquidation proceeding
	d.	be approved by at least one-half the number of claimants in a class, and those approving must represent at least two-thirds of the value of the claims in a class; and
	e.	normally be approved by all claimants in any class whose interests are impaired by the plan, although a court can still approve a plan without this consent, if it determines that all persons within an impaired class are treated fairly

Chapter 13 - Regular Income Plans

29.   Any individual, other than a stockbroker or commodity broker, may proceed under Chapter 13 of the Bankruptcy Act if:
    a.   he or she has a regular income, and
    b.   his or her unsecured debts are less than $100,000, and
    c.   his or her secured debts are less than $350,000

30.   Chapter 13 proceedings can be commenced *only* by the debtor. The filing of the petition also automatically stops creditors from taking any action against the debtor.

31.   Under Chapter 13 proceedings, the debtor proposes a plan for the payment of creditors from future income. Only the secured creditors, however, vote to approve the plan.

32.   Although unsecured creditors do not vote on the debtor's plan, they must receive at least the amounts they would have received under Chapter 7 liquidation proceedings. Each claimant within every class of unsecured creditors must also be treated the same.

33.   The plan must ensure that all claims entitled to priority are paid in full.

34.   The plan normally must provide for payments over three years, although they can be extended to five with court approval.

35.   The debtor's future income will be subject to control by a trustee to ensure the plan is properly implemented.

Chapter 12 - Relief for the Family Farmer

36.   This chapter was added to the Bankruptcy Code to aid family farmers with a regular annual income of which over 50 percent of the gross income must be from farming. This chapter is similar to Chapters 11 and 13 in that the farmer remains in possession of assets and files a reorganization plan within ninety days for approval. The plan must pay all priority claims in full within three years (five years with court approval). It also must treat all claims within a class the same unless a claimant has agreed to accept less. A trustee takes control of future income to carry out the approved plan.

Ethics Box: Any Ethical Obligation After Discharge?

37.   After a person's debts are discharged in bankruptcy there is no legal obligation to pay them. Since this is a result that the creditors have no choice but to accept, a debtor most likely does have an ethical obligation to pay, if the creditors were hurt and he or she now can do so without significant harm to his or her interests. However, since there is often pressure on a bankrupt debtor to reaffirm debts and pay them, the bankruptcy laws require that for a reaffirmation of discharged debts to be legally binding, the court must conduct a hearing at which the debtor is informed of the consequences of such an action.

In addition, it must determine that the reaffirmation would not impose an undue burden on the debtor and would be in the debtor's best interests.

Preventive Law: Actions to be Taken by a Creditor of a Chapter 11 Bankruptcy Reorganization

38.   A creditor is well advised to take the following steps before and after the filing of a Chapter 11 reorganization petition by one of its debtors.
   a.   If there are reasonable doubts regarding the financial stability of a debtor, a creditor can:
      i.   obtain additional collateral and perfect the security interest; and
      ii.   although a trustee may be able to set it aside if it occurs too close to the filing of the petition, agree to accept a partial payment in excess of what one would expect to receive in reorganization in exchange for cancelling the balance due
   b.   After a petition is filed by a debtor:
      i.   make sure proofs of all claims are timely filed;
      ii.   immediately determine if goods delivered within ten days of the filing can be reclaimed by the creditor filing for them within ten days after the debtor's petition was filed
   c.   Obtain the debtor's petition and talk to the other creditors to become informed of the debtor's assets and liabilities
   d.   Keep informed of the bankruptcy court proceedings.

MAJOR POINTS OF CASES

In re Johns-Manville Corporation (p. 618)

This case captured public attention for several years because it involved an otherwise financially strong company that sought bankruptcy protection from contingent product-liability claims and lawsuits stemming from exposures to asbestos manufactured by the company. In this case the court affirmed the bankruptcy judge's decision that the debtor's insurance coverage was part of the estate, and, therefore, the insurers were protected by the stay from claims filed against them as Manville's insurer. Further, it held that the stay also stopped discovery proceedings by co-defendants against the debtor. Both rulings were necessary to give the company the time to reorganize its affairs.

In the Matter of CHG International, Inc. (p. 621)

This case revealed the extent to which real-estate loans fit within the scope of preferential interest and are thus voidable in the event of a bankruptcy filing. The court ruled that the 1984 Amendments to the bankruptcy law, although eliminating the 45 day period that determined voidable preferences, were not intended to more than substantially contemporaneous exchanges. Past rulings as well as a lack of legislative history to the contrary provided the court's reasoning.

Applying this ruling to the facts of the case, the court reversed the District Court's decision and held that CHG's long term loans to Barclays were indeed voidable preferences. Consequentially, the court ordered CHG to return Barclays' interest payments so as to protect other creditors from unfair and unequal treatment.

Belcher v. *Turner* (p. 624)

The court in this case stated that the Bankruptcy Act recognizes the applicability of exemptions created by the state law in connection with bankruptcy proceedings. The court also stated that "the scope and application of such exemptions are defined by state courts and we [the federal courts] are bound by their interpretations."

In regard to the facts of the case, the court indicated that Kansas cases have established that the test to be applied in determining whether a homestead exemption is applicable is whether the structure is used or occupied as a residence. In applying the rule to the facts, the court agreed with the district court that only half of the duplex unit had been used as a residence, and consequently it permitted the half that was used as Belcher's residence to be exempted from the bankrupt estate. It ruled, however, that the other half of the duplex was part of the bankrupt's estate.

Matter of Horton (p. 627)

This case illustrates the rule that a discharge cannot be granted to a petitioner who has failed to keep adequate records of his or her financial transactions unless such failure is deemed to be justifiable under the circumstances.

Upon an examination of the facts, the court held that Horton, who dealt almost exclusively in cash in connection with his business transactions, had kept inadequate records. The court also stated that even though his daughter had kept records, they were not clear and her testimony was inconsistent. Furthermore, they did not help Horton because he had an obligation to maintain his own records. As a result, the court ruled that the district court's refusal to grant a discharge was correct.

In re Duersam (p. 633)

This case dealt with "good" and "bad" faith plan proposals under Chapter 13. The court made a holding on two points. First, student loans cannot be filed under Chapter 7 under most circumstances. Secondly, a proposal under Chapter 13 is in "bad" faith if the proposer has not made any effort to repay the loan in full, especially when she or he has acquired economic benefit from that loan.

With its holding, the court determined that Doersam's proposal under Chapter 13 was not made in good faith. Although she attained a position paying $24,000 per year as a result of the education that she received with the help of student loans, she filed her proposal before the loans even came due, indicating her lack of effort in attempting to repay them in full.

PRACTICAL CONSIDERATIONS

A debtor who becomes embroiled in serious financial difficulties should evaluate his or her situation carefully and precisely before attempting to decide on an appropriate course of action. A voluntary petition for bankruptcy (liquidation), while convenient, should be considered only as a last resort, since other quite viable alternatives now exist. Certainly, if creditors are unwilling to cooperate in good-faith efforts to avoid liquidation and leave the debtor no alternative, a petition for bankruptcy will probably be in order.

Conversely, the creditors might be well advised to consider the consequences of refusing to cooperate with the debtor. If they cooperate and allow the debtor a reasonable opportunity to satisfy his or her indebtedness, they may receive a substantial portion, if not all, of the money owed them. If, however, they insist on immediate payment and leave the debtor no alternative but to file for bankruptcy, then, unless they are secured creditors, there is a strong probability that they will receive very little payment on the indebtedness. Clearly, the financial difficulties of debtors affect others besides themselves, and from the viewpoint of creditors, it may sometimes be said that discretion is the better part of valor.

SELF TEST

True-False Questions

_____ 1. Railroads are not subject to liquidation or straight bankruptcy proceedings.

_____ 2. The filing of a voluntary petition for bankruptcy automatically subjects the debtor to the jurisdiction of the bankruptcy court.

_____ 3. In order for an involuntary petition for bankruptcy to be properly filed, the total amount of unsecured claims against the debtor must amount to at least $3,000.

_____ 4. A bankruptcy judge is prohibited from being present at the first meeting of unsecured creditors when they convene after a petition for bankruptcy is filed.

_____ 5. The debtor is generally not present at the first meeting of unsecured creditors.

_____ 6. As of the date of the filing of a petition for bankruptcy, the trustee has the status of a lien creditor.

_____ 7. Under the federal bankruptcy laws, a debtor's principal place of residence is completely exempt from bankruptcy proceedings and cannot be used by creditors to satisfy any indebtedness.

_____ 8. A partnership cannot be discharged from its debts under a Chapter 6 liquidation proceeding.

_____ 9. A petition for the reorganization of a business may be filed by the creditors of that business.

_____ 10. A debtor will be denied a discharge from his or her debts if he or she intentionally defrauded one of his or her creditors up to three years before the petition for bankruptcy was filed.

Multiple-Choice Questions

_____ 11. Bankruptcy judges are appointed by the President of the United States and serve in that capacity for:
a. ten years
b. twelve years
c. fourteen years
d. twenty years
e. their lifetimes

_____ 12. Which of the following is considered to be a bankruptcy proceeding?
a. reorganization
b. regular income plan
c. liquidation
d. only a and c are correct
e. a, b, and c are all correct

_____ 13. If a debtor has more than twelve creditors, a petition for involuntary bankruptcy must be initiated by at least:
a. one creditor
b. three creditors
c. five creditors
d. six creditors
e. seven creditors

_____ 14. In connection with a bankruptcy proceeding, which of the following activities will usually occur at the first meeting of the creditors?
a. the election of a permanent trustee
b. the election of a temporary trustee
c. a physical inspection of the assets of the debtor
d. an examination of the debtor by the bankruptcy judge
e. a and b are both correct

15. Which of the following is a function of the trustee in bankruptcy
    a. to collect the assets of the debtor
    b. to liquidate the assets of the debtor
    c. to pay off the debts of the debtor
    d. only a and b are correct
    e. a, b, and c are all correct

16. If a debtor's estate has been liquidated, the court will usually deny a discharge from remaining debts if:
    a. a prior discharge was granted within the six years immediately preceding the filing of the petition
    b. the debtor is an individual
    c. the debtor unintentionally concealed the existence of an asset
    d. the unpaid debt is over $300
    e. b and d are both correct

17. Which of the following types of businesses may not use the liquidation method of bankruptcy?
    a. retail institutions
    b. railroads
    c. steel companies
    d. manufacturing companies
    e. c and d are both correct

18. During the first 120 days following the filing of a petition for reorganization, a reorganization plan may be filed by:
    a. the creditors only
    b. the debtor only
    c. either the debtor or the creditors
    d. the debtor and creditors filing jointly
    e. the trustee in bankruptcy

19. Chapter 13 plans may be used by an individual whose unsecured debts must amount to less than:
    a. $50,000
    b. $75,000
    c. $100,000
    d. $200,000
    e. $350,000

_____ 20. A transfer of assets to a creditor by the debtor will be considered to be a preferential transfer if:

    a. it was made within ninety days before the filing of a petition for bankruptcy

    b. the debtor was insolvent at the time of the transfer

    c. the creditor was given more than he or she would have received through a bankruptcy proceeding

    d. all of the above are necessary elements for a transfer to be regarded as preferential

    e. only a and c are necessary elements

Completion Questions

21. The person who is responsible for administering the estate of a debtor in a bankruptcy proceeding is the _____.

22. In a voluntary bankruptcy petition, the _____ initiates the proceeding by filing the petition.

23. The bankruptcy proceeding in which the assets of the debtor are turned into cash and then distributed to the creditors is referred to as _____.

24. A(n) _____ _____ is a creditor whose debt or claim is secured by a lien on specific property.

25. In order for creditors to be able to initiate involuntary bankruptcy proceedings against a debtor, the total amount of unsecured claims against that person must be at least _____.

Chapter 35

THE AGENCY RELATIONSHIP

It is sometimes impossible for a person to perform a task that must be done. In such cases, the only alternative is to have someone else perform that task or function on behalf of the party who is unable to do it.

This chapter deals with the relationship that is created when one person asks another to act on his or her behalf in dealing with a third party. The relationship is commonly known as an agency relationship and is frequently used in the business environment. The chapter considers the nature of the relationship and various ways in which it is created. It also discusses the various types of authority that an agent may possess and distinguish an agent from various other parties who superficially appear to act in a similar role. The chapter also discusses the representative contractual activities of the agent and the rights and obligations that relate to the interaction between the principal and his or her agent.

When one considers the fact that some business entities can function only by means of the agency relationship, it is easy to understand why these materials are so important.

CHAPTER OBJECTIVES

After reading Chapter 35 of the text and studying the related materials in this chapter of the Student Mastery Guide, you will understand:

1. The nature of an agency relationship
2. The ways in which an agency relationship is created
3. The contractual features of an agency relationship
4. The rights and obligations of the parties to an agency relationship

MAJOR POINTS TO REMEMBER

Agents Defined

1. An agent, when authorized, may legally bind the principal to a contract with a third party.

2. An agent can be classified as a:
    a. general agent, if he or she has general authority to act on behalf of the principal in certain continuing activities
    b. special agent, if he or she is authorized to act on behalf of the principal in connection with a particular purpose or a particular occasion

3. Principals can be described as being:
    a. disclosed, if the principal's identity is known to the third party
    b. undisclosed, if neither the identity of the principal nor the fact that the agent is acting on behalf of another person is known to the third party

4.   If the agent is acting for an undisclosed principal, the agent is considered to be a party to the contract along with the principal.

Generally, if the agent is acting for a disclosed principal, the agent will have no liability for the contracts he or she negotiates or consummates.

Agency Distinguished

5.   The substance of a relationship, not labels given to it by the parties, determines whether an agency or other type of legal relationship is involved. The primary factor distinguishing an agency relationship is the power of control retained by the principal over the agent's activities.

6.   Distinguishable from agents are independent contractors who are hired by the job to accomplish certain results, but are not subject to the employer's power of control as to the details of how the results are to be achieved. Employers are not liable for the contracts made or torts committed by independent contractors, except that for torts the employer will be held liable if the independent contractor was hired to perform very dangerous activities or by statutes the duties involved are nondelegable.

Creation of Agency Relations

7.   Any person who has the capacity to consent can be a principal or an agent. However, one cannot do through an agent anything that the principal could not legally accomplish alone. Further, if a person must be licensed to perform certain activities, then he or she cannot act as an agent to perform such activities without the required license.

8.   Generally, no formalities are required to create an agency, although putting the delegated authority in writing is advantageous. The authorized acts of a gratuitous agent are as binding on the principal as those of a compensated agent.

Rights and Duties Between Principal and Agent

9.   Absent an agreement to the contrary, an agent is entitled to the following rights in connection with an agency relationship:
      a.   compensation unless clearly intended to be gratuitous
      b.   to have the principal keep and render an account of compensation owed (where practicable)
      c.   reimbursement
      d.   indemnification
      e.   to perform duties without unreasonable interference or hindrance by the principal

10.   In the event that the principal fails to compensate, reimburse, or indemnify the agent appropriately, the agent may impose a lien or a security interest on goods or money that belong to the principal but that are in the agent's possession.

11.   A fiduciary (which an agent is considered to be) is under a general obligation to act for the benefit of the party he or she represents. A fiduciary is held to a very high standard of good-faith conduct in acting solely for the benefit of the party to whom one is a fiduciary.

12.   An agent has certain obligations to his or her principal by virtue of their relationship. These obligations include:
       a.   loyalty
       b.   obedience
       c.   the duty to use reasonable skill and judgment
       d.   the duty to communicate information to the principal
       e.   the duty to account to the principal

13.   An agent may not enter into direct competition with his or her principal.
              If, however, the agent has informed the principal and received his or her consent, the agent may work for a competitor of the principal.

14.   All money that comes into the possession of the agent on behalf of the principal must be given to the principal.

15.   The agent is required to follow and obey all reasonable directives given to him or her by the principal.

16.   An agent must make a reasonable attempt to communicate to the principal any information he or she receives concerning transactions in which he or she is acting on behalf of the principal. In addition, agents must keep proper records and make accounting to the principal of all funds received for or from the principal.

17.   An agent must not commingle his or her funds with those of the principal unless the principal authorizes the agent to do so.

18.   An agent in the performance of his or her obligations must do so with the reasonable and ordinary skill, care, and judgment possessed by a person engaged in that business or occupation. But if the agent claims certain special skills, then the agent is held to that higher standard of performance.

Preventive Law

19.   Although generally not legally required, agency contracts should be in writing to reduce the chance of disputes arising. To this end, the contract should expressly explain, among other matters, the basis for and amount of compensation to be paid to the agent, which party will pay various expenses, which party will bear the risk of loss from third-party claims, and what will happen in the event of a breach of the contract.

Ethics Box: The Agent in the Middle

20.   Agents sometimes confront serious ethical issues in their attempt to remain loyal to the principal. A prime example is a travel agent who serves a large corporate client. Such a principal may demand that the agent takes advantage of fare loopholes that are prohibited by airline rules. As an "agent" of both the corporation and the airline, the travel agent is caught in the middle.

MAJOR POINTS OF CASES

Douglas v. *Aztec Petroleum Corp.* (p. 643)

This case states the general rule that an agent is a fiduciary who owes the principal duties to act with the utmost good faith, truthfulness, and loyalty. Further, if an agent willfully and deliberately breaches the agency contract, then the agent is not entitled to compensation, even for properly performed services, and is liable to pay the principal compensatory and punitive damages for the commission of a tort.

The agent here was found to have used money advanced to him by the principal for his personal benefit without authorization. He also failed to keep proper records and make a truthful accounting of expenditures. As a consequence of these breaches of the fiduciary duty, he was not entitled to receive any compensation for his services, and he was liable for damages caused to the principal by his wrongful acts, as well as exemplary or punitive damages.

Markland v. *Travel Travel Southfield, Inc.* (p. 646)

Leaning on precedent, the court in this case ruled that a travel agent is responsible for his or her principal's vacation problems only to the extent that the agent could have foreseen these problems. Applying this ruling to the facts of the case, the court held that Travel Travel was not liable for the extra expenses incurred by the Marklands as a result of the bankruptcies of Eastern and Flyfaire. The court reasoned that because the travel agency derived its information about Eastern's problem from the same sources as the Marklands, it had no "inside information" and thus no special responsibility for the couple's unfortunate vacation occurrences.

McKeehan v. *Wittels* (p. 648)

This case demonstrates the manner in which a court will approach the issue of an agent's responsibility to his principal. The court stated that an agent must follow the instructions given to him by his principal and that his failure to do so will render the agent liable for any damages that the principal sustains as a result. Likewise, the agent is also obligated to "disclose material facts to the principal, strictly avoid misrepresentation and. . . act with utmost good faith."

When the court examined the facts, it found that Malcolm and Jacob Wittels had knowingly disregarded the instructions of the plaintiff and that they also failed to inform her of material facts regarding her investments. They also, according to the court, occupied an antagonistic posture with respect to her. As a result, the court found that they had breached their fiduciary obligations to the plaintiff and were liable to her for damages as a result. The court stated that it found no evidence that Ilene Wittels participated in the creation of the relationship or in the breach of duty. Therefore, the court held that she was not liable to the plaintiff and reversed the judgment against her.

PRACTICAL CONSIDERATIONS

If a principal directs an agent to do something that is either morally or ethically improper, the agent must decide whether to follow the directive (even though he or she may not be legally bound to do so) or refuse to follow the orders given. Even though it may be legally improper for a principal to discharge an agent for such a reason, refusal is likely to terminate the relationship. Further, the agent must decide whether grounds for a lawsuit for wrongful discharge would exist, and if so, how valuable or effective a lawsuit of that type would be under the circumstances.

Example: Jerome, a rent-collection agent, is informed by his principal that since the tenants in apartment 4F are ten days late in their rent payment, he wants Jerome to demand that they pay the rent within one hour of his visit. Jerome is also told that in the event that they fail to pay him the rent, he is to remove their furniture and possessions from the apartment and bring them to the landlord's (the principal's) warehouse. He is also told to change the lock on the door of the apartment and not provide the tenants with a key. When Jerome goes to the apartment, he is informed by the tenants that their rent payment has been delayed because their ten-month-old child is in the hospital and they need the money for medical expenses.

Presented with the facts of the situation, Jerome must now decide what course of action is the most appropriate under the circumstances. He realizes that if he refuses to remove the furniture and possessions as directed, he will probably be terminated as the authorized rent agent. He also realizes that he probably has no right to enter the premises and do as he was directed, and that if he does follow directions, he may have further legal difficulties because of his potentially wrongful conduct. Jerome's decision will be difficult and he must weigh the alternatives very carefully.

SELF TEST

True-False Questions

_____   1.   An independent contractor may never be considered to be an agent.

_____   2.   An agent who is acting on behalf of an undisclosed principal may be held personally liable for a contract he or she has negotiated with a third party.

_____   3.   An agent is always entitled to receive compensation for the services he or she renders.

_____   4.   The principal-agent relationship is considered to be a fiduciary relationship.

5. If a principal fails to reimburse an agent for expenses, the agent may impose a lien on any property of the principal's that is in the agent's possession.

6. An agent may never work for another party who is engaged in competition with his or her principal.

7. The standard of skill and care required of an agent is that degree of skill and care ordinarily possessed by persons engaged in the same business or occupation.

8. An agent who represents that he or she has certain special skills is held to a higher standard of performance than other persons acting as agents.

9. All agency contracts must be in writing to be enforceable.

10. All persons can be principals or agents for any purpose.

Multiple-Choice Questions

11. An agency relationship can usually be described as:
    a. an irrevocable contractual relationship
    b. a fiduciary relationship
    c. a Socratic relationship
    d. an artificial legal personality
    e. a and c are both correct

12. Which of the following is an obligation by the agent to the principal?
    a. obedience
    b. loyalty
    c. total and complete honesty
    d. only a and b are correct
    e. a, b, and c are all correct

13. Which of the following is an obligation owed by the principal to the agent?
    a. compensation
    b. reimbursement
    c. indemnification
    d. a and b are both correct
    e. a, b, and c are all correct

14. Which of the following signatures will identify the existence of a disclosed principal?
    a.   A. Club by Sam Spade, as agent
    b.   Sam Spade, as agent for A. Club
    c.   Sam Spade (aaf A.C.)
    d.   a and b are both correct
    e.   a, b, and c are all correct

15. An agent can be held personally liable on a contract made for:
    a.   a disclosed principal
    b.   an undisclosed principal
    c.   a general principal
    d.   a special principal
    e.   none of the above is correct

16. An agent who willfully breaches his or her fiduciary duty to the principal is entitled to:
    a.   no compensation
    b.   partial compensation
    c.   full compensation
    d.   statutory fees
    e.   a lien on the principal's property for unpaid compensation

17. A breach of a fiduciary duty by an agent can constitute:
    a.   a breach of contract
    b.   a tort
    c.   a violation of professional business ethics
    d.   only a and c are correct
    e.   a, b, and c are all correct

18. A willful breach of a fiduciary duty by an agent that causes harm to the principal can subject the agent to liability for:
    a.   liquidated damages only
    b.   compensatory damages
    c.   punitive damages
    d.   only a and b are correct
    e.   only b and c are correct

19. An agent who acts for a principal without the intention of being paid is known as a(n) _____ agent.
    a.   special
    b.   general
    c.   gratuitous
    d.   undisclosed
    e.   fiduciary

_____ 20. In order to be legally binding, an agency relationship must be:
- a. in writing
- b. gratuitous
- c. based on expressly promised compensation to be paid to the agent
- d. all of the above are correct
- e. none of the above is correct

Completion Questions

21. _____ is the legal relationship in which one person is authorized to act on behalf of another person in dealings with a third person.

22. An agent who is authorized to act on behalf of a principal in connection with a particular purpose is referred to as a(n) _____ agent.

23. A _____ _____ is one that is authorized to act on the behalf of a principal in certain continuing activities.

24. An agent is a _____ in regard to his or her principal and, thus, must act in good faith solely for the benefit of the principal in transactions affecting the agency relationship.

25. A person who undertakes to provide a finished product and who is generally not under the control of the party who hires him or her is known as a(n) _____ _____.

Chapter 36

THE EFFECT OF AGENCY RELATIONS

This chapter continues the examination of agency relationships. It discusses the various types of authority that an agent may possess. The chapter also discusses the representative contractual activities of the agent and the effect on the principal of the agent's tortious conduct. Finally, the concept of the termination of the agency relationship is discussed.

Because principals can be held responsible under certain circumstances for the contracts made by agents, or the injuries caused by their tortious conduct, this chapter is significant in explaining the risks created by using agents to transact one's business affairs.

CHAPTER OBJECTIVES

After reading Chapter 36 of the text and studying the related materials in this chapter of the Student Mastery Guide, you will understand:

1. The types of agency authority that can exist
2. The potential contract and tort liability a principal can incur from an agent's actions
3. The ways in which an agency relationship is terminated and the effect of such termination.

MAJOR POINTS TO REMEMBER

1. An agency relationship can be created by:
   a. express agreement
   b. implication
   c. ratification
   d. necessity

2. Actual authority is the power of an agent to affect the legal relations of the principal by acts for which the principal has given consent.

3. Actual authority may be either express or implied.
   a. Express authority is that authority given to the agent by means of the words of the principal.
   b. Implied authority is the authority given to the agent by means of the actions or conduct manifested to him or her by the principal.
   c. Apparent authority is the authority an agent appears to have been given in the eyes of a reasonable third person. It should be noted that apparent authority cannot be established by the agent's statement alone.

4. One type of express authority is the power of attorney, which is a formal written instrument conferring authority upon an agent. Other less formal means of granting express authority exist, including the use of exculpatory clauses in form contracts that expressly limit the agent's contractual authority to the terms of the written contract. Such clauses protect the principal by giving the third party notice of the agent's actual authority. An agent's act outside of this authority creates personal liability for the agent.

5.   The principal implicitly authorizes the agent to do whatever is ordinarily required to accomplish the job. If an emergency develops that threatens the principal's business and it is impractical to communicate with the principal, then the agent has the necessary authority to act to protect the principal's business.

6.   An agent's apparent authority is actual authority, and actions taken within that authority are binding on the principal.

7.   When an agency has been created by means of ratification:
     a.   it is essential that the act being ratified is one that originally could have been authorized by the principal
     b.   a principal who ratifies the unauthorized act of the agent must ratify the entire act and not just a part of it
     c.   any action or conduct by the principal that manifests his or her complete affirmance of the unauthorized act will constitute a ratification.

8.   All information that becomes known to the agent which is related to agency transactions is treated as being known by the principal, whether or not the principal has actual knowledge. Although the agent has the duty to communicate all relevant information to the principal, if the agent fails to do so, knowledge of that information is nonetheless imputed to the principal.

Contractual Dealings: Agents and Third Parties

9.   An agent will normally not be deemed a party to a contract he or she negotiates on behalf of a disclosed principal. Consequently, the agent will usually have no liability for the contract.
          An agent who engages in nonauthorized negotiations or transactions, however, may be held liable on the contract that is created.

10. An agent who engages in a transaction or contract on behalf of an undisclosed principal will be treated as a party to the transaction or contract together with the principal, and as a result could be held liable for any damages incurred by the third party in connection with it. The agent, however, does have the right to look to the principal to be repaid for any money he or she is obligated to pay to the third party.

11. An agent who signs a contract and represents that he or she is acting on behalf of a principal makes an implied warranty to the other party that he or she is authorized to act on behalf of the principal. Breach of this warranty results in liability for the damages caused to the third party.

Agent's Tortious Activities

12. If an agent commits a tort while acting within the scope of his or her authority, both the agent and the principal may be held liable for any damages sustained by a third party. This

liability on the part of the principal is frequently referred to as vicarious liability. (It is also sometimes referred to under the doctrine of respondeat superior.) (See the *Mauk v. Wright* case for an examination of the meaning of "scope of authority or employment.") Agents are not relieved of the personal liability to the tort victim by the vicarious liability. This concept simply makes the principal liable along with the agent.

Principal's Criminal Responsibility

13.   An agent who commits a crime while acting on behalf of a corporation will be personally liable and responsible for the criminal conduct.

The fact that a person is an officer of a corporation does not by itself normally render that person responsible for the criminal conduct of the corporation. If, on the other hand, the criminal act is performed under the direction of or with the permission of the corporate executive, then such person may be held criminally responsible for the act.

Termination of Agency

14.   An agency relationship can be terminated by:
   a.   the accomplishment of the objectives of the agency
   b.   events or conditions that destroy the agent's power to act on behalf of the principal
   c.   mutual agreement
   d.   the unilateral act of either party
   e.   the death or incompetence of the principal
   f.   the lapse of time

15.   Either the principal or the agent can unilaterally terminate the agency relationship. There is a distinction between the power to end an agency relationship and the right to end it. The person who unilaterally terminates the relationship may be held liable to the other for breach of contract if he or she did not have the right to terminate it.

16.   When an agency relationship is terminated, notice must be given to third parties so that they will not be able to hold the principal liable for the conduct of the agent.

Actual notice must be given to those third parties with whom a general agent has had prior dealings.

With respect to third parties with whom the agent has not had prior dealings, reasonable notice of the termination of the agency is required.

18.   Certain types of agencies may not be revoked by the principal, such as an agency coupled with an interest.

Preventive Law: Exculpatory Clauses

19.   In this age of consumer protection the enforcement of exculpatory clauses to limit a principal's liability for the actions of an agent raises serious questions, since consumers may not appreciate their legal effect. Since people are generally expected to read,

understand, and be bound by their contracts, if it is shown that a person was aware of the exculpatory clause, then the clause is likely to be enforced. This awareness can be shown by the conspicuous placement of the clause in the contract, evidence that the third party read it, or evidence that it was called to his or her attention by the agent. By statute, however, in many states home solicitation consumer sales can be canceled within three days of their making. As a result of this uncertainty as to the legal effectiveness of such clauses, a company should train its agents to stay within their express powers. It should also require them to point out this clause to third parties, explain it to them, and have them sign to show that they were aware of it.

Preventive Law: Signing on Behalf of a Principal

20.   Because of the different holdings by the courts of states regarding the admissibility of parol evidence to explain an ambiguous signature, an agent who signs a contract should always clearly designate his or her agency capacity and the identity of the principal in order to avoid personal liability on the contract.

Ethics Box: The Opportunistic Agent

21.   In many instances it may as a practical matter be difficult for a principal to monitor an agent's performance, due to the agent's specialized knowledge or other factors. This places the agent in a position to take advantage of the principal or to not fully perform. Such behavior is not only a breach of professional business ethics, it is also illegal.

MAJOR POINTS OF CASES

State Security Insurance Co. v. *Burgos* (p. 655)

This case concerned the circumstances under which somebody may be considered an "authorized agent" for an insurer. The court held that an agent has apparent authority where a principal creates a reasonable impression that the putative agent has been granted authority to perform certain acts. In cases where an insurer leads the insured to believe that a broker has authority to perform certain acts, the insurer cannot deny the broker's authority to perform those acts. For the establishment of the broker's apparent authority, the court held acquiescence by the insurer to be sufficient.

Applying its ruling to the facts of the case, the court affirmed a decision in favor of the defendant. Although the Burgoses did not directly inform the plaintiff for two years of the shooting covered by the policy, the court stated that their notification of the broker constituted informing the plaintiff "as soon as practicable". Due to actions on the part of the plaintiff, the court held that it was reasonable for the defendant to conclude that the broker had apparent authority to take their claim.

Pailet v. *Guillroy* (p. 657)

The court in this case states that implied authority of an agent is actual authority that derives from that which is necessary or incidental to the agency assignment. In contrast, apparent authority of an agent arises when the principal clothes the agent with the appearance of authority to perform certain acts and a third party justifiably relies on that apparent authority.

In this case the agent did not have the implied authority to cancel a lease based on the express authority to collect rent and make minor repairs. Neither did the court find the agent was clothed with apparent authority to cancel the lease, since the principals had signed the lease and a subsequent consent to its assignment. Finally, the court found that the principal had not ratified the agent's cancellation of the lease through her inaction for nine months, since inaction does not show a clear and absolute intent to ratify.

Mauk v. *Wright* (p. 661)

This case deals with the element of respondeat superior (vicarious liability), which requires sufficient proof that the employee or agent was acting within the scope of his or her employment or authority at the time the tort was committed in order for the employer or principal to be held liable for the harm suffered by the victim. This requirement essentially requires that the employee's or agent's tortious actions were taken at a time when the employee or agent was acting on the behalf and to the benefit of the employer or principal. Under such circumstances the employee or agent is also legally within the control of the employer or principal.

The facts of this case are unique in that the accident involved a professional football player in summer training camp. The players had only about two hours of personal free time per day. The accident occurred during this free time. Normally, an employer is not liable for an employee's torts that are committed outside the time in which the employee is working. However, the standard player's contract gave the employer the right to discipline or terminate players for conduct during their free time. Because of this clause in the contract, the court concluded that there was an actual question of fact regarding whether the player involved in the accident was at that time acting within the scope of employment. Since a question of fact existed that needed to be decided, the granting of a summary judgment for the employer was reversible error and a trial must be conducted.

Charles Webster Real Estate v. *Rickard* (p. 664)

Because agency relationships are personal and fiduciary, they are terminated by the death or renunciation of the agent or the death or revocation of the principal unless the agent has an interest in the subject of the agency. Because the principal in this case had died and the executor had not accepted or ratified a sale procured by the real-estate broker, the agency relationship was terminated prior to the sale by the executor and no commission was owed.

PRACTICAL CONSIDERATIONS

1. The legal concepts of apparent authority and vicarious liability (respondeat superior) significantly increase the risk of contract liability and tort liability, respectively, of a principal to third parties. Employers must hire competent and honest employees and

agents to minimize these risks. They also need to provide adequate training and clear statements of agency authority. The public-policy rationales for each of these concepts clearly place the burden of controlling employees and agents on their employers. It is not an impossible task for employers. Apparent authority to contract is based not on the agent's actions but instead on the words and conduct of the principal that cause a third party to reasonably conclude that certain agency authority exists. Although an employer cannot avoid vicarious liability by simply telling its employees and agents not to commit torts, it can provide training to inform employees and agents of the reasonably foreseeable harm that could be caused to others from their work activities, how to minimize the risks of harm to others, and the importance of safety.

2. In a situation in which respondeat superior seems to apply, a plaintiff should, if possible, sue both the employer and the responsible employee or agent. Even though the employer is the party most likely to be able to pay, the employee or agent can also be held liable and may be covered by personal-liability insurance. It is always possible, particularly with small employers, that a plaintiff will not be able to collect from the employer. In addition, at least in some states, the effectiveness of discovery can be enhanced by joining the employee or agent as a defendant in the lawsuit.

SELF TEST

True-False Questions

_____ 1. When a principal terminates a general agency relationship, notice by publication in a newspaper of general circulation is sufficient to inform all third persons of the termination of the agent's authority to act on his or her behalf.

_____ 2. An agent's authority to act on behalf of a principal will always be terminated by the death of the principal.

_____ 3. The president of a corporation can never be held criminally responsible for the criminal act of one of the agents of the corporation.

_____ 4. If an agent has apparent authority, then he or she also has actual authority.

_____ 5. Apparent authority is established by the conduct or words of the agent.

_____ 6. Implied authority of an agent is that authority which is defined by statutory law.

_____ 7. In order for ratification to occur, the principal must accept the entire act of the agent.

313

_____ 8. Employers are liable for all torts committed by their employees or agents.

_____ 9. Generally, death of the principal will terminate an agency relationship.

_____ 10. A principal cannot revoke an agency contract, if the agent has an interest in the subject matter of the agency.

Multiple-Choice Questions

_____ 11. An agency relationship may be created by:
   a. express agreement
   b. implication
   c. the actions or conduct of a third party other than the principal
   d. a and b are both correct
   e. a, b, and c are all correct

_____ 12. If an agent commits a tort while acting on behalf of the principal, the injured party:
   a. may sue only the agent
   b. may sue only the principal
   c. may sue only the principal and the agent
   d. must sue both the principal and the agent together
   e. may sue either the principal or the agent but not both

_____ 13. When a general agency relationship is terminated by the principal, notice of the termination must be given to:
   a. the agent only
   b. third parties only
   c. either the agent or third parties
   d. the agent and third parties
   e. no notice is required

_____ 14. An agency coupled with an interest may be terminated without liability by the principal:
   a. at any time
   b. only when the interest is satisfied
   c. by the death of the principal
   d. within a reasonable time after the principal's death
   e. b and c are both correct

15. Which of the following will automatically terminate the agent's authority to act on behalf of the principal?
    a. the bankruptcy of the principal
    b. the insolvency of the principal
    c. serious physical injury to the principal
    d. the physical illness of the agent
    e. b and c are both correct

16. Principals are liable for the torts of their agents:
    a. in all situations
    b. only if the agent is compensated
    c. only if the agent is acting gratuitously
    d. that are committed within the scope of their authority
    e. none of the above is correct

17. If a principal is held liable on a contract that the agent made without actual authority, because the other contracting party reasonably believed from the principal's conduct or words that the agent possessed the authority to so contract, then this is:
    a. express authority
    b. implied authority
    c. apparent authority
    d. only a and b are correct
    e. none of the above is correct

18. Apparent authority of an agent is based on the:
    a. principal's conduct
    b. agent's conduct
    c. third party's subjective belief
    d. any of the above is correct
    e. none of the above is correct

19. A principal can ratify:
    a. future acts of an agent
    b. prior acts of an agent
    c. only entire acts of an agent
    d. only a and b are correct
    e. only b and c are correct

_____ 20. If an agent signs a contract and represents that it is done on behalf of a principal, but he or she lacked the actual authority to do so, then:
  a. the agent has breached an implied warranty
  b. the agent is liable to the principal for any loss caused by the unauthorized act
  c. the other contracting party can recover only for breach of contract against the principal
  d. the principal can never be bound to the contract
  e. only a and b are correct

Completion Questions

21. _____ authority is the authority an agent appears to possess in the eyes of a reasonable third person.

22. A principal's subsequent approval of an unauthorized act of another person who claimed to be acting on behalf of the principal is referred to as _____.

23. An employer is liable for the torts of its employees or agents that were committed within the scope of their authority under the concept of _____.

24. A principal cannot revoke an agency that is _____ _____ _____ _____.

25. Agency authority that is stated in words is _____ authority.

Chapter 37

FORMS OF BUSINESS ORGANIZATION

In selecting a form of business, the entrepreneur's choice has both short and long run implications by virtue of various factors. Some factors like cash flow and bottom line profile are quite obvious. At the same time, other factors such as both tax and management control are less apparent.

This chapter examines the three major forms of business: single proprietorship, partnership, and corporation. Included in this examination are the factors to be weighed in selecting one of these forms as well as the advantages and disadvantages of each. The chapter concludes with an overview of some specialized forms of business that are in frequent use today.

CHAPTER OBJECTIVES

After reading Chapter 37 of the text and studying the related materials in this chapter of the Student Mastery Guide, you will understand:

1. The different forms of business organization, including:
   a. single proprietorship
   b. partnership
   c. corporation
2. The relevant factors in selecting a form of business organization

MAJOR POINTS TO REMEMBER

Single Proprietorship

1. A single proprietorship is usually a small business operated and controlled by one or two people who receive all profits from and assume full liability for the debts of the business.

Partnership

2. A partnership is a form of business organization in which two or more individuals agree to be co-owners in a business operated for profit. A partnership agreement may be either implicitly or explicitly formed, and, in the case of the latter, the Uniform Partnership Act (UPA) determines the responsibilities and liability of the partnership.

3. In a limited partnership, general partners are personally liable for all debts; while limited partners, who have contributed less investment capital and do not play an active role in managing the business, are usually responsible for losses up to the amount of their capital contributions.

317

Corporations

4.   A corporation is a business entity created for the primary purpose of making profit and requiring:
   a.   one or more officers
   b.   a board of directors
   c.   shareholders

Factors to be Weighed in Selecting a Form of Business Organization

5.   Relevant factors in choosing a form of business organization include:
   a.   managerial control
   b.   extent of personal liability
   c.   transferability of interest
   d.   taxation
   e.   legal status

Advantages and Disadvantages of Each Major Form of Business Organization

6.   The advantages of a single proprietorship are that there is a single owner who retains all profits, enjoys easy start up, and pays only ordinary personal income taxes. However, its disadvantages are that the proprietor has unlimited personal liability for the debts of the business and can expand operations only with personal wealth or a loan.

7.   A partnership has certain advantages including the easier raising of capital, spread liability, and certain tax advantages. Its disadvantages are that each partner is liable for the other's actions and the partnership is dissolved upon one partner's death.

8.   The major advantage of a corporation is that it can raise capital and expand by selling shares, which are easily transferable on the stock market if the corporation is publicly owned. Also, the corporation has a separate legal status from that of its shareholder-owners.

Specialized Forms of Business Organizations

9.   The major goals of special forms of business organizations are to raise capital quickly, mass produce goods and services, and market these goods and services in the least costly manner.

10.   Specialized forms of business organizations include:
   a.   joint venture
   b.   cooperative
   c.   syndicate
   d.   joint stock company
   e.   franchising
   f.   limited liability company

11. Individuals or corporations agreeing to pool their capital and labor for various purposes for a limited time period constitute a joint venture.

12. The purpose of a cooperative is to market products at the best prices.

13. A major advantage of syndicates is that they can quickly raise large amounts of capital by bringing individual parties together to finance a purchase. However, members of a syndicate can face individual liability.

14. Joint stock ownership among partners in the absence of partnership liability constitutes a joint stock company.

15. The terms and conditions of the franchisor's agreement may include:
    a. the hours a franchisee's store will be open
    b. the products to be sold
    c. the percentage of gross profits to go to the franchiser
    d. the health and sanitary conditions that will prevail
    e. the grounds for terminating the franchisor-franchisee relationship

16. Because many franchisors have, in the past, overpromised potential sales to franchisees and failed to disclose all the terms of the agreement, the Federal Trade Commission now regulates this relationship.

17. Limited liability companies offer entrepreneurs and small businesses some important advantages not currently enjoyed by partnerships, which, along with joint ventures, may be replaced by limited liability companies in the future.

MAJOR POINTS OF CASES

Siegel v. *Chicken Delight, Inc.* (p. 644)

In its decision, the court further specified the conditions under which a given arrangement may be considered a tying arrangement, which is illegal under the Sherman Act. The court held that the "marketing identity" purpose is not and should not be an absolute justification for a tying arrangement. To recognize that a franchisor has a responsibility to ensure that products sold under its trademark bear a likeness in distinctiveness, uniformity, and quality to the franchisor's own product, the court stated, is not to say that every means employed by the franchisor to meet this responsibility is justified.

Applying its ruling to the facts of the case, the court affirmed the decision that the requirements made of Siegel by Chicken Delight constituted a tying arrangement. Contractual requirements that franchisees purchase certain cooking equipment, dry-mix food items, and trade-mark bearing packaging were not found by the court to be justified under the "marketing identity" exception to otherwise illegal tying arrangements.

SELF TEST

True-False Questions

_____ 1. The owner of a single proprietorship assumes full personal liability for business debts.

_____ 2. Partnership agreements may be either explicit or implicit.

_____ 3. Limited partnerships are legal in only 48 states.

_____ 4. Corporate shareholders assume full liability for the debts of the business.

_____ 5. Personal liability is greatest for a cooperative.

_____ 6. A joint stock company is somewhat comparable to a partnership.

_____ 7. Another name for a syndicate is a union.

_____ 8. In a franchising agreement, there are three parties: franchisor, franchisee, and mediator.

_____ 9. The Federal Trade Commission regulates the franchising agreement to some extent.

_____ 10. Limited liability companies are quickly replacing partnerships.

Multiple-Choice Questions

_____ 11. (An) Advantage(s) of partnerships include:
   a.   partners do not pay Social Security taxes
   b.   partners do not pay a self-employment tax
   c.   each partner is not liable for any other partner's actions
   d.   all of the above
   e.   none of the above

_____ 12. The purpose of a joint venture is to:
   a.   eventually form a merger
   b.   produce and sell goods, securities, or commodities
   c.   market products
   d.   all of the above
   e.   none of the above

_____ 13. A joint syndicate is:
   a. a group of people or businesses that pool capital and labor
   b. a nonprofit business created to market products
   c. a union
   d. an investment group created for the purpose of marketing a product
   e. none of the above

_____ 14. A limited liability company offers advantages to:
   a. large corporations
   b. entrepreneurs and small businesses
   c. syndicates
   d. all of the above
   e. none of the above

_____ 15. (An) Advantage(s) of single proprietorships is/are:
   a. no corporate income taxes
   b. easy start up
   c. limited personal liability
   d. all of the above
   e. a and b only

_____ 16. The factor most disadvantageous to the owners of single proprietorships is:
   a. taxation
   b. transferability of interest
   c. managerial control
   d. extent of personal liability
   e. legal status

_____ 17. An advantage not enjoyed by corporations is:
   a. separate legal status from ownership
   b. no personal liability for shareholders
   c. expansion via selling shares
   d. owners, managers, and directors usually protected from personal liability
   e. none of the above

_____ 18. Another name for a syndicate is:
   a. a union
   b. capital joint venture
   c. purchasing agent
   d. investment group
   e. none of the above

_____ 19. Tying agreements:
   a. are comparable to joint ventures
   b. are another name for a partnership
   c. have been scrutinized as a possible restraint on trade under the Sherman Antitrust Act
   d. are relevant to cooperatives
   e. none of the above

_____ 20. A disadvantage of partnerships is that:
   a. they must pay Social Security taxes
   b. they hold divorced legal status from the partners themselves
   c. each partner is personally liable
   d. they do not contain much potential for raising capital
   e. none of the above

Completion Questions

21. A _____ _____ is an agreement between two or more people to operate a business in which there are both general and _____ partners.

22. _____ are business entities.

23. A _____ aims to market products at the best prices.

24. A _____ is a nonprofit group.

25. _____ _____ _____ are a new kind of business organization.

Chapter 38

NATURE AND FORMATION OF PARTNERSHIPS

This chapter is concerned with the nature and formation of partnerships. It considers the question of what a partnership is, the factors that are important in establishing a partnership, and the various ways in which a partnership may be created. Additionally, the text discusses the formal requirements that attend the formation of a partnership and the nature and specific rules that apply to limited partnerships.

A full and complete understanding of the nature and formation of a partnership is essential to a comprehension of the operational mechanics that guide the partnership through its business activities.

CHAPTER OBJECTIVES

After reading Chapter 38 of the text and studying the related materials in this chapter of the Student Mastery Guide, you will understand:

1. The nature of the partnership relationship, including:
   a. the aggregate theory
   b. the entity theory
   c. the Uniform Partnership Act approach
2. The factors considered in determining the existence of a partnership relationship and the ways in which a partnership is created
3. The formalities that must be followed in creating a partnership

MAJOR POINTS TO REMEMBER

Nature of Partnerships

1. A partnership is "an association of two or more persons to carry on as co-owners a business for profit" (Uniform Partnership Act, Section 6[1]).

   A joint venture is an association of two or more persons for a single undertaking or a series of transactions. The legal rules that govern partnerships apply also to joint ventures.

2. Partnerships can be described as:
   a. general
   b. limited

3. All partners in a general partnership have unlimited personal liability for the activities of the partnership.

4. In a limited partnership, the liability of some of the partners is limited. Additionally, limited partnership must have at least one general partner, and also must have at least one limited partner who contributes capital and who shares in the profits of the business but

323

who takes no active part in the management or operation of the business activities of the partnership.

5. Every partner is an agent of the partnership as well as a principal.

6. There are two legal concepts of partnership:
   a. the aggregate theory, which states that it is an association of persons who are co-owners and who are individually responsible for the legal obligations created. The partnership is not a separate legal entity from the partners.
   b. the entity theory, which treats the partnership as a separate legal entity from the partners that has its own legal rights and obligations.

7. The Uniform Partnership Act combines the aggregate and entity theories. Generally, it treats a partnership as an aggregate, but for some purposes, such as property transactions, it is considered a separate entity.

Partnership Formation

8. There is no particular or specified procedure that must be followed in forming a general partnership.

9. Generally, a partnership can be created verbally or in writing.
   If the partnership is created by a writing, the writing is usually referred to as a "partnership agreement" or "articles of partnership."

10. In determining whether a business is being conducted as a partnership, the intent of the parties will be specifically considered.

11. The consent of all the partners in a partnership is required in order for a new partner to be admitted to the business.

12. Any person who possesses contractual capacity may become a partner in a business.

13. Under Section 2 of the UPA, a person "includes individuals, partnerships, corporations and other associations." The trend is to permit a corporation to become a partner in a partnership.

14. A person may become a partner in a partnership even though he or she has not made a capital contribution to it, if that person shares ultimate control in the firm's operation.

15. A partnership must be formed as a business. A business includes every occupation, trade, or profession.

16. While the sharing of profits is prima facie evidence of the existence of a partnership, Section 7(4) of the UPA provides that it will not be considered to give rise to a partnership if the profits are:
    a. paid or received in order to discharge a debt
    b. received as wages or rent
    c. paid to a widow or an estate as an annuity
    d. paid for the purchase of a partnership asset

    Share of losses may also be sufficient to establish partnership status.

Partnership Established by Representation

17. A partnership by estoppel exists when two or more persons (who are not partners) represent themselves or permit themselves to be represented as partners to others who rely on the representation. By such circumstances the person representing themselves or being represented as partners will be treated and will be liable as if they were partners.
    A person seeking to hold another liable as a partner by estoppel must have extended credit in reasonable reliance on the representation of that person as a partner.

Formalities

18. Generally, a partnership may select and use any name it wants provided that name is not prohibited by statute and also provided that fraud, trade-name infringement, and unfair competition are not involved. No particular terms or phrases need to be included in the name of a general partnership.
    A fictitious name is one that does not disclose the surnames of all the firm's partners. A business may use a fictitious name, but most states require the name to be registered.

19. A partnership is generally not required to have a written agreement. However, if the contractual nature of the partnership falls within the requirements of the Statute of Frauds, then the partnership contract must be in writing in order for it to be enforceable. A written agreement is usually required when:
    a. the partnership is to continue for more than one year
    b. an interest in real estate is transferred either to or by the partnership
    Frequently the parties enter into a written contract called the "partnership agreement" or "articles of partnership."

20. The Uniform Limited Partnership Act, which has been adopted by many states, provides that a limited partnership must file a certificate of limited partnership with a designated governmental official when it is formed.

21. Technical defects in the certificate filed by a limited partnership will not destroy the effective formation of the partnership. However, if a limited partner knows that a statement contained in the certificate is false, that partner may lose his or her protection as a limited partner.

22. Under the ULPA, a limited partnership can include the surname of a limited partner in its name only if:
   a.   the partner whose name is included is also a general partner, or
   b.   the partnership operated under that name before that person became a limited partner

23. The ULPA provides that the name of each limited partnership must contain the words "limited partnership."

   Further, the partnership is not permitted to include in its name any words or phrase which indicate or imply that it is organized for some purpose that is not specified in its certificate of limited partnership.

Preventive Law: Controlling Against Unintended Partnership Status

24. Creditors, seeking to protect their financial interests, may want to assume certain controls over a debtor's business. If this assumption of control is limited to that which is reasonably necessary to protect a creditor's legitimate interests, no problems should arise. However, if the creditor's participation is greater than necessary to protect its interests, there is a risk that the creditor will be deemed a partner with unlimited personal liability. Unfortunately, there is no clear rule to determine how much control is too much.

Preventive Law: Drafting Partnership Agreements

25. Although not generally required, a well-drafted written partnership agreement can still be very important. A written partnership contract:
   a.   establishes proof of the partnership's existence and its terms
   b.   can cause partners to consider and plan for potential problems and
   c.   can help avoid future legal disputes

MAJOR POINTS OF CASES

McKinney v. *Truck Insurance Company* (p. 681)

This case deals with the conflicting theories that exist with reference to the nature and character of partnerships. The court stated that prior decisions in Missouri had established that the aggregate theory of partnership had been recognized as being applicable in the state, so that a partnership is deemed to be made up of its members and not separate from them. However, the court also stated that for some purposes, it is proper to recognize a partnership as being an entity in itself.

According to the court, the facts of this case rendered it proper to consider the partnership to be a separate entity. The intention of the parties was that the insurance policy involved would apply only to the activities of the partnership - that is, the sale and repair of glass - and not to the separate business ventures of the individual partners. Consequently, at least for purposes of the insurance policy involved, the partnership should be distinguished from its members. The coverage provided by the insurance policy extended only to the activities of the partnership unit.

Commonwealth v. Campbell (p. 684)

This case dealt with the boundaries of the definition of partnership in adjudication. The court rules that for any entity to be considered a partnership for legal purposes, it must have been formed for the purpose of making a profit.

Applying its ruling to the case, the court found that Campbell was convicted under the wrong statute and, thus, was not guilty. The statute under which she was convicted concerned the reporting of false financial statements for partnerships. Even though she did make false financial statements, Campbell was found to be not liable under this statute, because the league was organized as a non-profit baseball league for young boys.

Lupien v. Malsbenden (p.686)

This case deals with the factors examined to determine if a partnership existed. The key ultimate conclusion which must be reached is that the parties intended a business relationship that meets the definition of a partnership, not that they specifically intended to form a partnership. If the relationship in fact is a partnership, then the parties' knowledge, intent, or characterization of the arrangement cannot change the legal result. A partnership is an association of two or more persons to carry on as co-owners a business for profit. Although no one factor is necessarily determinative, the sharing of profits, losses, and management control are clear indications of a partnership.

The court found that the defendant was a partner in a business and, thus, personally liable for its legal obligations. He had contributed capital to the business and exercised management control for several years in exchange for a share of any profits. This constituted a partnership.

Smith v. Norman (p. 689)

The court ruled in this case that a person cannot be claimed as a partner by estoppel unless that person is thought to be a partner prior to or at the time of a contract. Reliance on a person's representation of his or her partnership after the contract has been established is not sufficient to justify claiming that person as a partner by estoppel and, thus, as a liable party. Applying this ruling, the court found the plaintiff's suit against Max Norman to be invalid, due primarily to the fact that both plaintiffs denied believing that Max Norman was a partner at the time of the contract formation.

PRACTICAL CONSIDERATIONS

While a written partnership agreement is not required by law for most partnership arrangements, it is often considered to be an indispensable document that relates directly to the core of the partnership relationship. Unfortunately, when partners initiate their relationship and their business activities, their foresight is often limited to the visions of instantaneous, unceasing, and ever-increasing profits they anticipate. Such tunnel vision, however, ignores reality. A new business venture normally requires several years of development before appreciable results are achieved, and some ventures never quite reach their goals or make a profit. When failure of the venture appears imminent, the relationship that the partners expected to be perpetually harmonious may become the basis of ferocious hostility. Without a prearranged, well-conceived plan setting forth the respective rights and obligations of the partners, chaos and complete failure of the business venture may result.

Consequently, the execution of a partnership agreement is generally advisable whenever a partnership relationship is initiated. The partners should not be reluctant to discuss the necessity for such an agreement, nor should they be reluctant to modify the agreement later if the circumstances warrant such action. Open communication between the partners is a key to the success of their common pursuits and is essential to harmonious cooperation. While disagreements are inevitable in a partnership, they can be useful and productive in advancing the interests of the partnership. An organized effort is essential, however, and in this regard the partnership agreement provides a source of unification.

In certain instances, two or more businesses may wish to participate in a single undertaking. These businesses may form a joint venture - a partnership limited in duration and scope. Joint ventures are for the most part governed by the same rules that govern partnerships.

Two organizations may wish to continue operating separately with respect to most facets of their businesses but to work together on special projects. Such agreements are fairly common in the real-estate business; two businesses may enter into a joint venture to construct a shopping center, for example. Joint ventures have become fairly common in the oil industry as well, because few companies can afford to incur alone the massive expenses associated with oil exploration.

SELF TEST

True-False Questions

_____ 1. A limited partnership must have at least one general partner.

_____ 2. A partnership is generally considered to be an aggregate of the co-owners, but for some purposes it is considered an entity.

_____ 3. The existence of a partnership agreement conclusively establishes that a partnership relationship exists.

_____ 4. A person cannot become a partner in a partnership if one of the existing partners objects to his or her admission as a partner.

_____ 5. When a partnership is initially created, each of the partners must contribute capital to the partnership.

_____ 6. A person who regularly receives a 10 percent share of the profits of a partnership will always be considered to be a partner in the business.

_____ 7. Persons who are not actually partners in the same business may sometimes be held liable to third persons as if they were partners.

_____ 8. A partnership may always use any name that it wants as long as the name is not currently being used by another firm.

_____ 9. If partners agree that the partnership shall continue for a period of fifteen months, there must be a written agreement between the parties to ensure that the relationship will be enforceable.

_____ 10. If a limited partner takes any part in the management of the business in which he or she is a partner, that partner will not be entitled to the limited liability normally provided to limited partners.

Multiple-Choice Questions

_____ 11. The legal theory that holds that a partnership is an entity that is separate and distinct from the individual partners is the:
   a. aggregate theory
   b. autonomous theory
   c. entity theory
   d. jurisprudence theory
   e. doctrinal theory

_____ 12. Which of the following persons is never considered capable of being a partner in a partnership, in any jurisdiction?
   a. an infant
   b. a partnership
   c. a seventy-five-year-old man
   d. a member of Alcoholics Anonymous
   e. an adjudicated insane person

_____ 13. The fact that the profits of a business are shared by two or more persons will not in itself give rise to the existence of a partnership if the profits are:
   a. received as wages
   b. received to discharge a debt
   c. paid for the purchase of a partnership asset
   d. paid to a widow as an annuity
   e. all of the above are correct

_____ 14. Which of the following is a characteristic of a partnership?
   a. there must always be at least two or more parties involved in the partnership
   b. limited liability
   c. co-ownership of the business by the parties
   d. a and c are both correct
   e. a, b, and c are all correct

329

15. A limited partner's liability for partnership activities is limited:
    a. by statute to $5,000
    b. to the amount of his or her capital contribution to the partnership
    c. to 50 percent of the value of the partnership assets
    d. even if he or she joins the partnership without making a capital contribution
    e. to $10,000 or the amount of his or her capital contribution, whichever is less

16. Which of the following factors will be considered by a court in determining whether a business is a partnership?
    a. the total amount of assets involved in the business
    b. the intent of the parties involved
    c. control of business operations
    d. only b and c are correct
    e. a, b, and c are all correct

17. Which of the following factors must be presented in order for a partnership by estoppel to be created?
    a. a partnership agreement
    b. a representation of partnership association
    c. reliance by a third party on a representation of the existence of a partnership association
    d. b and c are both correct
    e. a, b, and c are all correct

18. Under the provisions of the revised Uniform Limited Partnership Act, the name of the partnership must include the words:
    a. Unincorporated Association
    b. Limited Partnership
    c. Public Limited Company
    d. Ltd.
    e. c and d are both correct

19. Which of the following provisions would be found in the terms of a partnership agreement?
    a. the purpose of the partnership
    b. the minimum age for admission as a partner
    c. the date on which the business will be incorporated
    d. only a and b would be found in the agreement
    e. a, b, and c would all be found in the agreement

_____ 20. Which of the following is a type of partnership?
- a. general partnership
- b. amalgamated partnership
- c. associated partnership
- d. a and c are both correct
- e. a, b, and c are all correct

Completion Questions

21. A(n) _____ _____ is an association of two or more persons for a single undertaking.

22. The _____ theory of partnerships holds that the partners are co-owners of the business and the property used in it.

23. The liability of a general partner in a partnership can be described as _____ liability.

24. A(n) _____ is an association of two or more persons to carry on as co-owners of a business for profit.

25. An agreement between partners that sets forth their respective rights and obligations in connection with the partnership is referred to as a(n) _____.

Chapter 39

OPERATION AND DISSOLUTION OF PARTNERSHIPS

Inasmuch as a partnership consists of an association of individuals, the relationship between the partners requires certain structural guidelines that may be referred to when internal problems or issues arise in the course of their business activities. These guidelines delineate and clarify their respective rights and obligations when the partnership agreement is silent on a particular issue.

This chapter considers the property rights that exist with reference to the partnership, the relationship among the partners, and the relationship that exists as a result of the interaction of the partners with third persons. The chapter also considers the rights and obligations of the partners when their relationship with each other changes and the partnership is dissolved.

CHAPTER OBJECTIVES

After reading Chapter 39 of the text and studying the related materials in this chapter of the Student Mastery Guide you will understand:

1. The relationship of the parties among themselves and their respective rights in partnership property and the partnership
2. Partner's responsibilities for partnership dealings with third parties
3. The nature and effect of the dissolution of a partnership
4. The winding up process and the termination of the partnership
5. The continuation of the partnership business after a dissolution

MAJOR POINTS TO REMEMBER

Property Rights in Partnership

1. Under the Uniform Partnership Act (Section 24), the partners in a partnership possess the following property rights:
   a. rights in specific partnership property
   b. the interest in the partnership
   c. the right to participate in the management of the business

2. While technically the partners in a business do not own the partnership property, they do collectively possess an ownership interest in it, which is referred to as a *tenancy in partnership*.

3. Under the terms of the UPA (Section 8[1], any property that is originally brought into "partnership stock" or subsequently acquired "on account of the partnership" is considered to be partnership property. Further, there is a rebuttable presumption that any property purchased with partnership funds is intended to be partnership property.

4. Unless otherwise agreed by the partners, a partnership may use partnership property only for partnership purposes.

5. A partner cannot assign his or her interest in *partnership property* to another person unless the rights of all the partners are assigned. A partner may, however, assign his or her *partnership interest* to another party without the consent of the other partners.

    A partner's interest in specific partnership property passes to surviving partners. It is not included in the deceased partner's estate.

6. A creditor of an individual partner may not seize an item of partnership property in order to satisfy the personal debt of the partner.

Partner's Interest in the Partnership

7. The UPA describes a partner's "interest" in the partnership as "his share of the profits and surplus." The statute also provides that a person's partnership interest is deemed to be personal property.

8. A partner's interest in the partnership is assignable, may be attached by his or her creditors, and becomes a part of the partner's estate upon his or her death.
    a. If a general partner assigns his or her interest in the partnership, the assignee does *not* acquire any right to participate in the activities of the partnership to inspect the partnership books, or to require information regarding the firm's transactions.
    b. If a limited partner assigns his or her interest in the partnership, the assignee may become a substitute limited partner.

9. A partnership agreement may provide that the interest of a deceased partner will pass to one or more surviving partners.

Relations Among Partners

10. A partnership is a fiduciary relationship under which the partners owe each other a duty of loyalty, good faith, and honesty, since they are agents to each other and the partnership.

11. Unless otherwise agreed:
    a. partners *share profits and losses equally* regardless of the nature or extent of the partners' capital contributions.
    b. all partners have equal rights in the *management* and control of the partnership's business activities
    c. no partner is entitled to reimbursement for acting in the partnership's business

12. Unless otherwise agreed by the partners:
    a. ordinary business decisions in a partnership relationship are determined by means of the vote of a simple majority of the partners
    b. major policy decisions of a partnership require the unanimous approval of the partners
    c. the majority must act in good faith for the firm's interest and not out of self-interest

13. No person may become a partner in a partnership without the consent of all the partners (UPA, Section 18[g]).

14. Each partner is entitled to receive true and full *information* on all matters affecting the partnership, and to this end is entitled to *inspect* the books of the partnership.
    If it is deemed necessary and appropriate, each partner may be entitled to a formal *accounting* even when the partnership is not being dissolved.

15. Limited partners in a partnership are not considered to retain a fiduciary relationship with one another. Limited partners are entitled to receive information about the partnership's activities but are not entitled to participate in the management of the business. If a limited partner does participate in management, that partner will lose the benefit of limited liability. The revised Uniform Limited Partnership Act permits more control over the affairs of the partnership than the original act did.

Relations with Third Persons

16. A partner may be authorized to enter into contracts on behalf of the partnership by means of:
    a. actual authority
    b. implied authority
    c. customary authority
    d. apparent authority

17. The partnership is liable for the torts of its partners if they are committed within the scope of the partnership activities or within the authority given to a particular partner. The individual partners will also be personally liable under such circumstances.

18. A partner who severs his or her relationship with the partnership will remain liable for partnership activities until some notice is given to third parties which indicates that he or she is no longer a partner.
    a. With respect to third parties with whom the partnership has had prior dealings, *actual notice* of the severance of the relationship is required.
    b. With respect to third parties with whom the partnership has not had prior dealings, *constructive notice* is sufficient, such as publication in a newspaper.

19. A new partner who joins a partnership in an existing business will be liable for any obligations that arise from activities that took place before his or her entry into the

business. Such liability, however, will be limited to the new partner's interest in the partnership property - that is, the new partner will not have unlimited personal liability in regard to obligations that arose before he or she joined the partnership.

Partnership Dissolution

20. Dissolution of a partnership does not automatically terminate the business enterprise that the partners conducted. It simply results in a change in the relations of the partners caused by the termination of any partner's association in the carrying on (as distinguished from the winding-up) of the business.

21. A partnership may be dissolved by:
    a.   the acts of the parties, which include:
        i.   completion of the partnership purpose
        ii.   the lapse of time
        iii.   the withdrawal of any partner from the partnership
        iv.   the expulsion of any partner from the partnership
        v.   mutual agreement of the partners
    b.   operation of law, which includes:
        i.   any event that makes it illegal to carry on the partnership business
        ii.   the death of any partner
        iii.   the bankruptcy of any partner or the partnership
        iv.   a decree of a court based on:
            (a)   the incapacity of a partner
            (b)   improper conduct
            (c)   indications that the business can be conducted only at a loss
            (d)   circumstances and equities that indicate a dissolution is necessary and appropriate.

22. A limited partnership will not be dissolved by the death, incapacity, bankruptcy, or withdrawal of one of its partners.

Winding Up the Partnership Business

23. During the winding up process:
    a.   assets are liquidated
    b.   money owed to creditors and partners is paid (to the extent possible)
    c.   accounts receivable are collected or the debts settled by agreement
    d.   capital contributions are returned to partners (if there are sufficient funds)
    e.   profits (if any) are distributed to the partners

24. Upon dissolution, the liquidating partner is endowed only with such authority as is necessary to perform the winding up process and bring about a termination of the business.

Distribution of Assets

25. Once a general partnership has been dissolved, claims against the partnership are paid according to the following priority schedule:
   a. claims of partnership creditors
   b. claims of partners for loans or advances
   c. partners' capital contributions
   d. distribution to the partners of any remaining profits and surplus funds

26. Upon distribution of the assets in connection with a limited partnership, limited partners receive their share of profits and other compensation as well as the return of their capital contribution after the creditors have been paid but before any loans or advances from general partners have been paid.

27. Under the doctrine of "marshaling of assets," the creditors of a partnership must first make a claim against partnership property before making a claim against a partner's individual assets.
   Likewise, a creditor of an individual partner must first make a claim against that partner's personal assets. Only when the individual partner's assets are insufficient to satisfy the indebtedness can the creditor make a claim against that partner's interest.

Continuing the Partnership Business

28. Under the UPA, partners may have the right to continue the business of the partnership even though a dissolution of the partnership has occurred and even though there is no provision for such action in the partnership agreement.

29. When a dissolved partnership is continued by the remaining partners, the creditors of the dissolved partnership become creditors of the continuing partnership.

Preventive Law: Partnership Property

30. Under the UPA, it is presumed that property bought with partnership funds is partnership property. A partnership agreement clearly stating a different intent of the partners, however, can overcome this presumption. Individual property "loaned," rather than contributed, to the partnership may be deemed partnership property, if the intent that it remain individually owned is not clearly stated in the agreement. Further, partnership accounting records should clearly distinguish between partnership property and that which is still owned by the individual partners.

Preventive Law: Partnership Agreement

31. The general rule of the UPA is that each general partner is entitled to equal participation in management and that most decisions are to be made by a majority of the partners, regardless of capital contributions or shares of earnings. If a different result is desired, however, the partnership agreement can provide for different rules for management

decision making and control, such as a "majority in interest" will control management and decisions. Through the agreement a partnership with many partners can still have centralized management.

Preventive Law: Dissolution of Partnership

32.   Partnerships are dissolved by the occurrence of several events. Dissolution, winding up, and termination can be damaging to an otherwise valuable business. It is sometimes preferable for the partners to agree that the remaining partners can buy the interest of the withdrawing partner and continue the business. The continuation agreement should establish, among other things, the valuation method to be used and the method for funding the purchase of the withdrawing partner's interest. For deaths of partners, such buy-sell agreements can be funded by purchasing life insurance.

MAJOR POINTS OF CASES

Stafford v. *McCarthy* (p. 697)

In this case, the court held that any court attempting to decide whether assets standing in the names of individuals should be treated as partnership property may make such a decision on the basis of the conduct and intention of such individuals. Examining such a basis, the court upheld the plaintiff Stafford's right to collect debt from Don McCarthy via his wife Pat's ownership of certain assets. Important to the court was that McCarthy claimed the assets were owned by "tenants by the entirety", a form of property ownership enjoyed exclusively by married couples. Not only were the McCarthy's not married when they bought the property, Don McCarthy attempted to dissolve his interest with an "Agreement to Dissolve Partnership", a task impossible when assets are owned by "tenants by the entirety". Thus, the Court affirmed the money judgment against Pat McCarthy.

National Biscuit Company v. *Stroud* (p. 704)

The UPA states that partners have "equal rights in the management and conduct of the partnership business." One partner cannot unilaterally restrict another partner from taking actions that are connected to the partnership business by giving notice to a third party of specific limitations or otherwise. Any such special restriction on the powers of the partners must be agreed on by a majority of the partners and notice given to affected third parties.

In this case a partner was held liable to a seller, even though he had given notice to the seller's agent that he would not be personally liable for any future purchases. This partner was bound by the purchase order made by his partner, since it was within the normal operations of the partnership business.

Kelsey-Seybold Clinic v. *Maclay* (p. 705)

This case illustrates the application of the rule that a partnership, as well as partners who have not participated in a tortious act, will be liable for the torts of its partners provided such acts are committed within the scope or ordinary course of the partnership's activities. It also demonstrates that the partnership will be liable for tortious conduct that was either authorized, consented to, or ratified by the partnership.

In this case, the court found that Dr. Brewer had been acting exclusively for his own benefit and "gratification." The court also assumed that his conduct was not consented to or ratified by the clinic. The court also stated, however, that the clinic owed "a duty to the family of its patients to exercise ordinary care to prevent a tortious interference with family relations." With respect to this last obligation, it was held that the clinic failed to establish that "it is not liable under any theory fairly presented by the allegations."

King v. *Stoddard* (p. 710)

Under the UPA, absent a partnership agreement to the contrary, the death of a partner causes a dissolution of the partnership. After dissolution a partner has no authority to enter into contracts that are binding on co-partners unless it is appropriate to the winding up of the partnership's affairs.

The court here concluded that the surviving partner had not acted appropriately to wind up the partnership by continuing to operate it for a considerable period of time after the death of the other two partners. His act of utilizing the accounting services of the plaintiff, thus, was not appropriate to his obligations to wind up the partnership affairs, given the period of time over which the services were rendered and that the services relevant to winding up the partnership could not be separated from other services rendered. The estates of the deceased partners, therefore, were not liable on the contract with the plaintiff's made by the surviving partners.

PRACTICAL CONSIDERATIONS

While the general law with respect to partnerships provides that the management of the partnership's activities shall be the equal responsibility of all the partners, many partnership agreements delegate specific responsibility for certain types of activities to individual partners who may have particular expertise in those areas. Once such a provision has been made, the other partners do not interfere in those specified activities and concentrate on other aspects of the business. Indeed, once such an agreement has been reached, the other partners in the partnership may have no authority to engage in the activities delegated to the particular partner. This type of arrangement, if properly implemented, can be extremely profitable and highly successful in the daily operation of a business enterprise.

Example: Willerby, Gateau, and Surrey form a partnership for the purpose of selling sports equipment on a wholesale and retail basis. Willerby has previously been a purchasing agent for a major sporting goods manufacturer. Gateau has been a professional baseball player and was offered a professional football contract as well. Surrey was previously employed as a professional sales executive for a national retail sporting goods organization.

When the partnership agreement is prepared, it is agreed that Willerby will have full responsibility for all matters related to the purchase of goods for inventory. Gateau will act as a public-relations representative for the partnership, and Surrey will have full responsibility for determining sales practices, procedures, and strategy. All other matters will be decided upon jointly by the partners.

This format may be appropriate because of the expertise possessed by both Willerby and Surrey in their respective fields. Gateau's public image as a professional athlete whose accomplishments have won him considerable acclaim may have a highly positive impact on the image the partnership wishes to project. By means of this plan, the partnership is seeking to use the talents of each partner to achieve the best results.

SELF TEST

True-False Questions

_____ 1. The ownership rights that the partners possess in partnership property are referred to as a tenancy in partnership.

_____ 2. Unless a contrary intention appears, property acquired with partnership funds will be considered to be partnership property.

_____ 3. A partner's use of partnership property is usually limited to partnership purposes.

_____ 4. A partner's interest in real property owned by the partnership is considered to be personal property.

_____ 5. A partner may assign his or her interest in partnership property without the consent of the other partners.

_____ 6. A partner may not enter into business transactions with the partnership for the sale of his or her own personal property if such a sale results in a personal profit to that partner.

_____ 7. A partner who enters into a partnership that is already in existence will have no liability for any activities of the business that occurred before he or she became a partner.

_____ 8. Unless otherwise provided, partners share equally in profits and losses realized by the partnership.

_____ 9. Upon the death of a partner, his or her spouse automatically becomes a partner in the business.

_____ 10. A limited partner possesses the same rights with respect to a partnership as a general partner does.

_____ 11. Which of the following is a right to which a partner in a general partnership is entitled?
    a.   loyalty
    b.   inspection of the partnership books
    c.   full information on partnership business
    d.   a and c are both correct
    e.   a, b, and c are all correct

_____ 12. Ordinary business decisions in a partnership business require the approval of:
    a.   all of the partners
    b.   two-thirds of the partners
    c.   a majority of the partners
    d.   half of the partners
    e.   three-fourths of the partners

_____ 13. A partner may be able to bind the partnership to a contract by the use of:
    a.   actual authority
    b.   gradiant authority
    c.   apparent authority
    d.   a and c are both correct
    e.   a, b, and c are all correct

_____ 14. Which of the following is a proper ground for the dissolution of a partnership?
    a.   the divorce of one of the partners
    b.   the bankruptcy of one of the partners
    c.   the serious illness of one of the partners
    d.   the indictment on criminal charges of one of the partners
    e.   a and b are both correct

_____ 15. A partner can seek a judicial accounting of the transactions of a partnership when:
    a.   the partnership is dissolved
    b.   he or she is wrongfully excluded from partnership business
    c.   at any time, provided he or she gives the other partners notice
    d.   a and b are both correct
    e.   a, b, and c are all correct

16. Dissolution by means of a court decree will be granted on which of the following grounds?
   a. the death of one of the partners
   b. the incapacity of one of the partners
   c. the bankruptcy of one of the partners
   d. the illegality of the business of the partnership
   e. a and d are both correct

17. Which of the following functions may the winding up partner(s) perform?
   a. sell partnership property
   b. conduct new business if it is a clearly successful venture
   c. purchase new inventory for the business
   d. a and b are both correct
   e. a, b, and c are all correct

18. When a partnership's liquidated assets are used to satisfy its outstanding obligations after dissolution has occurred, which of the following claims will be given priority over a claim of a partner for repayment of a loan he or she made to the partnership?
   a. claims of partnership creditors
   b. a claim by a partner for the return of his or her capital investment
   c. a claim for the payment of undistributed profits to the partners
   d. a and c will both have priority
   e. a, b, and c will all have priority

19. Major policy decisions of a partnership require the approval of:
   a. three-fourths of the partners
   b. two-thirds of the partners
   c. all of the partners
   d. four-fifths of the partners
   e. a majority of the partners

20. The Uniform Partnership Act requires that a partnership must maintain which of the following:
   a. a balance sheet
   b. a statement of partnership income
   c. an accounts-receivable journal
   d. all of the above are required to be maintained
   e. the act does not require any specific books to be maintained

341

Completion Questions

21. The _____ of a partnership is a change in the relationship between the partners caused by the termination of any partner's association with the carrying on of the business of the partnership.

22. A court-ordered investigation into a partnership's transactions and activities is referred to as a(n) _____.

23. The process of finalizing and ending the affairs of the partnership is referred to as the _____ _____ process.

24. The form of ownership by which partners own property rights in partnership property is known as _____ _____ _____.

25. The winding up partners of a partnership may also be known by the term _____.

Chapter 40

LIMITED PARTNERSHIPS

This chapter examines the nature of limited partnerships. The material includes an overview of the laws governing limited partnerships as well as the proper means of achieving the formation of a limited partnership. Besides discussing the manner by which limited partnerships are financed, this chapter also pays considerable attention to the rights, privileges, and responsibilities of both the limited and the general partners in a limited partnership agreement. This chapter also provides some of the legalistics of a limited partnership agreement, including how fiscal considerations are distributed, the proper way for a partner to withdraw from a partnership, and the manner by which a partnership may be dissolved.

CHAPTER OBJECTIVES

After reading Chapter 40 of the text and studying the related materials in the Student Mastery Guide, you will understand:

1. the laws governing limited partnerships
2. the certificate of limited partnership's role in the formation of such a partnership
3. the financing of a limited partnership
4. the rights and responsibilities of both limited and general partners in a limited partnership
5. the dissolution of a limited partnership

MAJOR POINTS TO REMEMBER

The Law Governing Limited Partnerships

1. All state limited partnership laws are based on the Uniform Limited Partnership Act (ULPA), which was originally written in 1916. However, some state's laws conform to the original writing, others to the 1976 version, and a majority to the 1985 revision.

Forming the Limited Partnership: The Certificate of Limited Partnership

2. The execution and filing of a limited partnership certificate with a state authority is both a necessary and a sufficient condition for the formation of a limited partnership. Any false statement made in this certificate is the general partner's responsibility.

Person Erroneously Believing Himself or Herself a Limited Partner

3. Persons who are general partners but believe themselves to be limited partners can be treated as limited partners if she or he had a good faith belief that his or her contribution to the business made him or her a limited partner in the enterprise, and if he or she either corrects the mistake by filing a certificate of limited partnership or gives notice and withdraws from future equity participation in the business.

Foreign Limited Partnerships

4. A foreign limited partnership, while formed under the laws of another state and subject to these laws in its organization, internal affairs, and liability, must register with an administrative authority of another state before transacting business there.

Financing the Limited Partnership: Contributions

5. Regardless of death, disability, et cetera, a partner is obligated to contribute cash, property, or services to the limited partnership so long as his or her promise to contribute is signed and in writing.

Limited Partners

6. A major advantage of being a limited partner is the limited liability that is involved. In return for not participating in the control of the partnership, a limited partner is liable only for his or her investment. When a limited partner participates in controlling the business, he or she loses this limited liability protection. However, there are a number of activities in which a limited partner may take part without surrendering limited liability.

7. A limited partner can lose limited liability by allowing his or her name to be used in the name of the limited partnership. Such an allowance makes the limited partner liable to creditors who extend credit to the limited partnership.

8. Limited partners do have a right to information about the business that is needed to protect their investment. Additionally, to the extent that the general partnership agreement allows them, limited partners have voting rights.

General Partners

9. At least one general partner is necessary to the existence of a limited partnership. Under the Uniform Partnership Act (UPA), general partners in a limited partnership have the same rights and responsibilities as those in a general partnership, including:
    a. the right to run day-to-day operations of the business
    b. the responsibility of personal liability for the partnership's obligations
    c. the responsibility of fiduciary duty of loyalty to both general and limited partners.

The Sharing of Profits, Losses, and Distributions in Limited Partnerships

10. In the absence of a written agreement to the contrary, profits and losses as well as cash and other assets in a limited partnership are allocated on the basis of each partner's capital contribution to the partnership.

Distributions and Withdrawal

11. As long as he or she follows the relevant rules of withdrawal, a withdrawing partner is entitled to any distribution stipulated by the partnership agreement. In the event that the agreement is silent, the partner is entitled to his or her interest in the limited partnership at the time of withdrawal.

Assignment of Partnership Interests

12. A partner may assign his or her interest in a limited partnership to another person; however, such an assignment neither dissolves the limited partnership nor entitles the assignee to become a partner, although certain procedures can be carried out to ensure the occurrence of the latter.

Dissolution

13. The causes of dissolution of limited partnership are fewer in number than those of general partnerships. Such occurrences as the death or incapacity of a limited partner or the outright withdrawal of a general partner does not dissolve the partnership.

14. The dissolution of a limited partnership happens:
    a. upon the completion of its terms or the occurrence of events specified in the partnership agreement.
    b. upon the written consent of all partners.
    c. upon the obtainment by a partner of a court-ordered dissolution.

MAJOR POINTS OF THE CASES

Briargate Condominium Assoc. Inc. v. *Carpenter* (p. 718)

In this case, the court held that a notice of withdrawal from a partnership effectively cuts off liability for any fees incurred after such notice. Additionally, the withdrawing partner is responsible for the losses of the plaintiff only to the extent that the plaintiff believed in good faith that the partner was general and not limited.

Applying this holding to the facts of the case, the court remanded the case back to the lower court. The court stated that the Association could not validly make a claim to being misled, to rely on Carpenter's assets, because the evidence suggests that the Association believed Carpenter to be a limited partner. The case was remanded to the lower court in order that there could be a further examination of Carpenter's good faith belief at the time of her investment that she was a limited partner.

Frigidaire Sales Corporation v. *Union Properties, Inc.* (p. 721)

With its decision, the court made the distinction between a corporation and the agents who work for this principal. The court held that it is the corporation, not its agents, that possesses general liability, regardless of whether or not the agents are already limited partners. To the extent that a contracting partner understands that the corporation is the general partner at the time of the contract, the liability cannot be shifted to the corporation's agents.

Applying this distinction to the case, the court affirmed the decision in favor of the respondents, who were being sued for general liability as agents of the corporation. The court ruled that because the respondents separated their actions on behalf of the corporation from their personal actions, and because the petitioner understood that the corporation as a separate entity held general liability, the respondents cannot be sued as general partners.

Woodruff v. *Leighton Avenue Office Plaza, Ltd.* (p. 725)

The plaintiffs asserted that the defendants' dissolution of the Leighton partnership constituted a breach of the limited partnership agreement, because the assets were sold without the consent of the limited partners. However, the court ruled that the limited partnership was dissolved upon the dissolution of the general partner, Gulf General Corporation. Upon this dissolution of the partnership, the court stated, the general partner was obligated to wind up the partnership's affairs, including selling the limited partnership's assets. Therefore, the court affirmed the decision in favor of the defendant.

SELF TEST

True-False Questions

_____ 1. A limited partnership need not have any general partners.

_____ 2. The basis for limited partnerships is found in common law.

_____ 3. A certificate of limited partnership is necessary for the formation of a limited partnership.

_____ 4. The general partner is liable for any false statements contained in the limited partnership certificate.

_____ 5. A good faith belief at the time of the partnership's formation that he or she was a limited partner is sufficient to exonerate a general partner from general liability.

_____ 6. Foreign limited partnerships are those partnerships formed in another country.

_____ 7. Limited partners acquire general liability upon participating in the control of the partnership.

346

_____ 8. A limited partner can lose the protection of limited liability by allowing his or her name to be used in the name of the limited partnership.

_____ 9. Limited partners can never have voting rights in a partnership.

_____ 10. The rights and obligations of a general partner in a limited partnership are different from those of one in a general partnership.

Multiple-Choice Questions

_____ 11. The causes of dissolution of limited partnerships when compared to those of general partnership are:
   a.   about the same in number
   b.   greater in number
   c.   fewer in number
   d.   vastly different
   e.   incomparable

_____ 12. Which of the following are legitimate reasons for the dissolution of a limited partnership?
   a.   the occurrence of certain events specified in the partnership agreement
   b.   written consent of all the partners
   c.   a court-ordered dissolution obtained by a partner
   d.   all of the above
   e.   none of the above

_____ 13. Upon the winding up of a limited partnership, the assets are first distributed to:
   a.   the cause of the winding up
   b.   the limited partners
   c.   the stockholders
   d.   the general partners
   e.   the creditors

_____ 14. A limited partnership consists of:
   a.   both limited and general partners
   b.   limited and often general partners as well
   c.   general partners and usually limited partners
   d.   neither general nor limited partners
   e.   none of the above

347

15. The limited partnership laws in the states are based on legislation from
    a. 1916
    b. 1976
    c. 1985
    d. all of the above
    e. none of the above

16. A general partner believing him or herself to be a limited partner is exonerated from personal liability if:
    a. he or she had a good faith belief that he or she had become a limited partner in the enterprise
    b. upon ascertaining that one is a general partner, he or she files a certificate of limited partnership
    c. he or she denies general partnership
    d. a and b only
    e. none of the above

17. A partner's contribution may be in the form of:
    a. cash
    b. property
    c. services
    d. all of the above
    e. a and b only

18. The financial risks of a limited partner are:
    a. his or her investment in the limited partnership
    b. his or her investment in the partnership as well as the value of his or her personal property
    c. the value of his or her real property
    d. his or her investments in all ventures
    e. none of the above

19. A limited partnership must have at least how many general partners?
    a. one
    b. two
    c. five
    d. ten
    e. none are required

_____ 20. Profits and losses in a limited partnership are usually allocated on the basis of:
   a. the status of a partner
   b. each partner's capital contribution to the partnership
   c. each partner's amount of time as a partner
   d. each partner's personal assets
   e. none of the above

Completion Questions

21. A_____ _____ may withdraw from a limited partnership at any time by giving written notice to other partners.

22. A(n) _____ of a partnership interest may become a limited partner.

23. State limited partnership laws are based on the _____ _____ _____ _____.

24. A(n) _____ _____ _____ is one that has been formed under the laws of another state.

25. A person becomes a _____ _____ by being named as one in the partnership records.

Chapter 41

INTRODUCTION TO CORPORATIONS

Corporate personality has bestowed upon the business community a protective cloak that enables business activities to be conducted without the inhibiting fear of personal liability. And there are many other reasons that this form of enterprise is highly attractive to modern businesspeople.

This brief introduction to corporations examines the features that identify and characterize the fictitious "person" that is known as a corporation. It includes an overview of the historical development of the corporate entity and discusses the characteristic elements that give the corporation its own personality. The text also distinguishes the various types of corporations.

The materials presented in this chapter are intended to provide the reader with a cognitive foundation for thinking about corporations. In the next chapter, a more extensive treatment of corporations will be given.

CHAPTER OBJECTIVES

After reading Chapter 41 of the text and studying the related materials in this chapter of the Student Mastery Guide, you will understand:

1. The historical development of the corporate entity.
2. The nature and classes of corporations, including:
   a. public and private corporations
   b. profit and nonprofit corporations
   c. public-issue and closely held corporations
   d. professional corporations
   e. foreign and domestic corporations

MAJOR POINTS TO REMEMBER

Nature of Corporations

1. The main features that characterize a corporation are:
   a. its entity status (juristic or corporate personality)
   b. limited liability of its owners
   c. continued (perpetual) existence
   d. transferability of its ownership
   e. centralized management

2. A corporation is a separate entity distinct from its members and/or owners.

3. The shareholders of a corporation enjoy the benefit of limited liability in connection with their investment in the corporation. As a result their personal assets may not be used or touched in order to satisfy corporate indebtedness in most cases. Likewise, the corporation is not responsible for the debts of its stockholders.

4. In most states, unless otherwise provided in the certificate of incorporation, a corporation will have perpetual existence.

5. While corporate ownership can generally be transferred rather freely from one stockholder to another, a restriction on such transfer that is contained in the appropriate corporate documents will be valid if the terms of the restriction are reasonable.

6. The management of corporate activities is usually accomplished through the board of directors and/or officers of the corporation.

Corporations and the Constitution

7. A corporation is considered to be a legal person in the eyes of the law. Consequently, it is entitled to the constitutional protections of due process and equal protection of the law.

8. A corporation is protected by the Fourth Amendment guarantee against unreasonable searches and seizures.
    A corporation is not entitled, however, to the protection of the privileges and immunities clause of the U.S. Constitution. Neither is it protected by the privilege against compulsory self-incrimination contained in the Fifth Amendment to the U.S. Constitution.

Ethics Box: Moral Accountability of Corporations

9. A corporation is an artificial legal entity, not a natural person. As such, some argue that a corporation cannot be unethical, since it is incapable of thinking or forming an intent. In contrast, others argue that, since corporations are an aggregate of human beings and have cultures that influence employees' behaviors, they can be held morally accountable for the consequences of their actions. The law increasingly accepts the latter argument of moral accountability of corporations.

MAJOR POINTS OF CASES

First National Bank of Boston v. *Bellotti* (p. 732)

In this case, the U.S. Supreme Court stated that a legislature may not dictate "the subjects about which persons may speak," nor may it limit or restrict the groups or categories of persons who may speak about a public issue. The Court also stated that it found no support for a rule that denies a corporation the benefits of the First Amendment protections simply because it cannot prove to the satisfaction of a court that the legislation it is addressing has a "material effect on its business or property.."
When the Court considered the state statute that was involved in this case, it found that while the protection of shareholders was a compelling interest, there was no "substantially relevant correlation between the government interest asserted and the State's effort to prohibit" the corporation from speaking on the issues enumerated in the statute. It also found that the provisions of the statute were both "under-and-over

inclusive" at the same time. Consequently, the Massachusetts statute was determined to be unconstitutional and the defendant's conviction was reversed.

Ex Parte Brown (p. 736)

In this case, the bench ruled that minority stockholders are entitled to fair treatment in the corporate decision-making process. The majority stockholders have a responsibility to act in the best interest of all shareholders, and a minority "squeeze out" is not a proper manner of corporate behavior.

Applying this ruling to the facts of the case, the Alabama Supreme Court reversed the decision formerly in favor of the defendant and remanded the case back to the trial courts. The court stated that the majority stockholders' failure to pay adequate dividends to the minority was prima facie evidence of a "squeeze out", and it directed the trial court to determine if this was indeed the case. The defendant's argument that the increase in the value of the minority shareholders' stock was a sufficient answer to charges of a squeeze out was deemed not cogent by the court.

Reisman v. Martori, Meyer, Hendricks and Victor (p. 738)

Corporations are incorporated in a particular state. If they are "doing business" in another state, corporations are normally required by statute to register in that state and receive a certificate of authority to conduct business there. What constitutes "doing business" in another state is a question of fact to be decided in each case. However, most state statutes have been interpreted by courts to require registration of foreign corporations only when continuous activities are contemplated, not for isolated, single transactions.

In this case the plaintiff law firm, organized as a professional corporation in Arizona, represented a client in Georgia. Even though it had represented two other persons in Georgia in the past, the court held that the plaintiff was not "doing business" in Georgia and, therefore, could sue the defendant in the Georgia state courts without first registering in that state.

SELF TEST

True-False Questions

_____ 1. The shareholder of a corporation may transfer ownership of his or her stock to another person by means of a provision in his or her will.

_____ 2. Shareholders of a corporation have direct control over the members of the board of directors and can give them specific directives on how the business is to be operated.

_____ 3. A closely held corporation will usually have a large number of stockholders.

_____   4.   Shareholders of a corporation are not usually liable for corporate debts beyond the amount of their investment in the corporation.

_____   5.   The creation of single-shareholder corporations is not permitted by state corporate law.

_____   6.   A corporation's status as a legal entity distinguishes it from all other business organizations.

_____   7.   The U.S. Supreme Court holds that a corporation is a "person" entitled to equal protection of the law as well as the privilege against self-incrimination.

_____   8.   Public issue corporations have management separate from their owners.

_____   9.   Management for the benefit of majority shareholders is more likely to occur in a private corporation than a public one.

_____   10. A corporation's income is taxed at the corporate as well as the shareholder level.

Multiple-Choice Questions

_____   11. Which of the following is a characteristic feature of a corporation?
                         a.   unlimited liability
                         b.   perpetual existence
                         c.   full control of business activities by its owners
                         d.   all of the above
                         e.   only a and b are correct

_____   12. Which of the following acts may be performed by a corporation?
                         a.   commence a lawsuit in its own name
                         b.   transfer ownership of property by means of a will
                         c.   enter into a contract with third parties
                         d.   all of the above
                         e.   only a and c are correct

_____   13. A corporation that is funded and created by the government to act as its instrumentality is:
                         a.   a public-issue corporation
                         b.   a professional corporation
                         c.   a public corporation
                         d.   a private corporation
                         e.   none of the above is correct

14. Which of the following is required in order for a corporation to quality as a Subchapter S corporation?
    a. there can be no more than twenty stockholders
    b. the corporation can issue only one class of stock
    c. all of the stockholders must consent to the corporation's treatment as a Subchapter S corporation
    d. all of the stockholders must be members of the board of directors
    e. only b and c are correct

15. Which of the following words at the end of a business's name will indicate that the business is a corporation
    a. Limited
    b. and Sons
    c. and Composite Group
    d. Associated
    e. only a and d are correct

16. Control of the business activities of a corporation is the responsibility of the:
    a. board of directors and the shareholders jointly
    b. stockholders alone
    c. board of directors and the officers of the corporation
    d. board of directors alone
    e. chairman of the board of directors only

17. Constitutional protections afforded the corporation include:
    a. equal protection of the law
    b. privilege against self incrimination
    c. protection against illegal searches
    d. all of the above
    e. only a and c are correct

18. The sphere of private corporations encompasses:
    a. all corporations except those that are public
    b. all corporations afforded protection from unreasonable searches
    c. corporations with either public or private interests
    d. all of the above
    e. none of the above

354

_____ 19. Corporations were originally conceived for the purpose of:
   a. breaking labor organizations
   b. avoiding the risks and discontinuities of partnership
   c. achieving business objectives beyond the reach of individuals
   d. only a and b are correct
   e. only b and c are correct

_____ 20. Shareholder control of corporations includes:
   a. electing the corporation's directors
   b. direct control over daily business of corporation
   c. approval of all changes in corporation's structure and operation
   d. all of the above
   e. none of the above

Completion Questions

21. A corporation created in Ohio that does business in Georgia is considered a _____ corporation in Georgia.

22. A corporation that is doing business in a state other than the one in which it was incorporated is known as a _____ corporation.

23. A corporation is afforded the constitutional status of a _____ _____.

24. A corporation whose stock has been sold to the general public and whose management rests in persons other than the owners of the company is referred to as a(n) _____ _____ corporation.

25. A(n) _____ corporation is a corporation that is formed for some purpose other than making a profit from business activities.

Chapter 42

FORMING THE CORPORATION

Chapter 41 provided basic information about the corporation, such as its history and composition. The materials presented in this chapter continue this treatment. The text discusses the varying degrees of government regulation that is exercised over corporations. It also examines the various stages of the incorporation process. Included in this examination is an identification of some of the difficulties that may be encountered during the process. Finally, consideration is given to the doctrine referred to as "piercing the corporate veil" and the consequences that can ensue from this doctrine's application.

The materials presented in this chapter are quite detailed. Because the corporate entity is a creature of significant global importance, the concepts presented should be considered carefully.

CHAPTER OBJECTIVES

After reading Chapter 42 of the text and studying the related materials in this chapter of the Student Mastery Guide, you will understand:

1. The extent to and the manner in which corporations are regulated.
2. The process of forming a corporation, including:
   a. preincorporation activities
   b. incorporation procedures
   c. incomplete incorporation considerations
3. The doctrine of disregarding the corporate personality (i.e., "piercing the corporate veil").

MAJOR POINTS TO REMEMBER

Regulation of Corporations

1. Virtually all corporations are incorporated under state statutes. The Revised Model Business Corporation Act (RMBCA) is the law primarily discussed in this and the next two chapters.

2. Federal law regulating various aspects of corporate activity is becoming increasingly important.

3. Except in the case of a Subchapter S corporation, a corporation is considered to be a taxpayer, and consequently it is required to file tax returns and pay income taxes on appropriate corporate taxable income.

4. In order for a corporation to quality as a Subchapter S corporation, it must satisfy the following requirements:
    a.   there may be no more than thirty-five individual stockholders
    b.   the corporation may issue only one class of stock
    c.   a statement containing the consent of all the stockholders to this tax status must be filed with the Internal Revenue Service

Corporate Formation

5. Promoters of a corporation have and maintain a fiduciary relationship with the corporation that they form. Consequently, a promoter must fully disclose to the corporation any dealings with the corporation in which the promoter has a personal interest, and must also enter any transactions with the corporation in good faith.

6. The promoter of a corporation is involved in the following activities:
    a.   planning the development of a corporate business venture
    b.   bringing together people who are interested in the business venture
    c.   effectuating the organization and incorporation of the corporation
    d.   establishing the corporation as a functioning business

7. A promoter who does not specifically state that he or she is acting on behalf of the corporation that is yet to be formed will be personally liable for any contract he or she enters into unless the corporation thereafter agrees to be bound by the contract and relieves the promoter of responsibility.
    A promoter may specifically state that he or she is contracting only in the name of the proposed corporation and not as an individual.
    The corporation is not bound to a contract the promoter has formed unless it consents to it and agrees to be bound by its terms.

Incorporation Procedure

8. Although individual state laws may vary, the name of a corporation must usually include one of the following terms or abbreviations:
    a.   Corporation (Corp.)
    b.   Incorporated (Inc.)
    c.   Limited (Ltd.)
    d.   Company (Co.)
    In the event of litigation, the law of the incorporating state will usually be applied to issues relating to the internal affairs of the corporation.

9. After the certificate of incorporation is issued, the board of directors must conduct an organizational meeting for the corporation.

10. A corporation will be considered to be a *de jure* corporation if it has substantially complied with the provisions of the statute that regulates the incorporation process.

11. A corporation will be considered to be a *de facto* corporation if the:
    a. state of incorporation has a law under which a corporation may be formed
    b. organization has made a good-faith effort to comply with the state law
    c. organization has conducted business as a corporation
    The RMBCA has eliminated the concept of a de facto corporation.

12. When a corporation has been defectively created and a third party deals with the organization as if it were properly incorporated, the third party may be prevented or estopped from challenging the status of the corporation after discovering, at a later time, that the corporation was not properly organized.

Disregarding Corporate Personality

13. A court will disregard the fact that an organization is incorporated and will hold its stockholders to be personally liable for its debts if the:
    a. creditors of the corporation have been defrauded
    b. corporation has evaded its statutory obligations
    c. public interest demands such action

14. If a parent company or the stockholders of a corporation conduct their activities in a normal manner and comply with all formal requirements, the "corporate veil" will normally remain intact.

Ethics in Corporate Restructuring

15. Corporate restructuring and its implications raise serious ethical questions about to whom the corporation is responsible as well as the extent to which this responsibility extends to all parties holding an interest in a given corporation.

MAJOR POINTS OF CASES

Coastal Shutters and Insulation, Inc. v. Derr (p. 744)

In this case, the court held that an entity is liable for preincorporation acts that are ratified or from which the entity derives benefits. To hold a corporation liable for a promissory note dated prior to its formation, the plaintiff needs only to demonstrate that the corporation agreed to the loan with the intention of attaining derivative benefits.

Applying this ruling to the facts of the case, the court denied the defendant's claim that it was exonerated from liability from a loan simply because it did not sign the promissory note before forming the corporation. The court stated that the extensions made on the promissory note by the corporation indicate not only that it was the borrower, but also that it intended to derive benefit from the loan.

Timberline Equipment Co., Inc. v. Davenport, Bennett et al. (p. 749)

In this case, the court stated that under applicable Oregon statutes, a de facto corporation can no longer exist in that state, and that any persons who seek to act as a corporation without a valid certificate of incorporation will each be held personally liable for all debts arising from or as a result of the corporate activities. The court also stated that under the doctrine of corporation by estoppel, the plaintiff must have believed that it was dealing "with a corporate entity."

In considering the doctrine of corporation by estoppel, the court held that inasmuch as the trial court found that the defendants failed to establish all the requisite elements, it was not necessary to determine the merits of that defense. With respect to the defense of the existence of a de facto corporation, the court held that the language of the Oregon statute (which provides for personal liability for persons acting as a corporation without having a valid certificate of incorporation) would be interpreted to "include those persons who have an investment in the organization and who actively participate in the policy and operational decisions of the organization" (emphasis added). Consequently, in view of the fact that Bennett was actively involved in the business venture, personal liability was determined to be appropriate.

W. M. Passalacqua Builders, Inc. v. Resnick Developers South, Inc. (p. 752)

In this case, the court implicitly offered factors to consider in determining the appropriateness of "piercing the corporate veil" of liability. The court ruled that such a piercing of Resnick Developers South, Inc. was permissible due to a number of factors. First, many of the officers and employees of one of the Resnick's various partnerships and corporations were also employees and officers for other corporate defendants. Secondly, the lines of corporate control and responsibility among Resnick controlled entities were often blurred. Third, the various corporate entities' financial transactions revealed a high degree of intermingling. Fourth, the various corporations did not deal "at arms length" with each other. Fifth, and finally, the Resnick corporations were not treated as individual profit centers.

SELF TEST

True-False Questions

_____ 1. Corporate law is statutory.

_____ 2. Incorporation procedures have become increasingly cumbersome.

_____ 3. The state of incorporation must also be the principal place of business.

_____ 4. A corporation is required to file an information tax return with the Internal Revenue Service but is not actually required to pay any income tax.

359

5. The promoter of a corporation is not considered to be an agent for it.

6. "Watered stock" is a term used to refer to stock issued by a corporation for consideration less than the stock's worth.

7. A de facto corporation has fully complied with all the formal requirements needed for proper incorporation.

8. A corporation's certificate of incorporation may limit its existence to a period of five years.

9. De jure corporation results only from the strictest compliance with the provisions of a statute authorizing corporation formation.

10. The promoter of a corporation is usually relieved of any liability for preincorporation contracts that he or she entered into on behalf of the corporation as soon as a certificate of incorporation is issued.

Multiple Choice Questions

11. Most federal regulation of corporation has occurred since:
    a. the enactment of the Sherman Antitrust Act
    b. the enactment of the Securities Act of 1933
    c. the war on poverty in the 1960's
    d. the Brown v. Board of Education decision in 1954
    e. the Panic of 1874

12. Generally, when a contract is made by a promoter with a third party, all of the following are contractually liable:
    a. the promoter
    b. the corporation
    c. the shareholders of a corporation
    d. a and c
    e. a and b

13. Today, preincorporation problems that arise result from:
    a. modern corporation laws
    b. conflicting court decisions
    c. the activities of promoters
    d. all of the above
    e. none of the above

14. A corporation has liability on a contract made by the promoter to the extent that:
    a. it incorporates
    b. the corporation expressly asserts in writing
    c. the corporation knowingly accepts the contracts benefits
    d. b and c
    e. none of the above

15. Which of the following are mitigating doctrines developed to shield shareholders from being treated like partners?
    a. de jure corporation
    b. de facto incorporation
    c. corporation by estoppel
    d. all of the above
    e. c and b only

16. Personal liability will be imposed on the stockholders in the event that which of the following occur?
    a. defraudment of creditors
    b. evasion of statutory obligations
    c. defeating the interest of the public
    d. all of the above
    e. none of the above

17. If a state law permits incorporation of a business and an organization makes a good-faith effort to incorporate in compliance with that law but fails to comply fully, when it conducts business as a corporation it will be considered to be:
    a. a de facto corporation
    b. a quasi corporation
    c. a private corporation
    d. a domestic corporation
    e. unincorporated

18. A corporation may be incorporated under the laws:
    a. of any state
    b. of the United States
    c. only of the state in which it initially does business
    d. only of a state in which it conducts business
    e. a and b are both correct

_____ 19. Which of the following is a function of a promoter of a corporation?
   a.   to purchase property on behalf of the corporation
   b.   to plan the development of corporate business ventures
   c.   to generate interest in the corporation among investors
   d.   b and c are both correct
   e.   a, b, and c are all correct

_____ 20. The doctrine under which a plaintiff may disregard the corporate status of a business and impose personal liability upon its stockholders is known as:
   a.   corporate dissolution
   b.   piercing the corporate veil
   c.   severing the corporate personality
   d.   decertifying the corporation
   e.   _lis alibi pendens_

Completion Questions

21.   The self-made rules by which the internal operations of a corporation are governed are referred to as the _____.

22.   After selecting the state of incorporation, the incorporators must draft and file the _____ _____ _____.

23.   The _____ is a person who undertakes the task of forming a corporation and advancing its interests.

24.   Where there are significant defects in the incorporation to prevent a de jure existence, courts may recognize the organization as a _____ _____ _____.

25.   Promoters are sometimes called _____.

Chapter 43

FINANCING THE CORPORATION

While corporations are frequently considered to be repositories of massive wealth and immeasurable financial potential, it must be recognized that not all corporations enjoy such a positive position. Even among those that do maintain a financially secure posture, the question of financing the business of a corporation is a serious one that merits considerable attention by those who control the corporate activities.

This chapter considers two major aspects of the financial integrity of corporate existence: (1) the various types of securities that can be issued by a corporation to raise funds and (2) the concept of stock subscriptions.

In examining these materials, remember that proper funding of a corporation is critical, for, as has already been discussed, the corporate identity may be disregarded when the corporation has been undercapitalized, and personal liability may be imposed on the principals of the business as a result.

CHAPTERS OBJECTIVES

After reading Chapter 43 of the text and studying the related materials in this chapter of the Student Mastery Guide, you will understand:

1. The various methods of financing corporate activities
2. The different kinds of corporate securities, including:
    a. debt securities
    b. equity securities
3. The nature and effect of stock subscriptions
4. The transfer of securities

MAJOR POINTS TO REMEMBER

In General

1. The process of gathering together funds by issuance of securities is referred to as financing or capitalizing the corporation. The funds are commonly called the corporation's capital.

2. Financing of the corporation may occur:
    a. when the corporation is initially formed, or
    b. after the corporation is formed and it needs additional funds for expansion, operation, or some other legitimate purpose

Kinds of Securities

3. Securities of a corporation can be described as:
    a. debt securities
    b. equity securities

4. Debt securities are those that evidence an indebtedness and include:
   a. notes
   b. debentures
   c. bonds

5. Two important characteristics of debt securities are:
   a. redemption: the right of a corporation to call in its obligations and pay them off at any time before they are due
   b. conversion: the right to change a debt security into an equity security at a certain ratio

6. Every business corporation is required to issue equity securities (usually called shares or stock) to its stockholders, who are the owners of the corporation. The right to issue equity shares is contained in the corporation's articles of incorporation.

7. A corporation will normally meet its financial obligations to creditors by using the funds that constitute its stated capital.

8. The return that investors in a corporation realize on their investment takes two forms:
   a. dividends
   b. capital gains

9. When a corporation issues stock to its stockholders, it usually issues either:
   a. common stock or
   b. preferred stock

10. Generally, the holders of common stock have a voting right in connection with corporate activities. Unless the certificate or incorporation (or other appropriate document) specifically provides otherwise, preferred stockholders do not have a voting right.

11. If a corporation declares a dividend, the preferred stockholders will receive their dividends in full before the common stockholders receive their dividends. If the corporation is liquidated, preferred stockholders will normally also be paid in full before common stockholders.

12. Debt securities have a significant tax advantage over equity securities, since the interest paid on debts is tax deductible by the corporation as a business expense, whereas dividends paid on equity securities are not deductible. It should also be noted that a corporation pays income taxes on profits before dividends are paid and shareholders pay income taxes on dividends received, thereby creating double taxation. Due to this advantage of debt securities, shareholders and corporations are tempted to have a high debt-to-equity ratio in the company's capital structure. If the IRS decides that the debt is excessive, it has the power for tax purposes to treat excessive debt as equity and the interest payments thereon as dividends.

13.   Stock options and rights give the holder the right to purchase stock at a fixed price for a specified period of time. If the option is negotiable, it is called a warrant, which is transferable. Stock options are often given as compensation to corporate executives. Shareholder approval is required under the Revised Model Business Corporation Act for stock options to be given to corporate executives.

Stock Subscriptions

14.   Preincorporation stock subscriptions are used to raise capital for the purpose of financing the business activities of a corporation that is being formed.

15.   A stock subscription entered into after a corporation has been formed is a contract between the corporation and the subscriber for the sale of shares of stock of the corporation.

16.   The modern rule of the RMBCA for preincorporation subscriptions is that they are irrevocable for a stated period of time, typically six months, unless the agreement provides otherwise or all subscribers consent to a revocation. Under the RMBCA a corporation must affirmatively act to accept preincorporation subscription offers.

17.   As soon as a stock subscription is made, the subscriber is vested with all the rights and obligations of a stockholder even though some of those rights may be suspended until the full subscription price has been paid. The subscriber's rights as a stockholder do not depend on the issuance of a stock certificate.

18.   Shares of stock that have been assigned a par value by the corporation may not be initially issued for less than par value.

    If shares of stock are issued to a stockholder at a price that is less than par value, the stockholder will be personally liable to the creditors of the corporation for the difference between the price paid for the stock and the par value.

    When payment for the shares is made in some medium other than money, a question may arise as to whether the corporation received value for the shares. A minority of states follow the true value rule: A shareholder is liable for any unpaid value if the assets given for the stock are worth less than the value of the stock. The Revised Model Business Corporation Act and most states follow the good faith rule in determining whether the corporation received good value for the stock.

Transfer of Securities

19.   Article 8 of the Uniform Commercial Code governs transfers of securities. Bearer securities can be transferred by delivery alone. Registered securities designate the name of the owner, and require delivery and indorsement for a transfer of ownership. Generally, owners of securities have the right to transfer them by sale, gift, or one's will at death.

20.	A corporation is obligated to make transfers of registered securities when they are presented by the owner with any necessary indorsement, provided the securities are not subject to valid transfer restrictions. Failure to do so makes it liable to the new owner.

MAJOR POINTS OF CASES

Lieberman v. *Koppers Co., Inc.* (p. 759)

This case illustrates the rule that a stock option plan provided to corporate employees as part of a deferred compensation plan is valid provided that the value of the services rendered by the employees bears a reasonable resemblance to the market value of the stock and as long as the plan serves a legitimate business purpose.

When the court considered the specific details of the plan involved in this case, it held that "while it may be established in the future that the ward of specific units under the plan may in an individual case ultimately pose the threat of payment of illegally excessive compensation, such a case is not before me now." Consequently, the court ruled in favor of the defendant and upheld the validity of the plan.

Coit v. *Amalgamating Company* (p. 764)

The Supreme Court in this case established the rule that if a corporate charter authorized the corporation to accept property as payment for shares of its stock and the shareholders acted "honestly and in good faith" in providing such property, the issuance would be deemed valid and for good value. It would also be considered fully paid. The Court also stated, however, that if actual fraud was involved in the transaction, creditors of the corporation could hold the stockholders responsible for the difference between the stock's worth and the value they had actually provided.

After examining the facts of the case, the Court held that the evidence did not support a finding of intentional and fraudulent undervaluation of the property that was given in exchange for the stock, except possibly for the value of certain chartered privileges. The Court stated, however, that even if the value of those privileges were deducted from the consideration provided for the stock, the remaining amount would still be so close to the value of the stock that a finding of good faith on the part of the stockholders could easily be made. Further, the plaintiff had not relied on the stock issuance transaction in dealing with the corporation. As a result, the Court held that Coit could not hold the stockholders liable to "pay in the amount of the stock, which . . . was . . . recalled and cancelled."

Estate of Crawford (p. 767)

In this case, the court ruled that in order for one to conclude that a transfer of stocks has not occurred, she or he must demonstrate that none of the formalities of the transfer has been completed. Applying this ruling to the case at hand, the court held in favor of the lower court's decision to return stocks from Dick to his brother Bill because the stocks had not yet been transferred upon their mother's death. Because the transfer had not occurred, Bill had rightful ownership of the stocks as it had been willed by Jo Ann

Crawford. The court determined that there had been no completion of the formalities of transfer by testing each of the ten subsections, each of which delineated what constituted transfer.

PRACTICAL CONSIDERATIONS

While most corporations do have the ability to raise substantial amounts of money quite easily, many prolonged and intense discussions take place regarding the most appropriate method to use to raise this money. The discussions often center on whether the board of directors should authorize the issuance of additional shares of stock or whether it should increase the corporate indebtedness by borrowing money. If the board decides to borrow the money, the next question for consideration is frequently whether to borrow it from an institutional lender (a bank or finance company) or to seek private investors who would be willing to make an investment loan to the company.

The answer to such a dilemma is not easily found. The solution will rest partly on the credit standing of the corporation, partly in the amount of funds needed, partly on the general economic condition of the country at the time the funds are needed, partly on the attractiveness of the company involved, and on numerous other economic and non-economic factors. The solution may also depend on the size, nature, and organizational structure of the company involved. If a company is a large conglomerate with worldwide holdings and diffuse ownership, the issuance of additional shares of stock will probably have no significant effect on the existing stockholders, yet it has the potential of raising large amounts of money. If, however, the company is a small corporation with only a few stockholders who have significant interest and input in the business activities of the company, the addition of new stockholders could have an overwhelming effect on the business and its operational integrity.

Obviously, the board of directors must consider all factors before deciding on the most appropriate financial plan. Indeed, after considering the various alternatives and weighing the merits of each under the corporation's individual circumstances, the board of directors may conclude that the most judicious approach is to defer any judgment to a later date. In matters of such importance and magnitude, haste can not only make waste, it can also lead to financial disaster. Caution and careful deliberation should be the rule in such matters.

SELF TEST

True-False Questions

_____ 1. Interest payment on bonds issued by a corporation are tax-deductible items for the corporation.

_____ 2. Every business corporation is required to issue equity securities.

_____ 3. Every business corporation is required to issue a dividend to its stockholders at the end of every fiscal year.

_____ 4. Preferred stockholders may never exercise a voting right in connection with corporate matters.

_____ 5. The owner of a warrant issued by a corporation may freely transfer it to another person.

_____ 6. Stock subscriptions may be executed only before a business has been incorporated.

_____ 7. The prime purpose of a preincorporation stock subscription is to raise capital that the corporation can use to finance its business activities once it has been duly incorporated.

_____ 8. All shares of stock issued by a corporation must have a stated par value.

_____ 9. A debenture is an equity security.

_____ 10. Preferred shareholders are entitled to receive a dividend issued by a corporation before common stockholders receive their dividend.

Multiple-Choice Questions

_____ 11. The process of assembling funds by the issuance of shares of stock is referred to as:
    a.   capitalization
    b.   regeneration
    c.   incorporation
    d.   a secured transaction
    e.   the assemblage process

_____ 12. The financing process consists of:
    a.   long-term financing
    b.   short-term financing
    c.   tax restructuring
    d.   a and b are both correct
    e.   a, b, and c are all correct

_____ 13. Equity securities include:
    a.   bonds
    b.   shares of stock
    c.   debentures
    d.   a and c are both correct
    e.   a, b, and c are all correct

14. Which of the following constitutes a return on the investment of
    a shareholder?
    a.   a cash dividend
    b.   a stock dividend
    c.   a capital gain on the sale of stock
    d.   b and c are both correct
    e.   a, b, and c are all correct

15. If no other provision is made in the articles of incorporation,
    voting rights will belong to:
    a.   common stockholders only
    b.   preferred stockholders only
    c.   both common stockholders and preferred stockholders
    d.   bondholders
    e.   bondholders and common stockholders

16. Under an executory contract for the purchase of shares of stock
    in a corporation, a person who previously owned no stock of the
    company will be deemed a stockholder:
    a.   when the contract is signed
    b.   when a stock certificate is issued
    c.   when the contract is accepted by the corporation
    d.   when a deposit on the contract is provided
    e.   a and c are both correct

17. The par value that is given to shares of stock may be assigned to
    those shares:
    a.   by the board of directors
    b.   in the bylaws of the corporation
    c.   in the articles of incorporation
    d.   a and c are both correct
    e.   a, b, and c are all correct

18. A characteristic of debt securities is that:
    a.   they are transferable to another party
    b.   they provide ownership rights in the corporation
    c.   they may be convertible into other securities
    d.   a and c are both correct
    e.   a, b, and c are all correct

_____ 19. An option, which is a negotiable instrument giving the owner the right to purchase stock of the corporation at a specified price, is known as:
a. a stock subscription
b. a debenture
c. a warrant
d. an illusory option
e. an allonge

_____ 20. Debt securities include:
a. debentures
b. bonds
c. notes
d. a and b are both correct
e. a, b, and c are all correct

Completion Questions

21. An unsecured corporate obligation that is backed by the general credit of a corporation or its assets is referred to as a(n) _____.

22. A _____ _____ is an agreement between a corporation and a prospective stockholder by which the corporation agrees to issue shares of stock to the subscriber in return for the payment of a sum of money.

23. The value that is assigned to shares of stock either by the board of directors or by the articles of incorporation is known as the _____ _____.

24. A(n) _____ is a document that generally evidences a long-term debt and is secured by a lien or mortgage on corporate property.

25. The owners of the corporation are the _____.

Chapter 44

MANAGING THE CORPORATION

A corporation may be described as a unique hybrid of fact and fiction. It is clear that a corporation is an entity in itself and that it has a personality that distinguishes it from all other forms of business organizations. Yet its very nature is built on the fiction that the corporation is a legal person. If a corporation is a person, then it would seem to follow that it could act for itself. The fact is, however, that a corporation cannot act for itself but must act only through others.

This chapter considers the mechanism by which a corporate structure not only exists but operates and functions. The text considers the purposes of the corporation and the powers it possesses. The chapter also discusses the nature, structure, and extent of corporate management and the fiduciary obligations owed by the corporate management to the corporation and the stockholders.

CHAPTER OBJECTIVES

After reading Chapter 44 of the text and studying the related materials in this chapter of the Student Mastery Guide, you will understand:

1. The purposes for which a corporation is created and the powers that it possesses
2. The roles performed by the different groups within the corporate structure, including:
   a. the stockholders
   b. the board of directors
3. The nature and extent of the fiduciary duty owed by the management of the corporation
4. The reasons for, and method of, dissolution and termination of corporations

MAJOR POINTS TO REMEMBER

Corporate Purposes and Powers

1. A corporation's purpose can be established by its articles of incorporation and by statutory law.

2. A corporation may be formed to engage in and conduct any lawful business. If, however, a corporation engages in activities that are not authorized by its articles of incorporation or acts in some manner that is not so authorized, it commits an "*ultra vires*" act.

3. The Revised Model Business Corporation Act (RMBCA) has codified most of the powers a corporation is permitted to exercise, including the:
   a. power to indemnify directors, officers, and other employees
   b. power to purchase and dispose of its own shares
   c. power to become a partner in a partnership
   d. power to perform any other act that is not inconsistent with the law and that furthers the business of the corporation

371

4. If a corporation commits an *ultra vires* act:
   a. the transaction in which the *ultra vires* act was committed may be enjoined or set aside either by the stockholders or by the state
   b. the corporation may be able to use the *ultra vires* doctrine as a device to set aside the transaction in which the corporation acted in an *ultra vires* manner

5. The RMBCA severely limits the application of the *ultra vires* doctrine by permitting it to be invoked only in:
   a. suits initiated by a state attorney general
   b. suits by the corporation against officers or directors who previously authorized an *ultra vires* act
   c. shareholder suits that seek to enjoin *ultra vires* actions

Corporate Management

6. The operational responsibilities of the corporation are shared by:
   a. shareholders
   b. officers of the corporation
   c. the board of directors

The Role of Shareholders

7. Shareholders usually do not take an active role in the business affairs of the corporation. Their principal corporate action is exercising a voting right at stockholders' meetings.

8. Shareholders in a corporation usually:
   a. elect the members of the board of directors
   b. vote to approve or reject certain transactions of the corporation that are considered extraordinary

9. The RMBCA and most state statutes at present require that shareholders hold an annual meeting at the time specified in the corporate bylaws. Notice of such meeting must either be sent to the stockholders before the meeting or be waived by the stockholder.

10. In order for a stockholders' meeting to be conducted, a quorum of the stockholders entitled to vote generally must be present.

11. Generally, voting rights of stockholders are exercised on the basis of one vote per share held. The cumulative voting method permits a shareholder to cumulate his or her votes. When authorized, cumulative voting thus modifies the voting structure to provide for increased minority voting rights and is generally available only for the election of corporate directors.

12. Stockholders can assign their voting rights to another by proxy. Those interested in gaining voting power, including corporate management, solicit proxies. The Securities Exchange Act of 1934 and Securities Exchange Commission rule regulates proxy solicitations in corporations with more than 500 shareholders and $1 million in assets to protect shareholders from misleading or concealed information in proxy solicitations.

13. Votes can also be combined by pooling or voting agreements among shareholders or by voting trusts.

14. Shareholders of a corporation are entitled to exercise a limited right of inspection, which permits them (under most statutes) to examine:
    a. a list of existing shareholders
    b. certain corporate records

15. Corporate dividends may be distributed in the form of:
    a. cash
    b. property (including the stock of another corporation that is owned by the corporation issuing the dividend)
    c. stock of the corporation issuing the dividend

16. Generally, dividends can be declared and paid only out of the earned surplus of the corporation. Although the RMBCA allows directors some discretion, dividends cannot be paid if the corporation is insolvent or would become insolvent.

17. The board of directors has the responsibility of deciding whether or not a dividend should be declared. If the directors refuse in "bad faith" to declare a dividend, a court may issue an order to compel the corporation to declare a dividend.

    If the articles of incorporation permit it, a shareholder may subscribe to a newly authorized issue of shares in the same proportion that his shares have to all outstanding shares, after the new shares are issued. This is called a preemptive right.

18. Shares are generally freely transferable. Article 8 of the Uniform Commercial Code provides that a stock certificate, in order to be validly transferred, must be:
    a. delivered
    b. indorsed by the registered owner

19. While shares of stock in a corporation are usually freely transferable, most states permit corporations to impose restrictions on such transfers, including the restriction known as the "right of first refusal." Restrictions can also be imposed to ensure compliance with the Securities Act of 1933 regarding private offerings. Restrictions must be conspicuously noted on the face of the stock certificate.

20. Under certain extraordinary circumstances, dissenting shareholders in a corporation are entitled to have the corporation purchase their shares at a fair cash value, provided that certain procedural steps are followed.

21. Shareholders in a corporation may institute two types of lawsuits in connection with their corporate interests:
    a.   direct lawsuits by shareholders on their own behalf
    b.   derivative suits on behalf of the corporation

The Role of the Board of Directors

22. The board of directors has the responsibility for establishing corporate policy and for providing direction to the corporation.

23. Directors of a corporation are generally elected at the annual meeting of the shareholders and usually hold office for a period of one year, and may be reelected.

24. Under common law, directors must be physically present at director's meetings and cannot vote by proxy.
    Statutory law in most states and the RMBCA, contrary to the common law, now permit board members to act on an informal basis without conducting a meeting when the written consent of all members of the board is provided.

25. Unless the articles of incorporation or the bylaws provide otherwise, a majority of the members of the board of directors must be present at a directors' meeting in order to constitute a quorum.

26. By the written consent of all directors, action can be taken on most matters without a formal meeting. The directors can also delegate their authority to committees of its members to act on other than extraordinary matters.

27. Today the trend is to allow shareholders to remove directors during their terms with or without cause.

28. In order to accommodate the needs of small corporations, under the RMBCA a corporation may have only one director.

The Role of Officers and Executives

29. The officers and executives of the corporation are responsible for the day-to-day managerial decisions that affect the corporation.

Management's Fiduciary Obligations

30. Directors and officers of a corporation occupy a fiduciary relationship with respect to the corporation. As a result, they owe the following obligations to the corporation:
    a.   duty of loyalty
    b.   duty of care

31.	A corporation has a prior claim over the directors and officers of the corporation to any opportunity for business and profit that may be considered as incidental to its business.

32.	Corporate officers and directors may be held personally liable for any loss sustained by the corporation as a result of their negligence.

33.	If, however, corporate officers and directors act in good faith to make informed decisions intended to be in the corporation's best interests, then under the "business judgment rule" they will not be held personally liable for corporate losses incurred from honest mistakes.

34.	The recent trend has been to recognize that directors and officers owe a fiduciary duty toward the shareholders, and not just the corporation. Further, even majority shareholders are today being increasingly held to have a duty toward minority shareholders to not abuse their controlling power to damage the minority interests for purely personal gain. Their obligation, although not clearly defined, is to act in the best interests of the corporation and all shareholders.

Ethics Box: Ethics and Board of Directors

39.	A few courts have ruled that they will accept the findings of litigation committees, comprised often of outside directors, regarding shareholder lawsuits. Use of such committees is advocated as being an efficient way to handle a suit. Opponents ask whether such committees have conflicting ethical and legal obligations. For example, can they divorce themselves from other directors? Is their obligation to the majority of shareholders or to render an independent judgment?

Issues and Trends

40.	Courts more often today are closely scrutinizing actions by directors and officers in "control" situations where outside investors or management is seeking to purchase the controlling interest in a corporation. In such situations it is helpful for the directors, officers, and shareholders to:
	a.	have outside directors analyze the fairness of buyout proposals and defensive response measures
	b.	enact defensive measures against attempts to take control of a corporation only in response to specific situations or in cases where such attempts are reasonably foreseeable
	c.	obtain reports on buyout offers from experts for use in the decision making
	d.	assume that directors will be sued and make sure that they are acting in good faith for the best interests of the shareholders

MAJOR POINTS OF CASES

Marsili v. Pacific Gas and Electric Company (p. 773)

The court in this case held that it is not proper for either a court or minority shareholders to substitute their own judgment for that of the board of directors of the corporation in connection with business matters unless the board has failed to act in good faith or to use its best business judgment on behalf of the corporation. The court also stated that the management of a corporation has discretionary authority to enter into any contract or transaction that is reasonably incidental to its business purposes unless it is expressly prohibited from doing so.

In this matter, the court found that no restrictions had been imposed on the authority of the board in connection with initiative or referendum proposals that affected the company, nor was the board prohibited from taking any actions related to political or legislative matters that were of concern to the corporation. As a result, the court found that inasmuch as the directors reasonably felt that the ballot proposition would have a direct adverse effect on the business of the corporation, they possessed the necessary authority to take action in opposing it.

Advance Concrete Form, Inc. v. Accuform, Inc. (p. 780)

The court held in this case that shareholders in a company do not have the right to investigate the books of that company if the purpose of such an investigation is to gain a competitive advantage for another company, namely their own. Applying this holding to the facts of the case, the court ruled that the plaintiff Advance, in wanting to investigate its competitor Accuform's books, had the intention of gaining a competitive advantage and thus did not have a right to the investigation. The court made the judgment on the basis of Advance's competitive relationship with Accuform. As a larger company, the court reasoned, Advance would be able to drive Accuform out of business by underbidding if they were allowed to investigate their books, ledgers, et cetera.

Guth v. Loft, Inc. (p. 787)

This case illustrates the extent of the fiduciary duty of loyalty that corporate officers and directors owe to the company. The court indicated that corporate officers and directors may not use their positions to advance their own private interests. They must refrain from doing anything that would be injurious to the corporation or that would deprive it of profits or advantages it might otherwise reasonably expect to have. The court also ruled that any officer or director of the corporation who violated his or her fiduciary obligations to it, and acquired any gains as a result, held those gains as a trustee for the corporation and was required to pay or hand over such gains to the corporation.

On the basis of the facts in the case, the court found that Guth had appropriated the Pepsi-Cola opportunity for his own personal interests and gain and had consequently placed himself in a competitive position with Loft in violation of his fiduciary obligations. As a result, the court held that it was proper to impress a trust upon those shares of Pepsi-Cola which were registered in the names of Guth and Grace.

***Smith* v. *Van Gorkom* (p. 789)**

       This case examines the relationship between the fiduciary duty of due care of corporate directors and officers and the protective business judgment rule. The court stated that the standard for determining whether a decision was not informed and not made with due care, and therefore outside the business judgment rule, is gross negligence. Further, officers are protected from personal liability for relying in good faith on reports made by officers, but these reports must be relevant to the subject matter of decision and sufficient to justify good faith, not blind reliance.

       In analyzing the facts of this case, the court found the directors to have been grossly negligent in accepting the buyout offer of the corporation. Gross negligence occurred from their approval of the offer at a relatively brief meeting held without prior knowledge of the offer, the substantive terms of the offer, or any significant financial analysis of its fairness. They had simply accepted their chairman's brief explanation and recommendation of acceptance without even questioning him extensively. Their decision to accept the offer was, thus, found not to be informed or made with due care. As such, the business judgment rule did not protect them from personal liability, even though the buyout was later approved by the shareholders.

PRACTICAL CONSIDERATIONS

       It is a well-recognized principle of law that only shareholders who are registered as the owners of shares in the corporation on the record date are entitled to exercise a voting right in connection with corporate matters. When shares of stock are transferred, difficulties with respect to voting rights may arise if the record date has already been declared and the transferor of the shares is considered to be the party entitled to exercise the voting rights. Such person no longer has an interest in the company (assuming he or she has transferred all of his or her shares) and is not likely to use such voting right. This could possibly have a disadvantageous effect on the new owner of the shares. In such a case, the new owner of the shares could effectively negate any possible adverse results by acquiring a proxy from the transferor of the shares. In this way, even if the transferor is deemed to be the owner of the shares for purposes of the vote, the transferee will still be able to exercise that vote in a manner that he or she deems to be appropriate.

SELF TEST

True-False Questions

_____   1.   A corporation can be formed to engage in any business that may lawfully be conducted for profit.

_____   2.   To satisfy the quorum requirement for a stockholders' meeting, a quorum must always be a simple majority of the shareholders entitled to vote.

3. A shareholder who transfers ownership of stock to another person will not be able to vote at a subsequent stockholders' meeting under any circumstances. (Assume that the shareholder does not thereafter have nor does he purchase any additional shares in the same company.)

4. If a money judgment is awarded in a stockholders' derivative action, the money must be paid to the corporation and will become the property of the corporation.

5. When a corporation engages in a transaction that is not authorized by its certificate of incorporation, it will be deemed to be acting *ultra vires*.

6. Corporate policy decisions are the sole responsibility of the shareholders.

7. When a stockholder gives another person a proxy in connection with his or her shares of stock, that proxy can always be revoked at any time.

8. Under the Revised Model Business Corporation Act, a voting trust must be in writing.

9. Dividends may be issued by a corporation out of its capital.

10. The Revised Model Business Corporation Act permits directors of a corporation to take actions on behalf of the corporation even though they have not had a formal meeting.

Multiple-Choice Questions

11. The doctrine of *ultra vires* can be used for which of the following purposes?
    a. as the basis for liability to enjoin a corporate act
    b. as a defense to liability on the part of a corporation
    c. as a basis of avoiding liability for an employee's tortious act
    d. only a and b are correct
    e. a, b, and c are correct

12. Which of the following groups is directly involved in the management of the corporation on a daily basis?
    a.   shareholders
    b.   officers
    c.   directors
    d.   a and b are both correct
    e.   a, b, and c are all correct

13. The Revised Model Business Corporation Act provides that a quorum for a stockholders' meeting must consist of at least:
    a.   one-third of the voting shareholders
    b.   half of the voting shareholders
    c.   two-thirds of the voting shareholders
    d.   three-fourths of the voting shareholders
    e.   four-fifths of the voting shareholders

14. Under the RMBCA, unless otherwise provided, a stockholder's proxy is generally valid for:
    a.   nine months
    b.   eleven months
    c.   twelve months
    d.   fifteen months
    e.   twenty-four months

15. A court will generally be able to compel a corporation to issue a dividend if:
    a.   the corporation has made a profit for the past two years but has not declared a dividend
    b.   there has been a bad faith refusal by the board of directors to declare a dividend
    c.   the corporation is solvent
    d.   the corporation has made a large profit in the current year
    e.   only c and d are correct

16. A class action may be initiated against a corporation by its stockholders for which of the following purposes?
    a.   to protect preemptive rights
    b.   to enforce a right of inspection
    c.   to enforce voting rights
    d.   only a and c are correct
    e.   a, b, and c are all correct

_____ 17. Under the RMBCA, a special stockholders' meeting may be called by:
- a. the board of directors
- b. 20 percent of the shareholders
- c. a person authorized to do so by the bylaws of the corporation
- d. only a and c are correct
- e. a, b, and c are all correct

_____ 18. Which of the following assets may be used by a corporation in distributing a dividend?
- a. capital funds
- b. the corporation's own stock
- c. stock owned by the corporation in another company
- d. only b and c are correct
- e. a, b, and c are all correct

_____ 19. Which of the following transactions does the Revised Model Business Corporation Act recognize as providing justification for an appraisal and buy outright?
- a. a merger
- b. an amendment to the articles of incorporation that materially affects the stockholders' rights
- c. a sale of all of the corporation's property that is not in the regular course of business
- d. only a and b are correct
- e. a, b, and c are all correct

_____ 20. A stockholders' derivative action may be taken to:
- a. require the corporation to issue a dividend
- b. protect preemptive rights
- c. recover improperly paid dividends
- d. a and c are both correct
- e. a, b, and c are all correct

Completion Questions

21. A(n) _____ _____ consists of the profits realized by a corporation in connection with its operations and investments.

22. A(n) _____ _____ is a contract agreed to by several shareholders by which they promise to vote their shares in a certain way.

23. When shares of a corporation have been issued and subsequently reacquired by the corporation, they are referred to as _____ _____.

380

24. A(n) _____ is a delegation of authority given by a shareholder in a corporation to someone else to vote the shares owned by the shareholder.

25. A party who is temporarily unable to pay his or her bills as they become due is referred to as being _____.

Chapter 45

CORPORATE MERGERS, DISSOLUTION, AND TERMINATION

The 1980's witnessed major corporate mergers and acquisitions that captured headlines while changing the face of the business world. Mergers occurred between direct competitors, between companies at different stages of the distribution chain, and between firms that operate in separate markets.

Mergers and acquisitions often raise antitrust law issues, which are discussed in later chapters. This chapter provides an overview of the basics of corporate structural changes. It also discusses the ultimate change in corporate structure: dissolution and termination of the corporation.

The text as a whole is a project and while each chapter has its own identity, the material in each is interrelated. Grasping the materials presented in this chapter is necessary to understanding the more extensive discussions of securities law and antitrust law in chapters 46 and 54.

CHAPTER OBJECTIVES

After reading Chapter 45 of the text and studying the related materials in this chapter of the Student Mastery Guide, you will understand:

1. Mergers and acquisitions, including:
   a. the rights and obligations of disappearing corporations
   b. appraisal rights

MAJOR POINTS TO REMEMBER

Mergers and Acquisitions

1. Mergers occur when one or more corporations are absorbed into existing corporations. A merger is distinct from a consolidation in that the former yields the survival of one of the merging corporations. Shareholder approval is generally a necessary condition for a merger to take place.

2. Under a short-form merger procedure, provided by many states, shareholders do not have to approve a merger if certain conditions are met.

3. Articles of merger must be filed with the secretary of state for the state in which the surviving corporation is incorporated.

Consolidations

4. A consolidation of two or more corporations yields a new corporation.

Rights and Obligations of Disappearing Corporations

5. Upon merger or consolidation, the rights and obligations of the disappearing corporations pass to the surviving corporation.

Purchase of Stock

6. Typically, the purchase of another company's stock to create a merger is accomplished by means of a tender offer. If enough shareholders agree to sell their shares to the purchasing company, the merger is completed.

Appraisal Rights

7. Shareholders who do not support a merger hold the right to receive "fair value" for all their shares in most states. To qualify for this appraisal, shareholders generally must:
    a. file a written notice of opposition to the merger prior to the shareholder vote
    b. issue a written demand for payment of fair value for the shareholders' shares after the merger or consolidation has been approved

Purchase of Assets

8. A corporation that purchases the assets of another company is not responsible for the selling corporation's liabilities if:
    a. the purchaser does not agree to do so
    b. the transaction is not equivalent to a merger or acquisition
    c. the purchasing corporation is not a continuation of the selling corporation
    d. the transaction is not entered into fraudulently to escape liabilities
        In the event that any one of these conditions does not hold, the purchasing company can be liable.

Dissolution and Termination of the Corporation

9. A corporation can be considered dissolved when it stops doing business and begins to liquidate its business.

10. After all the assets of corporation have been liquidated and creditors and shareholders have received the proceeds, that corporation can be considered terminated.

Voluntary Dissolution

11. Before a corporation begins business, a majority vote of its incorporators or initial directors is sufficient to dissolve that corporation. Once business has begun, the board of directors must adopt a dissolution revolution which then must be approved by a majority of the shares outstanding.

Involuntary Dissolution

12.   Involuntary dissolution can occur through either court action or administrative decree. The latter is permissible when it can be demonstrated that the corporation either abused its authority or was fraudulently conceived. Shareholders can obtain court-ordered dissolution in the event that either the shareholders or directors are harmfully deadlocked or the directors are acting contrary to the best interests of the corporation.

MAJOR POINTS OF CASES

Spinnaker Software Corp. v. *Nicholson* (p. 797)

This case considers what constitutes "fair value" in settling with minority dissenters to mergers and consolidations. The court ruled that, consistent with American Law Institute standards, the aggregate price accepted by the merging or consolidating corporation can be considered the fair value of that corporation only to the extent that the plaintiff cannot demonstrate otherwise.

In making this ruling, the court denied the merit of the case precedent offered by the defendant to persuade the court that the plaintiff is entitled to a settlement strictly according to the accepted aggregate price. Reviewing the testimony of the plaintiff's expert witness, the court upheld the higher settlement decided by the lower court. The court added that the appellate court will reverse valuations of property only if they are clearly erroneous.

County of Cook v. *Mellon Stuart Co.* (p. 799)

In this case, the court ruled that among corporations purchasing assets, each corporation can be held liable for the selling corporation's liabilities to the extent that the assets purchase is deemed a de facto merger as well as to the extent that each corporation plays an integral role in the common enterprise. Applying this ruling to the case, the court held that Baker Engineering was properly made a party to Cook County's lawsuit. The court stated that the resolution of questions of law and fact favor Cook County's assertion that the transfer of assets from Mellon Stuart to MBC constituted a de facto merger. Thus, the court concluded, Baker Engineering's integral role in the common enterprise of itself, MBC, and MSCI makes it liable for Mellon Stuart's deficient work.

Martin v. *Martin's News Service, Inc.* (p. 802)

This case involved the explication of circumstances under which a corporation can be involuntarily dissolved through a court order. The plaintiff offered Krall v. Krall as an appropriate precedent for the court's judgment. It stipulated that a corporation can be dissolved by the Supreme Court for "any good and sufficient reason", regardless of whether that corporation is being run profitably and successfully.

The court found the circumstances surrounding Martin's News Service, Inc. to be "good and sufficient reason" to dissolve this corporation. The court stated that by virtue of the fact that the business was being run as a sole proprietorship, there had been no corporate meetings for almost a decade, and there had been no input from one of the two fifty percent shareholders, the corporation appropriately could be dissolved.

SELF-TEST

True-False Questions

_____ 1. A consolidation is another name for a merger.

_____ 2. A short-form merger procedure restricts the rights of shareholders in approving mergers.

_____ 3. With a disappearing corporation, its rights and obligations disappear as well.

_____ 4. A tender offer can be either hostile or friendly.

_____ 5. Appraisal rights of the shareholder apply only to mergers.

_____ 6. Shareholders always have a right to the "fair value" for their shares when they dissent from a merger.

_____ 7. A corporation that sells its assets can remain in existence.

_____ 8. A corporation that purchases the assets of another corporation does not have to gain shareholder approval in most states.

_____ 9. Voluntary dissolution is allowed only before a corporation begins business.

_____ 10. Shareholders have no means of dissolving the corporation.

Multiple-Choice Questions

_____ 11. The most common degree of shareholder approval needed for a merger is:
a. 1/2 + 1
b. 3/4
c. 3/5
d. 2/3
e. 5/8

12. Which of the following do not need shareholder approval?
   a. mergers
   b. consolidations
   c. short-form mergers
   d. short-form consolidations
   e. c and d are correct

13. Shareholders hold appraisal rights:
   a. in all states
   b. in most states
   c. with respect to both mergers and acquisitions
   d. a and c are correct
   e. b and c are correct

14. The major advantage of purchasing the assets of a company rather than effecting a merger or consolidation is that:
   a. the purchasing company does not have to gain shareholder approval.
   b. the target company does not have to acquire shareholder approval.
   c. the purchasing corporation is not liable for the liabilities of the selling corporation.
   d. the selling corporation can remain in existence.
   e. none of the above

15. All of the following are true of corporate dissolutions
   a. they can be voluntary or involuntary
   b. they occur prior to termination
   c. upon dissolution, creditors and shareholders receive proceeds
   d. all of the above
   e. a and b only

16. A corporation is voluntarily dissolved after it begins business when:
   a. there is a majority vote of the shareholders approving the dissolution ressolution
   b. a court ordered dissolution is obtained
   c. the board of directors adopts a dissolution resolution
   d. a and b are correct
   e. a and c are correct

_____ 17. Involuntary dissolution can be achieved by the following means:
   a. court action
   b. administrative decree
   c. statutory provision
   d. purchase of assets
   e. a and b are correct

_____ 18. Which of the following is not true of a consolidation?
   a. a new corporation is formed
   b. articles of consolidation are filed with the secretary of state
   c. the new corporation is liable for the disappearing corporations' debts
   d. all of the above
   e. none of the above

_____ 19. A tender offer is a means of:
   a. involuntarily dissolving a corporation
   b. purchasing the stock of a corporation
   c. consolidating corporations
   d. voluntarily dissolving a corporation
   e. none of the above

_____ 20. The purchaser of assets is not liable for the selling corporation's debts unless:
   a. the purchaser implies an intention to assume liability
   b. the transaction amounts to a merger or consolidation
   c. the purchasing corporation is merely a continuation of the selling corporation
   d. the transaction is entered into fraudulently to escape liability
   e. all of the above

Completion Questions

21. A _____ constitutes the absorption of one corporation into another.

22. A _____ results in a new corporation.

23. The shareholder's _____ _____ ensures him or her "fair value" for his or her shares in the event that he or she dissents from a consolidation or merger.

24. A _____ _____ _____ is a alternative to a merger or consolidation.

25. Dissolutions can be both _____ and _____.

Chapter 46

SECURITIES REGULATION

For the common good and the protection of investors, extensive legislation has been introduced and implemented to regulate trading in corporate securities. Corporations are subjected to careful scrutiny and are required to follow detailed reporting procedures in order to minimize the possibility of fraudulent or abusive trading practices.

This chapter examines the major legislative enactments that have shaped the regulation of corporate securities. It discusses the Securities Act of 1933, the Securities Exchange Act of 1934, the Foreign Corrupt Practices Act of 1977, and various state securities laws.

In reviewing the text, careful note should be made of the fact that the Securities Act of 1933 regulates the issuance and registration of corporate securities, while the Securities Exchange Act of 1934 regulates trading practices.

CHAPTER OBJECTIVES

After reading Chapter 37 of the text and studying the related materials in this chapter of the Student Mastery Guide, you will understand:

1. The nature of securities regulation and the role of the Securities and Exchange Commission
2. The nature and provisions of the Securities Act of 1933
3. The nature and provisions of the Securities Act of 1934
4. The nature and provisions of the Foreign Corrupt Practices Act of 1977
5. The nature and effect of state securities laws

MAJOR POINTS TO REMEMBER

In General

1. The primary purpose of the Securities Act of 1933 is to compel publicly held corporations to make full disclosure of all material information to potential investors in the corporation.

   The Securities Exchange Act of 1934 regulates the trading of securities after they have been issued by a corporation.

The Securities Act of 1933

2. The Securities Act of 1933 (Section 2[1] defines a security in far-reaching terms that include stocks, bonds, debentures, investment contracts, voting trust certificates, and numerous other types of investment items.

3. In the case of SEC v. W.J. Howey Co., the U.S. Supreme Court established a test that is used to determine whether an instrument of transaction can be termed a "security." The criteria to be applied are:
    a. a contract or scheme must exist whereby a person invests money in a common enterprise
    b. there must be an expectation of profit by the investors
    c. the profits must be derived solely from the efforts of persons other than the investors

4. Two securities markets that exist for the purpose of trading securities are the:
    a. New York Stock Exchange (NYSE)
    b. over-the-counter (OTC) market

5. The only persons who are authorized to buy or sell securities on the trading floor of a stock market are registered specialists (commonly known as stock brokers).

6. In order for a security to be offered to the public or sold through the mail or by other means in interstate commerce, it must either be an exempt security or transactions or be registered with the Securities and Exchange Commission.

7. Under the Securities Act of 1933 a company that desires to issue securities not exempted by the Act generally must complete the following procedures:
    a. File a registration statement and prospectus with the SEC (the latter of which must also be given to every purchaser), which discloses fully and truthfully all information regarding the company and the securities that would be material to a reasonable person in making an investment decision.
    b. The SEC staff has a waiting period of twenty days when sales cannot occur to examine the registration statement for deficiencies. The company will receive a refusal order for serious deficiencies or a deficiency letter for lesser deficiencies. The registration becomes effective automatically twenty days after filing if the SEC does not give notice of deficiencies.
    c. The SEC examination of a registration statement does not evaluate the merit or worth of the securities, but instead looks only to the adequacy of disclosure.
    d. During the twenty-day waiting period, newspaper notices of the offering are allowed and oral offers by underwriters to dealers and the public are allowed, but not written offers or sales.
    e. Once the registration is effective sales can occur. Often the securities are marketed by issuers through underwriters and dealers.
    f. As an alternative to going through the above-described procedures for each new issuance of securities, under Rule 415 of the SEC large publicly held corporations are allowed to file single "shelf registrations" with the SEC, which are effective for two years. This allows such companies to sell new securities during the covered period by simply referring investors to their annual or quarterly reports without providing them with a new prospectus.

8. Certain types of securities and security transactions are wholly or partially exempted from the registration requirement but the anti-fraud provisions of both the Securities Act of 1933 and the Securities Exchange Act of 1934 still apply.

9. The following are exempted from registration under the Securities Act of 1933:
    a. commercial paper that arises out of current transactions, does not mature for at least nine months, and is not advertised for sale to the public
    b. small offerings of securities not exceeding $5 million
    c. small public offerings not exceeding $1.5 million over a twelve-month period, although an offering circular and notice to the SEC are required
    d. any security that is part of an issue sold within the boundaries of a single state and sold only to residents of that state, if the issuer is a resident or incorporated in the same state and 80 percent of its gross revenues come from operations in that state
    e. securities issued by the U.S. government, nonprofit organizations, and domestic banks as well as those regulated by other agencies.

10. Securities transactions exempted by the 1933 Act include:
    a. those by other than an issuer, underwriter, or dealer
    b. those issuances of securities that do not involve any public offering (i.e., a private placement), which under Regulation D, Rules 50-1506, of the SEC includes:
        i.   sales of not more than $500,000 in a twelve-month period to accredited or nonaccredited investors (Rule 504)
        ii. sales of up to $5 million of securities in a twelve-month period to any number of accredited investors and up to thirty-five nonaccredited investors (Rule 505)
        iii. sales of an unlimited amount of securities to any number of accredited investors and up to thirty-five nonaccredited investors, if the issuer believes that each nonaccredited investor, individually or with a representative, has sufficient knowledge or experience in business and finance to evaluate the offering.

    "Accredited investors," generally, are those who have the knowledge or experience in business and finance and the wealth to not need the protection afforded by the 1933 Act registration.

    Other restrictive requirements apply to offerings of securities under Regulation D.

11. To prohibit companies from breaking essentially one large offering of securities into several smaller ones in order to qualify for an exemption from registration, the SEC has adopted rules of integration and aggregation. However, generally the SEC does not require integration and aggregation of any offering made six months before or six months after another offering.

12. Under the 1933 Act, besides other civil sanctions, any person who purchases securities in reliance on material misstatements or incorrect information provided by or through an issuer can recover damages from:
   a. the issuer
   b. all who signed the registration statement
   c. lawyers, engineers, and accountants who participated in the preparation of the registration statement
   d. every director
   e. every underwriter

   However, except for the issuer, all others will not be held liable if they exercised due diligence in their work. What constitutes due diligence depends on a person's expertise and relationship to the issuer.

   The issuer and other persons of unregistered, nonexempt securities may be held liable to any person who purchases them and sustains damages in connection with the purchase.

   Any person who aids in the commission of any fraud in connection with the offer or sale of securities may be held liable for damages.

   Criminal sanctions can be imposed for willful violations of the 1933 Act.

The Securities Act of 1934

13. The Securities Exchange Act of 1934 provides that all companies with assets of $1 million or more and a class of equity securities that has at least 500 shareholders of record must register two classes of securities: debt and equity.

14. The Securities Exchange Act of 1934 governs the trading of securities on the national exchanges. It focuses on providing investors with continuous current information material to investment decisions by requiring the filing of annual, quarterly, and other reports with the SEC. There are civil penalties for failing to file these reports and civil liability in damages to purchasers who rely on misleading or incorrect information in such reports.

15. A company issuing proxies must file a proxy statement with the Securities and Exchange Commission ten days before mailing copies of it to shareholders.

16. The solicitor of proxies must:
   a. furnish shareholders with all material information in connection with the matter being submitted to them for their vote
   b. provide the shareholders with a form by which they can indicate their agreement or disagreement
   c. furnish an annual report to the shareholders when the proxy is solicited for the purpose of voting for directors

17. Shareholder-proposed resolutions and other matters under certain circumstances must be placed on the agenda of the annual meeting and on the proxies, together with the proponent's short supporting statement if management opposes the proposal, to allow

shareholders to vote on them. Management need not do this, however, if the proposals are not significantly related to the company's business or relate to ordinary business operations.

18. There can be civil liability for failure to comply with the regulations on proxy statements and solicitations.

19. Any person or group of persons who acquire more than 5 percent of a class of registered securities must file a statement with the Securities and Exchange Commission and the issuing company within ten days. If this is an opposed hostile takeover attempt, the targeted company must also file a statement explaining its efforts to defeat it.

20. It is unlawful for any person to misstate or omit a material fact or to engage in any fraudulent or deceptive practices in connection with a tender offer.

21. If the securities of a corporation are registered with the SEC or a national exchange, the directors, officers, and any persons who own 10 percent or more of the shares of the corporation are prohibited from realizing a profit in connection with them by purchasing and selling them within a six-month period (i.e., a short swing profit).

22. Under Section 10(b) of the Securities Exchange Act of 1934, it is illegal to use or employ any manipulative or deceptive device or contrivance that is in contravention of SEC regulations in connection with the purchase or sale of any security.

23. Rule 19b-5 promulgated by the SEC makes it illegal for any person to use the mails or any other means or instrumentality of interstate commerce or any facility of a national securities exchange for the purpose of perpetrating a fraud in connection with the purchase or sale of any security.

   Rule 10b-5 applies to any purchase or sale of any securities by any persons. The exempted securities and transactions previously noted are subjected to Section 19(b) and Rule 10b-5.

24. Corporate directors and officers in companies targeted for a hostile takeover bid sometimes establish defenses to such takeovers by providing:
    a. "golden parachutes" to management
    b. "poison pills," which involve new classes of stock at prices above the market
    c. "greenmail," which is the buying out of a hostile shareholder at prices above the market
    d. "porcupine provisions," which are super majority voting requirements
    e. issuing Treasury Stock to friendly parties
    f. moving to states with "shark repellent" laws that are antitakeover oriented
    g. bankrupting a company, called a "scorched-earth" policy
    h. attempting to find a "white knight" to buy it out

25. Generally, defensive strategies are allowed under the business-judgment rule, if the strategies advance the best interests of shareholders, does not waste assets or result in significant conflicts of interest. However, Section 10(b) and Rule 10b-5, the antifraud provisions, of the 1934 Act can be applied to limit the fraudulent use of such strategies.

26. It should be noted that Section 10(b) and Rule 10b-5 apply to all purchasers and sellers of any security, regardless of exemptions from registration. However, civil liability is imposed only for true fraud, which requires proof of scienter (including intentional, knowing, or reckless conduct).

27. Rule 10b-5 has been frequently applied to cases of insider trading, corporate misstatements made in connection with securities transactions for a "wrongful purpose," and corporate mismanagement when the fraud is connected to a securities transaction.

28. Illegal insider trading involves the buying and selling of securities of a corporation by individuals who have access to nonpublic material information and use it to their benefit in trading with persons to whom the insider owed a fiduciary obligation. Insiders include directors, officers, some employees, major shareholders, and tippees who receive nonpublic material information from a company source under circumstances in which they should have known that the disclosure or the use of the information was wrongful.

29. Under Rule 14e-3, as adopted by the SEC, it is illegal for any person who is in possession of nonpublic information that is material in regard to a prospective tender offer to purchase or sell a security if he or she knows or has reason to know that the information comes from the offering person or the issuer of the security or anyone acting on behalf of either.

30. Under Rule 10b-5, overoptimistic profit reports or press releases about earnings are prohibited if they would affect the prudent judgment of potential investors. Pessimistic statements have also been prohibited.

31. The Insider Trading Sanctions Act of 1984:
    a. provides for treble damages against any person who violates the 1934 Act while in the possession of material nonpublic information
    b. increased the criminal penalties for insider trading
    c. authorizes the SEC to take administrative actions against responsible individuals within companies violating the act, including the management

The Foreign Corrupt Practices Act of 1977

32. Under the Foreign Corrupt Practices Act, all domestic corporations are prohibited from offering or authorizing corrupt payments to a:
    a. foreign official or representative
    b. foreign political party or one of its officials
    c. candidate for political office in a foreign country

33. The Foreign Corrupt Practices Act applies to all corporations, including those that are not registered with the SEC.

34. The Foreign Corrupt Practices Act is enforced by the:
    a. Securities Exchange Commission
    b. Department of Justice

35. A payment is "corrupt" under this Act if its purpose is to get the recipient to act or refrain from acting so that the company can retain or get business.

36. The Act provides for criminal penalties. It only requires proof that a corporate official knew or had reason to know a payment would be a violation of the Act. It applies to offers and promises, as well as actual payments. But small gifts to officials and "grease payments" to clerical or ministerial employees are not illegal under the Act.

37. All publicly held, registered companies must have internal accounting systems adequate to detect payments illegal under this Act.

State Securities Law

38. States have the right to regulate securities transactions that are intrastate in nature.

39. Registration methods used by states in connection with securities include:
    a. notification to a state official
    b. qualification by approval of the state of the securities' merit or worth
    c. coordination that requires a prospectus

40. Most states exempt securities and transactions that are exempted from registration under the Securities Act of 1933 and securities listed on major stock exchanges.

41. When state "blue-sky" laws irreconcilably conflict with federal securities laws, attempt to regulate matters preempted by federal law, or violate the Commerce Clause of the U.S. Constitution, they are invalid.

Issues and Trends: International

42. In contrast to the Securities and Exchange Commission in the United States, Great Britain has deregulated its securities markets. The securities industry in Great Britain is self-regulated through the Securities and Investment Board. Great Britain recently also opened its securities markets to foreign securities and investors.

Ethics Box: Ethics and International Issues

43. Some argue that insider trading should not be illegal and is not unethical, since it provides information to improve the efficiency of the markets, can enhance the performance and motivation of executives, and is too costly to regulate, given the benefits involved. Japan,

Great Britain, and Germany, in comparison to the United States, pay little attention to insider trading. These reasons alone do not support the argument that insider trading is not unethical, since it often occurs when a fiduciary takes advantage of superior knowledge to the detriment of a person to whom the fiduciary duty is owed.

MAJOR POINTS OF CASES

SEC v. *Glenn W. Turner Enterprises* (p. 807)

The court in this case held that in order to determine whether a scheme is an investment contract (which falls under the registration requirements of the SEC), the test to be applied is whether it "involves an investment of money in a common enterprise" in which the profits realized are *solely* the results of the efforts of persons other than the investors.

In considering the facts of the case, the court held that the definition of securities should be flexible. Consequently, even though the investors in the scheme were required to expend some effort of their own, all the other requirements for an investment contract were present. As a result, the court held that in substance, if not in form, Adventures III and IV were investment contracts and were required to be registered as such with the SEC.

United States v. *Naftalin* (p. 813)

The Supreme Court held in this case that under the language of Section 17 of the Securities Act of 1933, it is unlawful for any person to use fraudulent means in the offer or sale of securities and that there is no requirement that the victim of a fraudulent scheme be an investor in the securities involved. The Act requires only that the fraud occur at some stage of the selling transaction.

In this matter, the Court found that although Naftalin did not sell any securities to the other brokers, his fraudulent conduct caused them to make commitments for the sale of the securities and also prevented them from being able to honor those commitments. As a result, the Court reinstated Natfalin's conviction on fraud charges.

Schreiber v. *Burlington Northern, Inc.* (p. 816)

The Williams Act added Section 14(e) to the Securities Exchange Act of 1934, which makes it a criminal offense for any person to misstate or omit a material fact or to engage in fraudulent or deceptive practice in connection with a tender offer. Shareholders can also bring lawsuits for damages, and SEC administrative actions can also be based on a violation of this section. A manipulative act under Section 14(e) requires misrepresentation or nondisclosure.

The Supreme Court ruled that under Section 14(e) Congress did not intend that courts judge whether the conduct was "artificial" or "unfair." Since the withdrawal of one and substitution of a new tender offer were not even alleged to have involved a misrepresentation or nondisclosure, there was no violation of Section 14(e).

Carpenter v. United States (p. 818)

The United States Supreme Court in this unusual case ruled that a conviction under section 19(b) and Rule 106-5 need not be based on inside information. Such a conviction could be based on the misappropriation of confidential information from another source if the information could have an impact on stock profits. In this case, the information was news in a Wall Street Journal (confidential) column that did influence investor behavior when published and that the writer had been required to keep secret until publication. Instead, he used that information to make trades based on how he believed investors would react to the information when it was published.

The court also upheld mail and wire fraud convictions, reaffirming that confidential information is property, and that when one misappropriates another's property, the property owner need not lose money from the misappropriation in order for fraud to have occurred.

Ernst & Ernst v. Hochfelder (p. 821)

The Supreme Court held in this case that no cause of action for fraud will exist under Section 19(b) and Rule 10b-5 of the Securities Exchange Act of 1934 unless it is shown that the alleged wrongdoer acted with an intention to deceive, manipulate, or defraud the investor. The Court specifically stated that the language and legislative history of the statute support the conclusion that liability under the Act cannot be imposed for "negligent conduct alone."

With respect to the facts of the case, the Court found that the failure of Ernst & Ernst to discover, in its audit, the fraudulent scheme used by Navy or to disclose it in the report to the Securities and Exchange Commission was not the result of an intent to deceive, manipulate, or defraud. Consequently, they could not be held liable under the provisions of Section 19(b) or Rule 10b-5 of the Securities Exchange Act.

Chiarella v. United States (p. 824)

The Supreme Court held in this case that under Section 19(b) of the Securities Exchange Act of 1934, a person's failure to disclose information obtained from the confidential documents of a corporation constitutes fraud only when that person has an obligation or duty to make such disclosure.

In this case, the Court held that inasmuch as Chiarella had no prior dealings with the corporation and did not occupy a fiduciary relationship with respect to it, he owed no duty of disclosure when he became involved in the market transactions even though he possessed nonpublic market information. Consequently, he was not guilty of fraud and his conviction was reversed.

Basic, Inc. v. Levinson (p. 826)

The United States Supreme Court in this case reaffirmed the fraud on the market theory, finding that whenever a firm publicly makes fraudulent misrepresentation, the investor who brings a 10b(5) action is entitled to the presumption that he relied on the misrepresentation. Of course, the defendant still has the opportunity to try to prove that the investor did not rely on the misstatements. Shifting the burden of proof to the defendant obviously put the plaintiff in a much better position.

The rationale for the presumption is the belief that most publicly available information is reflected in the market price.

CTS Corporation v. *Dynamics Corporation of America* (p. 831)

An Indiana statute attempted to regulate the hostile takeover of corporations chartered in Indiana with a specified level of shareholders in that state by imposing requirements that would in effect delay the consummation of tender offers made in a takeover attempt beyond the time in which this could be accomplished under the federal Williams Act and its implementing regulations. The Supreme Court found that the basic purpose of the Indiana Act was the same as that of the Williams Act. It also held that the Indiana Act did not discriminate against or impose an undue burden on interstate commerce in violation of the Commerce clause of the U.S. Constitution. The Court further held that since corporations and the voting rights of shareholders are matters of state creation and contra, states can continue to regulate corporations charged in their states and the voting rights to be given shareholders even though there may be some effect on interstate commerce. The Court, thus, held that the Indiana Act can be enforced to allow shareholders of the target Indiana corporation to collectively determine whether to accept a hostile tender offer, since it neither irreconcilably conflicts with the Williams Act nor violates the Commerce clause.

PRACTICAL CONSIDERATIONS

While the prohibition against insider trading has extended to the activities of stock brokerage firms, a clear distinction should be made between the brokerage firm that acts on nonpublic information which has been provided to it and the astute brokerage firm that is able to follow the business activities of a particular company and effectively predict the success or failure of that company's ventures. In the latter case, there is clearly no violation of either Rule 10b-5 or Rule 14e-3 for the firm would be using only its own intuitive instincts and business expertise to gain an advantage for its clients. In the first case, however, the firm would be using material, nonpublic information in improperly obtaining an advantage. This conduct is prohibited under the relevant rules.

Example: James owns the Caveman Stock Broker firm. His brother is a director of Multico Inc., a major international corporation whose stock is traded on the major stock exchanges. Through the efforts of his broker, James is asked to become a director of Multico. James accepts the position. Thereafter, Multico negotiates a major contract with a firm in South America that is worth millions of dollars in potential profits. Before knowledge of the transaction is made known to the general business community, James informs the brokers and employees of his brokerage firm about the contract. Based on this information, several major clients of the brokerage are contacted and are asked if they wish to purchase stock in Multico. They all decide to purchase 1,000 shares and authorize the Caveman stock brokerage to arrange for the purchase. After the purchase is made on behalf of these clients, news of Multico's contract becomes widely known and the value of its stock increases by 50 percent.

Based on the foregoing facts, Caveman has clearly acted in violation of the insider trading rules. It has acquired material, nonpublic information that it has used in connection with the sale and purchase of certain shares of stock. The information was acquired by the fact that James was a director of Multico.

If James had not been a director of Multico and his brokerage firm simply had been following the activities of that company, any information that it could glean from such activities could likely be used in advising their clients and would not involve a violation of the insider trading rules. Further, the fact that James' brother was a director of Multico, in itself, would not necessarily cause the activities of the brokerage firm to be improper.

SELF TEST

True-False Questions

_____ 1. Anyone who possesses the technical knowledge that is required to operate in the New York Stock Exchange may buy and sell shares of stock on its trading floor.

_____ 2. The Securities Act of 1933 forbids the public sale of shares of stock in a corporation through the mail unless the stock has been registered with the Securities and Exchange Commission.

_____ 3. The SEC will conduct an investigation into the merit or worth of securities registered with that agency.

_____ 4. Registration of securities will always automatically become effective twenty days after a registration statement is filed with the Securities and Exchange Commission.

_____ 5. If securities are sold before the filing of a registration statement, the purchaser of the securities may hold the issuer liable for any damages sustained by him or her in connection with the issuance.

_____ 6. The willful violation of the Securities Act of 1933 can result in the imposition of criminal sanctions upon the wrongdoer.

_____ 7. States have the right to regulate securities transactions that are interstate in nature.

_____ 8. Before a corporation mails a proxy statement to its shareholders, the statement must be filed with the Securities and Exchange Commission.

_____ 9. A company can be held civilly liable for issuing to its shareholders a proxy statement that is misleading.

_____ 10. The Securities Exchange Act of 1934 has no application at all to corporations which have no shares of stock that are required to be registered with the Securities and Exchange Commission.

Multiple-Choice Questions

_____ 11. Which of the following factors is considered in determining whether an instrument is a security?
    a. there must be an expectation of profit by the investors in the instrument
    b. any profits realized must be derived from the sole activities of persons other than the corporate representatives
    c. there must be a contract or scheme whereby a person invests money in a common enterprise
    d. a and c are both correct
    e. a, b, and c are all correct

_____ 12. The minimum time between the registration of securities with the SEC and the effective date of the filing is:
    a. twenty-four hours
    b. forty-eight hours
    c. sixty hours
    d. seventy-two hours
    e. ninety-six hours

_____ 13. When a corporation files a registration statement with the SEC, the statement must include:
    a. a prospectus
    b. a proxy
    c. an efficiency letter
    d. a and c are both correct
    e. a, b, and c are all correct

_____ 14. Which of the following is considered to be a security?
    a. a voting trust certificate
    b. an investment contract
    c. a certificate of deposit for a security
    d. a and c are both correct
    e. a, b, and c are all correct

15. If a corporation intends to mail a proxy statement to its shareholders, it must file the statement with the SEC:
    a. at least five days before the mailing
    b. fourteen days before the mailing
    c. ten days before the mailing
    d. within fourteen days after the mailing
    e. within five days after the mailing

16. A corporation is required to register two classes of securities with the SEC if:
    a. it is a publicly held corporation
    b. it has assets of $1 million or more
    c. a class of equity securities has 500 shareholders of record
    d. a and b are both correct
    e. a, b, and c are all correct

17. When a proxy statement is solicited by a corporation, the solicitor of the proxy must:
    a. furnish the shareholders with all material information concerning the matter being submitted to them for a vote
    b. furnish the shareholders with a formal prospectus
    c. amend its certificate of incorporation
    d. a and c are both correct
    e. a, b, and c are all correct

18. If a shareholder requests that an item be placed on the agenda of the corporation's annual meeting, the corporation may refuse the request if:
    a. the matter is moot
    b. the matter involves ordinary business operations
    c. the request is not supported by at least 15 percent of the stockholders
    d. a and b are both correct
    e. a, b, and c are all correct

19. When a corporation has engaged in deceptive stock trading practices, a lawsuit for damages may be brought against it by:
    a. the SEC
    b. the Federal Trade Commission
    c. any private person who has been injured by the deceptive trading practice
    d. a and c are both correct
    e. a, b, and c are all correct

_____ 20. Under Rule 10b-5, insiders include:
a. anyone who receives nonpublic material from a corporate source
b. corporate officers only
c. corporate directors only
d. major stockholders only
e. corporate directors and officers only

Completion Questions

21. Laws that are established by states for the regulation of securities are commonly referred to as_____ _____ laws.

22. A(n)_____is a written document by which the holder of registered securities gives another person permission to vote the shareholder's shares at a stockholders' meeting.

23. The period of time between the filing of a registration statement and its effective date is referred to as the _____ _____.

24. A(n)_____ _____ is a letter of comment issued by the Securities and Exchange Commission that indicates what corrections, if any, need to be made with respect to the documents submitted in connection with a corporation's application for the registration of securities.

25. The act that regulates the trading of securities after they have been issued by a corporation is the _____ _____ _____ _____.

Chapter 47

PERSONAL PROPERTY

This chapter discusses the nature of the different categories of property, the concept of bailments, and the rules that relate to bailments. It also discusses the various ways in which title to property may be transferred by an owner to someone else. Carefully note that title to different types of property is conveyed in various ways that depend on the nature of the property involved.

CHAPTER OBJECTIVES

After reading Chapter 47 of the text and studying the related materials in this chapter of the Student Mastery Guide, you will understand:

1.   The nature of the different types of property, including:
    a.   real property
    b.   personal property
    c.   fixtures
2.   The nature of a bailment relationship and the rights and obligations of the parties to it
3.   The various ways in which title to property can be transferred, including:
    a.   sale
    b.   gift
    c.   inheritance

MAJOR POINTS TO REMEMBER

Types of Personal Property

1.   Tangible personal property is personal property that has substance.

2.   Intangible personal property consists of legal rights that a person has that represent value, such as corporate stocks or bonds.

3.   Intellectual property is a form of intangible property that is generally created through mental rather than physical efforts, including patents, trademarks, copyrights, and trade secrets. (See Chapter 7 of this Student Mastery Guide for a review of the property rights.)

Fixtures

4.   A fixture is an item of personal property that has become attached to real property in such a way as to become part of it. Examples of fixtures are a chandelier, kitchen cabinets, a smoke detector.

5. Factors that are considered in determining whether an item of property is a fixture include the:
    a. intention of the party who attached the item
    b. manner in which the item is attached
    c. application and use of the item as a permanent part of the real property

6. Generally, in the absence of an agreement between a landlord and a tenant, a tenant who has made permanent improvements to leased property may not remove a fixture at the end of the lease.

    Trade fixtures (those used in connection with carrying on a business), however, may usually be removed from leased property at the end of the lease period.

Bailments

7. In order to have a valid bailment:
    a. the bailor must relinquish possession and control over the property to the bailee
    b. the subject matter of the bailment must be personal property
    c. there must be an expectation that the same property will be returned in the same or only slightly altered condition.

8. When possession of personal property is transferred but control over it is not transferred, no bailment exists. The relationship that is created is referred to as a licensor-licensee relationship.

9. When possession of real property is transferred to another person but title is retained by the owner, no bailment exists. The relationship created is that of landlord-tenant.

10. Any person may be a bailor, and that person does not necessarily need to be the owner of the personal property.

11. A thief may be a bailor.

12. In the case of fungible goods, the bailor does not necessarily have to receive the same property back at the end of the bailment. It is sufficient that the bailee return goods of similar quality when the bailment is ended.

13. A deposit of money in a banking institution does not give rise to a bailment inasmuch as money is not deemed to be fungible goods.

14. The different types of bailments are:
    a. bailment for the sole benefit of the bailor
    b. bailment for the sole benefit of the bailee
    c. mutual-benefit bailment
    d. constructive bailment

15. The degree of care that the bailee is required to take with respect to the bailed property in part depends on the type of bailment involved. The degree of care traditionally required was as follows:
    a. bailment for sole benefit of bailor: slight care
    b. mutual-benefit bailment: ordinary care
    c. bailment for sole benefit of bailee: extraordinary care
    However, the trend today is to consider the type of bailment as one of several factors in determining the degree of care required.

16. The rights of the bailee are the right:
    a. of possession
    b. to use the bailed property for the bailment purpose
    c. to insure the bailed property
    d. to receive compensation for services
    e. to impose a mechanics' lien
    f. to sue third persons who damage the bailed property or cause it to be damaged or lost
    g. to have the bailor retake possession of the property at the end of the bailment

17. The obligations of the bailee are to:
    a. use the necessary skill required for the bailment
    b. use the proper degree of care required for the bailment
    c. redeliver the bailed property to the bailor on demand or at the end of the bailment

18. The rights of the bailor are the right to:
    a. have the bailed property returned to him or her
    b. compensation in some cases
    c. sue third persons who damage the bailed property or cause it to be damaged while in the possession of the bailee

19. The obligations of the bailor are to:
    a. reimburse the bailee for any expenses incurred on behalf of the bailor
    b. indemnify the bailee
    c. inform the bailee of the condition of the goods

20. If the contents of the bailed property are such as would ordinarily be expected to be found inside it, then the contents of the bailed property are also deemed to be part of the bailment.

Transfer of Title

21. Title to personal property may be acquired in the following ways:
    a. by purchase
    b. by gift
    c. by inheritance
    d. by accession
    e. by confusion

Gifts

22. In order to make a valid gift, there must be:
    a. donative intent
    b. delivery
       i. actual
       ii. symbolic (any item that symbolizes or represents the gift, such as a key to a car)
    c. acceptance by the donee

23. A gift can be categorized as a:
    a. gift inter vivos: a gift made between living persons without consideration of the possible death of the donor
    b. gift causa mortis: a gift made in contemplation of death
    c. conditional gift
       i. condition precedent
       ii. condition subsequent

24. A gift inter vivos is irrevocable once it has been made.

25. The conditions for a valid gift causa mortis are:
    a. donative intent
    b. delivery
    c. death of the donor before the donee
    d. death of the donor due to the cause feared or one related to it
    e. revocability of the gift if the donor survives the event or cause feared

Judicial Sale

26. Title to property can also be transferred by a sale ordered by a court. The judicial order of sale may be to satisfy a judgment for monetary damages or to satisfy a debt for which the property was security. (See Chapter 32 for personal property and Chapter 49 for real property.) However, state statutes provide for certain property that is exempt from judicial seizure and sale. (See Chapter 34.)

Abandoned, Lost, and Misplaced Property

27. Personal property can be distinguished as
    a. lost, if a person parts with physical possession of an item of property involuntarily without any knowledge as to where or exactly when possession was parted with
    b. misplaced, if a person voluntarily parts with physical possession of property and forgets or fails to retake possession
    c. abandoned, if a person voluntarily parts with physical possession of property with no intention of reacquiring possession

28.	The finder of lost property acquires rights to it that are good against the whole world except the true owner.

As to the true owner, the finder of lost property becomes a bailee by operation of law.

The finder of misplaced property becomes a bailee by operation of law with respect to the property found. Such person acquires no rights of ownership.

The finder of abandoned property acquires title to it even as against the prior owner. The prior owner may not reacquire title to the property from the person who finds it.

Changing Concepts of Property

29.	The legal concept of property is continuously evolving. One significant trend has been to limit property rights where they conflict with basic civil rights, such as freedom from racial discrimination in housing. A second trend has been to recognize property rights in employment, including necessary degrees or licenses.

Preventive Law: Steps a Bailor Should Take When Entering into a Bailment Relationship

30.	In establishing a bailment relationship, the bailor should take care to:
	a.	identify the transaction as a bailment
	b.	classify it in regard to who is benefited
	c.	determine if the bailee is relying on the bailor's special expertise
	d.	establish the standard of care to be exercised by the bailee
	e.	expressly state the duties of the bailee

MAJOR POINTS OF CASES

George v. *Commercial Credit Corp.* (p. 842)

This case stands for the rule that in order to determine whether personal property becomes a fixture to real property, three considerations should be evaluated:
	1.	actual physical annexation to the real property
	2.	use of the property for the purpose for which it is intended
	3.	the intention of the owner permanently to attach the personal property to the real property

This court placed its primary emphasis on point 3. The owner's intention to affix the mobile home to the land met the conditions to qualify the property as a fixture.

Mercedes Benz Credit Corporation v. *Shields* (p. 846)

This case demonstrates that even though there may be an implied warranty of fitness for goods loaned by a bailor, such warranties may be explicitly waived by the parties. In this case, there was a clear provision in the lease agreement stating that the lessor made no express warranties as to the condition of the vehicle, its merchantability, or its condition. The lessor was therefore bound to the agreement and was liable for the full amount of the lease, despite the car's being defective.

Fireman's Fund Insurance Co. v. *Wagner Fur, Inc.* (p. 848)

This case demonstrates the application of the law of conversion to bailment. Any unauthorized misdelivery of bailed property, despite the bailee's good faith, constitutes a conversion. The conversion need not be willful, nor must it benefit the bailee.

Therefore, when Wagner delivered the furs to the wrong address and was unable to recover them, Wagner was liable for conversion even though Wagner did not in any way benefit from the misdelivery.

In re the Estate of Alfred v. *Sipe, Deceased* (p. 850)

The principle illustrated by this case is that in order to establish a valid gift, there must be (1) donative intent, (2) delivery of the gift, and (3) acceptance of the gift by the donee.

The fact that the appellant in this case had not signed a signature card creating the joint savings account did not control the disposition of the case in light of the fact that all three of the elements needed to establish a valid gift were present.

Memphis Development Foundation v. *Factors Etc., Inc.* (p. 853)

The personal right to acquire profits as a result of the publicity that attaches to the name of a public personality does not constitute a property right. Therefore, such a right may not be inherited or transferred, as the exclusive right to publicity does not survive a celebrity's death.

In the case, the court held that the exclusive right to the publicity surrounding Elvis Presley's death was not a property right that was capable of passing through his estate by inheritance.

PRACTICAL CONSIDERATIONS

It is well recognized that in a bailment relationship, the bailee has the right to impose a mechanic's lien in connection with money that may be due to him relative to the bailed property. It is also well recognized that the mechanic's lien is a possessory lien, and that once possession is relinquished to the bailor, the lien no longer exists. However, an ill-informed or perhaps unscrupulous person may try to impose a mechanic's lien on another person's property even when he clearly does not have the right to do so. His motive for doing so will normally be his desire to collect a debt that is due him.

Example: John brings his car to Dan's service station for repairs. After Dan completes the repairs, John asks him if it would be agreeable if he paid the repair bill the following week. Because John is a regular customer of Dan's, Dan consents to the request. Three weeks later, John returns to the garage for additional repairs. When Dan completes those repairs, John pays him for them but Dan refuses to release the car until John pays the other bill, which has not yet been paid.

Clearly, Dan has no right to retain the car. The reality of the situation, however, is that Dan will keep the car until John pays the outstanding bill. If John needs the car immediately, he will have no alternative but to pay the bill forthwith, even though Dan is acting improperly.

SELF TEST

True or False

_____ 1. There can never be a bailment of real property.

_____ 2. Trade Fixtures can generally be removed from leased property at the end of the lease period.

_____ 3. A deposit of money in a savings account is considered to be a bailment.

_____ 4. A thief may be a bailor of property he has stolen.

_____ 5. A gift inter vivos may be revoked by the donor after it has been made.

_____ 6. In a bailment for the sole benefit of the bailor, the bailee is required to use extraordinary care.

_____ 7. The bailee of a car can use it for any purposes he or she wants in all cases.

_____ 8. In order for a gift causa mortis to be valid, the donor must have a donative intent.

_____ 9. The finder of misplaced property becomes the owner of it by operation of law.

_____ 10. A bailee is entitled to receive compensation for services rendered by him or her in connection with a mutual-benefit bailment.

Multiple-Choice Questions

_____ 11. Which of the following would be considered to be personal property?
   a. a pair of skis
   b. a yacht
   c. an airplane
   d. only b and c are correct
   e. a, b, and c are all correct

408

12. In determining whether an item should be treated as a fixture, a court will consider:
   a. the size of the item
   b. the manner in which the item is attached to the real property
   c. the shape of the item
   d. only a and c are correct
   e. a, b, and c are all correct

13. In a bailment for the sole benefit of the bailee, the bailee is required to:
   a. use slight care in taking care of the bailed property
   b. use ordinary care in taking care of the bailed property
   c. use extraordinary care in taking care of the bailed property
   d. inform the bailor of the condition of the goods
   e. guarantee that the property will not be damaged

14. Which of the following is required in order to have a valid bailment?
   a. it must involve personal property
   b. there must be an expectation that the same property will be returned to the bailor in all cases
   c. the bailor must relinquish control of the bailed property
   d. only a and c are correct
   e. a, b, and c are all correct

15. Which of the following is considered to be real property?
   a. a built-in (below-ground) swimming pool
   b. a tree growing in a forest
   c. a furnace
   d. only a and c are correct
   e. a, b, and c are all correct

16. Which of the following is an obligation that the bailee owes to the bailor?
   a. to indemnify the bailor
   b. to reimburse the bailor
   c. to use the necessary skill required for the bailment
   d. to inform the bailor of the condition of the goods
   e. a, b, and d are all correct

17. Title to personal property may be obtained by:
   a. accession
   b. confusion
   c. inheritance
   d. only a and b are correct
   e. a, b, and c are all correct

_____ 18. Which of the following is required in order to have a valid gift?
          a.   delivery of the subject matter of the gift to the donee
          b.   donative intent
          c.   acceptance by the donee
          d.   only a and b are correct
          e.   a, b, and c are all correct

_____ 19. When a person parts with physical possession of an item of property involuntarily, without any knowledge as to where or when possession was parted with, that property is referred to as being:
          a.   lost
          b.   misplaced
          c.   abandoned
          d.   donated
          e.   rescinded

_____ 20. Which of the following is considered to be a fixture?
          a.   a chandelier
          b.   the basement of a house
          c.   a house plant placed on a window sill
          d.   b and c are both correct
          e.   a, b, and c are all correct

Completion Questions

21. _____ _____ are those goods of which any one item is the same as the next within allowable variations.

22. The person to whom a gift is made is referred to as the _____.

23. A gift that is made in contemplation of death is referred to as a(n)_____ _____ _____.

24. A(n)_____ is a legal transfer of possession of personal property from one person to another when ownership is not transferred.

25. The person to whom possession of personal property is transferred but who does not become the owner of the property is referred to as the_____.

Chapter 48

INTERESTS IN REAL PROPERTY

The ownership of land has often been thought of as a measure of wealth and an indication of at least a modicum of economic success. The degrees of ownership rights in land, however, are numerous and varied. Additionally, the control a person may exert over a parcel of land or an item of real estate will be determined by the nature and degree of the ownership rights and interests that person possesses in the property.

This chapter considers the nature and scope of real property. It discusses the various estates in land, leasehold estates, and nonpossessory interests in real property. It also examines the significance of and the distinctions between the various forms of co-owners of property. Finally, the text discusses the importance of land as it relates to the law and the legal system.

CHAPTER OBJECTIVES

After reading Chapter 48 of the text and studying the related materials in this chapter of the Student Mastery Guide, you will understand:

1. The nature of real property and the different types of interests in it, including:
   a.   estates in land
   b.   leasehold estates
   c.   nonpossessory interests
2. The different types of leasehold interests and the rights and obligations of the respective parties
3. The nature and extent of the different forms of co-ownership of property, including:
   a.   joint tenancy
   b.   tenancy in common
   c.   tenancy by the entirety
   d.   tenancy in partnership
   e.   community property
   f.   condominiums and cooperatives
   g.   real-estate investment trusts

MAJOR POINTS TO REMEMBER

Scope of Real Property

1. Generally, the rights of the owner of real property are limited with respect to the air space directly above that property and extend only to that area which he or she can reasonably use and enjoy.

Estates in Land

2. Ownership rights in real property may be categorized in various groups, which include:
    a. fee simple estate (fee simple absolute)
    b. fee simple defeasible estate
    c. life estate

3. A fee simple estate provides for total, unlimited, unrestricted, and unconditional ownership rights in real estate.

    A fee simple defeasible estate provides for total, unrestricted ownership rights in real property that, however, can be divested from the owner upon the occurrence of a specified event.

    A life estate is one in which the duration of the ownership interest in real property is measured by the life of a person.

4. A life estate in which the duration of the owner's interest is measured by the life of another person is referred to as a life estate pur autre vie.

Leasehold Estates

5. A leasehold estate is commonly referred to as a landlord-tenant relationship or a lease.

6. A leasehold interest is created when the owner of real property conveys possession and control of that property to another person (commonly referred to as the tenant or lessee) in return for the payment of rent. The owner retains title to the property.

7. Leasehold estates can be classified as:
    a. term tenancy (estate for years): one that exists for a fixed period of time; it begins and ends on specific dates
    b. periodic tenancy: a rental agreement that will continue for successive periods of time, such as month to month
    c. tenancy at will: one that exists when no specific rental period is provided
    d. tenancy at sufferance: one in which a person initially occupies the premises lawfully but thereafter occupies them unlawfully

8. A periodic tenancy will continue in existence until one of the parties gives the other proper notice of termination of the lease.

9. A tenancy at will can be terminated by either party to the lease by means of any action, conduct, or notice that informs the other party that the lease is being terminated.

10. In most states, a holdover tenant is treated as a lessee under a periodic tenancy.

11. The rental charge in connection with the lease of commercial premises can be determined by means of any or all of the following devices:
    a. a percentage lease: rent is set as a fixed percentage of the gross sales or net profits from the business operated on the premises
    b. a net lease: a fixed rent is charged and in addition the tenant pays the taxes, insurance, and maintenance expenses
    c. a revaluation or appraisal lease: rental payments are adjusted on the basis of period revaluation of the property.

12. Under the common law, unless it was otherwise agreed by the parties to a lease, the landlord has only a limited obligation to repair and maintain the property being rented. In most states the common-law rule has been modified for residential property. These states require the property to be maintained in a habitable condition.

13. During the term of the lease, a tenant (lessee) has the right to be in possession and control of the property and also has the right to use the property for any reasonable purpose unless that purpose:
    a. is illegal
    b. violates public policy
    c. results in substantial or permanent damage to the property
    d. is limited by the terms of the lease agreement

14. The landlord, however, has the right to enter premises, absent agreement to the contrary, to:
    a. collect the rent
    b. inspect the premises and make repairs
    c. prevent material damage or loss to the property

15. Some rent-control laws exist in various places in the United States. For example, in the city of New York a landlord cannot, except for certain reasons, evict a residential tenant who is paying the rent. Landlords are also restricted in the situations in which they can increase the rent on residential rental property.

16. A tenant can transfer his or her rights and interests in a leasehold by means of:
    a. assignment: all the remaining interest of the tenant is conveyed to another person
    b. sublease: less than the tenant's remaining interest in the lease is transferred to another person; for example, a tenant whose lease expires in July may sublet it to another for the month of May

17. A lease may be terminated by:
    a. expiration of the term specified in the lease
    b. condemnation of the premises
    It may also sometimes be terminated by agreement if the:
    c. premises are destroyed
    d. tenant files for bankruptcy
    In most states, death does not terminate the obligations of the parties.

18. The various leasehold tenancies terminate, generally, as follows:
    a. a term tenancy automatically terminates at the end of the term without notice
    b. to terminate periodic tenancies the notice often required is:
        1. ten days for a week-to-week tenancy
        2. thirty or sixty days for month-to-month tenancies
        3. six months for year-to-year tenancies
        4. thirty days for a tenancy at will

Nonpossessory Interests in Real Property

19. An easement, or a nonpossessory interest in land, can be either of two types:
    a. an easement appurtenant - an easement that usually involves two adjoining parcels of land and permits the possessor of one parcel to use the other
    b. an easement in gross - an easement that exists independently of a dominant estate

20. An easement can be created by:
    a. an express grant
    b. a reservation in a deed
    c. prescription
    d. necessity

21. Easements appurtenant usually run with both parcels of land such that transfers of the dominant or servient estates do not terminate the easement.

22. Generally, only commercial easements in gross are transferable.

Co-Ownership

23. When two or more persons have ownership rights in the same property, they may hold their interest as:
    a. joint tenants
    b. tenants in common
    c. tenants by the entirety
    d. holders of community property.

24. A joint tenancy exists when two or more persons own property together with the right of survivorship. Each owner possesses an undivided interest in the property.

25. In a tenancy in common, two or more persons own property together but do not have a right of survivorship. As in a joint tenancy, each owner possesses an undivided interest in the property.

26. A tenancy by the entirety exists when a husband and wife own property together with the right of survivorship. Each party possesses an undivided interest in the property. Neither party can sever the tenancy without the consent of the other.

27. A tenancy by the entirety is automatically terminated by a divorce of the parties. Upon divorce, their interest in real property is converted into a tenancy in common.

28. Under community property statutes, a husband and wife each obtain a one-half interest in property acquired by the skill or labor of either party during the marriage.

Condominiums and Cooperatives

29. A person who purchases a condominium acquires ownership rights in the unit purchased. The purchaser also obtains ownership rights, as a tenant in common with the owners of the other units, of the common areas of the condominium.

30. A person who purchases a cooperative unit acquires control over the unit purchased, but the ownership of the land and building of which the cooperative unit forms a part vests in some type of association (usually a corporation). The purchaser of the cooperative unit (i.e., the tenant) becomes a shareholder in the association.

Real Estate Investment Trust (REIT)

31. REITs must have at least 100 beneficial owners. They have a tax advantage over corporations, since there is no double taxation. The income of a REIT is not taxable to the trust, but instead the beneficiaries of the trust are taxed on their distributed share of the income.

32. In a recent incident a plane flew over a new methanol manufacturing plant being constructed by Du Pont to take photographs. A chemical engineer could from such photographs determine Du Pont's manufacturing process. This action might constitute the torts of trespass and trade-secret infringement. From an ethical standpoint this practice may constitute unfair competition.

Preventive Law: Co-Ownership of Property

33. In creating joint ownership of real property, one should clearly indicate whether the parties are:
    a. joint tenants with the right of survivorship
    b. tenants in common
    c. tenants by the entirety
    d. owners of community property
    One must remember that in most states real property owned by two or more persons who are not spouses is presumed to be shared as tenants in common unless another type of ownership is clearly specified.

415

MAJOR POINTS OF CASES

Sauls v. *Crosby* (p. 857)

The court held in this case that in Florida a person who acquires an ordinary life estate in real property is entitled to use that property for the duration of his or her life but may not do anything that will permanently diminish or change the value of the future estate to which the remainderman is entitled. The court also stated that if such life tenant does cause the value of the property to be diminished or change, unless specifically excused from responsibility, the life tenant will be liable for damages for the tort of waste. Further, it was also held that an ordinary life tenant has no right to cut down or remove from the property any timber that exists on it when such conduct is done for purely commercial reasons.

In the case before the court, the court ruled that under the facts presented it was improper for the life tenant (Sauls) to cut down the timber unless the proceeds realized from its sale were held in trust for those persons entitled to the estate after Sauls's death.

Solow v. *Wellner* (p. 858)

While the court in this case points out that every case alleging breach of the warranty of habitability depends on the specific facts of the case, this case provides an illustration of when conditions are bad enough to be a threat to the health and safety of the tenants, thereby constituting a breach of the warranty of habitability. Conditions in this case included: 60-70 bags of garbage piled up at the entrance, mice and roach infestation, inoperative locks to the building, four to five inches of standing water in the boiler room, and a collapsing ceiling in one laundry room.

Bostonian Shoe Co. v. *Wulwick Associates* (p. 863)

This case explains that an assignment of a lease occurs when a lessee transfers its entire remaining interest in a lease, whereas a sublease occurs when a lessee transfers anything less than its entire remaining interest in a lease. The original lessee in this case transferred all but one day of the remaining period of its lease, thereby creating a sublease. Since the lease agreement only prohibited assignments, the original lessee's sublease was valid as against the lessor.

Bijou Irrigation District v. *Empire Club* (p. 865)

This case demonstrates that holders of an easement cannot use property in a manner beyond that permitted by the easement. Nor can owners use the servient property in a way that interferes with the use of the easement.

In this case neither party was allowed to use the reservoir for recreational purposes because such use by the landowners could interfere with the rights of the water district under its easement, and recreational use by the District was beyond the scope of the easement.

Milian v. *Deleon* (p.869)

Two unmarried individuals otherwise competent to contract can agree to own real property as joint tenants without regard to the amount of financial contributions and development efforts made by either. In the partition of a joint tenancy, it is proper to order the sale of the property and the proceeds to be divided equally even though the joint tenants' contributions, financial and otherwise, may not be equal. Since a tenancy in common could involve unequal ownership rights in real property, a sale on partition might properly result in a unequal distribution of the proceeds.

The court found that there was substantial evidence to support a finding that the parties agreed to a joint tenancy. Consequently, an equal distribution of the partition sale proceeds between the parties was properly ordered.

Ritchey v. *Villa Nueva Condominium Association* (p. 873)

This case involved a situation in which a condominium association discriminated among its membership on the basis of age. The court concluded that restrictions based on age in connection with condominium communities are not per se unreasonable, and that under the applicable civil law of California restrictions imposed on members of a condominium project were valid and enforceable as long as they were reasonable. The court also held that restrictions on the alienation of a condominium unit could be based on the age of the purchaser, lessee, or a member of such person's family.

On the basis of its conclusions of law, the court held that the condominium association acted properly in this matter and did not exceed its authority in establishing a restriction on ownership based on age.

PRACTICAL CONSIDERATIONS

1. The owner of a life estate in real property acquires a transferable interest in the property and consequently may convey that title to another person during his or her lifetime. It may be extremely difficult for a life tenant to convey his or her interest, however, because the purchaser of such an interest will be able to own and use that property only as long as the life tenant remains alive. Upon the death of the life tenant, the purchaser of that party's interest faces the very real possibility of being involuntarily removed from the premises. The risks involved in the purchase of such an estate are obviously very high and the benefits that may be derived could be very small indeed. Consequently, even when a purchaser for a life estate can be found, the actual financial value of the life tenant's interest may be much less than expected.

2. While it is certainly true that a leasehold interest (a lease) of real property may be assigned to another person, most residential and commercial leases provide that the lease may not be assigned unless the landlord consents to the assignment. The usual provision also indicates that the landlord's consent shall not be unreasonably withheld.

    The practical effect of such a provision is that a landlord possesses a great deal of flexibility in deciding whether or not to permit a tenant to transfer the lease to another person. This is important in a fluctuating real-estate market, where rental value of property increases and decreases periodically. If the rental value of the property involved has decreased and the landlord can currently rent the premises only at a lower rate, it will probably be to his or her advantage to permit an assignment of the lease. Conversely, if the rental values have increased, it may be to the landlord's advantage to withhold consent to the assignment unless the tenant and the assignee of the lease agree to a modification of the periodic rental charge. Additionally, a landlord will often refuse to permit the assignment of the lease but will be willing to terminate the lease and enter into a new one with another person (who may or may not have been introduced to him or her by the tenant) at a higher rental charge and for an extended rental term.

It seems apparent that a landlord is in an advantageous position with reference to the assignment of a leasehold interest. If the issue is approached sensibly and reasonably by both parties, however, the tenant can usually receive a benefit as well.

SELF TEST

True-False Questions

_____ 1. A life estate in real property may be sold to another person during the life of the life tenant.

_____ 2. A term tenancy automatically terminates at the end of the time period specified in the lease.

_____ 3. An assignment of a lease and a sublease are identical legal concepts.

_____ 4. An easement in gross cannot exist independently from a dominant estate.

_____ 5. If A and B own real property together as joint tenants and A dies, B will become the owner of the property and A's heirs will not be entitled to any interest in it.

_____ 6. If H and W own property together as tenants by the entirety and they subsequently become divorced, the tenancy by the entirety will automatically be converted into a joint tenancy as soon as the divorce is granted.

_____ 7. When a person purchases a cooperative unit, that person acquires title to that part of the building which the apartment actually occupies.

_____ 8. The interest of a person who owns a fee simple absolute estate in real property may be transferred to another person by means of a will.

_____ 9. In order for a lease to be valid, it must be in writing in all cases.

_____ 10. A landlord has the right to enter the rented premises in order to prevent loss or damage to the property resulting from the tenant's negligence.

Multiple-Choice Questions

_____ 11. Which of the following terms describes an ownership interest in real property?
a. a fee simple defeasible estate
b. a fee simple absolute estate
c. a life estate pur autre vie
d. a and b are correct
e. a, b, and c are all correct

_____ 12. A lease that provides that it shall commence on June 1 and terminate on May 31 of the following year is considered to be:
a. a periodic tenancy
b. a month-to-month tenancy
c. an estate for years (term tenancy)
d. a tenancy at sufferance
e. a tenancy at will

_____ 13. A leasehold interest that can be terminated at any time by either party upon proper notice is:
a. a term tenancy
b. a tenancy at will
c. a periodic tenancy
d. a tenancy at sufferance
e. an estate for years

_____ 14. A commercial lease under which the tenant is obligated to pay a fixed rental charge plus the cost of taxes, insurance, and maintenance is known as:
a. a net lease
b. a percentage lease
c. a revaluation lease
d. an appraisal lease
e. a and c are correct

_____ 15. A lease will be terminated:
   a.   if the landlord sells the property that is the subject of the lease
   b.   if the leased premises are condemned
   c.   if the landlord dies
   d.   b and c are both correct
   e.   a, b, and c are all correct

_____ 16. When two or more persons own property together without the right of survivorship, their interest in the property is described as a:
   a.   joint tenancy
   b.   tenancy by the entirety
   c.   tenancy pur autre vie
   d.   tenancy in common
   e.   tenancy in partnership

_____ 17. An easement may be created by:
   a.   an express grant
   b.   a reservation in a deed
   c.   prescription
   d.   a and c are both correct
   e.   a, b, and c are all correct

_____ 18. When title to real property is conveyed to H and W, who will own the property together as husband and wife, their interest is referred to as a:
   a.   joint tenancy
   b.   tenancy in common
   c.   tenancy by the entirety
   d.   tenancy by marriage
   e.   communal tenancy

_____ 19. A periodic tenancy is also known as:
   a.   a month-to-month tenancy
   b.   a year-to-year tenancy
   c.   a holdover tenancy
   d.   only a and b are correct
   e.   a, b, and c are all correct

_____ 20. Which of the following is considered to constitute a nonpossessory interest in real estate?
   a. an easement
   b. a license
   c. a profit a prendre
   d. only a and b are correct
   e. a, b, and c are all correct

Completion Questions

21. A(n)_____ _____ _____ estate is an interest in real property that provides for total, unrestricted ownership rights in the property, which can be divested from the owner, however, upon the occurrence of a specified event.

22. An interest in land by which a person has the right to enter upon the property and take something of value from it is referred to as a(n)_____.

23. The parcel of land over which an easement is exercised is referred to as the _____ _____.

24. A(n) _____ is a personal privilege granting a person permission to enter upon the land of another for a particular purpose.

25. A commercial lease under which the rental charge is determined by a fixed percentage of the gross sales of the business that is conducted on the premises is commonly called a(n) _____ lease.

Chapter 49

ACQUISITION, FINANCING, AND CONTROL OF REAL PROPERTY

This chapter discusses the various ways in which title to real property can be obtained by members of the private sector as well as by the government. The discussion covers the financing of a purchase of real property, including the various theories that relate to the nature of a mortgage and the various alternate methods of financing, and considers the foreclosure procedures available when a default in required payments occurs. Finally, the text examines the control of land use.

CHAPTER OBJECTIVES

After reading Chapter 49 of the text and studying the related materials in this chapter of the Student Mastery Guide, you will understand:

1. The various methods available to acquire title to real property, including:
   a. adverse possession
   b. eminent domain
   c. purchase and sale
   d. gift
   e. inheritance
2. The nature of the various types of deeds, including:
   a. warranty deeds
   b. bargain and sale deeds
   c. quitclaim deeds
3. The use of real property as a means of security for an indebtedness
4. The nature and types of foreclosure proceedings
5. The methods of controlling the use of land

MAJOR POINTS TO REMEMBER

In General

1. Title to real property may be obtained by:
   a. purchase
   b. gift
   c. inheritance
   d. eminent domain
   e. adverse possession

Purchase and Sale of Real Property

2. When a contract for the sale of real property has been fully completed, the purchaser will acquire equitable title even though actual legal title has not yet been conveyed to him or her.

3.   While a buyer holds equitable title, states are split as to whether risk of loss to the property is on the buyer. This issue should be expressly resolved in the parties' written contract.

All states require under the Statute of Frauds that a contract for sale of real property be in writing to be enforceable.

4.   The title closing is either done directly through the parties or through an escrow agent.

5.   There are several types of deeds by which title to real property can be conveyed. They include:
     a.   warranty deed
     b.   bargain and sale deed
     c.   quitclaim deed

6.   A warranty deed conveys title to real property to the grantee and warrants that the title is good and that it is free of any liens and encumbrances.

7.   Covenants that are usually contained in a warranty deed include a covenant:
     a.   of seisin - a guarantee that the seller has good title and the right to convey it
     b.   against encumbrances
     c.   of quiet enjoyment
     d.   of general warranty

8.   A bargain and sale deed conveys title to real property to the grantee, but unless express covenants are specifically provided, this deed contains no warranties.

9.   A quitclaim deed conveys to the grantee only that interest in real property which the grantor possessed, if any. The grantor does not warrant that he or she is the actual owner of the property being conveyed.

10. In order for a deed to be valid, it must:
     a.   contain words of conveyance
     b.   identify a competent grantor and grantee
     c.   provide a legal description of the property
     d.   be properly signed and executed
     e.   be delivered to and accepted by the grantee

Recording Statutes

11. The purpose of recording statutes is to provide notice to third persons of the nature and extent of interests that exist in a particular piece of land.

The fact that an instrument is not recorded does not affect is validity. An unrecorded deed or mortgage is enforceable between the original parties.

12.   If a person has actual or constructive notice of the conflicting interest of another person, he or she does not acquire interest in good faith and consequently his or her interest in the property is subject to the interest of the other party.

Adverse Possession

13.   Adverse possession can be described as the acquisition of title to real property by means of the actual, exclusive, open, hostile possession of land for a continuous period of time as specified by law.

14.   In order to obtain title to real property by means of adverse possession, a person must show that his or her possession is:
   a.   open and notorious
   b.   hostile, i.e., the person in possession of the property claims to occupy it as the owner
   c.   actual
   d.   continuous for the period of time specified by law, typically five to eighteen years
   e.   exclusive

Eminent Domain

15.   In order for a governmental body to seize title to real property without the owner's consent by its exercise of eminent domain, it must:
   a.   use the property for the common public good
   b.   adequately compensate the owner of the property being seized
   c.   take the property only by due process of law

Real Property as Security

16.   Two documents are principally involved in a mortgage loan transaction. They are:
   a.   the bond (or note): the document that contains the terms of the loan and creates the obligation to repay the debt
   b.   the mortgage: the document that provides the lender with a security interest in the real estate

17.   State laws governing mortgages follow one of two theories:
   a.   title theory, which provides that title to the land that is being secured by the mortgage will be held by the mortgagee until the loan has been completely repaid, at which time the title will vest in the borrower
   b.   lien theory, which provides that title to the land immediately vests in the borrower, and the lender (mortgagee) acquires a lien on the property to ensure repayment of the loan.

Deed of Trust

18.   Under a deed of trust, the borrower conveys title to the property that he or she has purchased to a trustee, who holds the title for the benefit of the borrower and the lender.

When the debt that is secured by the deed of trust is fully paid, the trustee must reconvey the title to the property back to the borrower.

Mortgage Provisions

19. The interest rate charged in a mortgage can be either fixed for the entire term or be variable with changes in the market.

20. To protect against rising interest rates during the term of the mortgage, the mortgagee may insert a due-on-sale clause in the contract which requires that if the secured property is sold, then the mortgagee must be paid in full. The enforceability of such clauses have been challenged, but in most states have generally been held to be enforceable.

Installment Land Contracts

21. Under an installment land contract, the seller retains title to the land and the buyer makes periodic payments to the seller over a period of time. At the end of the time period and after all payments have been made to the seller as required by the contract, the seller must convey title to the property to the buyer.

Foreclosure

22. Two types of foreclosure procedures are:
    a. judicial foreclosure
    b. power-of-sale foreclosure

Control of Land Use

23. The use of land can be regulated and restricted by means of:
    a. restrictive covenants
    b. zoning ordinances

24. A restrictive covenant can be terminated by:
    a. an agreement in writing
    b. condemnation of the property
    c. failure to enforce it when it is violated

Preventive Law: Purchase of Real Property - Points for Purchasers

25. The purchase of real property is a major investment, and for many people the purchase of a house is their biggest investment. The assistance of an attorney is appropriate. Legal advice should be sought before even making an offer to purchase. Once an offer is accepted, a legally enforceable contract arises, and it may be too late to protect one's valid interests.

425

MAJOR POINTS OF CASES

Jorgensen v. *Crow* (p. 900)

This case illustrates that mere physical possession of a deed does not necessarily constitute delivery of the deed. There must be physical transfer of the deed plus some act or declaration of intent to transfer possession.

In this case, while there was a physical transfer, there was in fact evidence in the contract of sale that transfer of the title was not to take place until certain conditions had been met. Because those conditions had not been met, there was no lawful delivery.

Davis-Wellcome Mortgage Co. v. *Long Bell Lumber Co.* (p. 902)

The issue in this case was the priority of liens of a mortgagee and a mechanic's lien holder where construction of houses on the real property covered by the mortgage started the day after the mortgage was executed and delivered, but before it was recorded. The court held that a mechanic's lien attaches to property on the date work is commenced or materials furnished. It also held that by statute a mortgage lien has no effect as to others until recorded or the party with the conflicting lien interest has actual knowledge of it. Finally, by statute a mechanic's lien has priority over all other subsequent liens or encumbrances.

Based on these rules, the mechanic's lien became effective on the day before the mortgage was recorded. Since Long Bell did not have actual knowledge of the mortgage, its mechanic's lien takes priority over the subsequently recorded mortgage.

Porter v. *Posey* (p. 905)

The court ruled in this case that in order for title of land to be obtained by means of adverse possession in Missouri, the occupation or possession of the property must be actual, open and notorious, hostile, exclusive, and continuous for a period of ten years. It also stated that the possession will be open and notorious if the occupancy or possession is conspicuous, commonly known, and manifested by a claim of ownership. Further, according to the court, title to the property is properly transferred if the title owner intended to transfer the property to the transferee and the transferee received or took possession of it.

After examining the facts, the court found that the Englemeyers, from whom the Porters acquired their interest, had been the only ones to maintain the property for more than eighteen years, had intended to possess it as their own, and had occupied it for their own benefit to the exclusion of others (including Posey). Further, the Englemeyers had intended to convey the property to the plaintiffs, and the fact that they had not quited title before the transfer did not negate the validity of the transfer. On the basis of these findings, Porter's claim of title to the property was affirmed.

Seawall Associates v. *City of New York* (p. 908)

This case provides an example of when a land use regulation has a severe enough impact on a property to constitute a taking that requires just compensation. While each case must be examined individually, a regulation constitutes an unlawful taking when it (1) denies an owner economically viable use of his property or (2) does not substantially advance legitimate state uses.

The law in question required owners of single room occupancy buildings to rehabilitate the buildings and lease every unit, with vacancies lasting over 30 days constituting a violation. The court found the owner's right to possess and use their property as they see fit violated the mandatory rehabilitation and rental provision. While the purported purpose of the law was to provide homes for the homeless, there is no evidence that the forced increase in SRO units would aid the homeless, because the law does not mandate that tenants be homeless or low income families. Thus there is no evidence the law substantially advances a legitimate public interest.

Elysium Institute, Inc. v. *County of Los Angeles* (p. 914)

This case demonstrates the impact of the right of privacy on zoning. The city's overly broad definition of a nudist camp violates the right to privacy.

PRACTICAL CONSIDERATIONS

While it is relatively easy to state the various requirements that must be satisfied in order to obtain title to real estate by means of adverse possession, the actual application of the doctrine is not quite so simple. It must be remembered that the land must usually be possessed for many years, and many factors and events may intervene to cut off the adverse possessor's claim to title. It must also be remembered that the adverse possessor is also a trespasser on the land and is subject to removal from the land at any time before title has vested in him or her. Additionally, there is always the possibility that the actual owner of the property may initiate criminal proceedings against such a person, which could result in imprisonment or the imposition of a fine. Further, it must be realized that the adverse possessor will eventually be required to initiate legal proceedings to quit title to the property and have a court declare that he or she is the owner of the property. Such proceedings can be lengthy and expensive, and there is no guarantee of a successful conclusion.

As a result of the difficulties inherent in the application of the doctrine of adverse possession, one would be well advised to approach any situation involving the doctrine with a great deal of caution and careful forethought. It is generally not recommended that a person rush out and occupy any vacant parcel of land with the thought of acquiring title to it at some time in the future with no expenditure of money. Anyone who does so may acquire more problems than he or she anticipated.

SELF TEST

True-False Questions

_____ 1. When the buyer of real property executes a written contract for the sale of that property, he or she acquires legal title to it immediately upon signing.

_____ 2. When the seller of real property gives the buyer a warranty deed in connection with the sale, he or she represents that the buyer will not be evicted from the property by someone who has a better title to the property than the buyer.

_____ 3. The person who conveys title to real property to a grantee by means of a quitclaim deed warrants that he or she is the owner of the property being conveyed.

_____ 4. In order to be valid, a deed must be recorded.

_____ 5. Generally, restrictive covenants imposed on the use of land run with the land.

_____ 6. A person who trespasses on the real property of another may, under certain circumstances, become the legal owner of that property.

_____ 7. A person who enters into real property with the permission of the owner can thereafter successfully claim title to the property by means of adverse possession even though that person never repudiates the owner's title.

_____ 8. An easement may be created by prescription.

_____ 9. When a deed of trust is used in order to secure the repayment of a loan in connection with the purchase of real property, title to the property will remain in the seller's name until the loan is paid in full.

_____ 10. A judicial foreclosure is usually accomplished by means of a court order directing that the mortgaged real property be sold in order to pay the debt that was due.

428

_____ 11. In which of the following ways can a person obtain title to real property?
- a. by gift
- b. by eminent domain
- c. by adverse possession
- d. a and c are both correct
- e. a, b, and c are all correct

_____ 12. In order for a deed to be valid, it must be:
- a. properly signed and executed
- b. supported by consideration
- c. recorded
- d. a and c are both correct
- e. a, b, and c are all correct

_____ 13. The purpose for which land can be used may be regulated by:
- a. an easement
- b. zoning ordinances
- c. a lis pendens
- d. collateral infringement
- e. a, b, and c are all correct

_____ 14. When the grantor of real property conveys title to the grantee by means of a warranty deed, he or she covenants that:
- a. the government will not seize the property by right of eminent domain
- b. he or she has the right to convey the property
- c. the premises are covered by proper insurance
- d. a and b are both correct
- e. a, b, and c are all correct

_____ 15. In order for a person to acquire title to real property by right of adverse possession, he or she must prove that his or her possession was:
- a. hostile
- b. continuous for a specified period of time
- c. actual
- d. open and notorious
- e. all of the above are correct

16. The person who borrows money from a lending institution and agrees to provide real property as security for the loan is referred to as the:
    a. grantor
    b. mortgagee
    c. mortgagor
    d. survey
    e. guarantor of payment

17. By the terms of a quitclaim deed, the person to whom it is given:
    a. receives a guarantee that he or she is getting good title to the property
    b. knows that the title he or she is receiving may be taken away at any time
    c. receives whatever interest in the property the grantor had
    d. receives a covenant of quiet enjoyment
    e. receives a guarantee that there are no liens on the property

18. Security interests in real property can be established by means of:
    a. a mortgage
    b. a restrictive covenant
    c. a deed of trust
    d. a and c are both correct
    e. a, b, and c are all correct

19. A restrictive covenant can be terminated by:
    a. condemnation
    b. unilateral action by the property owner
    c. payment of a fee to a specified state agency
    d. refinancing of the real property that is subject to the covenant
    e. all of the above are correct

20. In order for a state government to obtain title to a person's property by right of eminent domain, it is necessary that:
    a. the landowner receive compensation for the land being acquired
    b. the property be taken away from the owner only by due process of law
    c. the property be used for some public purpose
    d. a and c are both correct
    e. a, b, and c are all correct

Completion Questions

21. The person to whom title to real property is conveyed is referred to as the_____.

22. The _____ is the person who is borrowing money from a lender and who agrees to provide specified real property as security for the loan.

23. The division of a geographic area into districts for the purpose of controlling the use of land is referred to as_____.

24. The process by which a government may acquire title to real property without the consent of the owner is known as _____ _____.

25. Under the _____ theory of mortgages, title to the property vests in the borrower, and the lender acquires a lien on the property.

Chapter 50

INTELLECTUAL PROPERTY AND COMPUTER LAW

Intellectual property stands as the next link in the chain of the evolution of property. In the nineteenth century, real property, such as the ownership of land and the attached buildings, was critical to many firms. This century has witnessed the increasing importance of tangible property such as cars, planes, and machines. And now, as we move into the twenty-first century, intellectual property -- i.e. intangible property created primarily by mental rather than physical effort -- is enjoying newly gained prominence. Paralleling the increased importance of intellectual property has been computer law. The past decade has yielded new laws to govern situations that have arisen as a result of the computer.

The materials in this chapter examine the four major types of intellectual property. Then, the law concerning the legal protection given to computer programs is reviewed, including an overview of several computer-specific legislative provisions. Finally, the applicability of criminal law to computers is evaluated.

CHAPTER OBJECTIVES

After reading Chapter 50 of the text and studying the related materials in this chapter of the Student Mastery Guide, you will understand:

1. The four types of intellectual property:
   a. trademark
   b. copyright
   c. patent
   d. trade secret
2. The emerging body of computer law
3. Computer law's relationship with criminal law

MAJOR POINTS TO REMEMBER

Types of Intellectual Property

1. There are four major types of intellectual property:
   a. trademark
   b. copyright
   c. patent
   d. trade secret

Trademarks

2. There are four basic types of trademarks:
   a. a trade name, such as IBM and Coca-Cola, which identifies goods originating from a specific company
   b. a service mark, which identifies a particular service and distinguishes it from other similar services

432

c. a certification mark, which is used by an attesting agency or firm to indicate that certain quality standards have been met for manufacturing or testing a product

d. a collective mark, which is used by a related group of people or businesses for mutual purposes

3. The most important piece of legislation dealing with trademarks is the Lanham Act, which established a system of federal registration for trademarks. Under the Act, registered trademarks are valid for twenty years, and this period can be doubled if the mark is still in commerce after twenty years. The Act also prohibits the unauthorized use of a trademark.

4. Trademarks generally fall into four categories of distinctiveness, including:
    a. arbitrary or fanciful mark
    b. suggestive marks
    c. descriptive marks
    d. generic marks

5. U.S. law allows trademarks to be acquired before they are put into use, with the only stipulation being that the trademark is used within six months of registration. Other countries, such as Canada and the Philippines, make use a necessary condition for acquiring a trademark.

6. The rights of a trademark are lost upon either abandonment of the mark or its becoming generic. The latter occurs when companies are successful in promoting a trademark to the extent that the trademark becomes a generic name for the product itself.

Preventative Law: Protecting Trademarks

7. Five basic steps can be taken to prevent one's trademark from being rendered "generic":
    a. use a descriptive term along with the trademark
    b. protest generic uses of the mark in publications
    c. follow up by writing suspected infringers and requesting that they change their practices
    d. put the words "trademark" or "registered trademark" next to the mark itself
    e. check the laws of any country where you might use the mark to see if you can register the mark before you begin using it

Copyrights

8. A copyright is effective in protecting the original work of a person for the life of that person plus fifty years. While a common-law copyright exists once a work is created, the creator of the work must attain statutory copyright protection before widely distributing the work lest it become part of the public domain. Such protection is acquired by distributing the work with a copyright notice.

9.	A major exception to the exclusive rights given to the copyright owner is the fair use doctrine, which stipulates that so long as the use is "fair", anyone may use material from a copyrighted work.

10.	Electronic copying represents a new frontier in the interpretation of copyright laws. In the most recent case, Atlas Telecom Inc. paid $100,000 in a settlement for electronically distributing within its firm about a dozen newsletters from Phillips Business Information Inc.

11.	Copyrights are obtained by notifying the public in a certain manner that copyright protection is being claimed.

Issues and Trend Box: What is Fair Use?

12.	The fair use exemption is generally narrower than most people interpret it to be. Contrary to popular belief, significant copying of musical recordings, books, et cetera is not permitted. Electronic copying has made it possible for a great number of people to have access to one's work at a very low cost. Publishers oppose this practice vehemently, and an increasing volume of litigation concerning this issue is likely to ensue.

Patents

13.	A patent can be obtained from the U.S. Patent Office for an invention involving a machine, chemical, design, process, or certain types of plants. A patent grants the owner of an invention the exclusive right to make, use, or sell the invention for a period usually of seventeen years.

14.	Patent infringement occurs when someone manufactures, uses, or sells a product or process that is substantially similar to that protected by a patent. The infringer can be held liable for damages caused to the patent holder.

15.	The patentability of a product is determined by answering the following questions. If the answer to all three are affirmative, then a product is patentable.
    a.	Is the invention new?
    b.	Is the invention useful?
    c.	Is the invention non-obvious?

16.	Securing a patent can be time-consuming and expensive due to the technical nature of the application process, which usually requires the services of a patent attorney. Between the application for and the issuance of a patent, the invention is often used with a public notice on it of "patent pending", which is used to discourage others from making use of the invention.

Trade Secrets

17. The two elements that must be present in order for there to be a trade secret are:
    a.   there must be some valuable information such as a customer list, a process for making a certain product, or a special recipe
    b.   such information must be kept secret

18. In contrast to other types of intellectual property, trade secrets are protected for the length of time that the information is valuable as well as secretive instead of for a specified period of time.

19. Owners of trade secrets are protected from wrongful appropriation, which includes bribing an employee of a firm to disclose a trade secret. However, reverse engineering or using trial and error to figure out a secret recipe are not considered wrongful appropriation.

20. Trade secrets are useful for protecting ideas for a longer period of time than patent protection affords.

Ethics Box: Ethics and Information

21. Questions of ethics arise anytime competitors employ methods to obtain information about other firms. One of the more ethically questionable of these methods is paying large consulting fees to former employees of competitors to supply information. Sometimes companies face ethical decisions without even looking for information. In a recent incident, a contract employee of 3M sent samples of a product under development to four competitors, none of which reported the information to 3M.

Computer Law

22. The sale of computer hardware as well as either the lease or the sale of computer equipment are subject to the Uniform Commercial Code (UCC).

23. In the sale of software and technical services, the court determines whether these are goods and thus subject to the UCC on the basis of one primary consideration: which is more important, the sale of the goods or the sale of the services?

Computer and Criminal Law

24. Examples in which criminal laws apply to computer-related crimes include:
    a.   when computers are used to embezzle funds
    b.   when hardware or software equipment is taken

25. Most states have passed specific statutes intended to deal with:
   a. the unauthorized access of a computer system
   b. the tampering with or causing damage to a system
   c. the invasion of data base records
   d. unauthorized copying of computer programs
   e. intentional introduction of computer viruses

26. The Computer Fraud and Abuse Act is the most important federal statute specifically addressing computer-assisted crimes. It protects computers used by the federal government, financial institutions, and those firms that operate in interstate commerce.

27. Other federal statutes that are aimed at the improper uses of computer resources include:
   a. the Electronic Funds Transfer Act
   b. the Computer Matching and Privacy Act of 1988
   c. the Semiconductor Protection Act (SCPA) of 1984

MAJOR POINTS OF CASES

Lois Sportswear, U.S.A., Inc. v. Levi Strauss & Co. (p. 901)

In this case, the court reviewed the district court's application of the Polaroid factors to a trademark dispute between Levi Strauss and Lois Sportswear. The court ruled that Levi Strauss's stitch pattern on the back of its jeans was a trademark to be afforded the greatest degree of protection because it can be classified as "arbitrary and fanciful". With this ruling serving as a threshold matter, the court next determined that the almost identical stitch pattern on the back of jeans imported by Lois Sportswear was likely to create confusion among buyers concerning the maker of the jeans. The court reasoned that the lack of sophistication of the buyers concerning knowledge of jeans would likely cause them to mistake Lois Sportswear jeans for Levi's. As a result of its findings, the court upheld the district court's decision.

Basic Books, Inc. et al. v. Kinko's Graphics (p. 906)

In this case, the court ruled that the copying and compilation of copyrighted work for the purposes of selling it to college students is not covered under the fair use exemption to copyright laws. Applying this ruling to the facts of the case, the court found in favor of several publishing companies who brought suit against Kinko's Graphics Corporation for copying excerpts of copyrighted work for sale.

Stiffel Co. v. Sears, Roebuck & Co. (p. 911)

In this case, the court had to settle two issues: the validity of a patent and whether unfair competition was undertaken. Concerning the first issue, the court found Stiffel's patent to be invalid due to a lack of originality. Sears, Roebuck & Co., against which Stiffel brought suit, offered a lamp in the early 1950's that the court did not find to be different in ornamental design aspects from the lamp patented by Stiffel in 1957. At the same time, the court did find Sears to be guilty of unfair competition. Sears' actions constituted such guilt, because it offered a lamp not clearly distinguishable from Stiffel's only after Stiffel mass marketed its product.

E.I. Du Pont de Nemours and Company v. *Christopher et al.* (p. 913)

If a person improperly discovers the trade secret of another person or company and thereafter discloses or wrongfully uses it, the person may be liable for such conduct.

The court held in this case that the disclosure of trade secrets obtained by aerial photography was, under the circumstances, improper, and the distribution to a third person of the photographs thus obtained was wrongful.

RRX Industries, Inc. v. *Lab-Con, Inc.* (p. 917)

A threshold decision for the court in this case was whether Lab-Con, Inc. breached its contract with RRX Industries. The court held that TEKA, whose software was marketed by Lab-Con, supplied software to RRX that never functioned properly, and which they failed to repair. Thus, there was a breach of contract.

The court then had to decide the appropriate extent of the damages for the breach of contract. Lab-Con contended that the contract was intended to provide services and thus the damages should be limited to the value of the contract. However, the court ruled that the sale of the software package was the primary feature of the contract, making the contract one of sale. As a result, the court held that RRX was entitled to consequential damages, or the full extent of the damages incurred by RRX as a consequence of TEKA's breach of contract.

U.S. v. *Riggs* (p. 919)

In this case, the court ruled on a number of charges brought against Riggs and Neidorf for their alleged scheme to defraud Bell South by stealing the specific details of its 911 services. The court found Riggs and Neidorf guilty of wire fraud in that they used computers, coded language, coded names, and other deceptive means in their effort to defraud Bell South. Secondly, the court found Riggs and Neidorf guilty of violating Section 2314 of the UCC, which prohibits the interstate transport of goods at a value $5,000 or more that are known to be stolen. The defendants' claim that what was transported was merely electronic pulses was rejected based on the fact that what was actually transferred was proprietary business information that constituted a "good, ware, or merchandise" within the meaning of the statute. Finally, the court denied the defendant's claim that applying Section 2314 undermines the Congressional intent behind the Computer Fraud and Abuse Act.

SELF-TEST

True-False Questions

_____   1.   Trade secrets are protected for a 17-year time period.

437

_____ 2. Arbitrary or fanciful marks are granted the widest trademark protection.

_____ 3. Under U.S. law, trademarks cannot be acquired until after a product is used for 6 months.

_____ 4. Trademark owners may lose the rights of their mark if they abandon it or if the mark becomes generic.

_____ 5. Common-law copyrights are sufficient to protect a product from being used by those other than the product's creator without authorization.

_____ 6. The fair use doctrine is an added bulwark to copyright protection.

_____ 7. The process for obtaining a patent is brief and relatively inexpensive.

_____ 8. Both patents and trade secrets can protect ideas.

_____ 9. Obtaining information about a competitor's strategies and products is always illegal.

_____ 10. The sale of computer hardware is not subject to the Uniform Commercial Code.

Multiple-Choice Questions

_____ 11. Which of the following is/are type(s) of intellectual property?
   a. trademark
   b. copyright
   c. trade secret
   d. patent
   e. all of the above

_____ 12. Which of the following is not true of the Landam Act?
   a. it establishes a system of federal registration for copyrights
   b. it makes copyrights valid for twenty years
   c. it makes unauthorized use of a copyright illegal
   d. all of the above
   e. none of the above

13.   The fair use doctrine concerns:
      a.   trademarks
      b.   copyrights
      c.   patents
      d.   trade secrets
      e.   all of the above

14.   Which of the following is <u>not</u> a question considered in determining patentability?
      a.   Is the invention new?
      b.   Has the invention been subject to a pending application in another country during the prior year?
      c.   Is the invention useful?
      d.   Is the inventionn non-obvious?
      e.   none of the above

15.   Which of the following does one normally acquire an attorney to obtain?
      a.   trademark
      b.   patent
      c.   copyright
      d.   trade secret
      e.   b and c

16.   What determines the period of protection afforded trade secrets?
      a.   the duration of time that the information is valuable
      b.   the Office of Trade Secrets, which currently sets the period at 7 years
      c.   the life of the person holding the trade secret plus 50 years
      d.   the duration of time that the secret is kept
      e.   a and d

17.   Computer crimes subject to criminal law include:
      a.   using a computer to embezzle funds
      b.   taking hardware or software equipment without authorization
      c.   passing oneself off as a legitimate user of stored data in order to gain access to a file
      d.   all of the above
      e.   none of the above

_____ 18. Which of the following does not directly address computer-assisted crime?
    a.   the Computer Fraud and Abuse Act
    b.   the Electronic Funds Transfer Act
    c.   the Computer Matching and Privacy Act
    d.   the Computer Crime Prevention Act
    e.   the Semiconductor Chip Protection Act

_____ 19. Intellectual property concerns:
    a.   computer law
    b.   cars, planes, and machines
    c.   intangible property created by mental effort
    d.   a and c
    e.   none of the above

_____ 20. Which mark is afforded the greatest protection?
    a.   arbitrary
    b.   suggestive
    c.   descriptive
    d.   generic
    e.   product

Completion Questions

21. _____ are acquired either by use or registration.

22. _____ _____ is a relatively new issue with which copyright law has increasingly had to deal.

23. A _____ is the most time consuming of all types of intellectual property to obtain.

24. The primary issue in adjudicating computer law is whether the sale of computer-related equipment is a sale of _____ or of _____.

25. A _____ is a picture, word, or design that identifies a manufacturer or merchant's goods from those of his competitors.

Chapter 51

WILLS, TRUSTS, AND ESTATES

To most people death is a frightening event, and most prefer not to think about it. Statistics and logic prove, however, that a little forethought and preparation can prevent a great deal of difficulty and unhappiness at a later date for those persons who survive the decedent.

The materials in this chapter are concerned with the consequences of death and also with the devices and methods available for planning in anticipation of the legal consequences of death. They discuss the concept of state intestacy laws, wills, estate administration, and estate planning.

As the materials in this chapter are examined, the wisdom of and need for advance planning to cope with the consequences of death will be come apparent. It is clear that planning can avoid severe and disastrous results.

CHAPTER OBJECTIVES

After reading Chapter 51 of the text and studying the related materials in this chapter of the Student Mastery Guide, you will understand:

1. The nature of a will and the requirements for validity
2. The nature and effect of state intestacy laws
3. The nature of estate administration
4. The nature and different methods of estate planning

MAJOR POINTS TO REMEMBER

1. State laws regulating the descent and distribution of a deceased person's estate are concerned with:
   a. testate distribution
   b. intestate distribution

2. Generally, the estate of a person who dies intestate will (by operation of law) be shared by the surviving spouse and children.

   If the decedent had no surviving children at the time of his or her death, the surviving spouse will generally be entitled to receive the entire estate. (This is not true in all states, however.)

Wills and Testamentary Laws

3. Property of a deceased person who has failed to leave a valid will can be distributed to his or her heirs by either:
   a. per-stirpes distribution
   b. per-capita distribution

4. If a person has no descendants, ascendants, or collateral relatives at the time of his or her death, that person's entire estate will go to and become the property of the state by means of a legal provision known and referred to as *escheat*.

5. In order to establish that a will is valid, it must be shown (in most states) that the decedent:
    a. possessed testamentary capacity at the time of executing the will
    b. had a testamentary intent in making the will
    c. complied with the statutory requirements established by state law relating to the execution of a will

6. In order for a testator to have testamentary capacity, he or she must:
    a. have attained the age specified by law (usually eighteen)
    b. be of sound mind

7. In order to be considered of sound mind, the testator must:
    a. know the natural objects of his or her bounty
    b. be aware of the nature and extent of the property he or she owns
    c. be able to plan for the disposition of that property

8. "Testamentary intent" means that the testator must intend:
    a. to transfer his or her property
    b. that the transfer shall take effect only upon his or her death

9. A person's testamentary intent may be invalidated on several grounds, including:
    a. fraud
    b. duress
    c. undue influence
    d. mistake

10. In order for a will to be valid, it must be properly executed. This means that (in most states) the will must usually be in writing, be signed by the testator or someone whom the testator has authorized to sign for him or her, and be properly witnessed.

    A will generally must be witnessed by two persons, although a few states require three witnesses. Such witnesses are used to verify the testator's signature and to attest that the testator has the intent and capacity to sign the will.

11. If a person is unable to sign a will himself or herself, such person may execute a will by:
    a. placing a mark (such as an X) in the place provided for the testator's signature
    b. authorizing another person to sign the will on his or her behalf

12. A will has no effect until the testator dies, and consequently it may be revoked or changed at any time before the testator's death.

Revocation of a Will

13.	A person can revoke a will by:
	a.	intentionally destroying it
	b.	making a new will
	c.	changing his or her marital status (in some states)
	Generally, a testator cannot disinherit a spouse. However, statutes generally do not provide for a forced share for the children of a decedent.

14.	A *codicil* is a document that changes or makes additions to the provisions of a will; it must be executed in the same manner as a will.

Estate Administration

15.	An estate is usually administered in accordance with statutory law and rules developed and overseen by state probate courts.

16.	In addition to the formal estate administration procedures that exist, an estate can be administered by alternate means, including:
	a.	trusts
	b.	life insurance policies
	c.	custodial accounts
	d.	joint tenancy agreements

Estate Planning

17.	Estate planning is the process of making plans and arrangements for the future distribution of a person's estate.

18.	The primary object of estate planning is to ensure that the testator's property is distributed to those persons (at the time and in the manner desired by the testator) whom the testator wants to receive it. Another function of estate planning is to attempt to minimize the taxes and fees that will be required to be expended from the estate.

19.	Several types of taxes affect the manner in which estate planning is conducted. They include:
	a.	federal estate tax
	b.	state inheritance or estate taxes
	c.	income taxes

20.	By the nature of a trust, title to the property that makes up the trust is vested in a trustee who holds the property for the benefit of the beneficiary. Two types of trust are:
	a.	an *inter vivos* trust: a trust created when the settlor of the trust property conveys or gives the property to the trustee while the settlor is alive
	b.	a testamentary trust: a trust that is established by means of a specific provision contained in a person's will

443

21. The settlor is the person who creates a trust, and the trustee is the person who manages the trust. The trustee has a fiduciary relationship to the beneficiary of the trust, the person for whom the trust was created.

22. When an irrevocable trust is created, title to the trust property irrevocably vests in the trustee of the trust.

23. A testamentary trust does not become effective until after the death of the testator. If for any reason the will is found to be invalid, the trust does not come into existence.

24. When joint property is used as an estate-planning device, title to the property involved is transferred by the owner to himself or herself and the other joint owner. Thus, the property does not become part of the probate estate.

25. Estate tax laws allow a person to transfer or make a $10,000 gift to a single donee or recipient each year without incurring any tax liability for the transfer.

26. A custodial account established for a minor child permits the donor to remove property from his or her estate and thereby reduce his or her estate tax liability. However, for children under fourteen the income above $1,000 per year from accounts established by parents will be taxed at the parents' rate.

27. Life insurance policies owned by a decedent that name a beneficiary other than the decedent's estate are generally not subject to estate and inheritance taxes, or probate. Life insurance is also used sometimes by a person in business to allow associates to acquire his or her interest in the company at death by providing the funds necessary to pay the decedent's heirs for the interest in the company.

Preventive Law: Estate Planning for Younger Individuals

28. Younger persons should develop estate plans and execute wills, if their assets are significant to them or they have children. These plans and wills need to be reviewed periodically to account for changes in persons' lives. Wills do not take effect until death, and many aspects of estate plans can be modified when the need arises.

Planning for Incapacity

29. A power of attorney gives one party the power to act on behalf of another under certain circumstances.

30. Living wills are documents that provide that artificial life support systems will not be used if a person becomes terminally ill or incapacitated. Requirements for living wills vary from state to state.

MAJOR POINTS OF CASES

Warpool v. Floyd (p. 927)

In this case, the court held that in Tennessee brothers and sisters of half blood share equally in the intestate distribution of a decedent's personal property along with the brothers and sisters of whole blood, and that no distinction is made between them. The court also held that the children of predeceased brothers and sisters share in the estate on a per-stirpes rather than a per-capita basis.

On the basis of the findings of law, the court stated that inasmuch as there was no legislative history providing otherwise, brothers and sisters of half blood share equally with full brothers and sisters in the intestate distribution of the decedent's personal property. Consequently, the decedent's estate was distributed accordingly.

Kenney v. Pasieka (p. 929)

This case involved the construction of a will. The court stated that the guiding principle in the construction of a will is the intention of the testator. In order to determine that intent, it is proper for a court to consider all the relevant surrounding circumstances. The court also stated that there is a legal presumption against intestacy and a court should try to construe an existing will in such a way as to give it validity. The court should not rewrite the will, however. In considering the will of Frank Pasieka, the court held that its provisions were so ambiguous that it was incapable of being construed in any meaningful way. Consequently, that part of the will which could not be effectively construed was ruled to be invalid and the part of the estate that related to those provisions was ruled to pass through intestate distribution. The balance of the will was held to be valid.

In re Estate of Lockwood (p. 932)

The court in this case stated that there is a presumption in the law that a person possesses the necessary testamentary capacity to make a valid will. If the testamentary capacity of a testator is challenged, the contestant has the burden of proving by a preponderance of the credible evidence that the testator was mentally unfit. Further, according to the court, once it has been shown that the testator lacked testamentary capacity as a result of mental disorder of a general and continuous nature, there is a reasonable inference that the incapacity continues to exist unless otherwise established.

On the basis of the testimony presented, the Court of Appeals held that the jury's finding that Mrs. Lockwood was in such a physically and mentally unsound condition that she was incapable of understanding the significance of her actions was justified. She lacked testamentary capacity at the time of execution of the codicil, and therefore the codicil was invalid.

In re Estate of Brown (p. 934)

This case involves the validity of a codicil. The court stated that under the law of Texas, unless otherwise provided, every will must be in writing and must be signed by the testator or by another person on his or her behalf and at his or her request. Further, a codicil must be executed with the same formality as a will. If a will or codicil is not wholly in the handwriting of the testator, it must also be witnessed by two or more witnesses. The court also stated that extrinsic evidence is not admissible in regard to terms or provisions that are necessary for the validity of an instrument but are missing from it.

In applying the enunciated rules of law to the facts of the case, the court found that the decedent's writing on the envelope expressed a testamentary intent. The court also held that it was proper to admit into evidence testimony that identified the circumstances surrounding the preparation of the writing. As a result, the court found that the document that was presented to the court for probate was a valid holographic codicil to the will of the decedent and that it was proper to accept it for probate.

Connecticut National Bank and Trust Co. v. *Chadwick* (p. 941)

This case involved the construction and interpretation of a provision contained in a testamentary trust that provided for the distribution of a portion of the trust among all living grandchildren at the time his last surviving child died. When the last child died, 2 biological grandchildren and four adopted grandchildren were alive. The two grandsons were adopted before the testators death and two granddaughters after his death. The court stated that the common law presumption is that adopted children are not considered to be benefices of a person who was not the actual adopting parent. However, this presumption is not irrebuttable. The court also stated that when the meaning of a trust is construed, the intention of the settlor is critical, and that such intention should be considered in light of all the surrounding circumstances. The testator had shown interest and concern for the grandsons, including concern for their financial situation. He also had ample time to exclude them from his will, which he did not do. This evidence was sufficient to reflect a desire to include them, and thus overcame the presumption of exclusion. With respect to the girls, even though they were not alive at his death, the girls' father (also father of the grandsons) had no natural children, so the testator would have known that any future grandchildren would be adopted. Therefore they were likewise intended to be included.

When the court considered the facts of the case, it concluded that there was no evidence that clearly established that Miss Hart had intended to give any meaning other than the ordinary meaning to the term "descendant." Consequently, it held that William S. Hills, by virtue of his adoptive status, was not intended to be included within the category of descendant for purposes of the trust.

PRACTICAL CONSIDERATIONS

Many people feel that it is not necessary for them to make a will because they simply do not own or possess sufficient assets to justify concern about how the assets they do possess will be distributed after they die. Most people do not fully appreciate that a will is not intended to provide only for the distribution of the assets they currently possess. It is also intended to provide for the distribution of any property they may acquire at any time in the future. It is also intended as a device that enables one's personal desires to be carried out with respect to the persons who will receive one's property upon one's death. Sometimes this can be an extremely important factor, as when a parent who has been severely abused by a child feels that it would be improper for that child to receive any of his or her property upon his or her death. If that parent did not execute a will, the child would receive a portion of the estate by virtue of the intestacy laws. Likewise, it is of critical importance for a person who has no living heirs to execute a will, because otherwise that person's property will escheat to the state rather than going to someone of his or her own choosing.

SELF TEST

True-False Questions

_____ 1. A will must always be in writing in order to be valid.

_____ 2. An insane person cannot make a valid will under any circumstances.

_____ 3. A will written on a paper bag will be considered valid if it satisfies all the other requisite elements for validity.

_____ 4. A witness to a will must read the document before signing it.

_____ 5. A will does not become effective until the death of the testator.

_____ 6. Estate planning is the process of making arrangements for the future disposition of a person's estate.

_____ 7. If a person dies without having executed a valid will, the property he or she owns at the time of death will be distributed to his or her heirs in a manner determined by statute.

_____ 8. The person who has the responsibility of distributing a person's estate under the laws of intestacy is referred to as the executor.

_____ 9. In order for a will to be valid, the testator must personally sign the document in all cases.

_____ 10. Any person who owns property may execute a valid will regardless of his or her age.

11. The person who has the responsibility for carrying out the provisions of a will is referred to as the:
     a.   administrator
     b.   executor
     c.   testator
     d.   trustee
     e.   settlor

12. In order to be of sound mind, the testator must:
     a.   know the natural objects of his or her bounty
     b.   be aware of the nature and extent of his or her property
     c.   be able to plan for the disposition of his or her property
     d.   only a and c are correct
     e.   a, b, and c are all correct

13. A will may be invalidated on which of the following grounds?
     a.   fraud
     b.   duress
     c.   undue influence
     d.   only a and b are correct
     e.   a, b, and c are all correct

14. In order for a will to be valid, it must usually be:
     a.   in writing
     b.   signed by the testator
     c.   shown to each of the beneficiaries upon execution
     d.   only a and b are correct
     e.   a, b, and c are all correct

15. A testator can revoke a will by:
     a.   physically destroying it
     b.   hiding it
     c.   executing a codicil
     d.   a and c are both correct
     e.   a, b, and c are all correct

16. Alternative methods of estate planning include:
     a.   trusts
     b.   life-insurance policies
     c.   joint tenancy agreements
     d.   only an and c are correct
     e.   a, b, and c are all correct

_____ 17. A trust that is established by means of a provision in a will is known as:
    a.   an inter vivos trust
    b.   a per-capita trust
    c.   a testamentary trust
    d.   a custodial trust
    e.   a documentary trust

_____ 18. Which of the following taxes will have an effect on the manner in which an estate plan is formulated?
    a.   income taxes
    b.   real property taxes
    c.   luxury tax
    d.   sales tax
    e.   only a, b, and c are correct

_____ 19. When an irrevocable trust is created, title to the trust property belongs to the:
    a.   settlor of the trust
    b.   trustee
    c.   beneficiary of the trust
    d.   administrator
    e.   testator

_____ 20. A testamentary trust becomes effective:
    a.   immediately upon the execution of the document by which the trust is established
    b.   when the trust document is filed with the registrar of deeds
    c.   upon the death of the testator
    d.   as soon as the beneficiary is informed of the existence of the trust
    e.   when the trustee pays the requisite fees

Completion Questions

21. A(n) _____ is a document by which the terms and provisions of a will may be changed or added to.

22. The person who is executing a will is referred to as a(n) _____.

23. A person who dies without having executed a valid will is considered to have died _____.

24. The property of a decedent who leaves no living heirs and who has not executed a valid will goes to the state by means of a process known as _____.

25.   The process by which a will is legally approved as valid and through which the estate is administered is known as _____.

Chapter 52

INSURANCE LAW

The study of property law is not complete without an examination of insurance law, since insurance policies are one important means by which to protect ourselves against financial losses caused by fortuitous events. This chapter begins by describing some of the common types of insurance that are available in the marketplace. Next, the nature of insurance contracts is discussed. The defenses of an insurer to the enforceability of an insurance contract are also explained, as well as the rules for interpreting insurance contracts. Finally, this chapter briefly discusses the basic types of insurance companies, and the differences between insurance agents and brokers.

CHAPTER OBJECTIVES

After reading Chapter 52 of the text and studying the related materials in this chapter of the Student Mastery Guide, you will understand:

1. The kinds of insurance available in the marketplace
2. The nature of insurance contracts
3. The defenses of the insurer, including:
   a. concealment
   b. misrepresentation
   c. warranty
4. The rules used to interpret insurance contracts, and the defenses of:
   a. waiver
   b. estoppel
   c. unconscionability
5. The types of insurance companies
6. The differences between insurance agents and brokers

MAJOR POINTS TO REMEMBER

In General

1. Insurance is a contractual arrangement by which one party agrees to pay the other a sum of money upon the happening of an event beyond the control of either party.

2. Insurance sales and contracts are primarily regulated by state law pursuant to the 1945 federal McCarran Act.

451

Kinds of Insurance

3. *Life insurance* contracts take a variety of forms, including:
    a. Whole life policies - which for premiums payable throughout life gives the insured death benefits and a type of savings or investment program that allows the insured to borrow against the cash surrender value of the policies
    b. Term insurance - which is solely life insurance for a specified period of time
    c. Universal life - which is a flexible policy in which part of the premium pays for life insurance with the remaining amount invested in market securities, and the amount paid can be varied with adjustments in the death benefits.
    d. Endowment and annuity contracts - the endowment policy pays the insured a lump sum of money at a specified date, whereas the annuity contract pays specific sums to the insured at periodic intervals after the insured reaches a specified age.

4. *Accident and health insurance* provides for payments to cover expenses associated with accidental physical injuries. Health insurance pays or reimburses some or all of the expenses for medical care incurred for certain illnesses. Group insurance plans are available to many people through employers at costs significantly lower than individual or family plans.

5. *Disability insurance* provides partial income continuation while the insured is too ill to work.

6. *Casualty insurance* protects against accidental damage to personal property by causes other than fire or the elements. Fire insurance covers real and personal property losses caused by fire.

7. *Homeowners insurance* protects the homeowner's residence and personal property. *Renters insurance* protects a renter's personal property.

8. *Automobile insurance* generally insures the car owner against damage to his or her car and liability.
    a. *Liability insurance* protects the insured for responsibility for losses suffered by others.
    b. *Collision insurance* covers losses to the insured's own care as a result of an accident, as well as theft.

9. *No-fault insurance* is available in some states to pay the insured for losses incurred in automobile accidents regardless of who was at fault for the accident.

10. *Credit insurance* protects the creditor and debtor by paying a debt in the event of the debtor's death.

11. *Title insurance* repays an insured for a loss arising from defects in the title to real estate.

12. *Business interruption insurance* pays for loss of income when a business is unable to operate due to an insured peril.

13. *Worker's compensation insurance* is required of employers to cover their employees for accidental injuries and illnesses arising out of employment without regard to who was at fault.

Nature of Insurance Contracts

14. Insurance contracts often are by necessity or state regulation standardized and not subject to normal negotiations.

15. Generally, in insurance contracts the customer makes an offer to purchase and the company decides whether to accept the offer. Insurance agents represent the company, and their statements and actions can affect the terms of the insurance contract. Typically, they can sign a "binder" for fire or casualty insurance to bind the company before it sees or accepts the application, but they cannot do so for life insurance.

16. To avoid gambling and immoral activities, a person must have an insurable interest in the subject matter to be insured in order to obtain an enforceable policy. For life insurance this must exist at the time of taking out the policy, but for other insurance it must exist at the time of loss.

17. Premiums charged for some insurance are regulated by states. Premiums are set based on the risks assumed, the costs of administration, interest to be earned, and desired profits.

Allocation of Costs Between Insurer and Insured

18. Costs are allocated to the insured through the use of deductibles, amounts the insured must pay before he can recover damages for a loss.

19. Coinsurance limits the percentage on the amount of the insured cost that an insurer is required to pay.

Subrogation

20. Subrogation prevents a party from collecting twice for the same damages.

21. In the insurance context, subrogation provides that an insurance company that has paid an insured's loss has the rights of the insured against the third party who caused his harm.

Defenses of the Insurer

22. Besides normal contract defenses, the three other primary defenses of insurers are:
    a. concealment
    b. misrepresentation
    c. breach of warranty

23. Concealment is the intentional failure of the insured to disclose a material fact to the insurer that would affect its willingness to accept the risk. This is a defense even though the insurer did not specifically ask for the type of information that was concealed.

24. If the insured intentionally or innocently misrepresents a material fact, either orally or in writing, regarding a subject matter asked of by the insurer, and the insurer justifiably and reasonably relies on this false representation, then the insurer can assert the defense of misrepresentation. Damages are available in cases of intentional misrepresentations, while only rescission can be obtained for innocent misrepresentations.

25. Incontestability clauses in insurance contracts limit the insurer's right to assert a misrepresentation as a defense to a set period of time (usually one or two years) after the policy is issued. However, a misrepresentation of one's age in a life insurance policy, regardless of when discovered, reduces the benefits to the amount the premiums paid would have purchased for a person of the actual age of the insured.

26. Warranties are express conditions stated in the insurance policy that must exist either before the policy becomes effective or before the insurer's promise to pay is enforceable. The trend is to require that the warranty conditions be material before they can constitute a defense.

Interpretation of Insurance Contracts

27. Defenses cannot be asserted by insurers when:
    a. a waiver (voluntary relinquishment of a known right) has occurred;
    b. estoppel applies due to the words or conduct of the insurer, which is inconsistent with its assertion of a defense and which was justifiably relied on by the other party; or
    c. the insurance contract or a relevant provision thereof is unconscionable

28. Insurance contracts can be terminated by:
    a. full performance
    b. exercising a right to cancel
    c. the nonperformance by one party of a material term of the contract, such as the payment of premiums or giving notice of the happening of an event insured against in a policy

Insurance Firms

29. There are two basic kinds of insurance companies, which are:
    a. stock insurance companies, which are established to sell policies for a profit with dividends being distributed to shareholders
    b. mutual insurance companies, which are owned by the policyholders

30. An insurance agent acts on the behalf of the insurer under a principal-agent relationship. An insurance broker represents the buyer of insurance in acquiring insurance from an insurer.

Ethics Box: An Ethical Problem for an Insurance Agent or Broker

31. Insurance agents have an ethical obligation to disclose known material facts to their principal, the insurer. Insurance brokers, although working for the buyer, have an ethical obligation to not knowingly conceal material information that the insurer would not otherwise be readily able to learn.

MAJOR POINTS OF CASES

Ranger Insurance Company v. Phillips (p. 953)

Generally, a parol contract of insurance is valid and enforceable when the parties have agreed on the essential terms. Any ambiguities in insurance contracts are to be construed against the insurer. Based on these rules, the court concluded that the agent's statements and the "set-up" that the insured heard and saw provided for insurance coverage, including student pilots. The agent later, without the insured's knowledge, deleted the coverage of student pilots, and the policy was so issued, but it was not delivered to the insured until after the airplane accident. Nonetheless, the contract was formed by the agent's representation of coverage even though the insured did not pay a premium based on that coverage. The question of whether passengers were also covered was unclear, but this ambiguity was resolved against the insurer.

Erie-Hauen, Inc. v. Tippmann Refrigeration Construction (p. 955)

This case examines the insurable interest of a lessor and lessee when a building is destroyed. The extent of the interest of each is determined at the time of the destruction. A Lessee has an interest to the extent of the unexpired term of the lease and in the improvements the lessee made. In this case, proof of extensive improvements made by the lessee entitled him to $57,546.56 out of the $179,594.14 proceeds from the insurance.

Mutual Benefit Life Insurance Co. v. JMR Electronics Corp. (p. 958)

If a fact that is material to the risk is misrepresented, the insurance company may avoid liability under the contract, regardless of whether the parties might have agreed to some other contractual arrangement had the critical fact been disclosed. By misrepresenting that the insured was a nonsmoker and paying non-smoker premiums when the insured was in fact a heavy smoker, JMR Electronics lost their ability to recover anything when the insured died, even though they probably could have insured him as a smoker for a higher premium.

Spindle v. *Travelers Insurance Cos.* (p. 961)

The malpractice insurance policy, including the master policy for the physicians' association, gave the insurer the right to cancel a physician's coverage at any time on thirty days' written notice. The plaintiff alleged that his policy was canceled maliciously by the insurer in an effort to influence members of the association to agree to a modification of the master policy that would allow the insurer to increase the premiums by an amount higher than allowed in the existing master policy. The plaintiff, thus, argues that this violates public policy to allow a cancellation that is not made in good faith.

The court noted that by statute, various kinds of insurance limitations have been placed on an insurer's right to cancel a policy. Further, it held that in every contract there is an implied covenant of good faith and fair dealing. As a result, the court concluded that the plaintiff's complaint had stated a cause of action and he was entitled to a trial to attempt to prove his allegations.

State Farm Mutual Automobile Insurance Company v. *Milam* (p. 963)

The insurance company refused to provide a defense for the son of its insured against a lawsuit arising from an automobile accident. The insurer's defense was that it had no obligation to defend, since it had not been given notice of the accident within the time required in the insurance policy. The court held that the critical issue in cases such as this is whether the insurer was prejudiced by the untimeliness of the notice.

Since the evidence showed that a thorough investigation was conducted by the police of the accident, and that there was no reason to believe there were any possible alternative causes for the accident, a more timely notice would not have placed the insurer in a better position than it currently occupied. Because there was no prejudice to the insurer, it cannot assert the lack of timely notice as a defense to the enforceability of its obligations under the policy. In effect, then, the insureds met their responsibility to give notice as soon as practicable, particularly since the insureds were unaware until the time of their notice that their son was covered by the policy.

PRACTICAL CONSIDERATIONS

1. Although the trend of the law is to be more restrictive of an insurer's right to assert the defenses of concealment, misrepresentation, and breach of warranty, information material to the risk for which insurance is sought should always be fully and truthfully disclosed. The risk of incurring a loss and having the insurance contract be unenforceable due to a failure to properly disclose material facts is simply too high. And, of course, it would be unethical not to truthfully disclose such information.

456

2. One might conclude that by incorporating a business to obtain limited liability for the company's legal obligations the need for liability insurance is eliminated or reduced. However, if a corporation is properly capitalized and operating profitably, it can have a substantial economic value. The limited liability of shareholders protects only their personal assets from third-party claims, not the corporate assets. If financially feasible, liability insurance should be carried by even small business corporations.

SELF TEST

True-False Questions

_____ 1. Ordinary life insurance policies only provide death benefits for a set period of time after which there are no benefits for the insured or the beneficiary.

_____ 2. Universal life insurance policies give the insured an investment that has the potential to earn value as determined in the marketplace.

_____ 3. An endowment policy generally requires that a lump sum of money be paid at a specific time.

_____ 4. Generally, in insurance contracts the insurer is the party who made the original offer.

_____ 5. Insurance agents never have the right or power to bind their principals, the insurance companies, to contracts.

_____ 6. All insurance contracts must be in writing and signed by both parties to be enforceable.

_____ 7. To obtain insurance one must have an insurable interest in the life or property being insured.

_____ 8. To be paid under a fire or casualty insurance policy, a person must generally have an insurable interest in the insured property at the time the loss occurs.

_____ 9. Premiums charged for some kinds of casualty and business insurance are regulated by some states.

_____ 10. A misrepresentation made by an insured in obtaining insurance can be raised as a defense by an insurer at any time during the term of a policy.

_____ 11. If an insurer specifically asks for certain information in an application for insurance, and the applicant fails to truthfully disclose the facts, then the insurer will have available to it the defense of:
    a.   concealment
    b.   misrepresentation
    c.   breach of warranty
    d.   waiver
    e.   estoppel

_____ 12. Statutes generally limit an insurer's right to use the defense of misrepresentation by requiring insurance contracts to contain a(n):
    a.   incontestability clause
    b.   waiver clause
    c.   estoppel clause
    d.   warranty
    e.   unconscionability clause

_____ 13. The right of a title insurer to assert the defense of misrepresentation:
    a.   exists only for intentional misrepresentations
    b.   is negated if the defect in the title was a matter of public record
    c.   exists for innocent misrepresentations
    d.   only a and b are correct
    e.   only b and c are correct

_____ 14. The trend is to allow insurers to assert the defense of breach of warranty for:
    a.   all misrepresentations
    b.   only material breaches
    c.   all conditions
    d.   only concealments
    e.   none of the above is correct

_____ 15. Courts can refuse to enforce insurance contracts, or provisions in such contracts, that are too one-sided and oppressive under the doctrine of:
    a.   waiver
    b.   estoppel
    c.   unconscionability
    d.   misrepresentation
    e.   incontestability

16. Implied in insurance contracts is the:
    a. obligation of fair dealing and to act in good faith
    b. right to cancel the contract at any time
    c. right to cancel the contract only on six months' written notice
    d. obligation to always give immediate notice of the occurrence of an insured event
    e. only c and d are correct

17. If a provision of a written insurance contract is ambiguous:
    a. the contract is void
    b. the ambiguity is construed against the insurer
    c. the ambiguity is construed against the insured
    d. the ambiguous provision is unenforceable
    e. none of the above is correct

18. The failure of an insured to give a timely notice of a loss to the insurer negates the insurer's obligation to pay:
    a. in all cases
    b. in no case
    c. when the failure is prejudicial to the insurer
    d. when the contract specified the time within which notice had to be given
    e. when the contract required notice within a reasonable time

19. An insurance company in which the policyholders are also the owners is a(n):
    a. mutual fund company
    b. insurance investment company
    c. ordinary life insurance company
    d. stock insurance company
    e. mutual insurance company

20. Insurance brokers represent the interests of:
    a. insurance companies
    b. insurance buyers
    c. independent agents
    d. only one insurance company
    e. the public

Completion Questions

21. _____ life insurance is a contract only for insurance for a given period of time.

22. An insurance company that voluntarily relinquishes a right to enforce a contractual provision cannot later enforce it under the _____ doctrine.

23. _____ occurs when a person fails to disclose a matter material to an insurer's risk in applying for insurance, even though the insurer never asked for the information.

24. _____ insurance provides for the partial continuation of a person's income when he or she is unable to work for an extended period of time.

25. A condition in an insurance contract that must exist before the contract is enforceable or the insurer is obligated to pay is a(n) _____.

Chapter 53

GOVERNMENT REGULATION AND THE ROLE OF ADMINISTRATIVE AGENCIES

Administrative agencies are hybrid organizations that perform functions commonly associated with the various branches of government. These agencies serve a vital function and are essential to the effective operation of the national and state governments.

This chapter discusses the history of government regulation of business, the nature of administrative agencies, and the constitutionally mandated separation of powers as it affects these agencies. The chapter also considers the work of administrative agencies and presents an evaluation of government regulation by these agencies.

CHAPTER OBJECTIVES

After reading Chapter 53 of the text and studying the related materials in this chapter of the Student Mastery Guide, you will understand:

1. The nature and role of administrative agencies
2. The functions performed by administrative agencies, including:
   a. the adjudication function
   b. the rule-making function
   c. administrative functions
3. The various factors that influence the way in which administrative agencies perform their functions.

MAJOR POINTS TO REMEMBER

History of Government Regulation

1. In response to the intense regulatory control of business in Europe, the United States first adopted a capitalistic economic system based on individual freedom, private property ownership, and a laissez-faire theory of government.

2. However, beginning with the Interstate Commerce Act of 1887 and the Sherman Antitrust Act of 1890, and escalating from the Great Depression to the current government, regulation has come to affect virtually every aspect of business operations. Much of this regulation is conducted through administrative agencies. The issue of whether government regulates business too much or not enough continues to be an important matter of public debate.

Administrative Agencies

3. Administrative agencies are governmental bodies, other than the courts and the legislatures, that carry out the administrative functions of government. They possess executive, legislative, and judicial powers. Administrative agencies have proliferated because:
    a. Congress cannot regulate everything
    b. there is a need for expertise
    c. agencies keep complex cases out of court
    d. Congress has wanted a means to implement its legislation

Administrative Agencies and Constitutional Separation of Powers

4. The major regulatory agencies are subject to extensive influence by the executive branch of government, even though some of the agencies do possess structural independence. Independent agencies are those that are not part of any department of the executive branch. Other agencies are part of the executive branch. Although structural independence from the executive branch is provided, the executive branch can influence agencies by:
    a. nomination of the agency heads
    b. political lobbying
    c. influencing public opinion
    d. influence on the budgetary process
    e. executive orders requiring agencies to conduct and consider cost-benefit analysis of all proposed rules

Judicial Review and Administrative Agencies

5. The actions and decisions of most state and federal administrative agencies are subject to review by the courts. When an agency acts in a legislative manner, the courts review the agency action to make sure that:
    a. the delegation of authority is constitutional
    b. the action is within the powers granted
    c. the agency does not violate any constitutional limitation or federal statute

6. When an administrative agency exercises its judicial powers, the courts may review the procedures followed by the agency to make sure that:
    a. they are constitutionally valid
    b. the agency possesses proper jurisdiction over the matter involved
    c. the procedural rules established by statute have been followed

7. Courts will set aside the decision of an administrative agency if that decision is determined to be arbitrary and capricious. Courts will also set aside an administrative agency adjudication if the decision is not supported by substantial evidence from the hearing.

Legislatures and Administrative Agencies

8. Administrative agencies acquire their authority from the legislature by means of enabling acts. These acts allow an agency considerable discretion to act and are based on very broad and general standards. However, more recently Congress has shown a willingness to exercise much greater oversight control over administrative agencies, as indicated by the FTC Improvement Act of 1980.

Work of Administrative Agencies

9. Administrative agencies perform several types of functions, which include:
    a. making rules that have the force of law
    b. settling disputes
    c. conducting hearings and deciding on violations of statutes or of their own rules
    d. administrative activities

10. In conducting adjudication proceedings, most agencies follow a procedure that consists of five stages:
    a. investigation
    b. complaint
    c. hearing
    d. order
    e. internal appeals

11. In an administrative hearing, questions of fact as well as issues of law are decided by an administrative law judge.

12. Congress has delegated the power to make rules to the agencies. The rules made by administrative agencies with respect to the segments of business that they regulate may be more susceptible to judicial attack than laws enacted by legislative bodies elected by the public.

13. Formal rule making is sometimes required of an agency by statute. This process normally entails:
    a. publication of the proposed rule in the *Federal Register*
    b. a public hearing conducted under rules of evidence with cross-examination of witnesses allowed
    c. formal written findings of fact and conclusions
    d. a decision to enact the proposed rule, modify it, or reject it, and, if adopted, publication in the *Federal Register*.

14. In most cases administrative agencies are allowed to use informal rule making, which entails:
    a. publication of the proposed rule in the *Federal Register*
    b. an opportunity for interested parties to submit written comments
    c. adopting the rule and publishing it in the *Federal Register*

Government Regulation and Administrative Agencies: An Evaluation

15. Administrative agencies have been subjected to industrial, legislative, and executive influences.

16. The Regulatory Flexibility Act of 1980 seeks to force all agencies to fit their regulations and information requirements to the size of the business affected. "Sunshine" or "open government" legislation generally requires administrative agencies to conduct most of their business in meetings open to the public after prior public notice has been given of the matters to be decided.

Ethics Box: Ethics and Government Regulation

17. The Ethics in Government Act of 1978 forbids an agency decision maker from participating in a rule-making decision after being the subject of an ex parte contact unless a full disclosure of the contact shows that it will not affect the agency official's decision. In an adjudication proceeding an agency official can be disqualified from decision making due to an ex parte contact. Ex parte contacts can also involve attempted bribery, which, of course, is illegal.

MAJOR POINTS OF CASES

Heckler v. *Chaney* (p. 975)

In this case, the Supreme Court considered the extent to which a government agency's decision not to enforce regulations should be subject to judicial review. The Court held that such a lack of action on the part of an agency is presumptively immune from judicial review. Reasons provided for this presumption include the agency's expertise in balancing priorities as well as the non-coercive nature of a refusal to act. The Court did state that this presumption of immunity can be abutted in the event that there exists meaningful legislative standards for limiting an agency's discretion in balancing priorities.

Applying this ruling to the facts of the case, the Supreme Court held that it had no power of judicial review over the Food and Drug Administration's failure to enforcement action concerning executions by lethal injection. Upon reviewing the Food, Drug, and Cosmetic Act, the Court concluded that there were no meaningful legislative restrictions on the FDA's discretion to act; therefore, a failure to act by this agency is not subject to judicial review.

Utica Packing Co. v. Block (p. 980)

The decision in this case dealt with administrative adjudication's relationship with due process rights afforded by the Constitution. The court ruled that while the requirement of a separation of functions is relaxed in administrative adjudication, the requirement of a fair trial before a fair tribunal is maintained. Necessary to upholding due process rights of the defendant is the appearance of fairness as well as the absence of a probability of outside influences on the adjudicator.

With this ruling, the court held that the earlier ruling of Campbell should be reinstated. On remand, Campbell had ruled that the mitigating circumstances constituted a justification for restoring Utica's meat inspection privileges. He was removed from his position by the Secretary of Agriculture, and his replacement reversed his decision. The court in this case ruled that such occurrences constituted an appearance of bias.

Florida Power & Light Co. v. United States (p. 983)

The court's judgment in this case required an interpretation of the Administrative Procedures Act in relation to the facts of the case. The court held that the Nuclear Regulatory Commission's cost base statement does not violate the APA because its omission of costs did not result in the remaining costs either not being reasonably related to the regulatory services provided by the NRC or not being associated with all operating licenses. The court also ruled that in light of the Congress's deadline for NRC action, the fifteen day period for comment was a sufficient amount of time.

Home Box Office Inc. v. Federal Communications Commission (p. 985)

This case examines the issue of to what extent ex parte contacts can be allowed in informal rule making. Due process of law requires procedural fairness and a reasoned decision. The satisfaction of these requirements cannot be determined when decision making is based on information provided in ex parte contacts that is not made public for interested persons to review for comment. However, balanced against these problems is the recognition that ex parte contacts are an important source of interaction between an agency and members of the public.

The court concluded the ex parte contacts made prior to publication of a proposed rule subject to informal rule-making procedures need not be publicly disclosed unless it becomes the basis for the decision rendered. Agency personnel responsible for the rule making should refuse ex parte contact after publication of a proposed rule. Those ex parte contacts that cannot be avoided must be publicly disclosed for comment. Since postpublication ex parte comments took place with all concerned industry groups, the court could not determine for the lack of a complete record whether the rule adopted met the due process requirement of reasonableness.

PRACTICAL CONSIDERATIONS

While courts are empowered to overturn an administrative agency's decision in a particular case on the ground that the decision is arbitrary or capricious, they do so infrequently because the term "arbitrary or capricious" is vague in meaning and extensive in scope. Before a court is willing to reverse the decision of an agency on such grounds, it will want to be convinced that the decision is one with which no reasonable person will or can agree. Obviously, such a decision is difficult to make, and before a judge rules that the conduct or decision of the agency is arbitrary or capricious, he or she will want to be sure that no other finding is possible.

Example: A applies to her state liquor authority for the issuance of a liquor license in connection with her delicatessen business. The state agency denies her application on the ground that she had been arrested for driving while intoxicated ten years earlier. A applies to the court to have the decision of the agency set aside on the ground that it is arbitrary and capricious.

The judge who must decide this case will probably have great difficulty in determining whether the agency's decision was arbitrary. He or she will have to decide whether the agency was justified in giving weight to the drunk driving charge in reaching its decision. The judge will also have to consider whether such an arrest is a proper matter for consideration in an application of the type made by A. The decision will clearly be a difficult one to make.

SELF TEST

True-False Questions

_____ 1. The Regulatory Flexibility Act of 1980 seeks to force all administrative agencies to fit regulations and information requirements made by the agency to the size of the business being regulated.

_____ 2. Many federal agencies are independent of the executive branch of the government.

_____ 3. Administrative agencies acquire their power of authority to act from legislation passed by the federal or state legislatures.

_____ 4. Administrative agencies operate only within the federal government.

_____ 5. In an administrative hearing, questions of fact are decided by a specially empaneled group of experts who are selected from among the members of the industry with which the hearing is concerned.

_____ 6. Administrative agencies have the authority to perform legislative functions.

_____ 7. Supervision of inmates at correctional institutions (jails) usually comes within the powers exercised by the judicial branch of the government.

_____ 8. Because administrative agencies have an independent existence, they are not influenced by pressures exerted by the legislative branch of the government.

_____ 9. The decisions of federal administrative agencies may not be reviewed by the courts.

_____ 10. A court may set aside a decision of an administrative agency if it finds that the decision was arbitrary.

Multiple-Choice Questions

_____ 11. In response to complaints of farmers that railroads were charging discriminatory rates, the U.S. Congress passed the:
    a.   Sherman Antitrust Act
    b.   Clayton Act
    c.   Interstate Commerce Act
    d.   Federal Trade Commission Act
    e.   Regulatory Flexibility Act

_____ 12. Administrative agencies are frequently referred to as:
    a.   commissions
    b.   agencies
    c.   boards
    d.   only a and b are correct
    e.   a, b, and c are all correct

_____ 13. Administrative agencies were created:
    a.   to keep large numbers of complex cases out of the federal courts
    b.   to provide employment
    c.   to provide legislative assistance to Congress
    d.   only a and c are correct
    e.   a, b, and c are all correct

_____ 14. The agency that has authority to fix the rates charged by companies involved in interstate commerce is the:
    a.   Federal Trade Commission
    b.   Interstate Regulatory Commission
    c.   Interstate Commerce Commission
    d.   Federal Communications Commission
    e.   Federal Aviation Authority

15. Which of the following is a stage in an administrative agency's adjudication proceedings?
    a. investigation
    b. complaint
    c. hearing
    d. order
    e. all of the above are correct

16. In an administrative hearing, questions of law are decided by:
    a. a superior court judge
    b. a special panel of lawyers
    c. a magistrate
    d. b and c are both correct

17. Which of the following is a factor that the courts will review when determining whether procedures used by administrative agencies are valid?
    a. whether there is a sufficient number of experts on the administrative hearing board
    b. whether the statutory rules controlling procedures have been followed
    c. whether the agency has proper jurisdiction
    d. only b and c are correct
    e. a, b, and c are all correct

18. Which of the following functions are administrative agencies empowered to perform?
    a. legislative
    b. judicial
    c. administrative
    d. only a and b are correct
    e. a, b, and c are all correct

19. The decision of an administrative agency may be overruled by a court on the ground of:
    a. abuse of discretion
    b. arbitrary or capricious decision
    c. concurrent jurisdiction with another agency
    d. only a and b are correct
    e. a, b, and c are all correct

20. An administrative agency may do which of the following?
    a. grant licenses
    b. administer tests
    c. make loans of money
    d. only a and b are correct
    e. a, b, and c are all correct

Completion Questions

21. _____ _____ are governmental bodies, other than courts and legislatures, that carry out the administrative tasks of the government.

22. The legislation that creates an agency is referred to as a(n) _____ _____.

23. The agency that has the authority to commence an action in order to stop or prevent false advertising or deceptive practices is the _____ _____ _____.

24. The _____ _____ _____ has the authority and responsibility to enforce rules made to protect buyers of corporate securities.

25. The radio and television industries are regulated by an administrative agency known as the _____ _____ _____.

Chapter 54

ANTITRUST LAWS: ENFORCEMENT AND CONTROL

Freedom of competition is a basic tenet of a capitalist society. Nevertheless, in order to keep the marketplace from becoming a jungle, it is sometimes necessary to impose certain restrictions on various industries. Sometimes these restrictions appear to affect only a few companies, and at other times they appear to influence the activities of an entire industry (as the recent rulings in regard to the telephone industry demonstrate) in a dramatic way.

This chapter considers the nature and extent of government regulation of business and its effect on anticompetitive practices. In examining this area of law, the text discusses the enforcement of antitrust laws, the exemptions that exist in connection with antitrust regulation, and the business behavior regulated by the antitrust laws.

CHAPTER OBJECTIVES

After reading Chapter 54 of the text and studying the related materials in this chapter of the Student Mastery Guide, you will understand:

1. The nature and extent of government regulation of business
2. The nature and effect of antitrust regulations
3. The types of business activities that are regulated by the antitrust laws

MAJOR POINTS TO REMEMBER

In General

1. If certain types of industry structures impair the mechanism that establishes prices, the government may be justified in restricting the formation of such structures and taking affirmative action to break up such firms.

Law and Economics in Setting Antitrust Policy

2. There are two basic schools of thought regarding how antitrust laws should be interpreted and applied:
   a. The Chicago School believes that all antitrust decisions by courts should be based on the sole criterion of economic efficiency to promote the maximization of consumer welfare through improved allocation of resources without impairing productive efficiencies. Under this approach the size of firms and their market share or control is less important.
   b. The Harvard School, in contrast, emphasizes the need to control firm sizes and market control to preserve markets with many smaller sellers, prevent concentrations of economic and political power, and protect against labor dislocations by greater local control.

Enforcement of Antitrust Laws

3. Actions under the antitrust laws may be initiated by:
    a. the Department of Justice in the regular court system
    b. administrative agencies that follow special procedures
    c. private citizens who seek compensation for injuries.

4. The Antitrust Division of the U.S. Department of Justice possesses special powers with respect to antitrust actions as they relate to administrative agencies.

5. The Federal Trade Commission has exclusive jurisdiction with respect to the enforcement of the Federal Trade Commission Act and possesses concurrent jurisdiction (together with the Department of Justice) for the enforcement of the Clayton Act.

6. In enforcing the various federal acts, the government uses:
    a. injunctions
    b. criminal sanctions
    c. fines

7. The Antitrust Improvements Act (1976) allows the attorneys general of the individual states to bring civil treble-damage lawsuits on behalf of the citizens of the state against defendants who have violated the antitrust laws.

8. Private plaintiffs can bring civil treble-damage lawsuits to enforce the Sherman and Clayton acts. Class actions can also be brought under appropriate circumstances.

Exemptions from the Antitrust Laws

9. Certain types of businesses and certain business and labor-union activities are exempted from the provisions of the antitrust laws. They include:
    a. regulated industries
    b. labor unions
    c. the insurance industry
    d. certain types of agricultural marketing arrangements

10. The Webb-Pomerence Act of 1918 provides that combinations of exporters are exempt from the application of the antitrust laws with respect to their international activities.

Sherman Act

11. Contracts, combinations, and conspiracies that restrain interstate trade are prohibited by Section 1 of the Sherman Act.

12. For purposes of analysis, cases arising under Section 1 of the Sherman Act are categorized as either:

  a. rule-of-reason cases in which the courts must balance the negative effects on competition against the positive affects to determine whether the business activity is an unreasonable restraint on trade and, therefore, illegal; or

  b. per se cases in which no extended economic analysis occurs, because the acts once proven are deemed in and of themselves illegal, including:

     (1) most horizontal price-fixing agreements

     (2) most vertical price-fixing agreements (although Department of Justice guidelines restrict its enforcement activities against such cases to explicit agreements to set specific prices)

     (3) most horizontal territorial market divisions or customer allocations

     (4) some group boycotts

13. Price-fixing arrangements are of two types:

  a. horizontal price fixing occurs when competitors on the same level of marketing structure agree to set prices

  b. vertical price fixing occurs when firms at different levels of the distribution system agree to set prices

14. Vertical territorial limitations are not deemed to be per se in violation of the antitrust laws. Each case involving such limitations is examined on its own merits.

15. If a group of people refuse to deal with a firm and make a concerted effort to induce others to stop dealing with that firm, courts will generally consider such conduct to be a per se violation of the Sherman Act.

16. A tying contract (i.e., one in which a purchaser is not permitted to buy a product unless he or she also buys another product at the same time) will be unenforceable if:

  a. control of the tying product has given the seller sufficient economic power to lessen competition in the market in which the tied product is sold

  b. a substantial amount of interstate commerce is affected, even if no actual injury to competition can be proved

17. Section 2 of the Sherman Act prohibits:

  a. monopolization

  b. attempts to monopolize

  c. combinations or conspiracies to monopolize

18. In determining whether a firm is engaged in a monopoly, a court will consider whether the firm has:

  a. overwhelming market power

  b. a general intent to monopolize

19. In order to determine whether a particular firm has overwhelming market power, courts consider the following factors:
    a.   the relevant product market
    b.   the geographic market

20. Modern cases hold that if a firm controls more than 80 percent of a relevant market, it is probably in violation of the Sherman Act. However, some courts now also consider efficiency and consumer welfare criteria.

21. An attempt to monopolize requires:
    a.   specific intent to monopolize
    b.   anticompetitive conduct
    c.   a dangerous probability of success

Mergers

22. There are three types of mergers:
    a.   a horizontal merger involves two competing firms on the same level of the distribution structure
    b.   a vertical merger involves two firms at different levels of the distribution structure that deal with the same basic product or process
    c.   a conglomerate merger involves noncompeting, unrelated firms

23. In order to evaluate the effect of a merger for regulatory purposes, it is necessary to define the product and geographic dimensions of a relevant competitive market.

24. In a horizontal merger, the courts will usually consider what:
    a.   postacquisition market shares, if any, are so insignificant that the merger can be considered clearly legal
    b.   market shares, if any, appear to be so anticompetitive that the merger may be considered to be illegal without any further investigation

25. In a vertical merger, courts will analyze the resulting market structure and the probable market behavior of the postacquisition firm. The purpose of doing this is to determine whether an actual or potential competitor will be excluded from a particular market.

26. The Department of Justice Merger Guidelines are useful to companies and their lawyers in evaluating whether a proposed merger would likely be challenged under Section 7 of the Clayton Act.

27. In Section 7 of the Clayton Act cases, the courts look at the potential effect on competition in the relevant competitive market (product and geographic) of a merger to determine whether the "effect of such acquisition may be substantially to lessen competition" or "tend to create a monopoly."

28. In regard to mergers, the courts have become more willing to consider efficiency factors in addition to structural factors and have required more substantial evidence of anticompetitive effects from proposed mergers.

Price Discrimination

29. Section 2 of the Clayton Act as amended by the Robinson-Patman Act, makes it illegal to sell, in interstate commerce, goods of like grade and quality to different buyers at different prices, if the reasonably probable effect is to substantially lessen competition or tend to create a monopoly. Buyers who knowingly induce and receive such discriminatory prices on purchased goods also violate this section.

30. Defenses to charges of illegal price discrimination include:
    a.   the price differential is justified by the differences in the costs of manufacturing, sale, or delivery to different buyers
    b.   changing market conditions have caused a need to change product prices
    c.   the sale at a lower price was made in good faith to meet the price being offered by a competitor

Issues and Trends

31. What legal affect do the U.S. antitrust laws have on foreign commerce? Generally, the cases seem to say that if U.S. or foreign private companies enter into an agreement that violates Section 1 of the Sherman Act, and it affects the foreign commerce of the United States, the U.S. courts have jurisdiction to enforce Section 1. Department of Justice guidelines state that U.S. antitrust laws apply to actions that have a "substantial and foreseeable effect" on U.S. commerce. Under the Act of State doctrine, however, U.S. courts will not decide the legality of acts of foreign nations or state-owned companies that occur within the foreign nation, even though U.S. commerce is affected.

Ethics Box: Matching Prices

32. Some people have questioned the ethics of offering "low price guarantees" vis-a-vis antitrust laws. Instead of being directed toward customers, these people speculate, such guarantees are implicit messages to competitors not to lower prices.

MAJOR POINTS OF CASES

National Collegiate Athletic Association, Petitioner v. Board of Regents of the University of Oklahoma and University of Georgia Athletic Association **(p. 999)**

This case involved the legal question of whether the NCAA was per se in violation of Section 1 of the Sherman Act by engaging in horizontal price fixing in selling rights to television broadcasts of all college football games. All colleges and universities as members of the NCAA voted on and were bound to a plan adopted that restricted the individual members from competing against one another in the selling of the rights to

474

televise their football games. The plan in effect artificially limited the number of games available on television for consumers and precluded any price competition. Such horizontal agreements to limit output and fix prices in other contexts have been held per se illegal.

The court in this case, however, found that the per se rule should not be applied to college athletics due to its legitimate needs for member cooperation to foster athletic competition. Nonetheless, it held that under the rule-of-season analysis the plan violated Section 1 of the Sherman Act, since its purpose of maintaining competitive balance was not proven to be advanced by the restraints on competition imposed. The plan, thus, was an unreasonable restraint on competition.

Continental T.V., Inc. v. *GTE Sylvania* (p. 1002)

The Supreme Court in this case specifically overruled the previous law with respect to vertical restrictions on territories. It stated that such restrictions should no longer be considered or treated as per se violations of the antitrust laws. However, they could still be carried out in such a manner as to render them in violation of the law. It also stated that the appropriate test to be applied in determining whether a vertical territorial restriction is proper is the rule of reason, which provides an adequate basis for regulation of the industries.

When the Court evaluated the claim in the instant case on the basis of the new standard that it pronounced should be applied, it found that Sylvania's marketing policy did not violate the rule-of-reason concept, and consequently it upheld the decision of the Court of Appeals denying damages to Continental T.V.

FTC v. *Superior Court Trial Lawyers Association* (p. 1005)

In this decision concerning boycotts, the Supreme Court made two rulings. First, it held that even if prices are fixed at a reasonable rate, the extent of reasonability never in and of itself provides immunity from prosecution under the Sherman Antitrust Act. Secondly, boycotts only can be considered political and exempt from the Sherman Antitrust Act when the participants seek no special economic advantage.

Applying this ruling to the facts of the case, the Supreme Court found "CJA lawyers'" boycott for higher wages to be an unjustifiable restraint on trade. The Court stated that the lawyers' reasonable financial demand does not provide exemption. Also, the Court dismissed the applicability of the Clairborne Hardware precedent in which African-American workers boycotted their place of employment in order that they could be afforded the freedom and equality guaranteed to them under the Constitution. Goals of freedom and equality, the court held, are not comparable to the goal of increased legal fees when analyzing the legality of boycotts.

Jefferson Parish Hospital District No. 2 v. *Edwin G. Hyde* (p. 1008)

This case illustrates a rule-of-reason approach to tying contracts. Whether two products or services are tied together or actually constitute a functionally integrated package is to be determined by whether there exists separate demand for each of the products or services. If the demand is separate, then a tying contract must be analyzed to determine whether the seller is using market power to force buyers to purchase that which they would not otherwise buy from the seller, and whether there is more than an insubstantial amount of interstate commerce involved. In the absence of clear proof of market power over the tying product, it must be proved that the contract is an unreasonable restraint on trade for a violation of Section 1 of the Sherman Act to exist.

In this case Jefferson Hospital required its patients to use the services of anesthesiologists under contract with it. Because Jefferson Hospital did not have dominant market power, this tying contract could not be a per se violation. Further, since the plaintiff had not proven that the price, quality, or the supply or demand for either the tying or tied product had been adversely affected by the exclusive service contract with the anesthesiologists or the tying contract offered to patients, there existed no violation of Section 1 of the Sherman Act.

(It should be noted that tying and exclusive dealing contracts may violate the Clayton Act, which is discussed later in this chapter.)

United States v. Du Pont & Co. (p. 1010)

This case involved the cross-elasticity test, which is applied to define relevant markets in connection with the monopolistic tendencies of a company. The Supreme Court stated that "monopoly power is the power to control prices or exclude competition." It also indicated that while every manufacturer can be considered to be the sole producer of the product it makes, its control over a relevant market depends on the availability of alternative products for buyers. It also stated that a factor related to cross-elasticity of demand between competing products is "the responsiveness of the sales of one product to price changes of the other."

In considering the various factors involved in this case, the Court concluded that Du Pont had no power to prevent competition from other wrapping materials and that it was required to deal with such competition. As a result, the Court found that the relevant market to be considered was the flexible packaging material market as opposed to cellophane, and that with respect to that market, Du Pont did not possess monopolistic control.

United States v. Grinnell Corp. (p. 1013)

The Supreme Court stated in this case that the elements of a monopoly are "(1) the possession of monopoly power in the relevant market and (2) the willful acquisition or maintenance of that power." It also considered whether a burglar alarm of the central-station type was interchangeable with other types of protective services so as to form only a part of a larger relevant market. After deliberation, the Court held that a central station was not interchangeable with other protective services and that it therefore formed a relevant market in itself.

On the basis of its conclusions of law, the Court examined Grinnell's control of the relevant market and concluded that it dominated that market in such a way as to be deemed to be in violation of the prohibition on monopolistic practices. As a result, the Court held that the order to have Grinnell divest its holdings in the three alarm companies was proper.

Brown Shoe Co. v. *United States* (p. 1019)

This case involved an evaluation of mergers between companies. In this case the Supreme Court held that the "area of effective competition must be determined by reference to a product market. . . and a geographic market" when one is considering a vertical merger. According to the Court, the outer boundaries of a relevant product market are determined by the test of cross-elasticity of demand in which submarkets are acknowledged to exist. It found the relevant product market to be men's, women's, and children's shoes. It characterized the geographic market as the nation.

With respect to horizontal mergers, the Court stated that their validity was to be gauged by their effect in an "economically significant market." It also said that the geographic market must "correspond to the commercial realities of the industry and be economically significant."

When the Court examined the details of the merger and considered the effect it would have on the market (a factor that the Court indicated was one of the most important to be considered in evaluating a merger), it concluded that the merger could have the effect of lessening competition in the shoe industry. On the basis of this finding, it held that the District Court was correct in refusing to permit the merger and upheld its decision.

Texaco v. *Hasbrouck* (p. 1023)

This case deals with the extent to which differential pricing for distributors and retailers does not constitute price discrimination. The court held that giving one lower prices than the other is only permissible if the buyer offered a lower price has marketing functions that warrant a discount. Also, the discount must be reasonably related to special expenses of the buyer, and the legitimacy of this relationship is subject to review.

Applying this holding, the Court found Texaco's offering of lower price to a distributor vis-a-vis a retailer to be price discrimination. The Court stated that there was no substantial evidence indicating that the discounts to Gull and Dompier were reasonably related to their actual marketing functions. Furthermore, the Court justified its ruling by citing the fact that Texaco was actively engaged in encouraging the downward integration of Dompier with the lower pricing, while at the same time inhibiting the upward integration of the respondents.

PRACTICAL CONSIDERATIONS

Participation in antitrust activities is not always voluntarily entered into by a merchant, who may truly wish to remain independent and conduct business on a competitive basis with other merchants. However, the reality of the marketplace is that certain outside pressures are often exercised in such a way that the merchant virtually may have no choice but to agree with the organized scheme of a group. The merchant's refusal to "join forces" with others in order to affect the price of a particular commodity may result in the supplier of that commodity refusing to deliver it to the merchant, or perhaps refusing to deliver it unless payment in cash is made at the time of delivery. Further, if the product is an industry-wide product, and the supplier is part of a group made up of other suppliers of the same or a similar product, that supplier may be able to arrange to have the other suppliers also refuse to deliver the product to the recalcitrant merchant.

The effect on the merchant is obvious. If the product involved is responsible for a major portion of the revenues, the merchant's continuing resistance to complying with the supplier's demands may eventually force the merchant to go out of business. Even if the product does not generate the major sales revenue of the business, profits will clearly be adversely affected nonetheless. Ultimately, the merchant may have little choice and few alternatives. The alternatives may even be useless or ineffective. Therefore, the merchant must use his or her best judgment in evaluating a situation of this type. Where possible, he or she should resist the efforts of the group of suppliers altogether while taking any other appropriate action to protect his or her interests. This will frequently be exceedingly difficult, but the alternative to not participating in the scheme is to participate in it with the knowledge that it is an illegal activity.

SELF TEST

True-False Questions

_____ 1. The Federal Trade Commission has exclusive jurisdiction to enforce the Federal Trade Commission Act.

_____ 2. The Sherman Act prohibits contracts that are unreasonable restraints of trade.

_____ 3. Courts consider price-fixing activities to be per se violations of the federal antitrust laws.

_____ 4. Boycotts are always considered to be in violation of antitrust laws.

_____ 5. Horizontal territorial limitations between business competitors are normally considered to be illegal.

_____ 6. Conduct that is considered to be monopolistic will always be considered to be in violation of antitrust laws.

_____ 7. In order to establish the existence of a monopoly, which is in violation of federal law, it is necessary to show that the company involved had a general intent to create a monopoly.

_____ 8. The only sanction available against a company that has been engaging in monopolistic activities is the issuance of an injunction.

_____ 9. Under the terms of the Clayton Act, a firm may never acquire 100 percent of the shares of the stock of another company.

_____ 10. Price-cutting practices by industry competitors are prohibited, under all circumstances, by the Robinson-Patman Act.

478

Multiple-Choice Questions

_____ 11. Which of the following is a remedy used by the government in connection with antitrust violations?
    a.   fines
    b.   injunctions
    c.   criminal sanctions
    d.   only a and b are correct
    e.   a, b, and c are all correct

_____ 12. Actions under the antitrust laws may be commenced by:
    a.   the U.S. Department of Justice
    b.   the Federal Trade Commission
    c.   the U.S. Senate
    d.   only a and b are correct
    e.   a, b, and c are all correct

_____ 13. Which of the following is exempt from the provisions of the federal antitrust laws?
    a.   the computer industry
    b.   labor unions
    c.   medical doctors
    d.   only b and c are correct
    e.   a, b, and c are all correct

_____ 14. In determining whether a company is engaged in a monopoly, a factor that will be considered is:
    a.   whether the firm has an intent to monopolize
    b.   whether the firm has an overwhelming market power
    c.   consumer welfare
    d.   only a and b are correct
    e.   a, b, and c are all correct

_____ 15. Section 2 of the Sherman Act prohibits:
    a.   certain boycotts
    b.   strikes by government employees
    c.   attempts to monopolize
    d.   whip-sawing
    e.   only c and d are correct

_____ 16. A merger that involves two competing firms at the same level of the distribution structure is referred to as:
    a.   a horizontal merger
    b.   a vertical merger
    c.   a diagonal merger
    d.   a conglomerate merger
    e.   an evolutionary merger

_____ 17. The prohibition of certain types of price discrimination has been achieved by virtue of the:
    a.   Clayton Act as amended by the Robinson-Patman Act
    b.   Sherman Act
    c.   Federal Trade Commission Act
    d.   Interstate Commerce Act
    e.   Antitrust Improvements Act

_____ 18. A tying contract will be unenforceable:
    a.   only if it involves monopolistic competition
    b.   if control of the tying product gives the seller enough economic power to lessen competition in the market where the tied product is sold
    c.   if a substantial amount of interstate commerce is affected
    d.   only if machine equipment is involved
    e.   only b and c are correct

_____ 19. Which of the following factors will be considered in determining whether a particular firm possesses overwhelming market power?
    a.   the size of the company
    b.   the relevant product market
    c.   the nature of the product
    d.   only a and b are correct
    e.   a, b, and c are all correct

_____ 20. A method of reducing competition whereby manufacturers and dealers or distributors agree to limit the territories in which the product will be sold is known as:
    a.   whip-sawing
    b.   horizontal territorial limitations
    c.   vertical territorial limitations
    d.   conglomerate merger
    e.   cross-elasticity

Completion Questions

21.   A(n) _____ is a court order that prohibits certain specified conduct.

22.   An industrial structure in which a few companies are able to control the activities of a business market is referred to as a(n) _____.

23.   A(n) _____ involves the acquisition by a corporation of the assets or stock of another corporation in such a way that the acquiring company gains control over the other.

24. A market condition in which a single business organization is able to exercise virtual control over the sale of a product or over the price to be charged for the sale of goods is referred to as a(n) _____.

25. _____ _____ is the process of selective price cutting in geographic markets for the purpose of affecting competition.

Chapter 55

CONSUMER PROTECTION LAW

In an area in which government regulation of business has been the subject of much debate, a great deal of attention has been focused on the need to provide protection to ordinary consumers when they are confronted by experienced businesspeople in the marketplace. As a result of the intervention of legislation in this area of the law, the doctrine of *coveat emptor* has been substantially modified.

This chapter deals with those rules that have been established for the protection of consumers and also with the agency that has been charged with the responsibility of supervising the consumer marketplace. The text considers the structure and functions of the Federal Trade Commission and examines it in its role as an administrative agency, in its dealings with unfair trade practices, and in connection with consumer protection laws.

CHAPTER OBJECTIVES

After reading Chapter 55 of the text and studying the related materials in this chapter of the Student Mastery Guide, you will understand:

1. The nature of the Federal Trade Commission and the functions it performs
2. The manner in which the FTC deals with unfair practices
3. The role of the FTC in the protection of consumer rights, including considerations of the:
   a. Truth-in-Lending Act
   b. Fair Credit Reporting Act
   c. Equal Credit Opportunity Act
   d. Fair Debt Collection Practices Act

MAJOR POINTS TO REMEMBER

The Federal Trade Commission as an Administrative Agency

1. The Federal Trade Commission serves as a consumer protection agency with authority to regulate business activities or practices that may be considered unfair or deceptive.

2. The FTC is made up, in part, of a chairman and four commissioners.
   The chairman is the executive and administrative head of the FTC. Other officers include the:
   a. executive assistant
   b. general counsel

3. The division of the FTC are the:
   a. Bureau of Competition
   b. Bureau of Consumer Protection
   c. Bureau of Economics

4. When the FTC issues a rule, it must do so in such a way as to make the rule applicable to an entire industry and not just to a portion of it.

5. Violations of the FTC rules subject the individuals or firms responsible for the violation to:
    a. fines
    b. temporary restraining orders or preliminary injunctions
    c. civil lawsuits (in some cases)

6. If after investigation the FTC staff believe a business has engaged in an unfair or deceptive practice:
    a. a voluntary admission or consent order will be sought
    b. should there be no such admission or consent order, a formal complaint is filed with an administrative law judge
    c. appeals from the judge's decision can be made to the full commission, which, upon a finding of a violation, issues a cease-and-desist order
    d. appeals of the commission's decision can be made within sixty days to a federal court of appeals

7. The FTC will, upon request, issue nonbinding advisory opinions on the legality of proposed business activities.

Unfair Trade Practices

8. The Federal Trade Commission Act, as amended by the Wheeler-Lea Act, prohibits trade practices that are unfair or deceptive. An advertisement is deceptive if it contains a material misrepresentation and would likely mislead an ordinary purchaser, acting reasonably under the circumstances, at whom the advertisement is directed or by whom it is expected to be read or received. A firm can be held in violation of the act even though it did not *intend* to deceive the public.

9. According to Section 5 of the Federal Trade Commission Act, advertising is unfair if it:
    a. offends public policy
    b. is immoral, unethical, or unscrupulous
    c. causes material or substantial harm to the consumer

10. The FTC requires a firm that advertises a product to keep on file data that support its claims regarding the quality, performance, and comparative price of its product.

11. The FTC can receive complaints from the consumers of products that fall under its jurisdiction and also can receive complaints from the competitors of the firm that makes those products. It is not required to take any action with respect to those complaints, however.

Remedies for Deceptive and Unfair Advertising

12. When conducting proceedings involving the adjudication of advertising issues, the FTC has the power to:
    a. issue cease-and-desist orders (injunctive relief)
    b. order a firm to issue corrective advertising

Deceptive Packaging and Labeling

13. The FTC requires that the package or label of a consumer product must bear the following information:
    a. the name and address of the manufacturer, packer, or distributor of the product
    b. the net quantity, which must be conspicuously placed on the front of the package
    c. an accurate description of what is contained in the package

Consumer Protection Laws

14. The Consumer Product Safety Act provides a framework for regulating potentially unsafe consumer products. The Consumer Product Safety Commission sets safety standards for consumer products and is empowered to ban those which it believes pose an unreasonable risk.

15. The Consumer Leasing Act imposes various requirements on lessors of consumer products leased primarily for personal, family, or household purposes.

16. The Consumer Credit Protection Act requires that a consumer who buys a commodity on credit must be provided with information concerning the cost of the credit. The Act prohibits unfair treatment of consumers in connection with credit applications and debt collection.

17. The Truth-in-Lending Act requires creditors to disclose to a consumer-debtor the terms and conditions of the credit being extended to him or her *before* such credit is actually provided.

18. A consumer credit transaction is one in which credit of less than $25,000 is provided to a consumer (a natural person) for personal, family, or household use.

19. The Truth-in-Lending Act requires those persons or firms that regularly extend consumer credit in the ordinary course of their business to make certain disclosures to the consumer-debtor, including the finance charge and the annual percentage rate (APR).

20. Pursuant to the terms of the Truth-in-Lending Act:
   a. the terms and conditions of credit must be disclosed in a clear and conspicuous manner and must be set out in a meaningful sequence
   b. nonrequired information may be disclosed provided it does not confuse the consumer
   c. the creditor must provide the consumer with a copy of the disclosure requirements at the time of disclosure of the credit information

21. Restrictions on advertising are imposed by the Truth-in-Lending Act and Regulation Z. One of the restrictions provides that lenders or sellers are not permitted to advertise terms of credit that are not usually or regularly extended to customers.

22. The Fair Credit Reporting Act requires consumer-credit reporting agencies to use reasonable procedures to meet the needs of lenders and at the same time to maintain the confidentiality, accuracy, and relevancy of the records they keep.

23. Consumer reporting agencies are regulated by the Fair Credit Reporting Act.

24. The rights of a consumer about whom a credit report has been requested or issued include the following:
   a. credit reports may not include inaccurate or obsolete information
   b. the consumer has a right to be notified that a reporting agency has relied on adverse information when credit has been denied
   c. upon request, the consumer has a right of disclosure

25. Remedies that are available to the FTC and consumers in dealing with violations of the Fair Credit Reporting Act include:
   a. cease-and-desist orders
   b. criminal sanctions
   c. civil actions for compensatory and punitive damages

The Equal Credit Opportunity Act

26. The Equal Credit Opportunity Act prohibits a creditor from discriminating against an applicant for credit on the basis of that person's:
   a. sex
   b. marital status
   c. race
   d. color
   e. age
   f. national origin
   g. receipt of public assistance
   h. exercise of rights under the Consumer Protection Act

27. The Equal Credit Opportunity Act can be enforced by the individual who has been adversely affected by the actions of a creditor or by the Federal Trade Commission. Actual and punitive damages can be awarded.

28. The Equal Credit Opportunity Act requires that notice be given of the lender's action, including disclosure of the basic provisions of ECOA, the name and address of the compliance agency, and the specific reasons for the action taken, or disclosure of the right to receive such a statement.

The Fair Debt Collection Practices Act

29. The Fair Debt Collection Act provides that:
    a. a debt collector may contact a person other than the debtor, the debtor's family, or the debtor's attorney only for the purpose of trying to locate the debtor
    b. a debt collector must contact the debtor only at convenient times
    c. a debt collector may not contact a consumer-debtor at all if he or she is aware that the debtor is represented by an attorney
    d. debt collectors may not engage in abusive, deceptive, misleading, or unfair conduct
    e. collections that require liens on real property may be pursued only where the property is located.

30. The Act does not apply to those companies that do their own debt collection.

31. The Act can be enforced either by the individual who has been adversely affected by the conduct of the debt collector or by the Federal Trade Commission. Actual damages, additional damages up to $1,000, attorney fees, and court costs may be awarded in connection with violations of the Act.

Ethics Box: Infomercials

32. Infomercials are an increasingly popular means of selling a particular product. Typically, several people sit around with a media star and discuss the positive attributes of a product. Sometimes these products are blatantly misrepresented. However, regardless of whether this deception occurs, infomercials raise interesting ethical questions about the way in which consumers are persuaded to engage in specific market activities.

Ethics Box: Ethics and Advertising

33. Television advertising directed toward children is particularly susceptible to claims of unfairness due to the alleged inability of children to separate puffing claims from reality. Ethically the actions of others beside the advertisers should be considered in this matter, including the television networks, researchers, and parents. It would seem that there exists the difficult question of what is the proper balance between the obligations of parents toward their children and those of the advertisers and networks in targeting children as viewers.

Ethics Box: Ethics and Bank Lending

34.   The Truth-in-Lending Act requires certain disclosures to be made in the extension and advertising of consumer credit. Ethical questions, however, can still arise regarding the obligations of lenders or sellers on credit who have superior knowledge to explain the possible risks in a transaction and the meaning of contractual provisions. Such issues have recently been raised concerning the advertising of home equity loans and the use of variable interest rates with no cap. Persons have used their home equity as collateral to obtain consumer loans. When the variable interest rates increase too much, some persons have then been unable to make the required payments. Their default in payments can cause the lender to begin foreclosure proceedings against the debtor's home.

MAJOR POINTS OF CASES

Kraft, Inc. v. *FTC* (p. 1032)

The Federal Trade Commission Act stipulates that it is unlawful for a company to engage in unfair or deceptive commercial practices. To the extent that commercial claims are false or misleading as well as material to prospective buyers, they are not permissible under FTC regulations. The FTC found this to be the case with Kraft, Inc.'s "Skimp" ads, a part of their "Five Ounces of Milk" campaign.

In this case, the court upheld the FTC's ban on these ads. The court states that Kraft's commercials were deceptive, because they strongly implied that the amount of milk used in their cheese made their slices superior to imitation and substitute cheeses in calcium content, which was not the case. The court further stated that the claims made by Kraft were material to buyers in that there was a nationwide concern for calcium deficiency and a great number of people expressed that they bought Kraft Singles because of their calcium content.

Federal Trade Commission v. *Mary Carter Paint Co., et al.* (p. 1034)

The Supreme Court stated in this case that the guides established by the Federal Trade Commission with reference to two-for-the-price-of-one offers require that the sales price for the two items be the customary or usual price for a single item of the same product. In the event that the advertiser had not sold the item before, then the standard to be applied to the pricing practice is the "usual and customary price for one in the relevant trade areas." The Court also stated that the FTC is often in the best position to determine if an advertising practice is deceptive under the Federal Trade Commission Act.

In reviewing the facts, the Court found that Mary Carter had no history of selling single cans of paint and that when it purported to sell two cans of paint for the price of one, it was merely allocating the cost of both cans to a single can of paint instead. Such advertisement was a misrepresentation, according to the Court. With respect to whether it was deceptive within the meaning of the Federal Trade Commission Act, however, the Court remanded the case to the Commission for a clarification of its order.

Warner Lambert v. Federal Trade Commission (p. 1036)

The court in this case stated that the Federal Trade Commission does possess the authority to order a company to issue corrective advertisements in order to remedy previous incorrect or unjustified advertisements. It also held that according to the rulings of the U.S. Supreme Court, the FTC is the expert body in the field of unfair or deceptive trade practices and that it has wide discretion in rendering judgments. Therefore, unless the remedy selected by the Commission in a particular situation has "no reasonable relation to the unlawful practices found to exist," the court should not interfere with the Commission's judgment.

In considering the facts of this case, the court held that the corrective remedy selected by the Commission was reasonable and appropriate under the circumstances and permitted the Commission's order to stand. It did, however, modify the language to be used in the corrective advertisement.

Williams v. Homestake Mortgage Co. (p. 1042)

The Truth-in-Lending Act (TILA) provides a framework of procedures to be followed in the event that an obligor wishes to rescind a loan. These procedures are designed to place the consumer in a stronger bargaining position than that in which she or he would otherwise be. However, the court ruled that, according to the Truth in Lending Simplification and Reform Act, another goal of these procedures is "to return the parties most nearly to the position they held prior to entering into the transaction." To ensure the attainment of the second goal, the court stated that Congress gave the courts the power to impose equitable conditions "at any time during the rescission process".

In this case, the court ruled, despite TILA's concern for the bargaining position of the consumer, it had a right to impose equitable conditions on the rescission process between Williams and Homestake Mortgage Co. The court reversed the decision formerly in favor of Williams and remanded the case for a determination of whether Ms. Williams should be required to return all or part of the loan proceeds. Without an imposition of equitable conditions, the statutory guidelines of TILA stipulated that she should be able to.

Bloom v. I. C. Systems, Inc. (p. 1046)

In this case, the court ruled on the scope of protection afforded by the Federal Debt Collection Practices Act (FDCPA). The language of the Act protects consumer and not business debt. The court ruled that in determining between these two types of debt, the debts must be examined in terms of end uses. If the debt is incurred for personal, family, or household purposes it is consumer in nature; otherwise, it is business.

Applying this ruling to the facts of the case, the court held that the plaintiff Bloom could not claim protection under the FDCPA for I.C. Systems, Inc.'s actions concerning his debt. Because end use is the important factor in characterizing debt, the court found not to be cogent the plaintiff's argument that his debt was consumer in nature because it was loaned to him by a friend informally for personal reasons. The court stated that the important point was that Bloom used the money to start up his software business. Furthermore, the court ruled that I.C. Systems, Inc. was not liable for its actions under the Fair Credit Reporting Act, because the information they disclosed was neither false nor supplied with malicious intent.

PRACTICAL CONSIDERATIONS

While Regulation Z was promulgated for the purpose of providing the public with specific information regarding the cost of credit extended to a borrower, the forms that have been developed are so complex that the average person is unable to comprehend their contents.

Most people's reaction to the requisite disclosure form is courteous acceptance followed by moderate to total confusion. It seems that most people tuck the disclosure statement away in some spot where it can be quickly forgotten.

The concept of full disclosure of the cost of credit and a detailed presentation of the items that determine the cost of that credit is well conceived. Until the public is educated in the law's subtleties, however, the full effect of the Truth-in-Lending laws will not be realized.

SELF TEST

True-False Questions

_____ 1. Litigation initiated by the Federal Trade Commission before the Trade Board is conducted by an administrative law judge.

_____ 2. Advisory opinions issued by the Federal Trade Commission regarding the legality of a firm's activity are binding on the Commission.

_____ 3. The Federal Trade Commission can issue rules that affect an entire industry.

_____ 4. The Federal Trade Commission forbids well-known personalities to endorse products they don't personally use.

_____ 5. Loans that are required to be repaid by means of a single payment can never be considered to be closed-end credit agreements.

_____ 6. The Truth-in-Lending Act is exclusively a disclosure statute.

_____ 7. A statement concerning credit made by a salesman to a specific client is considered to be an advertisement for credit under the Truth-in-Lending Act.

_____ 8. Before asking a credit reporting agency for an investigative report on an applicant for credit, a creditor must notify the applicant of his or her intention to use the services of the agency.

_____ 9. The Equal Credit Opportunity Act prohibits a creditor from discriminating against an applicant for credit on the basis of the applicant's employment status.

_____ 10. A debt collector may never contact a neighbor of a delinquent creditor in connection with the collection of a debt.

Multiple-Choice Questions

_____ 11. The chairman of the Federal Trade Commission is appointed by the President of the United States for a period of:
   a. three years
   b. five years
   c. seven years
   d. ten years
   e. fourteen years

_____ 12. The bureau of the Federal Trade Commission that investigates potentially unfair or deceptive practices is the:
   a. Bureau of Consumer Protection
   b. Bureau of Competition
   c. Bureau of Economics
   d. Bureau of Standards
   e. a and d are both correct

_____ 13. The Federal Trade Commission may investigate a trade practice that is:
   a. offensive to public policy
   b. deceptive
   c. unscrupulous
   d. only a and b are correct
   e. a, b, and c are all correct

_____ 14. In proceedings involving the adjudication of unfair and deceptive advertising practices, the Federal Trade Commission has the power to:
   a. order a firm to issue corrective advertising
   b. order a firm to pay money damages to a consumer who sustains a loss as a result of the advertisement
   c. issue a cease-and-desist order
   d. only a and c are correct
   e. a, b, and c are all correct

15. A consumer commodity that is packaged or labeled must bear which of the following items of information?
    a. the name and address of the manufacturer
    b. the year in which the product was made
    c. the weight of the product
    d. only a and b are correct
    e. a, b, and c are all correct

16. A consumer credit transaction is a loan made to a natural person for personal, family, or household use in an amount that is less than:
    a. $10,000
    b. $15,000
    c. $25,000
    d. $30,000
    e. $50,000

17. Which of the following transactions is exempt from the application of the federal Truth-in-Lending Act?
    a. a loan to a corporation
    b. a personal consumer loan in the amount of $30,000
    c. a loan that must be repaid in three payments
    d. only a and c are exempt
    e. a, b, and c are all exempt

18. Which of the following constitutes an open-end credit arrangement?
    a. a bank credit card
    b. the purchase of an automobile where the buyer is required to make thirty-six equal payments in order to pay the credit amount
    c. a credit account with a department store
    d. only a and c are correct
    e. a, b, and c are all correct

19. Under the Fair Credit Reporting Act, in most cases information relating to a person's credit is considered obsolete (except in connection with information related to bankruptcy) if it is older than:
    a. five years
    b. seven years
    c. nine years
    d. ten years
    e. fifteen years

_____ 20. The Equal Credit Opportunity Act prohibits discrimination against an applicant for credit based on:
    a. the applicant's receipt of public assistance
    b. a filing of a bankruptcy petition by the applicant three years before the application for credit
    c. the applicant's divorce six months before the application for credit
    d. only a and c are correct
    e. a, b, and c are all correct

Completion Questions

21. The bureau of the Federal Trade Commission that investigates unfair or deceptive practices is the Bureau of _____.

22. _____ _____ credit is a credit arrangement in which credit is extended for a specified period of time and in which the number of payments and the total amount due to the creditor have been agreed upon by the borrower.

23. The abbreviation APR stands for _____ _____ _____.

24. In order for a transaction to be considered a consumer credit transaction, the amount of credit extended to the borrower must be less than $ _____.

25. The _____ _____ _____ Act requires creditors to make certain disclosures regarding the terms and conditions of consumer credit arrangements before extending credit to a consumer-debtor.

Chapter 56

FAIR EMPLOYMENT PRACTICES

Within the scope of laws governing business, a major concern for any business is equal employment opportunity law. This type of law, to some extent, determines for businesses who can and cannot be hired or fired and for what reasons. A basic premise of equal employment opportunity law is that fundamental principles such as fairness and economic opportunity should be embedded in the way we think about and indeed carry out employment practices. Because of the scope of equal employment opportunity law, it is important not only to business executives but also to employees, union leaders, and all citizens in general.

This chapter examines the various federal statutes that prohibit discriminatory employment practices. Included in this examination is an explication of the meaning of discrimination. Also, the material discusses the nondiscrimination rule as well as its exceptions. Furthermore, the text covers equal employment opportunity principles such as affirmative action and reasonable accommodation. Finally, it closes with a discussion of the specific protection afforded by equal employment opportunity statutes.

CHAPTER OBJECTIVES

After reading Chapter 56 of the text and studying the related materials presented in this chapter of the Student Mastery Guide, you will understand:

1. The basic laws governing equal employment opportunity.
2. The meaning of discrimination.
3. Exceptions to the nondiscrimination rule.
4. Equal employment opportunity principles such as affirmative action and reasonable accommodation.
5. The specific protections of equal employment opportunity law such as race, national origin, religion, sex, age, and disability.

MAJOR POINTS TO REMEMBER

An Overview of Federal Statutory Law

1. Important federal civil rights laws promoting equal employment opportunity practices include:
   a. Title VII of the Civil Rights Act
   b. Civil Rights Act of 1866
   c. Executive Order 11246
   d. Age Discrimination in Employment Act
   e. Americans With Disabilities Act
   f. Family and Medical Leave Act

The Meaning of Discrimination: Disparate Treatment and Disparate Impact

2. Because federal statutes generally fail to define the meaning of discrimination, the U.S. Supreme Court has developed the disparate treatment and disparate impact models for determining whether unlawful discrimination has occurred.

3. The disparate treatment model of analysis addresses cases where discrimination is overt or intentional. To establish a prima facie case of unlawful discrimination under this model, the plaintiff must prove the following considerations:
    a. that he or she is a member of a protected group
    b. that he or she applied for and was qualified for the job the employer had open
    c. that despite his or her qualifications, the individual was rejected for the job
    d. that the employer continued looking for others with the individual's qualifications after rejecting that individual

    If the individual proves these considerations, then the employer is required to state a legitimate nondiscriminatory reason for rejecting the individual. If she or he can do this, then the individual plaintiff must show how the employer's stated reason is a pretext for discrimination.

4. The disparate impact model addresses discrimination that is not intentional, and it was designed to ferret out the discrete discriminator who uses practices having a discriminatory effect.

5. To make a case for discrimination under this model, the individual must show that an employer's practice or policy excludes members of a protected group. The employer can answer this charge with the justification of business necessity. The individual can then return with a demonstration that there is a less discriminatory alternative reasonably available to the employer for the same objective.

Exceptions to the Nondiscrimination Rule

6. Title VII provides a number of exceptions to the nondiscrimination rule, including:
    a. professionally developed tests to discriminate among employees as long as the test is not intended to discriminate against a protected group
    b. bona fide seniority systems
    c. discrimination on the basis of sex, national origin, or religion where each of these is a bona fide occupational qualification reasonably necessary for the normal operation of the employer's business

7. The bona fide occupational qualification exception justifies an employer's discrimination if the employer can show that all or substantially all of the members of a protected group who are excluded from the job are not able to perform that job's essential duties.

Other EEO Principles: Affirmative Action and Reasonable Accommodation

8. The purpose of affirmative-action programs is to effectuate equal employment opportunity laws.

9. Under affirmative-action programs, employers are required to:
   a. eliminate all current discriminatory practices and conditions
   b. take affirmative steps to increase the number of women and minority group members employed by the company

10. Under affirmative-action programs, employers are required to evaluate their work force to determine whether women and minority-group members are appropriately represented in all positions.

11. An essential characteristic of affirmative-action plans is the determination by the employer of goals and timetables and the relativeness of those goals and timetables to local work forces.

12. Affirmative-action plans voluntarily adopted by public-sector employers have been upheld by the Supreme Court as not being in violation of Title VII or the equal-protection clause of the Constitution, but the use of specific quotas in such plans has been held invalid.

13. Affirmative-action plans that also give preference to women in employment opportunities have been held valid by the Supreme Court.

14. The concept of "reasonable" accommodation found in Title VII of the Civil Rights Act stipulates that an employer has an obligation to accommodate particular needs of protected groups to the extent that such an accommodation does not levy "undue hardship" on the business.

Race

15. A major difference between the Civil Rights Act of 1866 and Title VII is that someone charging racial discrimination under the latter must file a charge with the EEOC.

16. Racial harassment is forbidden by both Title VII and the Civil Rights Act of 1866.

Natural Origin

17. Title VII is protection against discrimination on the basis of national origin does not encompass the protection of people against discrimination on the basis of citizenship.

18. Certain qualifications for a job, such as that the employee speaks a particular language or is a certain height and weight, can be deemed discriminatory on the basis of national origin under the disparate impact model and must be justified by the employer.

19. The Immigration Reform and Control Act prohibits employers from knowingly employing aliens who are not authorized to work in the United States.

Religion

20. Religious protections are afforded to employees in two ways:
    a. employers are prohibited from discriminating against either employees or applicants on the basis of religion
    b. employers are required to reasonably accommodate an employee's religious practice or belief to the extent that such an accommodation does not cause undue hardship on the employer's business operations.

Sex

21. Title VII of the Civil Rights Act forbids sex-based discrimination in nearly all aspects of employment. Within the scope of Title VII's protection, employers cannot discriminate against employees on the basis of pregnancy, childbirth, or related medical conditions.

22. The Equal Pay Act focuses on sex-based employment compensation. Employers cannot pay men and women differently for jobs that are essentially the same. Title VII's non-discrimination exemptions also hold for the Equal Pay Act.

23. There are two types of sexual discrimination under EEOC guidelines:
    a. quid pro quo sexual harassment occurs when an employer acts in a sexual manner towards an employee and then makes submission or rejection to such conduct either a condition of employment or a factor affecting employment decisions affecting the individual.
    b. hostile work environment occurs when a workplace has a hostile climate because of the pattern of conduct that is harassing to members of one sex.

Ethics Box: Ethics and Sexual Harassment

24. Although law is playing an ever-increasing role in regulating sexual harassment, responsibility for monitoring such conduct at the workplace continues to rest primarily with managers. Their ethical values determine the workplace environment concerning sexual issues.

Age

25. Under the Age Discrimination in Employment Act (ADEA), workers who are forty years of age and older cannot be discriminated against on the basis of their age. Courts use both the disparate treatment and the disparate impact models to determine the existence of such discrimination.

26. Defenses against age discrimination suits include:
    a. age is a bona fide occupational qualification (BFOQ)
    b. the employer used reasonable factors other than age in determining the employment status of a worker
    c. the employer followed a bona fide seniority system in making employment decisions
    d. the plaintiff was discharged or disciplined for good cause.

Ethics Box: The Incompetent Prof

27. A situation in which an employee is quite incompetent and happens also to be over forty years of age creates an ethical quandary for the parties concerned. The employer wants to get rid of the incompetent employee but faces the challenge of developing a legal "excuse" the truth of which is indisputably nonexistent. Also, to the extent that an employee is cognizant of his or her incompetence, the employee faces this question: Should I stay on my job and remain gainfully employed, which the ADEA will allow me to do or should I depart for the good of all concerned?

Disability

28. The Americans With Disabilities Act prohibits discrimination against disabled workers in the areas of job applications, hiring, promotion, termination, compensation, training, benefits, at cetera in places of employment with fifteen or more employees. Employers are also required to make reasonable accommodations to the needs of existing or potentially disabled employees but do not have to hire an employee whose disability prevents him or her from performing essential aspects of the job, even with reasonable accommodation.

The Family and Medical Leave Act

29. The scope of the Family and Medical Leave Act covers employers with 50 or more employees, each of which must be employed for at least 12 months and not less than 1250 hours to be entitled to protection under the Act.

30. Under this Act, qualified employees are entitled to unpaid family leave of 12 weeks in any 12-month period in the event of the birth or adoption of a child, the serious health condition of a family member, or their own serious health condition. An employee is also entitled to job restoration at his or her former position if he or she is salaried, is among the top 107 of the employees within 75 miles of the facility, and his or her restoration will not cause the employer economic hardship.

MAJOR POINTS OF CASES

Griggs v. *Duke Power Co.* (p. 1055)

The Supreme Court indicated in this case that the objective of Congress in enacting the 1964 Civil Rights Act was to achieve equality in connection with employment opportunities and to eliminate those practices that have previously favored white employees over others. It also stated that an employment practice that excluded African-Americans was to be prohibited unless the policy could be shown to be related to job performance.

On the basis of the record before the court, it held that the requirements of completion of high school and a satisfactory score on a general intelligence test bore no demonstrable relationship to successful performance of jobs for which these criteria were used. As a result, the practice could not be continued or permitted.

Johnson v. Transportation Agency, Santa Clara County, California (p. 1057)

The Court in this case determined the extent to which employers under voluntary affirmative action plans may figure sex as a relevant factor in employment decisions. The plaintiff charged that he was passed over for promotion strictly on the basis of his sex, while the employer argued that the hiring of a woman instead of the plaintiff was consistent with the Transportation Agency's goal of remedying inequities in employment patterns through affirmative action hiring and promotion. The defendant noted that both applicants were deemed to be qualified by the interviews, and that sex was only one factor in determining who should be promoted.

The Court upheld the defendant's actions on a number of bases. First, Steelworkers v. Weber upheld the legitimacy of voluntary affirmative action plans designed to eliminate racial injustices, which the Court said applied to sexual injustices as well. Secondly, because both applicants were qualified, the Court ruled that it was appropriate to take one single factor, namely, sex, into account in making the final promotional decision.

United Auto Workers v. Johnson Control, Inc. (p. 1061)

The Court ruled in this case that employer policies designed to protect employees are not acceptable if they are sex-based even if they are benign. The Court stated that employers must direct their concerns about a women's ability to perform her job safely and efficiently to those aspects of the woman's job-related activities.

Applying this ruling to the facts of the case, the Court found Johnson Controls, Inc.'s policy of not hiring fertile women in occupations in which employees are subjected to substantial exposures to lead discrimatory. The Court noted that no policy was formed in relation to men whose reproductive system can also be harmed by such exposure. Also, the Court pointed to the Pregnancy Discrimination Act (PDA) of 1978. This Act brought pregnancy-based discrimination into the purview of sex discrimination itself.

Harris v. Forklift Systems (p. 1063)

In this case, the Court considered the definition of a hostile or abusive work environment in determining the validity of sexual harassment suits. It held that for a work environment to be rendered hostile two conditions must exist. First, the work environment must be objectively hostile; i.e. any reasonable person would consider it as such. Secondly, the employee him or herself must perceive the work environment to be hostile. Furthermore, whether a work environment is hostile, the Court stated, is determined by looking at all of the circumstances of which the effect on the employees's psychological well-being is but one.

Applying this ruling, the Court found Charles Hardy's conduct towards the plaintiff to be sexual harassment. Not only did Hardy's behavior create an environment so hostile as to prompt the plaintiff to leave her job, the Court also judged that such behavior would cause any reasonable employee to respond as the plaintiff had responded.

SELF-TEST

True-False Questions

_____ 1. The Civil Rights Act of 1866 prohibits federal contractors from discriminating against either employees or applicants on the basis of race, sex, religion, or national origin.

_____ 2. The disparate treatment model of discrimination addresses overt discrimination.

_____ 3. Reasonable accommodation protects all employees except those who are disabled.

_____ 4. The Civil Rights Act of 1866 is limited to intentional discrimination.

_____ 5. Title VII's protections against discrimination on the basis of national origin includes a reference to citizenship.

_____ 6. Courts and the EEOC take a narrow view of what constitutes religious beliefs.

_____ 7. The Equal Pay Act protects women from compensation discrimination.

_____ 8. The Equal Pay Act exempts wage differences based on any factor other than sex.

_____ 9. The Pregnancy Discrimination Act of 1978 has no BFOQ exemption.

_____ 10. For a work environment to be rendered hostile, women must suffer psychological damage from someone's unwanted sexual advances.

_____ 11. Executive Order 11246 applies to:
   a. all contractors
   b. all federal contractors
   c. all government contracts
   d. unions
   e. none of the above

_____ 12. Which of the following is/are not (an) exception(s) to the nondiscrimination rule?
   a. bona fide seniority systems
   b. professionally developed ability tests
   c. BFOQ (bona fide occupation qualification)
   d. all of the above
   e. none of the above

_____ 13. All of the following are true of legal affirmative action plans, except:
   a. the plan is generally prepared by someone with responsibility for the company's human resource management
   b. the plans are required for federal government contractors
   c. utilization analysis is the first step in preparing the plan
   d. hiring quotas are a primary characteristic of affirmative action plans
   e. companies sometimes adopt affirmative action plans voluntarily

_____ 14. The doctrine of reasonable accommodation stipulates that:
   a. employers must hire a reasonable number of women and minorities
   b. employers need only to hire women and minorities at a rate 90% of their composition of the workforce
   c. an employer has the duty to accommodate the special needs of targeted groups to the extent that such accommodation is not a grievous burden for the business
   d. employers need only to hire women and minorities who are reasonable
   e. none of the above

15. All of the following characteristics are afforded protection under Title VII of the Civil Rights Act, except:
    a. race
    b. sex
    c. age
    d. national origin
    e. none of the above

16. Included in Title VII's protection against national origin discrimination are:
    a. an employee or applicant's marriage association
    b. an employee or applicant's membership in organizations promoting national groups
    c. an employee or applicant's citizenship
    d. all of the above
    e. a and b only

17. Which of the following is the most extensively litigated area involving religion?
    a. blatant discrimination on the part of the employer
    b. discrimination against those professing a belief in the Jewish religion
    c. work scheduling issues regarding an employer's duty to accommodate an employer's religious practices
    d. discrimination on the part of fellow employees
    e. discrimination against those adhering to the Islamic religion

18. Outside the purview of Title VII's protections relating to sex discrimination is/are:
    a. pregnancy
    b. medical conditions related to pregnancy and childbirth
    c. virtually all aspects of employment
    d. b and c only
    e. none of the above

19. Which of the following is/are not type(s) of sexual harassment?
    a. quid pro quo
    b. quo qua quo
    c. that which stems from a hostile work environment
    d. all of the above
    e. none of the above

_____ 20. The ADEA protects employees in what age group
        a. thirty to fifty-nine
        b. forty-five to seventy-five
        c. forty and older
        d. fifty and older
        e. fifty-five and older

Completion Questions

21. The American with Disabilities Act applies to employers with _____ or more employees.

22. The most comprehensive of the equal opportunity laws is _____ of the Civil Rights Act.

23. To determine whether there has been overtly unlawful discrimination, the court employs the _____ _____ model.

24. The doctrine stipulating that an employer must be sensitive to the special needs of protected groups is known as _____ _____.

25. The _____ _____ _____ provides for equal pay for equal work.

Chapter 57

ENVIRONMENTAL LAW

For much of United States history, concern for environmental quality resided in a very narrow scope of interest. However, with the arrival of the 1970s, this scope broadened greatly as people realized that air, water, and land degradation are not necessary consequences of progress. With this realization, have come a body of regulations commonly known as environmental law, whose intent is both to clean up and to protect the environment.

This chapter explains environmental law, especially it's implications for business. After discussing the history of environmental regulation as well as the primary agent of environmental law enforcement, the Environmental Protection Agency, the chapter identifies the two pieces of legislation from which our nation's policies for protection of the environment have derived. These are the National Environmental Policy Act and the Pollution Prevention Control Act. Then, the chapter provides a lengthy discussion of the legislative acts regulating air and water quality as well as hazardous waste and toxic substances.

When reading the chapter, you should examine the nature of United States environmental law both extrinsically and intrinsically. Concerning the former type of consideration, it is important to understand how environmental law affects business operations. Also, you should examine the laws themselves. Consider not only what the laws do, but also what they do not do.

CHAPTER OBJECTIVES

After reading chapter 57 of the text and studying the related materials in this chapter of the Student Mastery Guide, you will understand:

1. The history and development of environmental law in the United States, including:
   a. The Environmental Protection Agency
   b. The National Environmental Policy Act
   c. The Pollution Prevention Act
2. Environmental Law's implications for business
3. The fundamental nature of environmental law in the United States, including the regulation of:
   a. water
   b. air
   c. hazardous waste and toxic substances

MAJOR POINTS TO REMEMBER

History of Environmental Regulation

1. Throughout most of their nation's history, Americans have not been very concerned with the health of the environment. The first attempts to control pollution were made through the tort action of nuisance, which targeted the unreasonable interference with someone else's use and enjoyment of his or her land.

503

Although this doctrine would seem to be a more than adequate remedy for environmental health, Boomer v. Atlantic Cement Company demonstrated otherwise. The court ruled that if the tort action of nuisances is to be applied, then the benefits of the injunction must outweigh its harm. With inadequate knowledge about the true costs of pollution, the court asserted that the injunction's potential harm to the company had far more gravity than its benefits.

2.   The 1970s was the environmental decade for the United States. Following important books by Rachel Carson and Paul Ehrlich as well as the Santa Barbara Oil Spill in 1969, 27 environmental statutes were passed between 1969 and 1979. The vast majority of these laws were "command and control" or "end of pipe" regulations. Typically, failure to install technology or limit the emission of pollutants results in the imposition of fines under the standards.

3.   The massive deregulation of the 1980's weakened environmental protection, especially because this deregulation involved budget reductions for agencies like the EPA. Yet, by the close of the decade, Congress began to run counter to these policies, strengthening environmental laws up for reauthorization.

4.   The 1990s thus far have witnessed the sustainment of the reinvigoration of environmental concern but with a new emphasis away from command and control strategies and toward market forces and voluntary programs as avenues toward environmental protection.

Enforcement of Environmental Law and Policy

5.   The EPA, our nation's largest federal agency, has the primary responsibility for the promulgation and enforcement of environmental regulations. Originally conceived of as an integrated force in the protection of the myriad aspects of the environment, the EPA failed in meeting this expectation. However, in July, 1993 EPA administrator Carol Browner made the move toward integration by moving all enforcement offices into one main office.

6.   Expecting careful scrutiny by the EPA, many businesses are following what is known as preventative law. Corporate compliance with environmental regulations is made more likely when businesses form policies and appoint officers to facilitate this compliance. Knowing the environmental regulations as well as making compliance with them a primary goal and standard can save businesses from the fines that non-compliance entails.

The Policy Acts

7.   The National Environmental Policy Act (NEPA) has been regarded by many as the most influential piece of environmental regulation. Its primary purpose and effect has been to reform the process by which regulatory agencies make decisions.

8.   Title II under the NEPA is an extremely important provision for it requires the preparation of an Environmental Impact Statement for every major legislative proposal

504

or agency action potentially having a significant impact on the quality of the human environment. The significance of an action's impact is determined by both its context and intensity. In one case, Metropolitan Edison Company v. People Against Nuclear Energy, the court ruled that a consideration of the significance of an action's impact or the human environment does not encompass its impact on the psychological health of community members. Generally, for an action's impact to be "significant" there must be a link to some actual, physical change.

9. In both the business and the environmental community, feelings about the effectiveness of the EIS process are mixed.

Regulating Water Quality

10. One of two pieces of legislation that controls water pollution is the Federal Water Pollution Control Act (FWPCA) which focuses on the quality of water in our waterways. Point source effluent limitations are one way in which this protection is provided. Point sources are distinct places from which pollutants can be discharged into water, while effluents are the outflows from these sources. Effluent limitations dictate the maximum amount of pollutants that can be discharged from a source within a given period of time. The EPA, or any comparable state agencies, provides discharge permits for pollutants, and then it is up to the company's responsibility to monitor their respective discharges and to report any excesses. Currently, effluent limitations must reflect the "best available technology economically achievable" (BAT) for toxic pollutants and the "best conventional pollutant control standard (BCT) for nontoxic pollutants. The EPA does have the authority to grant individual sources variances from BAT standards.

11. The FWPCA also establishes a subsidy program for the construction of publicly owned water treatment plants that meet a state-of-the-art standard and are cost effective.

12. The Safe Drinking Water Act (SDWA) set standards for drinking water supplied by a public water supply system, which is defined as having at least 15 service connections or serving 25 or more persons. Under 1986 amendments, the EPA is required to establish maximum contaminant level goals (MCLG's) as well as maximum contaminant levels (MCL's). The former are levels at which there are no potential adverse health effects, and these levels are that to which we aspire. At the same time, the MCL's are enforceable standards, because they account for the feasibility and cost of adhering to a given standard. Violators uncovered by typically monthly monitorings are punished by administrative fines and orders.

Regulating Air Quality

13. The Clean Air Act promotes protection of both human health and the human environment by regulating the amount of pollutants in the air.

14. National Air Quality Standards (NAAQS's) provide guidelines for air pollution control. Primary standards are set to protect public health, while secondary standards are designed to protect the public welfare. Both of these standards can change upon the attainment of new scientific evidence.

15. Each state is required to submit a state implementation plan (SIP) to the EPA. Such a plan explains how the state will ensure that the pollutants in the air within a state's boundaries will not exceed NAAQS's.

16. In Union Electric Company v. Environmental Protection Agency, the court ruled that claims of technological and economic infeasability are only legitimate in conforming to SIP's to the extent that such claims do not substantially interfere with the prompt attainment of the national air quality standards.

17. The principle of the prevention of significant deterioration (PSD) disallows air quality in areas already in line with NAAQS's from deteriorating to maximum levels of air pollution under these guidelines.

18. Under the 1990 amendments to the Clean Air Act attempts are being made to use market forces to some extent to regulate air pollution. The EPA auctions a given number of sulfur dioxide allowances each year, and these allowances can be either saved, sold, or redeemed. The success of this program cannot be determined at this time.

19. One particular problem in analyzing any aspect of the Clear Air Act is that causal factors like the economic climate and weather conditions also play a role in determining the number of pollutants emitted.

Regulating Hazardous Wastes and Toxic Substances

20. Hazardous wastes and toxic substances have been shown to adversely affect human beings, including inflicting them with cancer, respiratory ailments, skin diseases, and birth defects. Yet, because so many people enjoy the comforts of technology and because there is a lack of scientific knowledge concerning the impact of many chemicals on human health, regulation is a difficult task.

21. The Resource Conservation and Recovery Act (RCRA) regulates waste disposal, not its creation. Under this Act, a manifest program (manifests are a particular type of records) provides a record of the location and amount of hazardous wastes, while also ensuring that such waste is properly transported and disposed. RCRA, in 1984 amendments, made landfills a last resort for the disposal of many types of waste. Although, if stringent enough, the states may enforce this act, the primary enforcer is the EPA.

22. The Comprehensive Environmental Response Compensation and Liability Act of 1980 (CERCLA), as amended by the Super-fund Amendment and Reauthorization Act of 1986 (SARA) is designed to both facilitate the cleaning up of leaks from hazardous waste disposal sites on the National Priorities List (NPL) and provide money for emergency

responses to hazardous waste spills, with the exception of oil. The EPA may sue those parties responsible for the transportation, generation, disposal and storage of waste; however, efforts to recover costs have been less than successful.

23.   The Toxic Substances Control Act (TSCA) regulates toxic substances that are integral parts of some products that we use daily. This regulation affects both existing and newly marketed chemicals. However, those chemicals currently in existence and previously used receive far less attention than new chemicals.

24.   The Federal Insecticide, Fungicide, and Rodenticide Act (FIFRA) regulates the use of pesticides in order to protect human health as well as the human environment. Having been registered and analyzed, pesticides may be used without restriction, restricted to some extent, or disallowed altogether. Pesticides must be registered every 5 years.

MAJOR POINTS OF CASES

Boomer v. *Atlantic Cement Company* (p. 1069)

The court maintained that before the traditional nuisance remedy can be applied (i.e. an injunction to halt pollution), the consequential harms of the injunction must be compared to its consequential benefits. In the event that the harms outweigh the benefits, an injunction to stop business operations (and thus pollution) is not appropriate.

Applying this cost-benefit consideration to the case, the court found that the harm done to Boomer by the Atlantic Cement Company's pollution was not sufficient enough vis-a-vis the costs that would be increased by an injunction to warrant such an injunction. However, the court did grant the plaintiff damages with the express hope that these costs on the Atlantic Cement Company "would itself be a reasonable effective spur to research for improved techniques to minimize nuisance." Thus, while the court was not willing to issue an injunction to stop the cement company's pollution, it did hope that economic incentives in the form of pecuniary damages would minimize this pollution.

Metropolitan Edison Company v. *People Against Nuclear Energy* (p. 1075)

The NEPA requires that when a government agency's actions substantially affects the human environment's quality, that agency must evaluate the "environmental impact" of its proposal. The court maintained that this NEAP requirement is applicable only when an agency's proposal will have <u>environmental</u> effects, which the court construes as being effects on the physical world.

Applying this interpretation of the NEPA, the court ruled against People Against Nuclear Energy's (PANE) contention that the reopening of the Three Mile Island plant should not be allowed because of the psychological harm that it would cause to the people's health. PANE argued that this psychological harm would result from the risk of a nuclear accident. However, the court ruled that a risk of a nuclear accident did not constitute a change in the physical environment but only a potential change. As a result, because PANE's claims to the adverse effects of the reopening were rooted in potential and not actual physical changes in the environment, the court held that these claims were not justifiable under the NEPA.

American Paper Institute v. *Environmental Protection Agency* (p. 1078)

In this case, the court established two principles. First, in determining the "best conventional pollutant control standard" (BCT), the court decided that the EPA must consider an industry cost-effectiveness test as well as a test comparing private industry, costs for reducing its effluent levels with those incurred by publicly owned treatment works (POTW's). At the same time, the court also ruled that under the FWPCA there was no established benchmark for determining the POTW comparison.

Applying these rules to the facts of the case, the court both affirmed and reversed in part the previous ruling. The court upheld the American Paper Institute's grievance that the EPA improperly ignored the industry cost-effectiveness test in determining the paper company's BCT. However, the court reversed the American Paper's Institute's previously upheld claim that the EPA was unjustifiably "arbitrary and capricious" in setting the POTW benchmark. According to the court, the FWPCA made no stipulations either in its legislative history or its actual text about a proper benchmark for the POTW.

Union Electric Company v. *Environmental Protection Agency, et. al.* (p. 1083)

This case related to the Clean Air Act of 1970, NAAQSs, and SIPs. In its decision, the court held that businesses must conform to the eight basic criteria set forth by the Clean Air Act and integrated into SIPs for controlling emissions, regardless of other factors.

Union Electric Company claimed that they could not meet the SIP's emission standards for sulfur dioxide because of economic and technological infeasability. Furthermore, Union Electric made the argument that these technological and economic difficulties arose more than 30 days after the SIP was approved and thus, its petition was valid (normally companies only have 30 days to file petitions for review). However, the court rejected Union Electric's claim on the ground that technological and economic difficulties do not excuse companies from conforming to the emissions criteria found in the Clean Air Act. Quite to the contrary, the court argued, this Act was intended to have a "technology-foreign character", which meant that companies must improve or alter the technological nature of their operations in order to conform to NAAQs.

SELF TEST

True-False Questions

_____ 1. The tort action of nuisance is a sufficient remedy for environmental pollution.

_____ 2. Most environmental statutes formed in the 1970's involved using market forces as well as voluntary programs to protect the environment.

_____   3.   States have the primary responsibility for the promulgation and enforcement of environmental regulations.

_____   4.   The National Environmental Policy Act's (NEPA) primary purpose and effect has been to reform the process by which regulatory agencies make decisions.

_____   5.   As determined by the court, an action must have a direct effect on the physical environment before it can be considered to have an "environmental impact" under the NEPA guidelines.

_____   6.   Under the FWPLA, effluent limitations of pollutants are uniform.

_____   7.   Under the Safe Water Drinking Act, businesses can legitimately appeal compliance to an SIP on the basis of technological and economic infeasability if consideration of this infeasability will not substantially interfere with Congress's primary purpose of promptly attaining national air quality standards.

_____   8.   The 1990 Clean Air Act Amendments are an example of the turn to market forces as a tool for protecting the environment.

_____   9.   The Resource Conversation and Recovery Act focuses on the reduction of waste.

_____   10.   In enforcing the Toxic Substitutes Control Act (TSCA), the EPA makes it a top priority to review chemicals that have been and continue to be in use.

Multiple Choice Questions

_____   11.   What are "command and control" or "end of pipe" regulations?
     a.   Laws dictating that businesses guilty of degrading the environment considerably must be taken over by the federal government.
     b.   Laws dictating that businesses guilty of degrading the environment considerably must be taken over by the state in which such a state is situated.
     c.   Laws mandating standards that if not complied with by a business can result in that business being seized by the EPA and subsequently auctioned off to the highest bidder.
     d.   Laws that mandate standards dictating either technology that must be installed or limits on the emission of pollutants.

_____ 12. The EPA is responsible for what type(s) of pollution?
    a. Air
    b. Water
    c. Pesticides
    d. All of the above
    e. a and c.

_____ 13. Who is required to prepare an EIS?
    a. Businesses
    b. the EPA
    c. the states
    d. those making legislative proposals or taking actions that would have significant impact on the human environment's quality.
    e. the Department of Energy

_____ 14. In determining the BCT for a business, what factors must be considered?
    a. industry cost-effectiveness test
    b. POTW comparison
    c. the amount of toxic pollutants currently emitted
    d. all of the above
    e. a and b only

_____ 15. What types of businesses primarily have been and continue to adopt the principles established by the Coalition for Environmentally Responsible Economics (CERES)?
    a. small, closely held firms
    b. large corporations
    c. businesses making products that in large part are consumed by United States citizens
    d. b and c
    e. a and c

_____ 16. Environmental statutes are driven primarily by
    a. aesthetic considerations
    b. human health considerations
    c. health considerations for all living species
    d. the desire by government to regulate business

17. In not complying to the basic criteria of the national air quality standards, a business's economic and technological considerations are:
    a. always legal justification
    b. sometimes legal justification
    c. never legal justification
    d. not important

18. What principle addresses those areas already in compliance with the air quality standards established by the Clean Air Act of 1970?
    a. MCLG
    b. BPT
    c. NAAQSs
    d. CERES
    e. PSD

19. A major obstacle in evaluating the effectiveness of the Clean Air Act is:
    a. that causal factors such as the economic climate also play a role in shaping the number of pollutants emitted.
    b. that the Act itself has not been around long enough for a thorough analysis to be done
    c. that its amendments changed it so drastically so as to make the Act virtually unrecognizable
    d. that we do not have adequate records about the quality of air before the Act was passed

20. Which Act seeks to reduce the extent to which waste is improperly disposed of?
    a. RCRA
    b. CERECLA, as amended by SARA
    c. TSCA
    d. FIFRA
    e. none of the above

Completion Questions

21. A primary tool for meeting the goals of the 1972 FWPCA amendments was the establishment and enforcement of _____ _____ _____.

22. Air pollutants include _____ _____ and _____ _____.

23. A pollutant especially targeted by the 1990 Clean Air Act Amendments is _____ _____.

24. _____ receive special regulatory treatment.

25. According to the Metropolitan Edison Company decision, _____ _____ is not a proper consideration for an EIS.

Chapter 58

INTERNATIONAL BUSINESS

The importance of international business trade and investment in today's world is ever increasing. All students of business law must be familiar with this area of law for their management educations to be complete. This chapter first discusses the environment of international trade and investment. It then identifies some of the primary sources of law affecting international business transactions. It concludes with separate examinations of the specific legal factors that impact on international trade and investments.

CHAPTER OBJECTIVES

After reading Chapter 58 of the text and studying the related materials in this chapter of the Student Mastery Guide, you will understand:

1. The nature and extent of international business trade and investments
2. The sources of law affecting international business transactions
3. The extraterritorial effects of national laws
4. The issues involved in conducting business transactions with foreign governments
5. The means of conducting, and the laws affecting, international business trade in the form of exports and imports
6. The nature of joint ventures and direct investments, and the laws that impact on these means of making international business investments

MAJOR POINTS TO REMEMBER

The International Environment

1. The United States now imports more goods and services than it exports.

2. International investment by firms is done for economic efficiency, competitiveness, and to avoid protectionist laws. It can involve portfolio investments and direct investments.

3. The increasing volume of international trade and investments can lead to conflicts with host governments. Host governments increasingly have sought to regulate such trade and investments, although there is little uniformity to their actions. Some have banded together in regional associations to deal with international trade and investment issues.

Sources of Law

4. Firms engaged in international business can be subject to:
   a. international law, which is based on custom and practices agreed upon by countries of the world, including those formulated by international organizations and multilateral agreements

b. regional laws, such as those enacted by the European Economic Community and the Andean Common Market

c. the national laws of the affected nations

5. Although attempts are to be made to reasonably interpret U.S. law consistently with international law, irreconcilable conflicts are resolved in U.S. courts by enforcing U.S. law.

6. Five basic principles for determining the jurisdiction of nations to decide international disputes are the:

a. territorial principle - jurisdiction is based on the place of the alleged wrong (used for economic regulation)

b. nationality principle - based on the nationality of the offender

c. protective principle - covers conduct that threatens national security or governmental operations

d. universality principle - custody of an accused criminal of worldwide interest provides jurisdiction

e. personality principle - based on the nationality of the victim

7. Because there are few international forums for resolving business disputes, businesses engaging in international transactions must often contend with national legal systems very different from those to which they are accustomed in their home country. Most national legal systems belong to one of the following major legal systems:

a. Romano-Germanic (civil legal system)

b. Socialist system (USSR and East European countries)

c. Common-law system (U.S., Great Britain, and Australia)

d. Islamic law (Middle Eastern countries)

There are significant differences both procedurally and substantively between these legal systems.

8. Laws of one nation can have extraterritorial effects, such as is the case with U.S. income taxes and antitrust laws.

9. Unlike in the United States, the heads of companies from many nations, particularly Communist nations, are government officials. When transactions involve a government or state-owned company, the enforceability of any resulting contracts can be affected by the doctrines of sovereign immunity and the Act of State doctrine.

International Business Trade

10. Some of the ways to conduct international business are through:

a. exporting

b. importing

c. licenses

d. joint ventures

e. direct investment

11. Exports are sometimes legally restricted for national public-policy reasons by requiring that a license be obtained authorizing a sale to be made to a foreign nation or a buyer therein. The Export Administration Act provides for three types of export licenses, which include a:
    a. general license, which is authorization to export without any application
    b. validated license, which requires an application for a specific product
    c. qualified license, which requires an application for multiple exports

12. The U.S. government has several programs to assist exporters, including the Exporting Trading Company Act of 1982, which provides for the granting of certificates of antitrust immunity upon application. This Act allows companies, including banks, to join together in forming an export trading company that will not be prosecuted for antitrust violations, if certain conditions are satisfied. Tax incentives are also made available to encourage exports from the United States.

13. Restrictions on imports can include bans of certain products, quotas, and tariffs. However, such restrictions are limited in those nations that are signatories of the General Agreement on Tariffs and Trade (GATT) or members of the International Monetary Fund (IMF).

14. Imports can also be subject to nontariff barriers both upon and after entry into a country.
    The nontariff barriers effective upon entry include licenses and foreign exchange controls.
    The nontariff barriers effective subsequent to entry can include procurement policies, taxes, subsidies, country-of-origin designations, and other practices designed to favor local products.

15. International business trade can also be conducted under licenses by which parties in a foreign nation are given the property right to manufacture and sell, or sell, lease, or use products, services, or technical assistance. The rights licensed can include patents, trademarks, copyrights, and designs.

16. Because of the differences in laws between nations, licensing agreements should cover what law is to govern, how and where disputes are to be resolved, and the effect of the agreement on competition.

17. License royalties may be subject to double taxation by the involved countries, unless a tax treaty exists between them.

International Business: Investments

18. International business investments, as an alternative to trade, can be in the form of:
    a. joint ventures
    b. direct investment

19. Joint ventures are the sharing of ownership and control of a limited-purpose business enterprise between two or more parties. They are becoming more common, as domestic laws in many nations become more restrictive of direct investments. These joint ventures involve complex legal issues, particularly regarding the form of the organization and its relationships to the joint venturers.

20. Direct investments in a foreign nation are typically complex. Factors in the source country that affect direct investments include:
    a. foreign investment laws, which may encourage or discourage this activity
    b. the form of business organizations allowed and the relationship to the parent company, such as a branch of the parent, a subsidiary foreign corporation, or a domestic corporation.
    c. foreign-exchange controls
    d. the tax laws of all involved governments
    e. the labor laws regarding wages, benefits, unions, rights to discharge employees, and the percentage of local citizens who must be hired
    f. the safety from the nationalization or expropriation of the local company and its assets
    g. the antitrust laws of the connected nations as well as the extraterritorial application of such laws
    h. the legal protection afforded patents, trademarks, copyrights, and trade secrets

Ethics Box: International Ethics

21. International business trade and investments can give rise to serious ethical questions. Ethical relativism is a concept that states that one is justified in meeting the standards of conduct which exist in a particular nation, even though the same conduct would be deemed unethical in another nation. In contrast, Universalists argue that some fundamental ethical obligations exist regardless of contrary customs or accepted practices in some nations, and that these fundamental obligations must always be met in order to be ethical.

MAJOR POINTS OF CASES

Consolidated Gold Fields PLC v. Minorco, S.A. (p. 1102)

In this case, the court held that the anti-fraud laws of the United States may be given extraterritorial reach if a predominantly foreign transaction has substantial effects within the United States. The court determined that Minorco's failure to disclose to Gold Fields' shareholders its ties to South African companies during its takeover constituted such substantial effects, because 2.5 % of the shareholders were American. This ruling reversed the lower court's decision. The Court of Appeals cited a precedent in which only a fraction of Americans were affected in comparison to the case at hand, but there was still determined to be an effect substantial enough to bring the case under the jurisdiction of U.S. anti-fraudulent laws. The court did abstain from determining whether enforcement jurisdiction should be enforced, because the District Court's record was insufficiently developed. Thus, the case was sent back to the District Court for such a determination.

Timberlane Lumber Co. v. Bank of America (p. 1104)

The primary issue of this case was whether the defendants' conduct, which occurred outside the United States, violated U.S. antitrust laws prohibiting acts and conspiracies that restrain foreign commerce. There is applied a three-part test to determine the extent of federal jurisdiction over claims alleging illegal antitrust behavior outside the United States. The three inquiries to be made are: (1) the effect or intended effect on the foreign commerce of the United States; (2) the type and magnitude of the alleged illegal behavior; and (3) the appropriateness of exercising extraterritorial jurisdiction in light of international comity and fairness, including analysis of (a) the degree of conflict with foreign law or policy; (b) the nationality or allegiance of the parties and the locations of principal places of business of corporations; (c) the extent to which enforcement by either state can be expected to achieve compliance; (d) the relative significance of effects on the United States as compared with those elsewhere; (e) the extent to which there is explicit purpose to harm or effect American commerce; (f) the foreseeability of such effect; (g) the relative importance to the violations charged of conduct within the United States as compared with conduct abroad; and (h) resolving the Seven Factor Test.

The court found that the first two inquiries had been met by the plaintiff, but that all but two of the factors of the third inquiry were against the court exercising jurisdiction. The effect of the defendants' actions in Honduras were minimal on U.S. foreign commerce, but the effect of the U.S. courts exercising jurisdiction could have substantial negative effects in Honduras. Thus, the plaintiff's antitrust suit was correctly dismissed.

International Association of Machinists, Etc. v. OPEC (p. 1106)

The IAM sued OPEC for allegedly engaging in price-fixing activities in violation of the U.S. antitrust laws. The doctrine of sovereign immunity states that the courts of one state generally have no jurisdiction to entertain suits against another state, except when a foreign state is engaged in commercial activities. The court did not find the exception to be applicable, because the control of natural resources has been deemed a governmental act, a view supported by both U.S. law and resolutions of the United Nations.

The Act of State doctrine was also crucial to the decision in this case. It states that a U.S. court will not decide a politically sensitive dispute which would require the court to judge the legality of the sovereign act of a foreign state. This doctrine is observed in order that U.S. courts do not interfere with the foreign-relations policies of the other branches of the U.S. government and the international community. Whereas the doctrine of sovereign immunity is a jurisdictional principle of international law that is recognized by statute in the United States, the Act of State doctrine is a principle of domestic law that recognizes the separation of powers under the U.S. Constitution. Under the Act of State doctrine the U.S. courts should not decide this case, because it could have a dramatic effect on U.S. relations with the member nations of OPEC.

Finally, the U.S. courts should also not decide this case for the reason that, although the alleged acts of OPEC could violate U.S. antitrust laws, these acts are not generally illegal throughout the world. For all these reasons, the court declined to decide this case and dismissed it.

Childcraft Education Corp. v. *United States* (p. 1111)

Tariffs are a tax on products being imported into a nation. They can be ad valorem or a flat rate. The plaintiff in this case is objecting to the product classification by the government of the products it imports, because the ad valorem tariff was much higher for toys than educational machines, and its imports had been classified as toys. The U.S. Court of International Trade upheld the classification, because the items were primarily for the amusement of children, although also educational. This court stated that, if sustained, the plaintiff's argument that, since children learned by using the items, they were educational, would make most products aimed at children educational due to their inherent lack of experience. Plaintiff's position could not be so sustained, and it did not meet the burden of proving that amusement was only an incidental by-product of the educational nature of the items.

PRACTICAL CONSIDERATIONS

As should now be obvious, engaging in international business trade and investments can be very complex. Part of the complexity is the product of having more than one sovereign nation with a legitimate interest in regulating such transactions. The affected nations may have very different legal systems and substantive laws. To minimize the potential risks from these factors, the parties to international business trade and investment transactions should explicitly consider and provide for in their written contracts, among other matters, the following:

1. Choice of Law clauses to define what laws shall govern their contract
2. Choice of Forum clauses to specify the nation's courts in which disputes will be resolved
3. Any alternative dispute-resolution technique and forum for resolving disputes, such as arbitration under the rules of the International Chamber of Commerce

SELF TEST

True-False Questions

_____ 1. Today the United States exports more goods than it imports.

_____ 2. Direct foreign business investments involve the purchase of stocks, bonds, and notes.

_____ 3. A firm does not need to own 100 percent of a foreign company for its investment to be classified a direct investment.

_____ 4. All nations strongly encourage direct business investments by foreign companies.

_____ 5. International business trade and investments are governed solely by national laws of the involved nations.

_____ 6. International laws are in part based on the customs and practices agreed to by nations of the world.

_____ 7. The role of the courts in a common-law legal system and a civil-law legal system are identical.

_____ 8. The legality of the commercial activities of foreign governments can sometimes be determined in the U.S. courts.

_____ 9. The Export Trading Company Act under certain conditions allows companies to export with immunity from prosecution for antitrust violations.

_____ 10. Tariffs can be based on a percentage of the value of imported goods or be a flat-rate tax.

Multiple-Choice Questions

_____ 11. International business investments are made by firms to:
   a. gain greater economic efficiency
   b. maintain or increase market shares
   c. avoid restrictive trade laws
   d. only a and b are correct
   e. a, b, and c are correct

_____ 12. Which U.S. laws can have an extraterritorial effect on companies engaged in international business transactions?
   a. income taxation laws
   b. antitrust laws
   c. both a and b are correct
   d. all laws
   e. no laws

_____ 13. A(n) _____ license for exporting is issued upon application to allow the holder to export multiple products.
   a. general
   b. validated
   c. qualified
   d. patent
   e. multiple

14. Under the sovereign immunity doctrine U.S. courts could have jurisdiction to decide the legality of acts of a foreign government, if those acts are:
   a.   commercial
   b.   governmental
   c.   administrative
   d.   discretionary
   e.   ministerial

15. Which of the following is a nontariff barrier to imports?
   a.   licenses
   b.   foreign-exchange controls
   c.   required country-of-origin designations
   d.   only a and b are correct
   e.   a, b, and c are correct

16. Licensing agreements should provide for:
   a.   which nation's laws will govern it
   b.   which nation's courts will be the forum for resolving disputes
   c.   how disputes are to be resolved
   d.   all of the above are correct
   e.   none of the above is correct

17. When two or more parties join together as co-owners of a business enterprise of a limited nature, they have formed a:
   a.   sole proprietorship
   b.   joint venture
   c.   partnership
   d.   corporation
   e.   subsidiary

18. When a company engages in international business by owning all or a controlling interest in a firm organized in a foreign nation, this is a:
   a.   direct investment
   b.   partnership
   c.   nationalization
   d.   licensing arrangement
   e.   portfolio investment

520

_____ 19. When a nation takes ownership of a company and its assets that were owned by a foreign company without its consent or payment of compensation, this is a case of:
- a. nationalization
- b. expropriation
- c. condemnation
- d. direct investment
- e. none of the above is correct

_____ 20. When considering a direct investment in a foreign nation, which of the following should be analyzed?
- a. foreign-exchange controls
- b. income and other taxes
- c. labor laws
- d. antitrust laws
- e. all of the above

Completion Questions

21. _____ is the nonconsensual, but compensated for, taking of ownership by a sovereign government of a foreign-owned company and its assets.

22. Under the _____ _____ _____ doctrine U.S. courts will not decide the legality of politically sensitive issues involving a foreign nation, if by doing so the courts would likely cause an interference in the foreign relations policies of the United States.

23. In a _____ _____ legal system judicial decisions are recognized as a source of law.

24. Goods that are sold to buyers in foreign nations constitute_____.

25. Laws that restrict the quantity of a product which is allowed to be imported are _____.

Chapter 59

ACCOUNTANTS AND PROFESSIONAL LIABILITY

The chapter traces the law regarding accountants common-law and statutory duties to their clients and society. It first explains the role of generally accepted accounting principles (GAAP) and generally accepted auditing standards (GAAS) in establishing the standards for performing accounting services. This chapter next discusses the contract and tort liability of accountants as well as the effect of accountants' professional opinions. Third, it examines the statutory liability of accountants and tax preparers. Fourth, it explains the government's access to accountants' records. Finally, it discusses the liability of accountants to third parties who rely on the product of accountants' professional services.

Accountants perform services that are intended to benefit government and the public. Managers rely on the work of accountants in making important decisions. Accountants, of course, must understand their legal obligations to clients and others. This chapter, then, is of substantial importance to many people.

CHAPTER OBJECTIVES

After reading Chapter 59 of the text and studying the related materials in this chapter of the Student Mastery Guide, you will understand:

1. The role of GAAP and GAAS in regard to the legal liability of accountants
2. The bases for legal liability of accountants, including:
   a. contract
   b. tort
   c. statutory
3. The nature and effect of accountants' opinions
4. The liability of tax preparers
5. The rights of government to gain access to accountants' records
6. The liability of accountants to third parties

MAJOR POINTS TO REMEMBER

Professional Standards

1. Compliance with GAAP and GAAS will help establish that an accountant has not acted negligently (has not committed malpractice), but such compliance is not an absolute defense. This is particularly true if there is reason to know that a client's affairs are not being properly and honestly conducted.

2. Accountants have at common law an obligation to exercise reasonable care and competence - the care and competence normally exercised by an accountant in the particular locality, according to accepted professional standards.

Accountant-Client Relationship

3. The work product immunity that applies to attorneys in their relationship to their clients does not apply to accountants and their clients. The Supreme Court upheld the difference in these two relationships despite an expressed concern that it may hinder the full disclosure of records by clients to accountants.

Contract Liability

4. An accountant can be held liable for breach of either the express or implied terms of his or her contract with a client. Impliedly these contracts require that accountants exercise the degree of skill and competence in the performance of a contract that is commonly exercised by members of the profession. Accountants also impliedly agree in their contracts with clients to perform their services without fraud.

5. When accountants are retained to render a professional opinion regarding a client's financial records and they cannot render an unqualified opinion, then they will issue one of the following:
    a. qualified opinion for material uncertainty or deviations from GAAP
    b. adverse opinion when financial statements do not fairly present the firm's position in conformance with GAAP
    c. disclaimer of opinion when there is insufficient information to form an opinion on the accuracy of audited statements

6. When accountants perform compilations based on records supplied by clients, no audit is performed to insure the accuracy of the records. A report is issued with the compilation explaining that no audit was performed and the accuracy cannot be assured.

7. A review is done to give a limited opinion that records of a client are not materially misleading. A report is issued with reviews explaining that a full audit was not performed.

Tort Liability

8. Besides breach of contracts, accountants can also be liable for negligence. Negligence occurs when a duty of care is owed, the duty is breached, the breach caused injury, and the breach was the proximate cause of the injury. The duty of care is the "skill, care, knowledge and judgment usually possessed and exercised by members of that profession in the particular locality, in accordance with accepted professional standards and in good faith. . . "

9. Accountants can be liable for other torts too, including fraud.

Liability of Tax Preparers

10. Contract and tort duties apply to the preparation of clients' tax returns.

Liability to Third Parties

11.   Many third parties rely on the work of accountants for important information upon which to make decisions. Traditionally, however, an accountant's liability for negligence is limited to those with contractual relationships with the accountant, known as privity of contract. This principle limiting accountants' liability to those with whom they are in privity of contract is known as the Ultramares Doctrine.

12.   Accountants can be held liable to third parties for fraud in rendering their services. Fraud occurs when an intentional, knowing, or reckless misrepresentation is made that is justifiably relied on by a person to his or her detriment. Some courts, though, have allowed fraud to be found in cases of gross negligence.

13.   In response to the Ultramares Doctrine, courts have extended the negligence liability of accountants to third parties that they actually foresee will be relying on their professional work. This view is now expressed in the Restatement (Second) of Torts, Section 552. A few courts have extended accountants' liability for negligence to third parties who should have been foreseen as relying on their professional work, but this is not the current prevailing view.

Statutory Liability

14.   Accountants can be held liable under state and federal statutory law. The Securities Act of 1933 and the Securities Exchange Act of 1934 are significant sources of such statutory liability for misrepresentations, omissions, and fraud in financial statements, registration statements, annual reports, proxy statements, and tender offers. Under the 1933 Act liability can be imposed for negligence, while under the 1934 Act scienter, including reckless conduct in many courts, must be proven. Accountants can also be held liable for aiding and abetting fraud.

15.   Under the Internal Revenue Code accountants can have civil liability for negligently preparing, or willfully making misstatements in, tax returns prepared for clients, as well as failing to furnish clients with a copy of their tax returns.

16.   Accountants can also incur criminal liability for willful violations of the Securities Act of 1933, the Securities Exchange Act of 1934, the Internal Revenue Code, the Federal False Statements Act, the Federal Mail Fraud Act, and the Conspiracy Statute. The courts allow the mens rea element (guilty mind) of willfulness to be inferred from an accountant's actions and do not require proof of malice.

Ethics Box: Accountants' Professional Responsibility

17.   Should the members of the accountancy profession be allowed to establish the standards for professional responsibility? Members of the profession have greater expertise regarding the tasks performed and have the incentive to weed out those who are incompetent or wrongdoers. On the other hand, there is also the possible incentive to

protect the profession and its members. The law is influenced by ethical standards in the profession, but the law establishes the minimum standards of professional conduct. The profession's standards can be higher.

Ethics Box: Ethical Dilemmas Facing Professionals

18.   Accountants, like other professionals, encounter clients who are engaged in wrongdoing. They obtain this information through their confidential relationships with the client. What legal and ethical principles should be used to guide their decision making as to whether to disclose the information of wrongdoing?

MAJOR POINTS OF CASES

United States v. *Arthur Young and Co.* (p. 1125)

In a criminal tax investigation the IRS sought the tax records of the client of the defendant and the firm's related workpapers. The defendant argued that its workpapers were immune from disclosure. The court rejected this argument, in part because the public responsibility of accountants transcends their obligations to a client. This is in contrast to attorneys whose role is to represent the best interests of their clients, a role that requires confidentiality of communications and workpapers. Ultimately accountants are public watchdogs who must maintain independence from their clients. As such, granting immunity from compelled disclosure for their workpapers is inappropriate.

Hall v. *Edge* (p. 1128)

In this case, the court examined the distinction between statements of fact and mere expressions of opinion. The court noted that the latter is not actionable as false representation in a fraud action under normal circumstances.

The court found Hall's action against Jackson to not be encompassed under the broad scope of normal circumstances. Hall claimed fraudulent action on the part of Jackson for poor financial advice offered to Hall by him. The lower court had determined that this claim was not actionable, because Jackson's statements were mere expressions of opinion. However, the court in this case ruled that by virtue of the relationship that existed between Jackson and Hall - - the former being an accountant and the latter a layperson - - Hall had reason to believe that Jackson's statements were factual in nature. Thus, the court held, Hall's action could not be dismissed on the grounds that Jackson's statements were expressions of opinion. The case was remanded back to the trial court so that a jury could judge the fraud claim on these new grounds.

Ultramares Corporation v. *Touche* (p. 1132)

The plaintiff sued an accounting firm which had issued an opinion that a corporation's financial records showing it to be solvent were "true and correct." The plaintiff loaned money to the corporation in reliance on these financial statements. The corporation was actually insolvent and defaulted on paying this loan. The defendant accounting firm did not know that the plaintiff would rely on its opinion, but it did know that its client would use the opinion to secure financing.

The court held that the defendant accounting firm was not liable to the plaintiff, a third-party creditor, for negligence, because such liability would create an indeterminable risk for the profession. Liability for negligence runs only to those in privity of contract with accountants. However, liability to third parties not in privity of contract will exist for fraud - international, knowing, or reckless misrepresentations.

First Florida Bank v. Max Mitchell & Co. (p. 1134)

In this case, the court ruled that accountants have liability for negligence with third parties where no privity exists under certain circumstances. To the extent that an accountant "knows" that a third party will rely upon his opinion, he or she is liable for the financial damages incurred as a result of such reliance.

Applying this ruling to the facts of the case, the court found Mitchell to be liable for the financial statements he gave to the First Florida Bank. Mitchell gave these statements to the bank to demonstrate that C. M. Systems should be given a $500,000 loan. C.M. Systems defaulted on the loan, and the financial statements were shown to be false. Because Mitchell gave these statements to the Bank with the intention of the Bank relying on them, the Court found Mitchell to be liable.

Resnick v. Touche Ross and Co. (p. 1137)

Plaintiffs had invested and lost money in the securities of a client of the defendant, allegedly in reliance on misinformation contained in financial statements certified by the defendant. They alleged violations of Section 10(b) of the Securities Exchange Act of 1934 and Rule 10b-5, and aiding and abetting violations of Section 10(b) and Rule 10b-5.

The court ruled that the scienter element of a Section 10(b) case includes intentional, knowing, or reckless misrepresentations. Further, the aiding and abetting claim requires allegations that the client violated the securities laws, the accounting firm knew of or recklessly disregarded the violations, and it substantially assisted the client in effecting the violation. The court concluded that the plaintiff's complaint adequately alleged both causes of action and should not be dismissed.

PRACTICAL CONSIDERATIONS

1. Third parties who rely on the opinions of accountants in making business decisions in regard to a company, particularly whether or not to extend credit, must carefully examine the exact nature of the opinion rendered. It is important for third parties to understand the differences among unqualified, qualified, adverse, and disclaimer opinions, as well as the limited assurances that are made with compilations and reviews. In each instance the opinions should be studied carefully before making a final decision.

2. Third parties cannot assume that, if they lose money by extending credit to a company based on an accountant's professional opinion regarding its financial statements, they will be able to recover their losses from the accountant. First, under current law they must

prove that they were actually foreseen by the accountant as a party who would rely on the accountant's professional work. Even if this "actually foreseen" test is met, a case based on allegations of negligence requires proof that the accountant failed to exercise the care and skill of a competent accountant in the locality, and that this failure was the cause of the person's losses. If fraud is alleged, the misrepresentation must have been made intentionally, knowingly, or recklessly and involve a material fact that was justifiably relied on to the claimant's detriment. However, the "actually foreseen" test is not applied in cases of fraud. Clearly, these burdens of proof can be difficult to satisfy in many cases. One should consider, at least in cases of significant amounts of money to be loaned, requiring that an accountant's opinion be obtained specifically as a condition for the loan, and that the accountant who is to render the opinion will know its purpose and that you will be the one relying on its accuracy.

SELF TEST

True-False Questions

_____ 1. Accountants cannot be held liable for losses caused to others, if they have complied with GAAP and GAAS in performing their professional services.

_____ 2. Accountants can have liability for losses suffered by their clients based on breach of contract.

_____ 3. Under the tort theory of negligence accountants have a duty to perform the professional services with the care and skill of a reasonable person.

_____ 4. Accountants can be held liable to clients for losses suffered due to the failure to perform services according to professional standards.

_____ 5. An accountant's contract for professional services with a client is normally governed by both express and implied terms.

_____ 6. Careless mistakes in performing professional accounting services cannot constitute a breach of contract.

_____ 7. An accounting firm can be held liable for the negligent or fraudulent acts of an employee that are committed within the apparent scope of authority.

_____ 8. In a compilation an accountant does not render an opinion assuring the accuracy of the subject financial statements.

_____ 9. When conducting a review, an accountant renders an unqualified opinion.

_____ 10. When conducting an audit and rendering an opinion, an accountant is liable for negligence or fraud to the client and actually foreseen third parties who justifiably rely on the financial statements to their detriment.

Multiple-Choice Questions

_____ 11. An accountant's opinion which states that a company's financial statements do not fairly represent its position in conformance with GAAP is a(n) _____ opinion.
    a.   unqualified
    b.   qualified
    c.   adverse
    d.   disclaimer
    e.   review

_____ 12. In performing a review, an accountant renders a(n):
    a.   unqualified opinion
    b.   assurance that the financial statements are not materially misleading
    c.   qualified opinion
    d.   review opinion
    e.   compilation opinion

_____ 13. Compliance with GAAP and GAAS by an accountant is:
    a.   an absolute defense to liability
    b.   no evidence of proper performance
    c.   some evidence of proper performance
    d.   of no relevance to cases before the courts
    e.   both b and d are correct

_____ 14. In performing professional services, an accountant has a duty to meet the standard:
    a.   of a reasonable person
    b.   of the care and competence normally exercised by accountants in the particular locality, according to professional standards
    c.   of how accountants anywhere in the United States would act
    d.   both a and c are correct
    e.   none of the above is correct

15. Accountants can be held legally responsible for the improper conduct of their professional services under:
    a. contract law
    b. tort law
    c. statutory law
    d. both a and b are correct
    e. all of the above are correct

16. Accountants can have statutory liability for the failure to properly perform their services under the:
    a. Internal Revenue Code
    b. Securities Act of 1933
    c. Securities Exchange Act of 1934
    d. common law
    e. a, b, and c are correct

17. When the government seeks to obtain the records of a client from an accountant, the client can successfully assert:
    a. the Fifth Amendment protection against compulsory self-incrimination
    b. the accountant-client privilege for confidential communications
    c. the Fourth Amendment protection against unreasonable search and seizures
    d. both a and c are correct
    e. none of the above is correct

18. In regard to an accountant's workpapers, the government:
    a. can properly require their disclosure
    b. cannot ever require their disclosure
    c. cannot obtain them in a criminal case
    d. can obtain them only for criminal cases
    e. only b and c are correct

19. Accountants can be held liable for negligence or fraud in performing their professional services to:
    a. only their clients
    b. clients and any third parties who relied on their work
    c. clients and third parties who were actually foreseen to rely on their work
    d. clients and third parties whose reliance on their work should have been foreseen
    e. only third parties

_____   20.   An accountant's legal responsibility for fraud is based on scienter, which means:
       a.   intentional acts
       b.   knowing acts
       c.   reckless acts
       d.   gross negligence
       e.   a, b, and c are all correct

Completion Questions

21.   In a(n) _____ opinion an accountant certifies that financial statements fairly reflect the client's financial position in conformance with GAAP.

22.   Under the _____ Doctrine an accountant's liability is limited to those in privity of contract with him or her.

23.   _____ of contract means a direct contractual relationship between two parties.

24.   In most criminal cases against accountants _____ _____ must be proven.

25.   In a(n) _____ an accountant prepares financial statements based on a client's records but does not render an opinion based on an audit under GAAS.

SELF TEST ANSWERS

CHAPTER 1   The Function and Sources of Law

True-False Questions

1. True
2. False
3. True
4. True
5. False

Multiple-Choice Questions

6. e
7. e
8. c
9. b
10. c

Completion Questions

11. Law
12. dicta
13. Codification
14. stare decisis
15. Statutory interpretation

CHAPTER 2 — Legal Systems

True-False Questions

1. True
2. False
3. False
4. True
5. False
6. True
7. True
8. False
9. True
10. False

Multiple-Choice Questions

11. d
12. e
13. e
14. c
15. d
16. c
17. e
18. b
19. d
20. e

Completion Questions

21. intermediate appellate courts
22. federalism
23. foreseeability
24. original jurisdiction
25. jurisdiction

CHAPTER 3   Civil Litigation and Alternative Dispute Resolution

True-False Questions

1. False
2. True
3. False
4. True
5. True
6. True
7. False
8. False
9. False
10. False

Multiple-Choice Questions

11. e
12. e
13. a
14. c
15. b
16. c
17. e
18. a
19. e
20. c

Completion Questions

21. petit jury
22. summary judgment
23. subpoena
24. summons
25. judgment N.O.V.

CHAPTER 4   Constitutional Law and Business

True-False Questions

1. False
2. True
3. False
4. False
5. False
6. True
7. True
8. False
9. False
10. True

Multiple-Choice Questions

11. d
12. d
13. d
14. a
15. e
16. c
17. e
18. c
19. a
20 e

Completion Questions

21. state action
22. quasi-suspect
23. preemption doctrine
24. commercial speech
25. Fourteenth Amendment

CHAPTER 5   Introduction to Criminal Law

True-False Questions

1. False
2. False
3. True
4. False
5. True
6. True
7. False
8. False
9. False
10. True

Multiple-Choice Questions

11. d
12. a
13. d
14. e
15. e
16. a
17. d
18. d
19. e
20. c

Completion Questions

21. plea bargain
22. white collar
23. Larceny
24. exclusionary rule
25. False pretenses

CHAPTER 6   Intentional Torts

True-False Questions

1. False
2. False
3. True
4. False
5. False
6. False
7. True
8. True
9. True
10. True

Multiple-Choice Questions

11. b
12. c
13. c
14. c
15. d
16. b
17. e
18. c
19. a
20. b

Completion Questions

21. tort
22. conversion
23. assault
24. libel
25. trespass

CHAPTER 7   Negligence and Strict Liability

True-False Questions

1. False
2. False
3. True
4. True
5. False
6. False
7. True
8. True
9. True
10. True

Multiple-Choice Questions

11. c
12. d
13. b
14. a
15. a
16. c
17. d
18. b
19. a
20. d

Completion Questions

21. tort feasor
22. negligence
23. contributory negligence
24. respondeat superior/imputed negligence
25. strict liability

CHAPTER 8   Business and Ethics

True-False Questions

1. True
2. False
3. True
4. False
5. True
6. True
7. False
8. True
9. True
10. False

Multiple-Choice Questions

11. b
12. e
13. c
14. e
15. c
16. a
17. b
18. c
19. c
20. a

Completion Questions

21. pareto superior
22. act utilitarianism
23. due care
24. categorical imperative
25. Ethical egoism

CHAPTER 9   Social Responsibility of Business

True-False Questions

1. False
2. False
3. True
4. True
5. False
6. True
7. False
8. True
9. True
10. False

Multiple-Choice Questions

11. e
12. e
13. a
14. c
15. d
16. d
17. b
18. e
19. c
20. a

Completion Questions

21. Civil Rights Act of 1964
22. shareholders
23. stakeholders
24. corporate moral accountability
25. voluntarism

CHAPTER 10   Introduction to the Law of Contracts

True-False Questions

1. False
2. True
3. True
4. False
5. False
6. True
7. False
8. False
9. False
10. False

Multiple-Choice Questions

11. e
12. d
13. b
14. c
15. a

Completion Questions

16. executed
17. common law, statutory law
18. quasi contract
19. express
20. void

CHAPTER 11   The Offer

True-False Questions

1. True
2. True
3. False
4. True
5. True
6. False
7. False
8. True
9. False
10. False

Multiple-Choice Questions

11. b
12. d
13. d
14. c
15. c
16. a
17. b
18. a
19. c
20. e

Completion Questions

21. promissory estoppel
22. offeree
23. counteroffer
24. option
25. offer

CHAPTER 12   The Acceptance

True-False Questions

1. False
2. True
3. True
4. True
5. False
6. False
7. True
8. False
9. False
10. True

Multiple-Choice Questions

11. b
12. c
13. a
14. b
15. c
16. b
17. a
18. c
19. a
20. c

Completion Questions

21. merchant
22. offeree
23. counteroffer
24. auction
25. acceptance

CHAPTER 13   Consideration

True-False Questions

1. False
2. True
3. False
4. False
5. False
6. True
7. True
8. True
9. True
10. False

Multiple-Choice Questions

11. e
12. d
13. b
14. c
15. e
16. c
17. b
18. d
19. e
20. a

Completion Questions

21. forebearance
22. requirements contract
23. legal detriment, bargained exchange
24. illusory promise
25. accord and satisfaction

CHAPTER 14   Genuine Assent

True-False Questions

1. False
2. False
3. False
4. True
5. False
6. True
7. True
8. False
9. True
10. False

Multiple-Choice Questions

11. b
12. d
13. a
14. b
15. d
16. c
17. a
18. d
19. b
20. a

Completion Questions

21. opinion
22. Scienter
23. undue influence
24. duress
25. Misrepresentation

CHAPTER 15   Capacity to Contract

True-False Questions

1. True
2. False
3. False
4. True
5. False
6. False
7. True
8. True
9. False
10. True

Multiple-Choice Questions

11. c
12. b
13. a
14. d
15. a
16. e
17. a
18. c
19. b
20. c

Completion Questions

21. Ratification
22. guardian ad litem
23. emancipation
24. infant
25. habitual intoxication

CHAPTER 16   Illegality

True-False Questions

1. True
2. True
3. False
4. False
5. True
6. False
7. True
8. True
9. False
10. True

Multiple-Choice Questions

11. d
12. b
13. c
14. e
15. a
16. c
17. d
18. d
19. e
20. a

Completion Questions

21. wagering contract
22. in pari delicto
23. unconscionable
24. exculpatory
25. regulatory statutes

CHAPTER 17   Legal Form

True-False Questions

1. False
2. True
3. False
4. True
5. False
6. True
7. False
8. False
9. True
10. False

Multiple-Choice Questions

11. a
12 e
13. d
14. b
15. c
16. b
17. c
18. e
19. a
20. b

Completion Questions

21. memorandum
22. promissory estoppel
23. Parol evidence
24. easement
25. Statute of Frauds

CHAPTER 18   Rights of Third Parties

True-False Questions

1. False
2. False
3. True
4. False
5. True
6. False
7. False
8. True
9. False
10. False

Multiple-Choice Questions

11. b
12. d
13. c
14. b
15. e
16. a
17. c
18. b
19. c
20. a

Completion Questions

21. creditor beneficiary
22. novation
23. assignment
24. obligor
25. assignor

CHAPTER 19   Performance Discharge and Remedies

True-False Questions

1. True
2. True
3. True
4. False
5. True
6. False
7. True
8. False
9. False
10. True

Multiple-Choice Questions

11. b
12. d
13. e
14. c
15. b
16. d
17. e
18. a
19. e
20. b

Completion Questions

21. specific performance
22. Liquidated damages
23. novation
24. injunction
25. punitive damages

CHAPTER 20   Introduction to Sales Contracts

True-False Questions

1. False
2. True
3. True
4. False
5. False
6. True
7. False
8. True
9. False
10. False

Multiple-Choice Questions

11. b
12. e
13. d
14. a
15. c
16. b
17. c
18. e
19. c
20. d

Completion Questions

21. Good Faith
22. "goods"
23. quantity
24. dealing
25. future sale

CHAPTER 21   Sales: Title, Risk of Loss, and Insurable Interests

True-False Questions

1. True
2. False
3. True
4. False
5. True
6. False
7. True
8. True
9. True
10. False

Multiple-Choice Questions

11. a
12. e
13. e
14. e
15. a
16. d
17. c
18 a
19. e
20 e

Completion Questions

21. document of title
22. negotiable
23. Entrustment
24. CIF
25. identification

CHAPTER 22   Sales: Performance

True-False Questions

1. False
2. True
3. True
4. True
5. False
6. False
7. True
8. False
9. False
10. True

Multiple-Choice Questions

11. b
12. b
13. e
14. c
15. a
16. d
17. a
18. c
19. b
20. e

Completion Questions

21. cover
22. commercial unit
23. seasonable
24. Conforming goods
25. acceptance

CHAPTER 23   Sales: Remedies

True-False Questions

1. False
2. False
3. True
4. True
5. False
6. True
7. False
8. False
9. True
10. False

Multiple-Choice Questions

11. e
12. e
13. d
14. b
15. c
16. a
17. e
18. a
19. e
20. b

Completion Questions

21. cover
22. consequential
23. Incidental
24. prospective
25. specific performance

CHAPTER 24   Warranties

True-False Questions

1. False
2. True
3. False
4. True
5. False
6. False
7. False
8. True
9. False
10. True

Multiple-Choice Questions

11. b
12. c
13. d
14. c
15. e
16. b
17. a
18. a
19. b
20. d

Completion Questions

21. puffing
22. privity of contract
23. implied warranty
24. express warranty
25. title

CHAPTER 25   Product Liability

True-False Questions

1. False
2. False
3. False
4. True
5. True
6. False
7. True
8. True
9. True
10. False

Multiple-Choice Questions

11. d
12. e
13. e
14. d
15. d
16. d
17. e
18. e
19. a
20. c

Completion Questions

21. proximate cause
22. Comparative negligence
23. Strict liability
24. justifiably relied upon
25. Assumption of risk

CHAPTER 26 Introduction to Negotiable Instruments and Documents of Title

True-False Questions

1. True
2. False
3. True
4. True
5. False
6. True
7. False
8. False
9. True
10. False

Multiple-Choice Questions

11. e
12. c
13. b
14. a
15. c
16. e
17. b
18. a
19. c
20. b

Completion Questions

21. Negotiation
22. demand instrument
23. cashier's check
24. bearer
25. drawer

CHAPTER 27   Negotiable Instruments: Negotiability

True-False Questions

1. True
2. False
3. False
4. True
5. False
6. True
7. False
8. True
9. True
10. False

Multiple-Choice Questions

11. c
12. e
13. e
14. b
15. b
16. d
17. b
18. c
19. e
20. b

Completion Questions

21. unconditional
22. Fixed
23. words of negotiability
24. handwritten terms
25. negotiable

CHAPTER 28   Negotiable Instruments: Transfer, Negotiation, and Holder in Due Course

True-False Questions

1. True
2. False
3. True
4. True
5. False
6. False
7. True
8. True
9. False
10. False

Multiple-Choice Questions

11. d
12. b
13. e
14. e
15. b
16. d
17. a
18. c
19. c
20. a

Completion Questions

21. depository bank
22. dishonor
23. allonge
24. special
25. Negotiation

CHAPTER 29   Negotiable Instruments: Liability, Defenses, and Discharge

True-False Questions

1. True
2. True
3. True
4. False
5. False
6. True
7. False
8. False
9. True
10. True

Multiple-Choice Questions

11. b
12. e
13. b
14. e
15. d
16. a
17. e
18. a
19. d
20. a

Completion Questions

21. fraud in the factum
22. Protest
23. presentment
24. foreign bill
25. maker

CHAPTER 30   Negotiable Instruments: Checks

True-False Questions

1. True
2. True
3. True
4. False
5. False
6. True
7. True
8. True
9. False
10. False

Multiple-Choice Questions

11. d
12. d
13. c
14. e
15. b
16. a
17. a
18. d
19. d
20. d

Completion Questions

21. check
22. Expedited Funds Availability
23. subrogation
24. post-dated
25. stale

CHAPTER 31   Electronic Fund Transfers

True-False Questions

1. True
2. False
3. True
4. False
5. True
6. False
7. True
8. False
9. False
10. False

Multiple-Choice Questions

11. a
12. b
13. d
14. e
15. b
16. c
17. e
18. b
19. c
20. b

Completion Questions

21. intermediary
22. security procedures
23. 205
24. Fed Wire
25. settling banks

CHAPTER 32   Secured Transactions

True-False Questions

1. False
2. True
3. True
4. False
5. True
6. True
7. True
8. False
9. True
10. True

Multiple-Choice Questions

11. d
12. d
13. a
14. c
15. b
16. d
17. c
18. b
19. c
20. e

Completion Questions

21. security agreement
22. secured party
23. chattel paper
24. collateral
25. purchase-money security interest

CHAPTER 33   Rights of Debtors and Creditors

True-False Questions

1. False
2. False
3. True
4. True
5. True
6. True
7. False
8. True
9. True
10. False

Multiple-Choice Questions

11. d
12. b
13. e
14. c
15. d
16. b
17. c
18. c
19. d
20. a

Completion Questions

21. receivership
22. lien
23. artisan's lien
24. ten
25. receivership

CHAPTER 34   Bankruptcy

True-False Questions

1. True
2. True
3. False
4. True
5. False
6. True
7. False
8. True
9. True
10. False

Multiple-Choice Questions

11. c
12. e
13. b
14. a
15. e
16. a
17. b
18. b
19. c
20. d

Completion Questions

21. trustee
22. debtor
23. liquidation
24. lien creditor
25. $5,000

CHAPTER 35   The Agency Relationship

True-False Questions

1. False
2. True
3. False
4. True
5. True
6. False
7. True
8. True
9. False
10. False

Multiple-Choice Questions

11. b
12. e
13. e
14. d
15. b
16. a
17. e
18. e
19. c
20. e

Completion Questions

21. Agency
22. special
23. general agent
24. fiduciary
25. independent contractor

CHAPTER 36   The Effect of Agency Relations

True-False Questions

1. False
2. False
3. False
4. False
5. False
6. False
7. True
8. False
9. True
10. True

Multiple-Choice Questions

11. d
12. c
13. d
14. b
15. a
16. d
17. c
18. a
19. e
20. e

Completion Questions

21. Apparent
22. ratification
23. respondeat superior or vicarious liability
24. coupled with an interest
25. express

CHAPTER 37   Forms of Business Organization

True-False Questions

1. True
2. True
3. False
4. False
5. False
6. True
7. False
8. False
9. True
10. False

Multiple-Choice Questions

11. a
12. b
13. e
14. b
15. e
16. d
17. e
18. d
19. c
20. c

Completion Questions

21. limited partnership, limited
22. Corporations
23. cooperative
24. cooperative
25. Limited liability companies (LLC)

CHAPTER 38   Nature and Formation of Partnerships

True-False Questions

1. True
2. True
3. False
4. True
5. False
6. True
7. False
8. True
9. True
10. False

Multiple-Choice Questions

11. c
12. e
13. e
14. d
15. b
16. d
17. d
18. b
19. a
20. a

Completion Questions

21. joint venture
22. aggregate
23. unlimited
24. partnership
25. partnership agreement

CHAPTER 39 Operation and Dissolution of Partnerships

True-False Questions

1. True
2. True
3. True
4. True
5. False
6. False
7. False
8. True
9. False
10. False

Multiple-Choice Questions

11. e
12. c
13. d
14. b
15. d
16. b
17. a
18. a
19. c
20. e

Completion Questions

21. dissolution
22. accounting
23. winding up
24. tenancy in partnership
25. liquidators or liquidating partners

CHAPTER 40   Limited Partnerships

True-False Questions

1. False
2. False
3. True
4. True
5. False
6. False
7. True
8. True
9. False
10. False

Multiple-Choice Questions

11. c
12. d
13. e
14. a
15. d
16. d
17. d
18. a
19. a
20. b

Completion Questions

21. general partner
22. assignee
23. Uniform Limited Partnership Act (ULPA)
24. foreign limited partnership
25. limited partner

CHAPTER 41   Introduction to Corporations

True-False Questions

1. True
2. False
3. False
4. True
5. False
6. True
7. False
8. True
9. True
10. True

Multiple-Choice Questions

11. b
12. d
13. c
14. e
15. a
16. c
17. e
18. a
19. e
20. a

Completion Questions

21. foreign
22. foreign
23. legal entity
24. public issue
25. nonprofit

CHAPTER 42   Forming the Corporation

True-False Questions

1. True
2. False
3. False
4. False
5. True
6. True
7. False
8. True
9. False
10. False

Multiple-Choice Questions

11. b
12. a
13. c
14. d
15. d
16. d
17. a
18. a
19. d
20. b

Completion Questions

21. bylaws
22. articles of incorporation
23. promoter
24. de facto corporation
25. preincorporators

CHAPTER 43   Financing the Corporation

True-False Questions

1. True
2. True
3. False
4. False
5. True
6. False
7. True
8. False
9. False
10. True

Multiple-Choice Questions

11, a
12. d
13. b
14. e
15. a
16. b
17. d
18. d
19. c
20. e

Completion Questions

21. debenture
22. stock subscription
23. par value
24. bond
25. stockholders

CHAPTER 44   Managing the Corporation

True-False Questions

1. True
2. False
3. False
4. True
5. True
6. False
7. False
8. True
9. False
10. True

Multiple-Choice Questions

11. d
12. b
13. a
14. b
15. b
16. e
17. d
18. d
19. e
20. c

Completion Questions

21. earned surplus
22. pooling agreement
23. treasury stock
24. proxy
25. insolvent

CHAPTER 45   Corporate Mergers, Dissolution and Termination

True-False Questions

1. False
2. True
3. False
4. True
5. False
6. False
7. True
8. True
9. False
10. False

Multiple-Choice Questions

11. d
12. c
13. e
14. c
15. e
16. e
17. e
18. e
19. b
20. e

Completion Questions

21. merger
22. consolidation
23. appraisal right
24. purchase of assets
25. voluntary and involuntary

CHAPTER 46 Securities Regulation

True-False Questions

1. False
2. True
3. False
4. False
5. True
6. True
7. False
8. True
9. True
10. False

Multiple-Choice Questions

11. d
12. b
13. a
14. e
15. c
16. e
17. a
18. d
19. d
20. a

Completion Questions

21. blue-sky
22. proxy
23. waiting period
24. deficiency letter
25. Securities Exchange Act of 1934

CHAPTER 47   Personal Property

True-False Questions

1. True
2. True
3. False
4. True
5. False
6. False
7. False
8. True
9. False
10. True

Multiple-Choice Questions

11. e
12. b
13. c
14. d
15. d
16. c
17. e
18. e
19. a
20. a

Completion Questions

21. Fungible goods
22. donee
23. gift causa mortis
24. bailment
25. bailee

CHAPTER 48 Interests in Real Property

True-False Questions

1. True
2. True
3. False
4. False
5. True
6. False
7. False
8. True
9. False
10. True

Multiple-Choice Questions

11. e
12. c
13. b
14. a
15. b
16. d
17. e
18. c
19. d
20. e

Completion Questions

21. fee simple defeasible
22. profit *a'prendre*
23. servient estate
24. license
25. percentage

CHAPTER 49   Acquisition, Financing, and Control of Real Property

True-False Questions

1. False
2. True
3. False
4. False
5. True
6. True
7. False
8. True
9. False
10. True

Multiple-Choice Questions

11. d
12. a
13. b
14. b
15. e
16. c
17. c
18. d
19. a
20. e

Completion Questions

21. grantee
22. mortgagor
23. zoning
24. eminent domain
25. lien

CHAPTER 50   Intellectual Property and Computer Law

True-False Questions

1. False
2. True
3. False
4. True
5. False
6. False
7. False
8. True
9. False
10. False

Multiple-Choice Questions

11. e
12. d
13. b
14. e
15. b
16. e
17. d
18. d
19. d
20. a

Completion Questions

21. Trademarks
22. Electronic copying
23. patent
24. goods, services
25. trademark

CHAPTER 51   Wills Trusts and Estates

True-False Questions

1. False
2. False
3. True
4. False
5. True
6. True
7. True
8. False
9. False
10. False

Multiple-Choice Questions

11. b
12. e
13. e
14. d
15. a
16. e
17. c
18. a
19. b
20. c

Completion Questions

21. codicil
22. testator or testatrix
23. intestate
24. escheat
25. probate

CHAPTER 52   Insurance Law

True-False Questions

1. False
2. True
3. True
4. False
5. False
6. False
7. True
8. True
9. True
10. False

Multiple-Choice Questions

11. b
12. a
13. d
14. b
15. c
16. a
17. b
18. c
19. e
20. b

Completion Questions

21. Term
22. waiver
23. Concealment
24. Disability
25. warranty

CHAPTER 53   Government Regulation and the Role of Administrative Agencies

True-False Questions

1. True
2. True
3. True
4. False
5. False
6. True
7. False
8. False
9. False
10. True

Multiple-Choice Questions

11. c
12. e
13. a
14. c
15. e
16. b
17. d
18. e
19. d
20. d

Completion Questions

21. Administrative agencies
22. enabling act
23. Federal Trade Commission
24. Securities Exchange Commission
25. Federal Communications Commission

CHAPTER 54   Antitrust Laws: Enforcement and Control

True-False Questions

1. True
2. True
3. True
4. False
5. True
6. False
7. True
8. False
9. False
10. False

Multiple-Choice Questions

11. e
12. d
13. b
14. d
15. c
16. a
17. a
18. e
19. b
20. c

Completion Questions

21. injunction
22. oligopoly
23. merger
24. monopoly
25. Whip-sawing

CHAPTER 55   Consumer Protection Law

True-False Questions

1. False
2. False
3. True
4. True
5. False
6. True
7. False
8. True
9. False
10. False

Multiple-Choice Questions

11. b
12. b
13. e
14. d
15. a
16. c
17. e
18. d
19. b
20. d

Completion Questions

21. Competition
22. Closed-end
23. annual percentage rate
24. $25,000
25. Truth-in-Lending

CHAPTER 56   Fair Employment Practices

True-False Questions

1. False
2. True
3. False
4. True
5. False
6. False
7. True
8. True
9. False
10. False

Multiple-Choice Questions

11. b
12. e
13. d
14. c
15. e
16. d
17. c
18. e
19. b
20. c

Completion Questions

21. 15
22. Title VII
23. disparate treatment
24. reasonable accommodation
25. Equal Pay Act

CHAPTER 57   Environmental Law

True-False Questions

1. False
2. False
3. False
4. True
5. True
6. False
7. True
8. True
9. True
10. False

Multiple-Choice Questions

11. d
12. d
13. d
14. e
15. a
16. c
17. b
18. e
19. e
20. b

Completion Questions

21. national permit discharge elimination system
22. lead, ozone, particulates
23. sulfur dioxide
24. toxic emissions
25. risk of psychological harm

CHAPTER 58   International Business

True-False Questions

1. False
2. False
3. True
4. False
5. False
6. True
7. False
8. True
9. True
10. True

Multiple-Choice Questions

11. e
12. c
13. c
14. a
15. e
16. d
17. b
18. a
19. b
20. e

Completion Questions

21. Nationalization
22. Act of State
23. common-law
24. exports
25. quotas

CHAPTER 59   Accountants and Professional Liability

True-False Questions

1. False
2. True
3. False
4. True
5. True
6. False
7. True
8. True
9. False
10. True

Multiple-Choice Questions

11. c
12. b
13. c
14. b
15. e
16. e
17. e
18. a
19. c
20. e

Completion Questions

21. unqualified
22. Ultramares
23. Privity
24. mens rea
25. compilation

NOTES

NOTES

NOTES